European Valuation Practice

OTHER TITLES FROM E & FN SPON

Competitive Cities
Succeeding in the global economy
H Duffy

**European Cities, Planning Systems
and Property Markets**
Edited by J. Berry and S. McGreal

**Housing Policy and Rented
Housing in Europe**
M. Oxley and J. Smith

The Idea of Building
**Thought and action in the design
and production of buildings**
S Groák

**Industrial Property Markets in
Western Europe**
Edited by B Wood and R Williams

Marketing the City
**The role of flagship developments
in urban regeneration**
H Smyth

**The Multilingual Dictionary of
Real Estate**
L van Breugel, R H Williams and
B Wood

**National Taxation for Property
Management and Valuation**
A MacLeary

Project Management Demystified
2nd Edition
G Reiss

Property Development
4th Edition
D Cadman and R Topping

**Property Investment and the
Capital Markets**
G R Brown

Property Investment Decisions
A quantitative approach
S Hargitay and M Yu

Property Valuation
The five methods
D Scarrett

Rebuilding the City
Property-led urban regeneration
Edited by P Healey, D Usher,
S Davoudi, S Tavsanoglu and
M O'Toole

**Risk Analysis in Project
Management**
J Raftery

**Spon's European Construction
Costs Price Book**
2nd Edition
Edited by Davis Langdon & Everest

Urban Regeneration
Property investment and development
Edited by J N Berry, W S McGreal
and W G Deddis

Effective Writing
**Improving scientific, technical and
business communication**
2nd Edition
C Turk and J Kirkham

Getting into Print
**A guide for scientists and
technologists**
P Sprent

Good Style
Writing for science and technology
J Kirkham

For more information on these and other titles please contact:
The Promotion Department, E&FN Spon, 2–6 Boundary Row, London SE1
8HN. Telephone 0171 865 0066.

European Valuation Practice

Practice

Theory and technique

Edited by

Alastair Adair
University of Ulster, UK

Mary Lou Downie
University of Northumbria, Newcastle, UK

Stanley McGreal
University of Ulster, UK

Gerjan Vos
University of Amsterdam, The Netherlands

Taylor & Francis
Taylor & Francis Group

LONDON AND NEW YORK

Taylor & Francis
2 Park Square, Milton Park, Abingdon, Oxfordshire OX14 4RN
711 Third Avenue, New York, NY 10017

First edition 1996

© 1996 Taylor & Francis

Typeset in 10/12pt Times by Saxon Graphics Ltd, Derby

First issued in paperback 2011

A catalogue record for this book is available from the British Library

Library of Congress Catalog Card Number: 96–67193

ISBN 978-0-419-20040-6 (hbk)
ISBN 978-0-415-51211-4 (pbk)

Contents

Contributors

Alastair Adair has a PhD in Land Management and is professor in Real Estate Investment in the School of the Built Environment at the University of Ulster and Convenor of the Property Investment Teaching Group. A chartered surveyor he is President of the European Real Estate Society. Main research interests include property valuation, market analysis and the financing of property development.

Sandrine Bardouil is a French chartered surveyor working at the Madrid office of Weatherall Green & Smith. As the 1994/95 Jones Lang Wootton travelling scholar, she compiled a report on local valuation approaches in Europe and contributed articles to *Estates Europe*. She is a graduate from the University of Paris, the London School of Economics and has a Master's degree in Estate Management from South Bank University.

André R. Bender has a PhD degree in Finance. He is professor of Finance in the Department of Management Studies of the University of Geneva and is the author of journal articles on financial analysis and real estate finance. He has also authored books on corporate finance.

Peter Byrne qualified as a geographer and is senior lecturer in Land Management and Development at the University of Reading. Main research interests include the development of computerized appraisal methods and risk and uncertainty in appraisal. He is the author of *Risk, Uncertainty and Decision-Making in Development Appraisal*.

Neil Crosby has a PhD in Land Management and is professor of Land Management in the Department of Land Management and Development at the University of Reading. He is co-author of *Property Investment Appraisal* with Andrew Baum (1995, 2nd edn). Main research interests include investment valuations and the impact of lease incentives. He is a member of the Surveying Courses Board and the Investment, Development and Use Research Committee of the RICS and was a member of the Mallinson Committee.

Mary Lou Downie has a degree in Mathematics and lectures in property investment at the University of Northumbria at Newcastle. She qualified as a chartered surveyor while working in the Inland Revenue's Valuation Office in Oxford. Afterwards she moved to Milton Keynes Development Corporation where she was involved in privately-funded development of commercial and industrial buildings. In 1993 she began researching valuation in mainland Europe, funded by the RICS.

Philippe Favarger has a PhD degree in Economics. He is assistant professor of Real Estate Economics in the Department of Architecture of the Federal Polytechnical School of Lausanne and at the Architecture Institute of the University of Geneva. He has authored several journal articles in property economics.

Nick French is Acacia Lecturer in Land Management and Laing Fellow in Real Estate at the University of Reading. He is Executive Director of the European Real Estate Society, editor of the *Journal of Property Valuation and Investment* and a member of the RICS GP Research Committee. He has written extensively on appraisal methods and the valuation of lease incentives.

Jan de Graeve is a Fellow of the Royal Institution of Chartered Surveyors, President of EUROVAL and Vice-president Chambre Belge des Experts Chargés de Mission Judiciares-CEJA. He is a past-president of FIG commission 1 and holds qualifications in town planning, infrastructure and surveying.

Martin Hoesli has a PhD degree in Finance. He is assistant professor of Finance and Real Estate in the Department of Management Studies of the University of Geneva and an associate professor at Groupe ESC Bordeaux. He has written journal articles on real estate investment and finance and is a member of the editorial board of the *Journal of Property Research*.

Colin Humphries qualified as a chartered surveyor with St Quintin in the City of London, where he has worked as an asset valuer responsible for South East England. In 1987 he moved to Belgium, working for Ketteridge St Quintin in Antwerp and Brussels, undertaking all aspects of investment agency and valuation. In 1993 he joined DePfa-Bank in Wiesbaden, Germany, in their valuation department, being responsible for overseeing all valuations in Benelux. Since joining DePfa's London office in 1994 he has been responsible for evaluating new loan proposals.

Tero Lahdes has an MSc(Econ.) degree and is undertaking research at the Helsinki University of Technology in the field of real estate valuation for his PhD.

Erik H. Larsen graduated as a civil engineer from the University of Newcastle upon Tyne in 1968. He has been in valuation practice since 1985. Currently he is Vice President of The Norwegian Surveyors Association and lectures at the School of Valuation. He has had previous work experience in the construction industry in both South Africa and Norway.

Kari I. Leväinen is professor of Real Estate Economics at the Helsinki University of Technology. He has more than 24 years of experience on real estate issues. Dr Leväinen has also worked as senior scientist of the Academy of Finland and as research engineer for the Association of Finnish Cities.

Stellan Lundström is associate professor in the Department of Real Estate and Construction Management at the Royal Institute of Technology, Stockholm. He is also serving as head of department. Professional interests include property management and valuation. Recent research has mainly focused on valuation of contracts and management control systems within the public sector.

Philippe Malaquin has been a real estate valuer since 1968 and became a Fellow of the Royal Institution of Chartered Surveyors in 1991. He has been Managing Director of EEIG Euroexport since October 1993 and currently is chairman of TEGOVOFA, The European Group of Valuers of Fixed Assets. He is also a member of the Board of TIAVSC, The International Asset Valuation Standards Committee.

Bryan MacGregor has a PhD degree in Land Economy and is MacRobert Professor of Land Economy at the University of Aberdeen. He has written extensively on property investment and land development and is editor of the *Journal of Property Research*. He is Chairman of RICS Investment, Development and Use Research Committee and is a member of the Built Environment and Planning Panel for Research Assessment Exercise 1992 and 1996.

Stanley McGreal is reader in Estate Management at the University of Ulster and Director of the Real Estate Studies Unit. His main areas of research include property market analysis, urban regeneration and housing. He is co-editor of *Urban Regeneration Property Investment and Development* and *European Cities, Planning Systems and Property Markets*.

José de Pablo Méndez is President of the Sociedad de Tasacion SA, which was the first valuation company in Spain. He received a university degree in civil enginering and business administration and is a member of TEGOVOFA and of several Spanish professional organizations such as ATESA.

Manfredo Montagnana has a degree in Mathematics. Formerly of the University of Geneva and one year at UC Berkeley, he works at the Politecnico di Torino where he is associate professor of Applied Mathematics at the Faculty of Architecture. Main research interests include mathematical models for real estate markets and regional planning.

Erik Persson is adjunct professor in the Department of Real Estate and Construction Management at the Royal Institute of Technology, Stockholm, and senior partner at Catella AB. Professional interests include valuation, market and information management.

Franco Prizzon is assistant professor of Appraisal at the House & Town Department of Turin Polytechnic. Main research interests include real estate market analysis and investment valuation.

Maria dos Anjos Ramos has a degree in Financial Administration and currently is Assistant to the Secretary of State for Housing and a member of the Board of Directors of the National Institute of Housing. She has undertaken appraisal work for the Bank Crédito Predial Português and the Inter-American Development Bank.

Karl-Werner Schulte Hon Assoc RICS is professor of Real Estate Management and Dean at the European Business School (EBS) in Oestrich-Winkel, Germany's oldest private university. He is Academic Director of the EBS Real Estate Academy, managing director of a postgraduate course in financial planning, president of the German Society of Property Researchers and heads the chapter Real Estate Investment Analysis. Main research interests include investment analysis, valuation and corporate real estate management.

Hans-Ulrich Stork was formerly a division manager for long-term financing at Citi Bank before moving to IKB-Deutsche Industriekreditbank. He joined the Board of Managing Directors of DePfa-Bank AG in April 1992 where he is mainly responsible for the public sector investment fund operation.

George ten Have is partner of Rodenburg Mulder ten Kate, Bedrijfsmakelaars BV, in Apeldoorn. He is a member of NVM, the Dutch Society of Real Estate Brokers, and has lectured on valuation at SBV/University of Amsterdam. He has written articles and books on valuation practice in the Netherlands.

Matthias Thomas is research assistant and lecturer at the European Business School (EBS) Real Estate Academy. He is a member of the German Society of Property Researchers and heads the section on International Comparison of Valuation Practice in Europe and the USA. Main research interests include property performance measurement, property index construction and property valuation.

Gerjan Vos is a senior lecturer in the Department of Real Estate Economics, University of Amsterdam. Main research interests include valuation and investment analysis, market research, feasibility studies and sector studies.

Ferruccio Zorzi is associate professor of Appraisal and Project Valuation at Turin Polytechnic. Main interests include appraisal, quanti-qualitative valuations and real estate trends, particularly forecasting models.

Foreword

In the uncertain hour before the morning,
near the ending of interminable night.

Time was when valuation was a non-controversial issue. The valuer cocooned by the occult systems of their profession and complacent of their competence and local knowledge bathed in the glory of a golden afternoon. The collapse of European property markets in the 1990s in London, Paris and Madrid, to cite only the more graphic examples, has thrown the old certainties to the winds. The breadth of knowledge required of those operating in property markets and the growth of cross-border business has created a more sophisticated environment.

European Valuation Practice: theory and technique is an important breakthrough in facilitating the Single European property market. The European Group of Valuers of Fixed Assets (TEGOVOFA) was established in 1977 with the objective of setting up European valuation standards. However, it is only in 1996, with publication of this book, that an authoritative comparative review has been available on European valuation techniques and standards in a global context.

This book has been published at a time when there is increasing focus on international solutions following the GATT accord and setting up of the World Trade Organization. At the same time, in Europe, east and west, debate on valuation has moved to centre stage. The EC Directive on the Annual Accounts and Consolidated Accounts of Insurance Undertakings, with its requirement for valuation in accordance with a standard European Union definition of market value, the current review of the derogation provisions of the Directive on a Solvency Ratio for credit institutions concerning the weighting of assets secured by mortgages and property leasing transactions and the needs of the privatization programmes in central and eastern Europe, have directed attention on standards, systems and consistency.

Publication is consistent with TEGOVOFA's 1994 decision to include methodology as an integral part of the establishment of standards and practice compatible with the needs of global corporate and real estate investors and lending institutions.

The scope of its content linking theory with practice make it a vital source of information to a wide range of users, including real estate professionals, financiers, institutional investors and their advisors, property researchers and students, and those involved in these issues at an institutional and policy making level.

C.P.M. CHAMPNESS
Secretary General
The European Group of Valuers of Fixed Assets
July 1995

The context of valuation practice in Europe

1

*Mary Lou Downie, Alastair
Adair, Stanley McGreal
and Gerjan Vos*

Stories of valuation eccentricities within Europe abound, their bizarre nature betraying ignorance of each other's valuation objectives, theory and practice. This unfortunate situation has been brought to the fore by the internationalization of property activity, stimulated by the inception of the Single European market for goods and services. Developers seek to expand their activities from their home base in pursuit of fresh profit opportunities while investors look for the potential of diversifying between economies and locations. Financial services organizations seek market share in other countries, while manufacturing companies relocate and expand their presence in strategically chosen locations to serve their new international markets. The result is that consultancies which service and feed off all these groups have to grapple with property values in unfamiliar locations, encompassing foreign business and legal systems, if they wish to retain their clients' instructions. This text, through examining valuation techniques in several European countries, seeks to highlight variations and, indeed, similarities, where these exist, in terms of practice and methodology.

1.1 INTRODUCTION

The response of property consultants to the challenges of cross-border opportunities and international expansion has been to cooperate or merge with an indigenous partner to overcome the disadvantage of lack of local knowledge, expertise and contacts. Most such international links have flourished on an agency basis, earning fees through letting, selling and buying property for clients, or on a brokerage basis. A period of active expansion in Europe in the years prior to the inception of the Single Market is now being followed by consolidation, dictated to some extent by economic recession and oversupply, particularly in office markets (Berry and McGreal, 1995). It remains to be seen whether the market for these services is now saturated.

European Valuation Practice. Edited by Alastair Adair, Mary Lou Downie, Stanley McGreal and Gerjan Vos. Published in 1996 by E & FN Spon, London. ISBN 0 419 20040 1

The well-established international property consultants, having established their presence with agency business, are likely to expand by introducing, among other services, commercial property valuation. This raises the question whether such operators will employ the methods and value concepts of the international property industry or adopt local methods. Despite much anecdotal evidence that the valuation process varies from place to place, very little research has been carried out to establish the nature or extent of such differences (Bell and Hobbs, 1993; Downie, 1993; RICS, 1993). In deciding whether to use indigenous valuation methods consultancies must identify whether they are equipped and qualified to value locally by local methodology, whether the fee potential of a country warrants the necessary investment in personnel and training, and whether restrictive local practices effectively close the market in valuation services to outsiders. The crucial issue however is likely to be their clients' requirements. They may opt for familiarity, the valuation formats they know and understand, or alternatively for a system which provides better for their particular needs than the one they have hitherto used. Many users of valuations are now expanding their business across their traditional borders and in so doing are exposed to the valuation culture of their new markets. As a consequence they find themselves using appraisals produced in the valuation cultures of several different countries and will undoubtedly evolve preferences for those which best serve their needs.

Business expansion across borders prompts the need for consistent valuation systems for accounting and stock market valuation purposes. This is already happening through the introduction of unified accounting rules in certain financial service sectors enabling meaningful cross-border comparison of values and performance. For example, the European Union Directive governing the reporting of Insurance Company Performance.

Several international associations of valuers have been formed with various objectives, including lobbying the European Commission, standardizing concepts and definitions of value, setting international practice standards and improving communication across borders. The overall agenda is to increase valuation business by offering an enhanced quality of service to clients on a wider geographical basis than before. The effectiveness of these organizations is not guaranteed, depending in part on their acceptance by national professional bodies, and there is potential for disagreement when cherished national systems of practice and theory have to be reconciled in creating an internationally accepted standard or definition. Examples are The International Asset Valuation Standards Committee (TIAVSC), The European Group of Valuers of Fixed Assets (TEGOVOFA) and The European Valuers Association (Euroval).

In addition to the proliferation of such associations, the Royal Institution of Chartered Surveyors (RICS) has extended its influence into mainland Europe by accrediting selected higher education courses and setting up national organizations. This is significant, since chartered surveyors have to apply the bases of valuation and follow the requirements of the 'Red Book' (RICS, 1990) in carrying out valuations for specified purposes and are subject to the institution's Code Of Practice. Such courses exist in Ireland, Germany and the Netherlands as well as the UK.

International consultants already carry out many valuations for their clients, often in connection with investment transactions and predominantly in the major investment locations: the large cities and localized growth regions. Many of these consultants have UK connections and therefore use UK-based growth–implicit valuation methods or the internationally accepted growth–explicit discounted cash flow method. Indeed, it is possible to foresee a situation where two tiers of valuation methods are applied by two distinct sets of valuers: international/UK methods applied by international consultants dominating the larger investment markets and indigenous valuers operating in the more provincial markets and for specialized functions such as providing court evidence.

This book attempts to clear some of the confusion by providing a framework within which different national valuation processes can be compared across 12 western European countries.

1.2 INVESTMENT VALUATION: PRICING AND APPRAISAL OF WORTH

It is of crucial interest to investors to be able to compare the worth of investments in different countries with their prices, i.e. the exchange value in the market. Research in this area tends not to be published, primarily because of its commercial sensitivity. The range, complexity and subjectivity of the issues to be incorporated in such a study are considerable. Quantifiable estimates must be made of the risk and return characteristics of investments, including the effectiveness of land registration guarantees, tenure norms, income certainty and growth potential, tenant and business risk, differences between the national and local economies, and many more. In addition to appraising investment worth, investors need to understand local pricing methods.

It is possible to conjecture that in markets as yet unexploited by international investors, price is dictated by the interaction of local users' and investors' perceptions of worth, and local valuers' pricing mechanisms. In some markets owner-occupation of commercial property is more usual than separation into occupation for use and ownership for investment purposes. In such circumstances local users' perceptions of worth will dominate (Coakley, 1994) with price expressed as:

$$\text{price} = f \text{ (local valuation practice, local user worth)}$$

If the scenario is developed to envisage newly-arrived international investors appraising and acquiring property in a subset of such markets, for instance major cities, then prices are likely to be influenced by their perceptions of worth and their pricing methods. Coakley characterizes this as the predominance of international views of property's exchange value (Coakley, 1994) with international price expressed as:

$$\text{international price} = f \text{ (international valuation practice,} \\ \text{international investment worth)}$$

The price at which properties are exchanged will depend on which of the functions gives the higher value. Prima facie, it would appear that pressure from outside investors may well increase demand and thereby push up values. Therefore, in internationally attractive investment locations, international methods may replace indigenous methods of valuation and of pricing. Conversely, in the markets not favoured by such investors, indigenous methods may persist.

There is anecdotal evidence that international investors are cautious about entering territory as yet unbroken by their peers. For example, investment in Dusseldorf is acceptable but Dortmund, despite possible high returns, is not. Therefore, international investment is restricted to a limited group of cities and as competition for investments there intensifies, prices rise and returns diminish. Concurrently, the advantages of widening the investment net also increase: product is more readily available elsewhere, it offers higher potential returns and it may offer returns disproportionate to the added risk since these may be relatively inefficient markets with prices unrelated to intrinsic worth.

It is the business of investors, but outside the scope of this book, to investigate relative levels of price and of worth. This study is confined to one aspect of the scenario: the different indigenous valuation processes. By elucidating this subject it is hoped to make a contribution to the overall picture of varying methods of appraisal and pricing, and spheres of influence of valuers, users and investors. However, a great deal more work will need to be carried out before investors have a secure understanding of the relationship of appraisal of worth and pricing to inform their acquisition and disposal decisions.

1.3   THE CULTURAL PROBLEM AND THE VALUATION PROCESS

Most valuation texts concentrate on the construction and manipulation of mathematical models designed to express chosen value concepts such as likely sale price or investment worth. These models have usually been evolved by practitioners and are constantly being criticized, refined, supplemented or replaced by new models proposed by practitioners and, increasingly, academics. Some may have been enshrined in law, or alternatively adopted by client or other professional bodies and explanation in the literature is invariably aimed at readers familiar with the national context in which they are used. This book, by examining valuation processes within and across national spheres of influence, addresses a more heterogeneous practice base and target audience. As a result, valuation processes rather than valuation methods alone are discussed.

The essential problem is the cultural nature of valuation. It is often said that valuation is an art rather than a science and, like all art, valuation cannot be fully appreciated without an understanding of its cultural context. This means the business or economic culture of the country, a concept of great complexity and subtlety. There are national expectations (low inflation in a stable economy in Germany, higher inflation and a severely cyclical economy in Italy and the UK), national laws on land registration, property ownership and occupation (rent indexation in Germany and France, upwards-only rent review in the UK), fiscal regimes, company law and norms (frequent take-over and merger of mainly quoted companies in the UK, a large privately-owned industrial base in Germany, with few take-overs) and, of course, different dynamics of politics and society, manufacturing and service industries and the property they use.

A practitioner or researcher operating in one country may misinterpret the valuation process in another through ignorance of this complex scenario of economic interactions and their social, legal and political backdrop. Therefore, this book does not confine itself to the technical aspects of valuation, as do many other national references, rather it supplements the details of law, mathematics and valuation concepts or definitions with an overview of clients, valuers' education and employment, tenure norms, data sources and philosophy. Unfortunately it is difficult for those steeped in their own national system to identify the cultural aspects which may be unique, and therefore interest the reader from another country, and few valuers are well educated in comparative economics or business studies. The book makes an attempt to address the question of the cultural context of valuation, but knowledge of this area is so underdeveloped at present that it can only be a tentative first step.

These cultural aspects can have profound repercussions for the practice of valuation. The accounting culture of many countries avoids revaluation of property for accounting purposes; assets are carried in the accounts at their cost to the business. By contrast, in the UK, which has a large publicly quoted equity market, property is regularly revalued for annual accounts, providing a substantial workload for valuers and wide-ranging debates about the appropriate methods of valuation for this purpose (RICS, 1994). Not only does UK accounting culture enhance the size of the valuation profession, but also its degree of sophistication in developing practice and theory. At present, the valuation profession enjoys varying degrees of development and coordination in different countries, resulting from such cultural factors.

Although the UK valuation profession may be considered as well developed, the debate reported by Mallinson (RICS, 1994) reveals areas such as loan security valuation where there is much to be learnt. Indeed, ideas from other valuation traditions may be able to contribute (Downie, 1993), particularly when looked at in the light of research into the nature of the economic forces driving shifts in value. The German concept of *Verkaufswert*, or 'sustainable value', ties in with Coakley's analysis of property pricing which characterizes property prices in a boom as being dissociated from use-value (Coakley, 1994). Viewed from this angle, the pressure for loan security valuations to be accompanied by forecasts can stem from the sustainability of the user-market and its ability to maintain rental growth. The possibility of learning from each other's valuation experience and theory is a strong reason for studying valuation processes in other countries.

1.4 ORGANIZATION OF THE BOOK

The book is divided into two parts. The first, consisting of four chapters, provides a rationale and parameters for the work, and sets the overall framework of definitions, concepts and client requirements for the valuation purposes discussed. The second part examines the theory and practice of valuation in 12 countries. The book concludes with a comparative chapter in which the editors take the opportunity of highlighting the major themes of the work and identifying issues for future research.

1.4.1   Part One: Theoretical basis of valuation

Many valuation texts are organized around definitions of value and valuation methods or models. There has, however, been very little systematic scrutiny of this classification framework until recently. The dramatic volatility in commercial property values which occurred in the UK during 1987–1994 precipitated not only a rash of litigation but also a review by the RICS of all aspects of commercial property valuation practice. The results of the Committee's work were published as *The Mallinson Report* (RICS, 1994) and provide a detailed and useful consideration of value concepts and valuation methods or models and their potential use by clients. The discussions reported suggest the scope for varied interpretation of apparently well-established concepts such as 'open market value', and this within just one country. As well as pointing to the need for clearly defined and appropriate value concepts, Mallinson highlights the indistinct boundary between concepts and methods: for instance, is the depreciated replacement cost a value definition or a valuation method? The importance of these issues for this text is that some common language of value definition and mathematical models is required upon which to base cross-border communication and analysis. Chapter 2 sets out to provide just such a framework of concepts, models and language which are then followed through in the succeeding chapters on valuation objectives and individual country processes.

At the same time it is important that the subtleties of national differences are not obscured. For instance, a bank lending on the security of property in the UK may seek an 'open market value under the *"White Book"*' (RICS, 1992) or an 'estimated realization price', and a German mortgage bank may seek a *Beleihungswert* based on 'sustainable value' defined under the Mortgage Bank Law. All three of these are different versions of the concept of exchange price or market value giving rise to different figures and yet all are required by apparently similar clients for apparently identical purposes, the security of a loan. The editors have been acutely aware of the dangers of neglecting such nuances and have sought to distinguish them throughout.

Valuation is carried out for many purposes, their relative importance varying from one country to another and from time to time. Obvious examples are:

valuation for	purchase and sale, including	for occupation
		for investment
		for (re)development
	accounts, including	for annual accounts
		for stock market flotation/merger
		for pricing of investment bonds/units
		for performance measurement
	letting	
	loan security	
	taxation, including	inheritance tax
		occupation tax
		capital gains on disposal

	wealth tax
statutory purposes, including	taxation on transfer
	compulsory acquisition
	by a public body
	replotting of land
	compensation for
	planning restrictions

Since it is not practical for a book of this size to cover all these valuation objectives, two fields of valuation activity have been chosen to provide a focus for the authors and thereby place limitations on the scope of the book. In selecting valuation for loan security and for investment purposes, the editors were influenced by the growth of activity in these fields in recent years.

The drive to internationalize investment has been explained and justified by Solnik (1991) in the wider context, and by Sweeney (1993) and Baum and Schofield (1991) in the field of property. These arguments were brought into sharp focus with the raised awareness of European markets resulting from the creation of the Single European market in 1993. Several catalysts to increased cross-border property investment activity have been identified. Sweeney applies the argument forwarded by Solnik in the context of equity markets: increasing diversification opportunities by expanding into economies with non-synchronous cycles, arguing that diversification between European national markets can improve portfolio performance. Baum and Schofield look at Europe as one market, to be balanced by global diversification. In contrast, Lizieri and Finlay (1995) question the long-term opportunities for diversification of the type posited by Sweeney, should the European economies converge under the impetus of monetary union and market unification.

Whatever the outcome of this debate, investors have been alerted to the possibility of improving portfolio performance by diversification across borders. The removal of restrictions on Swedish investment precipitated a rush of money into German, UK and other markets in the late 1980s which demonstrated the desire of investors to expand from the limitations of their national investment product.

Whilst there can be little doubt about the interest of investors in markets outside their own, many have found the practical hurdles numerous and hard to overcome (DTZ Debenham Thorpe, 1993). Among these is the cultural diversity of property markets mentioned above. This manifests itself in problems as diverse as uncertainty over how floorspace is measured for quotation of rental values, through to complex taxation rules and the variation in leasing practice with all its implications for income growth and risk (Adair *et al.*, 1995). Added to this is the lack of historical performance data for most European property markets, the crucial basis of investment understanding, expectations and strategic decision-making. This has been noted by Nabarro and Unsworth (1992) and Sweeney (1993) and is, as yet, a major unresolved problem. The search is therefore underway for time series valuation data from reliable and consistent sources in European countries.

In the UK the problem has largely been solved by the major investing institutions, insurance companies, pension funds and property unit trusts, pooling information through the Investment Property Databank (IPD). In addition, various valuation-based performance indices are produced commercially by larger property consultancies (Society of Property Researchers, 1993). The data produced in the UK is of a high standard viewed in the European context, and yet the reliability of its output has been queried on the basis that it is valuation rather than transaction based (Brown, 1991). The debate has centred about two issues: firstly that of serial correlation of valuations, the result of valuers looking back at past evidence and values and so failing to mirror the true volatility of property prices (Cullen, 1994). A secondary issue has been the dominance of valuation by large property consultants, which might take a unified view of value movements and so unduly influence the overall performance figures. This last issue has been answered by the monitoring of valuations to ensure that no one valuation consultant produces more than 25% of the valuation of the IPD Index (Society of Property Researchers, 1993).

Judging by the evolution of these crucial time series in the UK, the issue of valuation will be important to the success of any attempt to initiate similar data series in other countries. Nabarro and Unsworth (1992) reported the difficulties of constructing a performance index for France and highlighted the difficulty of using valuations already produced for accounting purposes. Apart from the scarcity of revaluations, in a country where most property is carried in accounts at cost, the lack of certainty about the basis of valuation of those figures which were available was identified as a significant problem. It was announced in autumn 1994 that IPD, working in conjunction with major investors in the Netherlands, is to produce a performance index series for the Dutch property market. It is likely that this was the most fertile of the other European markets for such an undertaking due to the structure of its property industry, which involves large contributory pension funds and insurance companies.

Where the series are to be used for purposes involving comparison of one national property sector's performance against another, as is inevitable in international diversification studies, the issue of internal consistency is exacerbated by the need for international compatability of valuation practice. The extent to which this is likely to be a problem is as yet unknown; this book contributes to the debate by highlighting differences in the valuation definitions and methodology.

The property investment industry has always been intimately involved with the banking system due to the suitability of property as loan collateral and from this relationship arises the need for property valuation. The discussion of this particular client need has probably reached its most sophisticated articulation in *The Mallinson Report* (RICS, 1994). Indeed, problems arising from loan security valuations were one of the motives for commissioning the report and have been under review by the UK courts following the property recession of the late 1980s and early 1990s. In particular, the Schneider 'Zeil-Galerie' collapse in Germany has increased interest in this area of valuation. Issues under review range from the appropriate concept of value to be used through to the acceptable valuation tolerance in a volatile market, the need for the valuer to forecast falls in value, valuation in a 'thin' market, where few transactions provide evidence of levels of value, undue influence of the borrower for business reasons, and the lack of understanding by the client of the implications of a valuation.

The issue is of more than passing interest due to the wide-ranging effects of bad debt on the stability of banking systems and the resilience of economies. Coakley (1994) expands this theme, showing the importance of bad property-secured debt in the UK, French, Swedish, American and Japanese economies. This analysis suggests that property took on the character of a quasi-financial asset during the 1980s, leading to increasingly volatile property prices. The simultaneous integration of international financial markets extended the property market crisis beyond the boundaries of the originating countries. Some commentators have suggested that this crisis is due in part to competition by the banks in pursuit of market share, resulting in incautious lending to the property industry. Whatever the relationship, the effect of the influx of overseas loans into the UK and the subsequent market collapse has been to export some of this financial instability to the banking systems of other countries. Governmental safeguards against imprudent bank lending vary from one country to another. In the UK the destabilizing influence of excessive lending to property companies was well advanced before the Governor of the Bank of England commented on it in May 1987. In contrast, the German Banking Supervisory Authority controls and monitors even the detail of the loan security valuation process.

Lending by overseas banks to the UK property industry was important in the late 1980s property boom. Relaxation of controls on cross-border activity by the German Hypothekenbanken in 1992 have led to increased activity outside Germany (DTZ Debenham Thorpe, 1993). This globalization of bank lending and other financial activity leads to the need for banking clients to understand the valuation processes indigenous to the markets which secure their lending. Problems with reconciling differences in practice may drive a move to unified and consistent valuation processes for loan security, just as in the fields of investment and accounting. This could be achieved by market forces in the sense that valuation users will opt for the system which best serves their business, or it may be initiated by the European Commission in the interests of financial stability or of free competition within the industry.

1.4.2 Part Two: Valuation practice in Europe

In considering valuation practice, experts from selected countries have provided accounts of their national systems. The editors, recognizing the importance of comparability and differences between the respective national contexts, identified a number of core issues for inclusion in these country specific chapters. These include the following:

1. an introduction to the practice of valuation in the country, the importance of investment and loan security valuation and the main client groups for each type of valuation;
2. the legislative or regulatory context within which the valuation practice is set;
3. other contextual influences such as the relationship of valuers and financiers, the influence of professional bodies and cultural issues;
4. property tenure and letting formats, including the duration of agreements or contracts, rent adjustment mechanisms, income growth patterns, income risk and gross to net income adjustment;
5. the theoretical basis of valuation techniques, including the concepts or bases of valuation, valuation methods and mathematical models;

6. database management with particular reference to data collection, methods of measurement, market transparency, reliability and information technology;
7. the practical application of the methods, namely assembly and analysis of comparables, determination of value, income growth – explicit and implicit approaches, incorporation of risk and reporting.

A specific limitation is a variation in the degree to which valuation practice is developed in each country. This may be influenced by such factors as volume and sophistication of client needs, the legislative requirement for valuations, the state of evolution of property investment and speculative development industries and the role of professional groups of valuers. For this reason some chapters may appear more highly developed and detailed than others, mirroring the varying development of valuation practice.

Although there is a considerable body of literature on property valuation available, within individual countries, some of which is referenced in the respective chapters, its use to researchers of international comparative valuation are frustratingly limited. The most testing problem is that of language, particularly technical language. *The Multilingual Dictionary of Real Estate* (van Breugel *et al.*, 1993), although helpful, cannot alone overcome this difficulty. Few, if any, translators can, even at great expense, provide an authoritative translation of the huge volume of specialist work required for an overview in which the researcher can have confidence. Thus, in this text local technical words, when first introduced, are accompanied by an English translation or by an explanation in instances where direct translation is not feasible. Furthermore, many of the accounts of national valuation processes include valuation examples to illustrate the methods which are discussed.

1.4.3 Part Three: European valuation perspective

The book concludes with a comparative analysis of valuation theory and practice in the countries described and recommendations for areas of further research. The comparative analysis examines variations in approach to the valuation of a standard prime office property for investment purposes across each of the European countries. Similarities and differences in approach, in terms of sources and utilization of market data, and in technique are discussed. Opportunities for harmonization of critical areas of valuation theory and practice are considered, for example bases of value, methods of measurement and standardization of techniques. In addition, the prospects for a common European valuation approach are discussed.

REFERENCES

Adair, A.S., Berry, J.N. and McGreal, W.S. (1995) Fiscal policy, taxation incentives and inner-city housing development. *Housing Studies*, **10** (1), 105–15.

Baum, A. and Schofield, A. (1991) Property as a global asset, in *Investment, Procurement and Performance in Construction* (eds Venmore-Rowland, *et al.*), RICS/E & FN Spon, London.

Bell, D. and Hobbs, P. (1993) The market for UK property consultants in Europe. Paper presented at the Conference 'European Real Estate: an Agenda for Research', Reading, UK.

Berry, J.N. and McGreal, W.S. (1995) *European Cities, Planning Systems and Property Markets*, E & FN Spon, London, p. 417.

Brown, G. (1991) *Property Investment and the Capital Markets*, E & FN Spon, London.

Coakley, J. (1994) The integration of property and financial markets. *Environment and Planning A*, **26**, 697–713.

Cullen, I. (1994) *The Accuracy of Valuations Revisited*. Proceedings of the RICS Cutting Edge Conference, London, pp. 91–101.

Downie, M.L. (1993) Property valuation in Germany: a different tradition. Paper presented at the Conference 'European Real Estate: an Agenda for Research', Reading, UK.

DTZ Debenham Thorpe (1993) *Money into Property*, DTZ Debenham Thorpe, London.

Lizieri, C. and Finlay, L. (1995) International property portfolio strategies: problems and opportunities. *Journal of Property Valuation and Investment*, **13**(1), 6–21.

Nabarro, R. and Unsworth, R. (1992) *European Property Investment Performance Measurement*. Henry Stewart Conference Proceedings, London.

RICS (1990) *Statements of Asset Valuation Practice and Guidance Notes ('Red Book')*, Royal Institution of Chartered Surveyors Books, London.

RICS (1992) *Manual of Valuation Guidance Notes ('White Book')*, 3rd edn (as amended), Royal Institution of Chartered Surveyors Books, London.

RICS (1993) *An Agenda for Research*, Royal Institution of Chartered Surveyors Books, London.

RICS (1994) *The Mallinson Report: Report of the President's Working Party on Commercial Property Valuations*, Royal Institution of Chartered Surveyors, London.

Society of Property Researchers (1993) *Property Indices Research Report*. SPR, London.

Solnik, B. (1991) *International Investments*, 2nd edn, Addison-Wesley, Reading, Mass.

Sweeney, F. (1993) Mapping a European property investment strategy. *Journal of Property Valuation and Investment*, **11**(3), 259–67.

Van Breugel, L., Williams, R. and Wood, B. (1993) *The Multilingual Dictionary of Real Estate*, E & FN Spon, London.

Theoretical basis of valuation

PART
1

Concepts and models of value

2

Nick French and
Peter Byrne

2.1 INTRODUCTION

Economic theory suggests various concepts of value which will apply to property as a factor of production. Valuation practice has interpreted these concepts and, in many countries, these have been developed into documented bases of value or definitions of value. The aim of such definitions is to communicate to users of the valuation the significance of the valuation figure and to achieve consistency of approach among valuers. Alongside the evolution of value concepts and definitions of value, practitioners in each country have developed valuation methodologies closely linked to the bases of valuation.

This chapter sets out a framework of value concepts, bases of valuation and valuation methodology. The objective is to provide a background to underlying concepts which underpin each country's valuation practice.

2.2 CONCEPTS OF VALUE

Land and property (any reference to property in this chapter is taken to mean real property or real estate) are factors of production. As with any other asset, the value of the land flows from the use to which it is put and, in turn, that is dependent upon the demand (and supply) for the product that is produced. If there is a high demand for the product (at a fixed level of supply) the price will increase and the economic rent for the land/property will increase accordingly. This is the underlying paradigm of Ricardian rent theory where the supply of land is fixed and a single good is produced. In such a case the rent of land is wholly an economic rent; 'the rent of land is high because the price of corn is high'.

The theory is rooted in classical economic tradition but has been developed and extended by Marxist economists on the one hand and neoclassical economists on the other. Classical theory generally distinguishes between two kinds of

European Valuation Practice. Edited by Alastair Adair, Mary Lou Downie, Stanley McGreal and Gerjan Vos. Published in 1996 by E & FN Spon, London. ISBN 0 419 20040 1

price – price of production (determined by the labour theory of value) and market price (determined by supply and demand). Neoclassical theory makes no such distinction and only recognizes market price. It is based on a coherent and consistent theory of value and price. The value theory is psychological, or subjective, in nature; price theory is market orientated. The neoclassical paradigm makes a distinction between what an asset is 'worth' to an individual and the asset's price of exchange in the market-place. In a perfect market, where any individual has access to the same information as all others in the market, price and worth should coincide. However, in a market where access to information is not uniform, such as the property market, it is more likely that the two figures will diverge. Furthermore, it is important to recognize that the price of an asset in the property market will differ according to the use to which the asset is to be put. Economic theory would suggest that where there is no demand for the good, then property as a factor in the production of that good has no value. It may however have a value in an alternative form of production and the property would be redeveloped or reutilized accordingly.

For any valuation or calculation of worth model to have validity it must produce an accurate estimate of the market price or worth of the property investment. The model should therefore reflect the market culture and conditions at the time of the valuation. It should be remembered that the model should be a representation of the underlying fundamentals of the market. It is important that the distinction between price and worth is not only recognized but also fully understood. However, there is a sizeable and vocal contingent who do not accept that there is a distinction between 'price' and 'worth'. They simply believe that a property is 'worth' what it can be sold for and thus 'worth' **must** be the same as 'price'. At first sight this proposition appears to be tenable, but it fails to recognize the underlying motivation of any investment decision. A rational investor will make the decision to buy an asset if the price in the market is equal to or below his/her assessment of the present worth (at the required target rate of return) of the future cash flow which is likely (or predicted) to be produced by that asset. Conversely, all other things being equal, a decision to sell will be triggered at a point where the price in the market is equal or greater than the individual assessment of worth. In other words, investors trade or retain on the basis of their own perception of the future and consequently their own yield requirement. Each of these will differ from investor to investor. If they did not there would be no market. Thus, to state that 'worth' is the same as 'price' is failing to appreciate the underlying motivation of all financial markets. In a perfect market where there is complete information available to all players, and that information is analysed in a uniform and consistent manner by all participants, the divergence in opinions and perceptions will be quite small. There will therefore be a grouping of 'worth' and if the price is ascertained with reference to this thought process, there will be a similar conformity in opinions of price. Again, an analogy would be the stock market. Where there is little difference between price and worth trading takes place based largely on the marginal differences of opinion between the investors. Market value is the best assessment of the trading price of the building, and appraised worth is the range of individual assessments of worth 'to each appraiser'. Thus, price sits in a wider set of possible values ascribed by individuals.

In a dispersed market there might be a large number of possible investors each of whom have their own information bases and their own interpretation of the attractiveness of the investment. As such there would be a large number of possible 'worths'. Price will therefore be one of many possible values. However, in a more perfect market there is a uniformity in the information available and thus less divergence in the calculations of worth. Price therefore will be found within a much smaller subset of possible values.

Thus, in the property market, what is often called 'a valuation' is the best estimate of the trading price of the building and appraised worth is the range of individual assessments of worth to a range of appraisers. This process is considered further in Chapter 3.

A number of issues arise from this consideration of price and worth; information availability, heterogeneous/homogeneous asset, liquidity/depth of market, implicit calculation of worth (comparable pricing) and explicit calculation of worth (components of future performance). In effect, for the market there is a single price and for an individual there is a preferred appraised worth. Trading occurs where these two differ. Investors will buy when appraised worth exceeds the price; they will sell if price exceeds their appraised worth.

In this context, the following convention is adopted: price is the actual exchange price in the market-place, market value is an estimation of that price were the property to be sold in the market and calculation of worth is used to assess the inherent worth to the individual or group of individuals.

1. **Valuation** – the process of determining market value. An estimation of the price of exchange in the market-place.
2. **Calculation of worth** – the provision of a written estimate of the net monetary worth at a stated date of the benefits and costs of ownership of a specified interest in property to the instructing party, and reflecting the purpose(s) specified by that party (this wording is the RICS definition of 'calculation of worth').

In a perfect market, where all investors have the same information, 'price' and 'worth' should produce the same figure. The role of the valuation is to model the thought process underlying the calculation of worth.

In many property markets it is commonplace for the ownership of property to be separate from its use. As a result these concepts of price and worth have to be applied to two separate, but interrelated, markets – the market in ownership for investment purposes and the market for owner-occupation. Often the price of exchange will be the same whether the purchaser has investment or occupation in mind, but none the less the view of the two groups of bidders will be different. An investor will view worth as the discounted value of the rental stream produced by the asset, whereas the owner-occupier will see the asset as a factor of production and assign to it a worth derived from the property's contribution to the profits of the business. No doubt both groups of bidders will also be mindful of its potential resale price to a purchaser from the other group.

The concept of the worth of a property is most important in markets which are underdeveloped in terms of liquidity and the separation of ownership and use rights. Here most transactions are based on owner-occupier's views of the worth of the property, i.e. the contribution it will make to business profit, as well as subjective issues such as status and feelings of security. Valuers, with hardly any transaction evidence, can only attempt to replicate these calculations of worth in arriving at an estimate of exchange price.

Interestingly, the other development of the worth concept has been more recent and in markets of a quite different character, the sophisticated institutional investment markets, characterized by higher turnover and separation of ownership and use. Here the idea that worth can be estimated from the subjective viewpoint of each investor has been utilized in giving investment advice to aid investors in deciding to buy, sell or hold property assets, as discussed in Chapter 3.

2.3 THE ESTIMATION OF EXCHANGE PRICE

It is apparent that the 'valuation professions' throughout Europe have tended to concentrate on the price of property assets in exchange and where worth has been considered it has looked exclusively at the investment aspect. This chapter inevitably reflects this view of the market in concentrating upon this investment 'culture'.

One of the paramount concerns of the profession is the need to ensure that information presented to a client is clear and unambiguous. Not only should all parties understand the terminology used, but it is also important that the client receives all other information that might be required to make a rational financial or investment decision. The latter point does not only concern the semantics of definitions of exchange price, but must also address the issue of valuation methodology. Given that clients are themselves becoming more sophisticated in the way they determine whether to buy or sell property, then the pricing model used to assess the most likely exchange price should reflect their thought process. This requires the valuer to better understand the client's requirements and leads to the adoption of more explicit valuation models which can reflect the increased level of data and information available.

2.3.1 Definitions of value

A definition of value is an attempt to clarify the assumptions made in estimating the exchange price of a property if it were to be sold in the open market. These assumptions can include the nature of the legal interest, the physical condition of the building, the nature and timing of the market and assumptions about possible purchasers in that market. Given that a compelling reason for using market value definitions is to ensure consistency in the process of valuation it is unfortunate that there are a number of such definitions. In the UK, for example, the country with which the authors are most familiar, there are currently eight different recognized market value definitions. The reason given for having such a large number is that it is desirable for the user of estimates of exchange price to have a detailed knowledge of the purpose and scope of the valuation. However, it must be recognized that a proliferation of definitions can be counter-productive as, obtusely, it increases the potential for misinterpretation. With only one definition, whilst there might be a period when people debate its precise interpretation, ultimately one consensus view will prevail and a universally acceptable definition will have been created. If, however, different definitions are proffered, the ambit for debate is extended. Not only will there be differences of opinion related to each individual definition but there will also be confusion over the distinction between them. In the short term the wish for clarity actually produces perplexity.

An illustration of this phenomenon has occurred recently in the UK, with the introduction of two new definitions of value related to financial loans secured on property assets. Until January 1996, there were two RICS manuals relating to the valuation of property. These were the *Statements of Asset Valuation Practice and Guidance Notes* (*'Red Book'*) and *Manual of Valuation Guidance Notes* (*'White Book'*). The *'Red Book'* provided mandatory statements to be applied to valuations that are to be published in financial statements. All other valuations were covered by the non-mandatory guidelines of the *'White Book'*. The existence of two manuals has caused significant confusion since their inception and they have now been merged into one document. The new document, *RICS Appraisal and Valuation Manual* (new *'Red Book'*) is a mixture of guidance (notes) and compulsion (practice statements) but applies to any written valuation. The new definitions were originally introduced in the old *'White Book'* in Valuation Guidance Note 12 (VGN 12), but have both been transferred to the new *'Red Book'*. The new definitions, of 'estimated realization price' (ERP) and 'estimated restricted realization price' (ERRP), were introduced as alternatives to the previously accepted definition of 'open market value' (OMV). To help illustrate the differences between each of these definitions, each is reproduced in full below. It should also be noted that a further variation is introduced when considering the market value of a property in owner-occupation. For this the definition of OMV is amended to include an additional assumption that the market value will be based on the existing use of the property continuing.

(a) Open market value (OMV) – Practice Statement 4.2 (RICS Appraisal and Valuation Manual)

An opinion of the best price at which the sale of an interest in property would have been completed unconditionally for cash consideration on the date of valuation, assuming:

1. a willing seller;
2. that, prior to the date of valuation, there has been a reasonable period (having regard to the nature of the property and the state of the market) for the proper marketing of the interest, for the agreement of price and terms and for the completion of the sale;
3. that the state of the market, level of values and other circumstances were, on any earlier assumed date of exchange of contracts, the same as on the date of valuation;
4. that no account is taken of any additional bid by a purchaser with a special interest;
5. that both parties to the transaction had acted knowledgeably, prudently and without compulsion.

The OMV definition assumes that the property has been marketed and that terms have been agreed, hence it represents an estimate of the price of exchange for the property had it been sold today. This might be different to the price that might be achieved if the property were placed on the market today and sold at a later assumed date. This alternative 'market value' has, in the UK, been defined as the estimated realization price (ERP).

(b) Estimated realization price (ERP) – Practice Statement 4.5 (RICS Appraisal and Valuation Manual)

An opinion as to the amount of cash consideration before deduction of costs of sale which the valuer considers, on the date of valuation, can reasonably be expected to be obtained on future completion of an unconditional sale of the interest in the subject property assuming:

1. a willing seller;
2. that completion will take place on a future date specified by the valuer to allow a reasonable period for proper marketing (having regard to the nature of the property and the state of the market);
3. that no account is taken of any additional bid by a purchaser with a special interest;
4. that both parties to the transaction will act knowledgeably, prudently and without compulsion.

In addition to the ERP definition, the RICS also introduced a further definition which defined market value if the property was being marketed from today but where the marketing period was curtailed due to necessity to sell within a short specified period. This is known as estimated restricted realization price (ERRP).

(c) Estimated restricted realization price (ERRP) – Practice Statement 4.6 (RICS Appraisal and Valuation Manual)

An opinion as to the amount of cash consideration before deduction of costs of sale which the valuer considers, on the date of valuation, can reasonably be expected to be obtained on future completion of an unconditional sale of the interest in the subject property assuming:

1. a willing seller;
2. that completion will take place on a future date specified by the client (and recorded in the valuer's report) which does not allow a reasonable period for proper marketing (having regard to the nature of the property and the state of the market);
3. that no account is taken of any additional bid by a purchaser with a special interest;
4. that both parties to the transaction will act knowledgeably, prudently and without compulsion.

This is the same as ERP but allows the lender to specify the period available to achieve the sale.

Discussion continues in the UK over the implementation of these definitions, the need for them and their suitability for different client needs. The extent to which the new definitions will be asked for by clients is also still uncertain.

The main distinction between the definitions quoted above is in the time frame during which the hypothetical transaction is conducted. A valuation, under any definition, is simply a 'snapshot' in time. It represents the best estimate of price for that property on the date of sale. There is a common misconception held by many clients (and some valuers) that valuations have a 'shelf-life'. The market value today may not be the same as the market value tomorrow. In a rising market it will be higher, in a falling market it will be lower. This relationship of price with time is well understood in other markets. In the stock market, the market value of shares will vary constantly as the market changes. No broker would guarantee that the price achievable today would be achievable tomorrow indeed, the futures market is based on the premise that prices will change over time – investors effectively trade on the basis that their respective expectations are different. Yet experience has shown that where property is concerned many clients believe that the valuation provided somehow acts as a safeguard against changes in the market.

2.3.2 International and European definitions of value

It is fair to say that the influence of UK valuation standards is quite far reaching and, in particular, the definition of OMV has been used extensively internationally as the basis of market value. However, in recent years, there have been a number of new international initiatives which have introduced alternative, and often conflicting, definitions of market value. The first of these is the new international definition of value – 'market value' (MV). This definition was introduced by the International Assets Valuation Standards Committee (TIAVSC) as part of its International Valuation Standards. The objective of this standard is to provide a common definition of market value. This standard also explains the general criteria relating to this definition and to its application in the valuation of property when the purpose and function of the valuation calls for estimation of market value. Market value is a representation of value in exchange, or the amount a property would bring if offered for sale in the open market at the date of valuation under circumstances that meet the requirements of the market value definition. In order to estimate market value, a valuer must first estimate highest and best use, or most probable use. That use may be a continuation of a property's existing use or some alternative. These determinations are made from market evidence.

Market value is estimated through application of valuation methods and procedures that reflect the nature of property and the circumstances under which given property would most likely trade in the open market. The most common methodologies of estimating market value are direct capital comparison, the investment method, the contractor's method and the profits method.

Market value is defined for the purpose of the Standards as follows *market value (MV) – Practice statement 4.1* (RICS Appraisal and Valuation Manual).

> The estimated amount for which an asset should exchange on the date of valuation between a willing buyer and a willing seller in an arm's length transaction after proper marketing wherein the parties had each acted knowledgeably, prudently and without compulsion.

This definition, although much shorter, is effectively the same as the UK definition of open market value and indeed the RICS has included the definition of market value alongside open market value in the *RICS Appraisal and Valuation Manual*. It is possible that market value might become the preferred definition in the UK bringing the RICS into line with the International Assets Valuation Standards Committee.

However, the new international definition is not the only alternative definition available. The European Group of Valuers of Fixed Assets (TEGOVOFA) have their own definition of market value:

> Market value is intended to mean the price at which an interest in a property might reasonably be expected to be sold by private treaty at the date of valuation assuming:
>
> 1. a willing seller;
> 2. a reasonable period within which to negotiate the sale, taking into account the nature of the property and the state of the market;
> 3. values will remain static throughout the period;
> 4. the property will be freely exposed to the market with reasonable publicity;
> 5. no account is to be taken of an additional bid by a special purchaser.

Interestingly, this European definition is forward looking and is akin to the new UK definition of ERP, albeit it does assume a static market between now and sale unlike the ERP definition. To add further complications, the European Community has standardized legislation relating to the valuation of assets held by insurance companies and this introduces a new definition of market value.

> Market value shall mean the price at which land and buildings could be sold under private contract between a willing seller and an arm's length buyer on the date of valuation, it being assumed that the property is publicly exposed to the market, that market conditions permit orderly disposal and that a normal period, having regard to the nature of the property, is available for the negotiation of the sale.
>
> Extract from SI 1993 No. 3246
> The Companies Act 1985 (Insurance Company Accounts) Regs 1993

Again, this definition, although worded differently, would equate to a forward-looking valuation and is akin to ERP in the UK.

The valuation profession internationally is therefore confronted with a range of possible definitions of market value. It is difficult to determine the appropriate basis when each definition is slightly different. However, it should be recognized that all the definitions cited above (OMV, OMVEU, ERP, ERRP, TIAVSC MV, TEGOFAVA MV and insurance MV) are price definitions. The distinction between each price definition in each case is slightly different. Confusion arises because of the profession's concentration on semantics. If the valuer stops viewing each definition as mutually exclusive it is possible to view each definition as a simple price definition. The distinction is then made as to the date of sale. If the property is being hypothetically sold today, open market value will apply. If it is to be sold at a future date after reasonable marketing, market value or ERP will be appropriate. Hopefully, over time, one definition will become prevalent and those definitions that are less used will be replaced by the preferred definitions.

2.4 MARKET VALUE AND COST

The above section has concentrated on the various definitions of market value. However, there are two recognized bases of valuation of land and buildings, market value and replacement cost. The latter is sometimes used for accounting purposes where a historic cost is to be used in a company's accounts, yet, as discussed earlier, it may be viewed as a valid valuation method in its own right. The basis of replacement cost valuations is the determination of the gross replacement cost less allowances for depreciation and obsolescence.

The 'cost method' therefore has two possible applications, one that may be used in market value estimates and one that is not. When the cost method is applied to market value estimates all elements of the method are derived from open market evidence. When a cost method is applied to non-market value circumstances, non-market elements are applied. This distinction between market and non-market elements is analogous to the difference between price and worth. If the market uses a cost model to assess market value, then the application of this method using market-derived information will produce an estimate of exchange price in that market. If, however, user-specific inputs are used in the model the resulting figure will represent the worth of that property to that user and this might not be the same as the exchange price in the market.

In further contrast, the 'depreciated replacement cost method' (DRC) combines market and non-market elements and cannot be regarded as market value. These different cost applications must not be confused or misconstrued in making, presenting or applying *market value* estimates.

Given that price should reflect the thought process of a potential purchaser it is not unreasonable that where there is no established trading market then cost of replacement will become the principal form of pricing. This proposition is strongly supported by the experiences of pricing in the emerging markets of the old Eastern bloc countries where transaction prices have been (initially) influenced by the replacement cost or contractor's method.

2.5 VALUATION MODELS

The purpose of any method of valuation is to model the thought process of the players in the market. The aim of a valuation is to determine the price at which it is expected that a property asset might change hands in the free market. The model should therefore attempt to reflect how the buyers in that market will assess the market value of that property.

If all property and all buyers were homogeneous there would be one method of valuation. On a *pro rata* basis all property would tend toward one unit price. An analogy to this hypothetical situation is the stock market. Any one share is priced the same as any other share in the same company and that price is determined by what buyers in the market are currently willing to pay. At a fundamental level, the buyers will assess the worth of the shares to them, based on their own perceptions and expectations on the future performance of that company. If they think the future cash flow to be generated from the dividends (and/or capital changes) will produce satisfactory returns they will pay a high price to receive that cash flow. If they believe the growth prospects are less attractive they will pay less for the shares. In other words, prices are determined by the buyers' perception of worth. The sale will occur at the point which reflects the worth of that share to the investor with the highest expectation of growth. That investor will outbid those with lower expectations. If the market is efficient it is likely that this price will reflect the consensus view.

A fundamental valuation model should therefore reflect this thought process of determining worth. However, in a market where there are frequent transactions it is possible to observe the level of prices without the need to interpret the underlying fundamentals. Price is determined by comparison.

2.5.1 The direct capital comparative method

The comparative valuation model is one step removed from an analysis of the buyer's intent. Comparison is a more detailed analysis of the original thought process. It can be an efficient method where markets themselves are efficient but can become less reliable when markets are thin or where information is not available universally to the market. In spite of this, comparison has become the principal method of determining price in the property market.

Property, unlike shares, is not a homogeneous asset. Each property is unique in a number of ways. For example, location, physical form, legal interest and permitted use. These parameters, in turn, will determine the potential cash flow of the property as an investment or its utility in owner-occupation. Price will then reflect the highest and best 'bid' for that property under those unique circumstances.

At the extreme, a valuation model will need to incorporate the beliefs and expectations of the individual players in the market. Just as in the stock market, where it is possible to determine price by observation of previous recent sales, it is also possible to assess property market values by comparison. In some submarkets within the overall property market there will be a degree of comparability. One house on a residential estate will be similar to another on the same estate. One square metre of office space in a central location will be similar to other office space in the same area.

The comparability is not exact but there are sufficient similarities for the price of one house to be determined by reference to the recent sale of another house in that location. Judgements will have to be made about the relative merits of the subject property and the comparable property. If the property being valued is considered to be 'better' than the comparable one then a higher price will be paid, if it is less attractive a lower price will result. At the residential level it is possible to analyse a cross-section of sales and thus allocate a market value to the component elements of the house. It is possible to determine the price difference between a house with a garage and one without, the price difference due to an additional bedroom, the market value of a larger garden, etc.

The skill of the valuer is therefore to take a representative cross-section of recent comparable sales and analyse them to determine the market value, the expected price of exchange, for the subject property. The greater the difference between the comparables and the subject property the greater the skill required by the valuer in adjusting the market value to reflect those changes.

2.5.2 The investment or income capitalization method

At its simplest level, the comparable model can be used to determine capital value directly. However, moving from submarkets where there is a high degree of similarity (for example, residential markets) the way in which comparison can be utilized needs to be modified.

In the investment market, for example, direct capital comparison is rarely appropriate because the degree of heterogeneity is much higher. As such, the comparison needs to be broken down further to look at rental (on a *pro-rata* basis) and the initial yield achieved on sale.

This distinction between the rental and the yield reflects an interesting interaction between two submarkets – the occupational market and the investment market. At its simplest level, property can either be owned and occupied by the same party (owner-occupied), or the owner can choose to pass the right of occupation to a third party by letting the property. The tenant will then pay the owner (the landlord) a rent to represent the (normal) annual value of the property to the tenant. The level of rent is determined by the supply of, and demand for, that type of property in the market. This returns to Ricardian rent theory, where the interaction of supply and demand in the occupational submarket produces an economic rent for the property. The level of the rent is in turn determined by the demand for the goods and services produced by the occupying tenant. The rent also represents the return or interest on the money invested in the property by the owner. It is the remuneration for the giving up of the use of the property. This rental income is simply a cash flow and as such the value of the rented property may be determined by the present value of the predicted cash flow.

The investment valuation model should therefore reflect the thought process of determining the worth of the cash flow. It is interesting to note that prior to the time when the 'reverse yield gap' phenomenon arose, when the yields on non-growth, low-risk investments (such as government stock) started to exceed the initial returns on the riskier growth investments (such as property), the investment method of valuation was truly that. It calculated the worth of the rental flow accurately and rationally by reference to the levels of returns of other investment media. The yield was fixed by reference to the government stock rate (say 3–4%) and increased to reflect the additional risk in property (5–6%). The cash flow also tended to be a fixed rent on a long lease (say 99 years). Thus, the valuation was the present worth of that annual net rental at the then current investment rate. It was a full-discounted cash flow method (DCF). This technique was corrupted in the 1960s and 1970s with the advent of rental growth. No longer were rents expected to remain fixed. The combination of inflationary pressure in the economy and real growth on individual property types, as demand outpaced supply, led property owners (investors) to introduce rent reviews to claw back this increased value. Valuers therefore needed to adapt to a 'growth' environment without having access to sufficient computing power or understanding of methodology to allow for growth assumptions explicitly. The traditional method became a short cut to the full DCF method. The capitalization of the initial income at a lower yield meant a higher multiplier [years purchase (YP)] and a corresponding higher market value to reflect the greater attractiveness of the growth investment. In reality, valuers were decapitalizing recent comparable sales and applying the same multiplier (low yield) to the subject property. The investment method ceased to be a rational analytical technique and was now one of simple comparison.

This scenario is perfectly acceptable in a market where there are frequent transactions. It is then possible to observe the level of prices without the need to interpret the underlying fundamentals. Price is determined by comparison. However, the investment method no longer looks at the underlying investment criteria and is now a crude form of benchmarking. It provides a reference point against which to base the subject valuation. The traditional investment method is a coarse, but robust, method of comparison. It does not attempt to analyse the worth of the property investment from first principles. As a result, the 'worth' of a property is effectively forgotten. The method is very capable, in normal markets, of estimating the most likely price of exchange but, given the imperfections of the property market, this is not necessarily the same as the property's inherent worth.

2.5.3   The profits method

The investment method, in this context, is therefore a good example of where valuation methodology has moved away from modelling the thought processes of the players in the market and instead assesses the market value of a subject property by reference to observed recent transactions of similar properties in the same area. It no longer looks at the fundamentals – i.e. the original reasons why the purchasers might be willing to buy at a certain price for such assets in the market. As previously noted, the price of a property asset should reflect the worth of that asset to the purchaser. It is therefore likely that the process of assessing worth will be a reflection of the use of the property to the business. If it is possible to observe the purchase of similar properties the comparables will be used to determine market value. However, if there are insufficient sales to determine a comparable value, and if there is no rent produced because the property is in owner-occupation, then the valuer must determine the value by returning to a detailed market analysis. For instance, the market value of a hotel in owner-occupation will be dependent on the potential cash flow to be derived from ownership. That cash flow will be determined by the number of bedrooms in the hotel, the room rate and the average occupancy rate for the year. In other words, property is simply viewed as a unit of production and it is the valuer's role to assess the economic rent for the property from first principles. This is calculated by assessing the potential revenue to be expected each year from the hotel and deducting all other costs of a prudent hotelier in realizing that cash flow. These costs will include direct costs such as catering, laundry and service. In addition, allowances will need to be made for the remuneration of the hotelier, interest on money borrowed to run the hotel and a return on capital for any equity tied up in the business. Having calculated the liabilities these are deducted from the revenue figure and the residue will be an estimation of the economic rent for the property. The capital value can then be derived by multiplying the annual rent by an appropriate multiplier.

This process reverts to a fundamental analysis of the worth of the property to the business. The economic rent is a derivative of the supply and demand for the final product, in this example the hotel rooms. The same principle will apply to any type of property where the market value of the property is intrinsically linked to the business carried out within that property. Other examples will therefore include restaurants, leisure centres, cinemas, theatres, etc.

2.5.4 The residual method

This analysis of understanding the market value of the land and property to the business can be extended to include the valuation of development property. If one views the process of (re)development as a business, it is possible to assess the market value of land and buildings in their existing form as part of that process. Development occurs where the current use of land and buildings is not the highest and best; by spending money redeveloping the site it is possible to release latent value, as the market value of the land is increased due to the demand for the new use commanding a higher price than the previous use. By viewing development in this way it can be seen that the residual method of valuation is very similar to the profits method.

With the residual method the valuer assesses the market value of the land in a redeveloped form (either by comparison or by the investment method) and deducts from this 'gross development value' all costs that will be incurred in putting the property into the form that will command that price. These costs will include demolition of the existing building (if not already a cleared site), infrastructure works, construction costs, professional fees, finance costs and a remuneration for undertaking the risk of development (developer's profit). By deducting these liabilities from the final market value a residue is produced. This residual represents the maximum capital expenditure for buying the land. It will therefore include all costs of purchase (taxation, legal fees, professional fees and finance). The net residual land value is determined by allowing for these additional land costs. It can be seen, therefore, that the residual land value is, as with any economic rent, dependent upon the supply and demand of the finished product, i.e. the developed property. The greater the demand for the finished property, the higher the gross development value and, if costs remain relatively static, the higher the market value of the land in its original state.

2.5.5 The contractor's method or depreciated replacement cost

The final way in which it is possible to estimate the market value of land and property is the replacement cost or contractor's method. If the property being valued is so specialized that properties of that nature are rarely sold on the open market then it will be effectively impossible to assess its value by reference to comparable sales of similar properties. Similarly, if there is no rental produced, the investment method will also be inappropriate. The profits method could be applied if the property is intrinsically linked to the business carried out in the property; however, where that business is one of production (rather than service) it is difficult to determine the contribution of the property to the overall usage. The plant and machinery contained within is likely to have a greater value to the business than the structure containing it. Thus, once again, the valuer must revert to understanding the thought process of the user of the building. This can be illustrated by reference to a property such as an oil refinery. Here the nature of the business is so specialized that there are no comparisons, the property would be owner-occupied so there is no rental and the plant and the machinery will be the important elements contributing to the value of the business. Thus, the owner of the building will simply assess the market value of the building by reference to its replacement cost. How much would it cost to replace the property if the business were deprived of its use. In simple terms, market value will equate to reconstruction costs. The valuer will assess the market value of the raw land (by reference to comparable land values in an appropriate alternative use), add to this value the cost of rebuilding a new building which could perform the function of the existing structure and, from this information, make subjective adjustments to allow for the obsolescence and depreciation of the existing building relative to the new hypothetical unit. It is reasonable to assume that this mirrors the thought process of the owner-occupier and thus should be viewed as a valid and rational method of valuation.

In the UK there is some confusion as to whether depreciated replacement cost is a method or a basis of valuation. It tends to be used exclusively for the valuation of specialized properties. Specialized properties are those which, due to their specialized nature, are rarely, if ever, sold on the open market to a single occupier for continuation of their existing use, except as part of a sale of the undertaking in occupation. DRC is a method of using current net replacement costs to arrive at the value to the undertaking in occupation of the property as existing at the valuation date, where it is not practicable to ascertain open market value for the existing use.

The DRC basis of valuation requires estimates of the market value of the land in its existing use and of the gross replacement cost of the buildings and other site works, from which appropriate deductions may then be made to allow for the age, condition, economic or functional obsolescence and environmental and other factors which might result in the existing property being worth less than a new replacement. The land is assumed to have the benefit of planning permission for the replacement of the existing buildings (or modern substitute buildings).

It is interesting that in countries where property investment is less prevalent, and where owner-occupation is the favoured method of property utilization, it is not only specialized properties which are valued by the contractor's method. If there is no investment market (i.e. properties will only exchange between owner-occupiers in the market) then the price of exchange will reflect the 'bottom line' cost to the purchaser. This bottom line will be the cost that will need to be incurred for a new-build relative to the existing property that is on the market. There will be a strong correlation between price and cost. However, if the occupation market is dominated by companies renting, and there is a degree of scarcity in the market, then price will be determined not by cost but by the supply and demand characteristics of the occupational market. In such a case, regardless of the nature of the property, the investment method will dominate as the favoured valuation model.

2.6 CONCLUSION

There is continuing debate about the interpretation of value concepts by means of definitions of value and their implementation by means of a valuation methodology. As valuers move from operating in their home country to the demands of a European and international market-place these issues are likely to become more complex. Conversely, the cross-fertilization of ideas provides an opportunity for improved theory and practice.

Market value and price are not one and the same and thus the models used must start to reflect these differences. It is clear that, in determining market price, the model adopted should mirror the thought process of the investors in the market. The information available should be used and analysed in the same way as it would be by other players in the market. If it is not then substantially different valuations may occur and this can only give rise to confusion as to market value in the minds of clients and valuers.

In view of the loss of confidence in the profession across Europe, following the collapse of several important submarkets, it is particularly important that these issues are resolved as soon as possible. The following chapters, which describe theory and practice in several European countries, illustrate the various indigenous applications of the basic concepts of market value, their associated definitions of market value and their application in practice.

FURTHER READING

Evans, A.W. (1988) *The Theory of Land Values – A Reintroduction*, The University of Reading, Department of Economics (Discussion Paper No. 34).

Lichtenstein, P.M. (1983) *An Introduction to Post-Keynesian and Marxian Theories of Value and Price*, Macmillan Press, London.

Ricardo, D. (1926) *Principles of Political Economy and Taxation*, Everyman, London.

RICS (1991) *Statements of Asset Valuation Practice and Guidance Notes (Red Book)*, RICS Books, London.

The Asset Valuation Standards Committee (1976) *The Statement of Asset Valuation Practice and Guidance Notes*, RICS Books, London.

Valuation of investment properties for acquisition, disposal and performance measurement

3

Neil Crosby and
Bryan MacGregor

This chapter examines the appraisal of investment properties for a variety of purposes excluding loan valuations, which are considered in Chapter 4. It is an overview of a subject which has been well documented elsewhere and references to these more detailed treatments are given in the text. In Brown (1991), there is a useful bibliography broken down under various topic headings relating to investment in property.

This chapter is divided into three parts. Section 3.1 examines the role and application of appraisal techniques to find both the value/worth of the investment and its open market value (defined in terms of an estimate of price), and discusses the objectives of investors and the characteristics of property as an investment. Section 3.2 examines property within the portfolio context. Section 3.3 examines the investment appraisal process at the individual property level and section 3.4 identifies the information needs of the appraisal process. Section 3.5 summarizes the chapter within the context of the role of models for property investment decision-making.

3.1 PROPERTY INVESTMENT

3.1.1 The role of investment appraisal

In Chapter 2 the debate regarding the possible distinction between price and value/worth is introduced. Both concepts are particularly important to valuations of investment property for the purposes of acquisition and disposal, performance measurement and financial statements. In a market which is not efficient the price of an asset at any point in time may not correspond with its value/worth.

European Valuation Practice. Edited by Alastair Adair, Mary Lou Downie, Stanley McGreal and Gerjan Vos. Published in 1996 by E & FN Spon, London. ISBN 0 419 20040 1

Arguably, the property investment market is efficient at the weak form level (see Brown, 1991; Clapp *et al.*, 1994), but the reality is a market in which transactions take time to complete and information is not readily available to all participants. These characteristics create opportunities for investors (or groups of investors) to identify assets whose prices are above or below their own estimates of the value/worth of the investments. Obviously, individual estimates of worth differ from one investor to another for two reasons; firstly, they may have different **individual** investment objectives, such as a different holding period, and, secondly, they may interpret **market** information differently, for example, rental value now and in the future, level of voids (periods when the whole or part of the property is not let) and so on. The clear distinction between worth/value to the individual and price can be complicated when the criteria of one investor are shared by other similar investors. If these investors dominate the market for this type of property, market price should equal the value/worth. In property markets this does not always follow.

Debates such as these are often undertaken in a climate of misunderstanding due to the terminology used. In this chapter price is the actual exchange price in the market-place, an estimation of what that price might be is termed market value (MV) (as formal definitions of MV are based upon price estimation) and value/worth is used to denote the value to the individual or group of individuals.

An additional problem with the property investment market is the identification of the price at any one time and to reconcile this single 'snapshot' of price with the marketing period for the type of property. Depending on the property and the state of the market, this period may range from weeks to years. This illiquidity is a major constraint to the acceptance of property as an institutional asset class and is reflected in the price.

Valuation technique has to satisfy two needs. Firstly, it has to identify the exchange price in the context of definitions of open market value, which often define the time period in such a way that price is actually unrealizable (see discussion on open market value definitions in Chapter 2) and, secondly, it has to identify the underlying value/worth of the property at a particular time. The roles may require different applications of technique (Baum and Crosby, 1995).

3.1.2 Objectives of investors and characteristics of property as an investment

Many investors in property are also investors in other asset classes and therefore property investment is a comparative process. Even investors whose main business is property may choose to invest in other (liquid) assets while awaiting property opportunities which have better risk/return characteristics than these short-term alternatives. Most investors require property investments to perform in comparison with these other assets. There are now few property market investors and analysts who believe that property can be appraised in isolation from an understanding of these other assets. As the global economy takes shape this understanding must cross national borders, including both international financial markets and overseas property markets. The property investor in Europe must be aware of the influence of different lease structures in, for example, London and Paris, as well as understanding the reasons why foreign investors invest in a certain property submarket at a certain time.

An investment objective could be to earn high returns with low risk. But as these two objectives are incompatible, investors have a combination of risk and return criteria: to maximize return for a given level of risk or minimize risk for a given level of return. Property must be able to compete with, or complement, other investment media to achieve an allocation of funds. Investors can achieve these objectives in a number of ways. At a portfolio level, they may attempt to spread their assets around the different asset classes. Theories regarding the composition of the optimum portfolio mix are outlined in section 3.2. Within property investment, investors normally diversify by investing in overseas property, by spreading assets across the regions of a particular country or by investing across different property types such as office, retail, industrial and residential.

In addition to risk/return criteria, different investors will have a number of additional objectives. An institutional investor may be an immature superannuation fund whose liabilities are not expected to exceed income flow for many years or may be a mature fund which may need to liquidate some assets in the near future. Matching asset growth to liability growth will be an important consideration for pension and life funds. This will also have an effect on some elements of an appraisal, for example, the prospective holding period.

The investor may be administering a unit trust and require competitive short-term performance to increase the number of investors rather than focus on investments which have poor short-term prospects but are expected to perform better over a longer term.

Being in competition for investment funds heightens the need for comparisons with the performance of other portfolios owned by similar organizations. Benchmarking portfolios against various performance measures and constructing portfolios which mimic competitors, or performance measurement services, is now a routine occupation for many investors. Therefore, in addition to risk/return criteria, investor objectives may also include liquidity criteria, matching assets to liabilities, cash flow considerations, income/capital growth needs and competitive benchmarking against appropriate measures (see MacGregor, 1990).

The main characteristics of a property investment are:

1. **Income flow** A property investment can produce a wide variety of initial yields. Depending upon property type, and/or lease structure, it is possible to obtain long-term fixed incomes or high-growth potential future cash flows. The investor is therefore able to find many combinations of initial yield and future growth structure to fit the objectives.
2. **Capital value** The same combination of attributes regarding rental income holds for capital values. Although property investments have generally been perceived to have growth potential, it is possible to find high yielding, no growth investments or, in the case of some tenures, investments which lose their capital value as they approach specified dates. Investors can therefore match their income and capital value objectives to the attributes of individual properties while still having a choice over location and property type.
3. **Illiquidity** One of property's main disadvantages when compared to other asset classes is the time and cost of buying and selling the asset. This is the

main reason why many investors have sought to create indirect property investment vehicles which do not have illiquidity problems. Investors with short-term investment horizons may find property less attractive than longer-term investors.

4. **Lot size** Another major problem is the difficulty in obtaining consistent lot sizes. Major property investments are beyond the means of many investors and often require shared-ownership, while other property investments are so small they have very little influence on portfolio returns. These factors tend to limit the number of investors in the market for many properties. Large properties also create difficulties in diversifying property portfolios (Brown, 1991; see section 3.2).

5. **The lack of central trading** The property market is actually a set of very small submarkets based on location, property type and, occasionally, leasing and tenure. Each submarket has a relatively low turnover of stock and the information flow is hindered by the lack of public records (or the speed at which transaction information reaches the market-place). Some of the required information is highly technical, localized and/or not in the public domain. This can restrict detailed knowledge within the market.

6. **Property valuations** The nature of the property market makes the valuation process particularly difficult. In contrast to some competing investments, where instant information is available on the trading prices of identical assets, pricing information is sparse and therefore reliance is placed on valuers producing information in the form of pricing or open market valuations. The accuracy of this information is open to some doubt (see Brown, 1985; Drivers Jonas/IPD, 1988, 1990; Lizieri and Venmore-Rowland, 1991; Brown, 1992; Matysiak and Wang, 1995). Worth calculations are also fraught with difficulty due to the nature of local markets and the difficulty of finding and processing relevant information to produce reliable forecasts of the performance of the particular market.

These factors provide problems, but also opportunities, for investors with different objectives to find a property asset at a competitive price. Whether property advisors can identify competitively priced assets to enable abnormally high returns to be consistently made from period to period is more debatable (Brown, 1991, p. 206).

Another important aspect of property investment is the availability of finance. Even though the worth of an investment may relate to the present value of future cash flows, the ability to participate in the market for many investors is dependent upon the availability of finance. The lending strategies of banks and other sources of finance can have a significant impact on property investment capitalization rates and prices.

Finally, these characteristics need to be set against the objectives of the fund bearing in mind expectations regarding the future economic climate. The different performance characteristics of different assets need to be related to a variety of economic scenarios or outcomes. For example, if future inflation is higher than expected, which asset types will perform better or worse? If real wages increase above expectation this will have significant impact on the liabilities of a pension fund which needs to have a defensive strategy for this outcome.

3.2 PROPERTY INVESTMENT AT THE PORTFOLIO LEVEL

Many investors hold portfolios of properties and wish to consider individual property investments in a portfolio context. This section considers property portfolio theory. It begins with 'modern portfolio theory' (MPT) (Markowitz, 1952, 1959) and then considers the 'capital asset pricing model' (CAPM) (Sharpe, 1970). These are analyses which were developed in the share market and have, only recently, been applied to property portfolios. For a more detailed review of MPT and CAPM, see Rutterford (1993), and for an examination of the application to property, see MacGregor and Nanthakumaran (1992).

MPT is a theoretical framework for combining assets and constructing the best combinations of risk and return (see section 3.1 for a discussion of investor objectives). It was developed for the equities market and has been applied to property portfolios, although with limited success. It begins from calculations of expected portfolio return and risk. In this context, risk is a measure of the expected volatility of returns, i.e. a measure of the uncertainty of the expected returns. As most investors hold portfolios of assets, rather than one asset, the return and risk of individual assets are important only because these are used to calculate the portfolio risk and return. As discussed in section 3.1, investors require higher expected returns for higher risk.

When assets are combined in a portfolio, the portfolio return is a simple value-weighted average of the individual asset returns:

$$E_\mathrm{p} = \sum^i w_i E_i$$

Risk is more complex and involves the correlations between returns:

$$S_\mathrm{p}^2 = \sum^i \sum^j w_i w_j S_i S_j \, \rho_{ij}$$

where E_p is the expected portfolio return, E_i is the expected return on asset i, w_i in the proportion of the portfolio in asset i and $\Sigma w_i = 1$; S_p is the portfolio risk (the standard deviation of expected returns), S_i is the risk of asset i and ρ_{ij} is the correlation coefficient between assets i and j.

The correlation coefficients (ρ_{ij}) take values between -1 and $+1$. If, and only if, these are all $+1$, then the portfolio risk is the weighted average of the individual risks. Otherwise it is less and, the lower the correlations, the lower the portfolio risk. Thus, an understanding of portfolio risk is essential if portfolios are to be constructed efficiently.

The objective of MPT is either, for a given level of risk, to achieve the maximum return or, for a given return, to minimize risk. The output of the analysis is the proportion of funds to be invested in each asset and a measure of the expected return and the risk. It is important to note that the analysis should be based on expectations of return and risk, i.e. forecasts: the use of historical data as a proxy is merely a convenience.

The first step in the MPT analysis is to estimate the return and risk of each individual asset which could be included in the portfolio. The second step is to calculate the return and risk of all possible weighted combinations of these assets. The result is a set of all possible return and risk combinations. Some of these will be suboptimal, i.e. it is possible to find a combination of assets which produces either a higher return for the same risk or lower risk for the same return. By eliminating the suboptimal points it is possible to construct the 'efficient frontier'. This comprises the set of return/risk points which, for any return, have the lowest risk and, for any risk, have the highest return.

The decision of which of the efficient return/risk combinations to choose depends on the trade-off an individual investor makes between risk and return, i.e. the indifference between risk and return. Risk-averse investors choose low return/low risk combinations; risk takers choose high return/high risk.

In order to undertake the analysis the portfolio has to be divided into asset classes, where the return and risk characteristics are similar within an asset class and are dissimilar between asset classes. In the equity market shares can be used as all shares of one type perform identically. This is not true for property and it is unrealistic to perform the analysis using individual properties as the asset classes.

The conventional way of dividing a property portfolio is into sector/region combinations, such as retail in Wales. This is on the basis that different sectors of the market perform differently, as do different regions. It is also a convenience because data for forecasting asset returns and undertaking value/worth appraisals is available at the regional and sector level but not readily available at the local or town level which has been argued to be more appropriate.

Generally, the higher the level of aggregation the less difficult it becomes to forecast property cash flows. Thus, national forecasts of rental change for the retail sector are easier than for an individual property.

As, unlike shares, no two properties are identical, the risk measure for property portfolios, divided into sector/region assets classes (accounting for systematic factors), has to be adjusted from the standard MPT measure. An additional factor in the calculation is the number of properties in the portfolio and their values: other things being equal, the greater the number of properties, the lower the portfolio risk.

While the basic principles of MPT have been accepted, the techniques were not widely used until the introduction of cheap and powerful computers. Even then, identifying the indifferences of investors is not easy. A further problem is that the objectives of investors are more complex than simple maximization on a year-to-year basis: these include beating competitors and matching liabilities (see section 3.1). One development of MPT in the investment analysis which tackles the former objective involves comparing a portfolio with the market average portfolio and forecasting its return and risk relative to the market.

Only recently has MPT been used for property portfolios and with only limited success. Problems arose from the absence of the necessary technical skills and poor quality data. A further complication arises in seeking to implement the results: it is difficult to buy and sell quickly large amounts of property in order to restructure the portfolio to a new optimum based on new forecasts.

As well as its use in property portfolio construction, MPT has also been used to argue for the inclusion of property in the multi-asset portfolio on the basis that, as property returns are lowly correlated with those of other assets, it offers diversification opportunities. Such analyses suffer from the relatively poor quality of property data and have been widely criticized (see MacGregor and Nanthakumaran, 1992, for a fuller discussion). Recently, various attempts have been made to transform total return data from property to enable more meaningful analysis to take place (see, for example, Blundell and Ward, 1987; Geltner, 1989; Barkham and Geltner, 1994).

While the basic ideas of MPT have been developed and elaborated many remain theoretical rather than practical. The practical applications are limited and the full techniques are not widely used in property investment. None the less, the basic ideas and concepts are of some value. However, it does not help to determine the appropriate risk premium for an asset: it leaves it up to the individual investor to apply their individual risk premium (see section 3.3).

The 'capital asset pricing model' (CAPM) was developed to overcome some of these difficulties with MPT. It is another way to consider the relationship between return and risk for an investment in a portfolio context: it considers the trade-off between return and risk to establish if an asset is correctly priced. In effect, it calculates an asset's correct risk premium.

As most shares are positively correlated, i.e. they tend to move up and down together, it was suggested that there was a common market response in their returns. This led to the proposition that the expected return on a security could be expressed as a linear function of the expected return on the market as a whole. This is called the market model:

$$E_i = a_i + b_i E_m$$

Using a time series of historical data, it is possible to estimate the parameters by calculating the regression line:

$$R_i = a_i + b_i R_m$$

where E_i is the expected return on asset i, E_m is the expected return on the market, a_i and b_i are constants specific to that asset, R_i is the (past) return on asset i and R_m is the return on the market.

The analysis can be extended to portfolios. The approach assumes that the only common factor affecting returns is the return on the market: it is assumed that there are no economic factors which affect only some sectors or some industries. This has the advantage of simplifying the calculations by relating the returns on any asset to a common index (the market as a whole) rather than to each other. The theoretical justification for this approach is provided by CAPM. CAPM introduces a risk-free asset and allows investment in this asset or borrowing at this risk-free rate. It also requires a number of further restrictive assumptions about the investment market (see, for example, Rutterford, 1993).

Underlying the market model and CAPM is the assumption that there are two components to risk: market risk, also known as systematic or non-specific, and non-market risk, also known as unsystematic or specific. Market risk cannot be diversified – it affects the entire market. In contrast, specific risk is a function of specific factors relating to individual assets rather than to the market as a whole. It can, therefore, be diversified away when the asset is held as part of a large portfolio. Total risk is the sum of the two.

The market and the non-market components of risk have to be considered separately. Market risk assumes greater importance as investors will only be rewarded for the risk they cannot eliminate through diversification, i.e. they are not compensated for all the risks they take. In a market dominated by holders of portfolios constructed using the Markowitz efficient frontier approach, the only risk rewarded with greater return is market risk. If the market is dominated by risk-averse investors who are able to hold representative samples of the market, then an asset is not less valuable merely because it is more risky: its value depends on its impact on portfolio risk. In other words, the risk of an asset for which an investor is compensated is determined by its effect on the riskiness of the market portfolio.

Any remaining risk (non-market or specific) will not be compensated by a higher return because it is only the risk of the portfolio which is important and because it is possible to diversify away this specific risk by holding more assets.

One important aspect of the CAPM analysis is its application to the pricing (or worth estimation) of an individual asset. It is possible to derive the equation, known as the security market line:

$$E_i = RF + \left[E_m - RF\right] COV_{im} / S_m^2$$

where E_i is the expected return on asset i; RF is the expected return on a risk free asset; E_m is the expected return on the market; COV_{im} is the covariance between asset i and the market, and S_m is the standard deviation (risk) of the market.

The term COV_{im}/S_m^2 is known as the 'β' of an asset and measures the volatility of the asset relative to the market. If β is 1 then the asset has the same risk as the market and the return will be the same as the return on the market; if β is 0 there is no risk and the return is the same as for the risk-free asset; if β is less than 1, the return is less than the market; and if β is greater than 1, the return is greater than the market.

The securities market line proposes a linear relationship between the market risk of an asset (as measured by β) and its expected return. β is a measure of the risk or volatility of a share relative to the market as a whole. It is a widely used, but not a widely understood, aspect of investment analysis, although it has been little used in property investment. β can be calculated from historical data: but this is a proxy for expectations. Figures for β are available for all quoted shares on all major stock exchanges and are regularly updated. This enables the CAPM analysis to be used as a pricing model. If the market risk of the investment and the expected market return are known then the expected return on the asset can be calculated and compared against the return which the asset is priced to deliver. This shows whether the asset is correctly priced. This adds a new dimension to the analyses set out in section 3.3.

Although CAPM is appealing as a pricing model, there is no reason to believe that it is possible to make the necessary assumptions to permit the analysis. For property, a further problem arises from the lack of data of sufficient quality to undertake the analysis, in particular the calculation of β from historical data. The estimates of β are not stable over time and depend on the period of analysis.

CAPM is a single index model, i.e. it assumes that the only common factor is the return on the market. It is not unreasonable to suggest that some factors affect some assets and not others. To overcome this problem, multi-index models have been developed which link returns on an asset to other common factors such as industry-specific factors.

Many of the concepts discussed above are of value in the construction and management of real portfolios in the property market, but the full analysis is unworkable and is of limited practical value.

3.3 PROPERTY INVESTMENT APPRAISAL AT THE INDIVIDUAL PROPERTY LEVEL

3.3.1 Pricing valuation ('open market value')

Most property investment appraisals are undertaken to identify the sum likely to be realized if there were a transaction in the property. Valuations for financial reporting and performance measurement are underpinned by definitions of 'market value', which are interpreted as price in the market-place throughout Europe.

The methods used to identify this price are usually based upon simple applications of discounted cash flow. The major exception to this is the use of direct capital comparison, which can be applied as the sole method of valuation or as a check to the valuation produced by investment/cash flow methods. However, most simple applications of discounted cash flow are in reality comparable methods, using investment yield as the unit of comparison (see below).

The courts and valuation tribunals in the majority of countries have endorsed the view that the best evidence of price is recent sales of similar property investments. At this simple level, the investment valuation model utilizes current rents payable and rental values and discounts (capitalizes) them into infinity at a yield which, in effect, 'hides' within it all the risks of the property investment. It has been termed the all-risks yield or capitalization rate for these reasons. Basic assumptions concerning the prospective levels of future rental growth, depreciation and obsolescence rates and their implications, and prospective vacancy rates are hidden within the calculations. As these factors are not explicitly assessed, the capitalization rate cannot be determined from first principles and is entirely dependent upon comparable sales data being available. Therefore, in markets where the assets are rarely traded or are of such an individual nature that sales are not comparable, the technique looses much of its credibility. As the property market is made up of a vast array of submarkets, on account of individual locations, physical characteristics, property types and tenures, it is possible to have one submarket with a constant flow of comparables in similar properties creating some objective pricing information, while in another market there are no sales over many years.

In addition, certain property types are less likely than others to generate quality comparables. High-rise multi-let office blocks and regional shopping malls are obvious examples where comparable techniques cannot be rationally used to assess price. In the absence of comparables, the pricing valuation model needs to be amended. In a rational market, price should tend towards value/worth over time and models used to assess worth should have an effect on price. In the absence of comparables, a pricing valuation should be based upon the models used to determine investment value/worth.

A pricing valuation is required for all of the purposes covered by this chapter. When acquiring or disposing of property it is essential to have an estimate of the likely exchange price. Part of the stock selection policy within a portfolio may relate to comparing market price with estimates of worth. However, definitions of market value do not actually provide the answer required by purchasers and sellers of property. For example, the TIAVSC (International) definition of market value assumes that the marketing period has finished and the sale is about to be completed (see Chapter 2). The purchaser or seller requires a future value, i.e. how much would the property be sold for if it was put on the market today and sold at the end of a reasonable marketing period? In contrast, the TEGOVOFA (European) definition and the insurance companies' valuation Directive from the EU assumes the marketing period is in the future, but that markets remain static into the future. Neither definition gives the likely exchange price if the marketing commenced at the valuation date unless markets are completely stable. This point has been debated recently in the UK in the context of loan valuations resulting in a new definition of exchange price called 'estimated realization price' (see Chapter 16).

Valuations for performance measurement require a periodic pricing valuation (often annual, but can be as frequently as monthly or quarterly) as a proxy for an actual acquisition and sale price of the property at the beginning and end of the measurement period. Depending on the ownership type, the detailed basis of valuation might be set by regulation but most performance measurement services specify market value under the normal definition, i.e. a pricing basis. Pricing valuations for acquisition/sale and performance measurement should differ slightly as the former are forward looking over the marketing period while the latter (depending upon the definition adopted by the particular country/ client) assume a completed sale at the valuation date. However, in practice many appraisers do not vary the approach.

The comparative investment method of valuation operates at varying degrees of complexity. At the simplest level, it is an initial yield approach where, if r is the current rent payable and i the initial yield, the valuation becomes:

$$\text{Capital value} = \frac{r}{i}$$

Slightly more sophisticated approaches include an assessment of current rental value and an assumption regarding the date of its receipt (at lease expiry or rent review). The model then becomes the present value of the existing rent until lease expiry or review plus the present value of the rental income receivable after lease expiry into infinity. If R is the rental value, k the capitalization rate and t the unexpired term of the lease or period to the next rent revision, the model becomes:

$$\text{Capital value} = \frac{r}{k} + \frac{R - r}{k\left[(1 + k)^t\right]}$$

The model can be applied with increasing sophistication. The above model assumes no growth in rental values into the future, therefore the yield implies any future growth prospects. More complex discounted cash flows can be adopted which are more explicit about this implied growth and other factors. However, as more attributes of the cash flow are made explicit, the interpretation and analysis of comparables becomes subject to more assumptions. For example, in order to determine the rate of return indicated by a transaction, assumptions would have to be made on virtually all the other inputs into the cash flow, including forecasts of rental growth and obsolescence rates.

Proponents of the two simple applications illustrated above argue that the simplicity makes them objective in the interpretation and use of comparable evidence, as no assumptions have to be made to calculate the return.

Example 3.1: Assume a retail property has been sold for £500 000. Its rental value is estimated to be £40 000 per annum and the rent payable under the current lease is £30 000, with no more rent revisions until the end of the lease in two years time. The two valuation models can be used to analyse the transaction as follows.

1. The initial yield is

    $$30\ 000/500\ 000 = 6\%$$

2. Yield analysis assuming reversion to current rental value at lease expiry date:

$$\frac{r}{k} + \frac{R-r}{k\left[(1+k)^t\right]}$$

$$500\ 000 = \frac{30\ 000}{k} + \frac{40\ 000 - 30\ 000}{k\left[(1+k)^2\right]}$$

$$k = 7.72\%$$

Advocates of more explicit models argue that the lack of detail has reduced complex future cash flows to a level of simplicity that hides some fundamental aspects which affect value. Valuers who rely solely on comparison indicators, such as the initial yield determined from comparable sales, will lag the dynamics of the market-place, producing backward looking valuations based upon historic transaction evidence.

However, if the above property were analysed using an explicit cash flow, only one variable could be objectively calculated, the others would have to be assumed. Assume the property was expected to be ready for redevelopment in 10 years time, with a forecasted land value of £700 000 at that time, and that rental growth would average 5% per annum over the next 10 years. The rate of return from the property would be 11.097% excluding all costs. This appraisal of market price is similar to an explicit appraisal of worth and the level of subjectivity in the appraisal is set against its ability to provide the investor with more information on the validity of the price.

3.3.2 Assessments of worth/value to the individual investor

When acquiring and selling investment property, the valuer ought to be asked for an appraisal of the worth of the investment to the client to enable the buy, sell or hold decision to be made. A worth calculation is based on a combination of market information and client specific information. This information can be incorporated into an appraisal with the ultimate objective of assessing the value to that individual. If the market value identifies the price that can be obtained or needs to be paid, the appraisal of worth identifies the value to the individual investor or group of investors.

The normal model for assessing worth is an explicit discounted cash flow. Theoretically simple, the application is fraught with uncertainty and, therefore, risk. A fundamental problem is the estimation of cash flows.

Worth calculations seek to determine the future behaviour of the cash flow and attempt to quantify all factors which will influence it. They have therefore developed as discounted cash flow calculations where the inputs have been made explicit; hence the term explicit DCF for this application of present value mathematics. The actual information needs of an explicit cash flow model are set out in section 3.4. Underpinning the application of the model is the risk/return trade-off.

There are two main approaches to appraising the return from investments using DCF. These are 'net present value' (NPV) (where the present value of the out-flows or costs are subtracted from the present value of the inflows or incomes) and 'internal rate of return' (IRR) (where the net present net value of the cash flow is zero).

The decision rule for NPV is that an investment is accepted if the NPV is zero or above, as it produces a return above the cost. NPV requires a target rate of return to be set and the level of discount rate is discussed later in this section and in section 3.4. The formula for NPV is:

$$\sum_{t=0}^{N} \frac{A_t}{(1+r)^t}$$

where A_t is the investment's cash flow at time t (where t ranges from 0 to N, the final cash flow) and r is the target rate of return.

The decision rule for IRR is that an investment is accepted if the investment's IRR is equal to or greater than some predetermined target rate, normally the same target rate as for NPV. The IRR is the value of r such that:

$$\sum_{t=0}^{N} \frac{A_t}{(1+r)^t} = 0$$

In the general financial literature, the debate concerning which approach to use has tended to be in favour of NPV. In real estate IRR is used frequently. A full treatment of the use of NPV and IRR is given in Lumby (1991).

If the investment cash flows were certain, the target rate of return could be set at the risk-free rate of return. However, given that most cash flows are uncertain, the appraisal model requires adjustment for risk. There are a number of risk adjustment techniques which can be applied and these are outlined below. Baum and Crosby (1995) give a more detailed account.

The first approach is to risk adjust the target rate of return by adding a risk premium to the risk-free rate of return. In practice, the choice is largely intuitive, although the previous section discussing portfolios outlined the application of capital market theory to determining risk premiums. Apart from the intuitive nature of the adjustment, another feature is the relative fall in the present value of cash flows as they become more distant. Increasing the discount rate puts more weight on near flows and could change a choice between two investments; one with substantial cash flows near the beginning of the investment and the other with the more substantial cash flows towards the end of the investment period.

In order to avoid this problem, an alternative is to risk adjust the cash flow rather than add a risk premium to the risk-free discount rate. This 'certainty equivalent' approach reduces the expected cash flow to an amount which the investor would trade for a risk-free or certain amount. The NPV and IRR decision rules can then be applied using the risk-free rate of return as the target rate.

Both of these methods of risk adjustment assume a single point estimate of cash flow and a single appraisal figure. Other risk adjustment techniques assume a range of possibilities for each of the (or at least the main) inputs into an appraisal. The most basic of these is sensitivity analysis.

In order to undertake a sensitivity analysis, the major inputs into an investment appraisal are given a range around the best estimate and a 'what if' question is asked (for example, if the rental growth rate changes by 1% per annum, both above and below the best estimate, what effect will it have on the appraisal?). A sensitivity analysis is often undertaken using two inputs and reported as a matrix. The matrix can be extended to include more observations.

To illustrate, a simple example of an analysis of price was given at the end of section 3.3.1 and the rate of return was found to be just over 11% assuming a 5% per annum rental growth rate and a reversion to site value in 10 years. The price of the investment was £500 000. A sensitivity analysis could easily be undertaken to assess the impact on NPV if the discount rate was 1% lower or higher than the 11% or the rental growth rate also varied by plus or minus 1%. The results are set out below and can be compared with the 0 NPV at a purchase price of £500 000.

Discount rate (%)	Rental growth rate (£)		
	4.00	5.00	6.00
10.000	14 633	39 262	66 094
11.097	–22 301	0	24 297
12.000	–50 130	–29 562	–7 153

Substantially more sophisticated techniques are available for testing the variation in NPVs caused by uncertainty regarding the level of the future cash flow in an appraisal. A number of them approach the problem by assigning probabilities to a range of values for each variable within the DCF. They then use means and variances of the various valuations produced to make the investment decision. They are outside the scope of this chapter and are fully set out in various texts (for example Morley, 1988; Hargitay and Yu, 1993; Baum and Crosby, 1995).

3.4 APPRAISAL INFORMATION NEEDS

3.4.1 Market valuations

The information needs for the assessment of open market value or exchange price in the market-place are market based and client's individual preferences or objectives are only important if they influence market price. The base information for pricing models is transaction evidence of rents and yields. This information has to be adjusted according to locational, physical and lease structure differences between comparables and the property to be valued, for example:

1. **Location** Accessibility at a national, regional and local level, etc.
2. **Physical characteristics** Size, shape, configuration, services, fittings, etc.
3. **Lease structure** Term, rent review pattern and basis, repairing liabilities, service charges, user clauses, improvements, etc.

In addition, price is affected by the level of supply in the market and information on trends in the development pipeline; take-up and vacancy rates are crucial to an informed opinion of the likely exchange price. Trends in the demand factors for the individual markets such as retail sales, manufacturing output and employment are also very important for interpreting the transaction evidence. Because of the individual nature of properties and the low transactions turnover, finding transactions which are recent, similar in location, physical characteristics and lease structure and do not include some form of special relationship or special purchaser is difficult. It is therefore virtually inevitable that most transactions evidence has to be substantially adjusted and interpreted for some, or all, of these differences before it is applied to the valuation of a similar property.

If near-perfect comparables can be found, then the investment valuation technique, incorporating analysis of all-risks yields from transactions, is an unnecessary process. Yield analysis within the simple yield capitalization model is solely to take account of different lease structures, especially different unexpired terms or rent revision dates and ratios of rents passing under leases to the estimated open market rental values. If investment properties are let on similar lease structures, more direct comparable techniques can be used without any recourse to present value mathematics. However, more complex multi-occupancy buildings require more sophisticated techniques. In markets dominated by large multi-occupancy buildings (for example, high-rise downtown offices), pricing valuations are often carried out by a fully explicit discounted cash flow approach.

Pricing valuation is a combination of transactions analysis and a wider feeling for the property market and the particular submarket (so that market movements since the latest transaction evidence can be incorporated). Slavish adherence to comparables as the sole evidence of price will inevitably lead to valuations which lag turning points in the market. In cases where transactions do not exist, or are isolated, models which can be used to determine market values from first principles are preferable to these which are based solely on market evidence.

3.4.2 Appraisals of worth

The information needs for an explicit DCF are a mixture of market and client-specific information. The market information, which can be broken down into current and future data, should not be affected by the specific criteria of clients and is an attempt to quantify such factors as the current rental value, future rental value change and depreciation rates, future redevelopment or refurbishment costs, an exit yield forecast, current lease structures and management, rent review, purchase and sale costs. The client-specific information includes factors such as holding period, loan facilities, taxation and target rate of return.

Many of these factors include overlaps between client-specific and market information (for example, holding period for an appraisal might be dominated by the current lease structure, the client might have specific redevelopment plans which do not match most profitable use or optimum time criteria, the client's costs may be different to the market standard and the exit yield may be affected by the client's view on holding period).

Due to the range of possible information that can be included in an explicit DCF, there is no accepted schedule of information or layout for this kind of valuation and a number of organizations within their individual countries have developed their own approach. However, as the model is a genuine attempt to create a forecast of what will actually happen to the property over the life of the actual, or prospective, ownership, over simplifications are discouraged. For example, cash flows within some implicit DCF (i.e. conventional pricing) market valuations are assumed to be paid annually in arrears even though rent payments may take place at lesser intervals than this and in advance. As the all risks yield is a comparison indicator, this is tolerated in practice; in explicit DCF, the timing of cash flows can be assessed precisely when they occur.

The basic information needs for a typical discounted cash flow are set out in Table 3.1.

Three aspects of the information needs require more detailed discussion. These are the forecasting of future values, depreciation/appreciation and obsolescence, and the choice of discount rate.

Table 3.1 Typical information requirements for appraisal of worth to individual

Type of information	Current information	Forecasts
Rents and yields	Estimated rental value	Existing property rental value forecasts
	Rents passing	Location rental value forecasts Exit yield forecasts
Depreciation	Costs of redevelopment or refurbishment	Site depreciation/appreciation Inflation in building costs Timing of redevelopment or refurbishment
Current lease	Number of tenants Lease expiry dates Rent review dates	Future voids Structure and timing of future leases
Holding costs	Management costs Review costs Purchase and sale costs	
Client specific information	Discount rate Taxation Loan/finance	

(a) Forecasting

The information for a growth explicit DCF set out in Table 3.1 is at the individual property level and this creates problems for the valuer. These problems relate to the forecasts of such factors as rental growth, the investment yield to be applied to the rent from the property at the end of the cash flow to determine terminal capital value, rates of depreciation and obsolescence and redevelopment cost increases. Forecasts of the market can be undertaken at a national, regional and local level. They are normally based upon econometric modelling of the economy and the property market, identifying relationships which have occurred in the past and using leading indicators or forecasts to produce an estimate of each variable in the future. There are inadequacies/deficiencies in the quality, quantity and availability of data at all levels, but generally the greater the level of disaggregation, the greater the data problems. National and regional forecasts are therefore easier than local level forecasts. Coupled with the demand-side data problems, local level forecasts suffer from the increased importance of supply-side influences and the difficulties of defining the market area (individual locations which can be grouped by prospective price movement).

Forecasts of property market movements therefore need informed qualitative adjustment at the individual property level from the available information at town centre or (more likely) regional level. Price movements within cities and towns can vary substantially from location to location over time, with retail property being the most locationally volatile. Some of these variations are caused by new development changing the relative quality of locations and it is very few owners who have large enough portfolios to diversify at town centre level.

The level and complexity of information required to undertake growth-explicit cash flows has raised questions of whether valuers, used to undertaking market valuations, are equipped to take on appraisals of value/worth. However, the forecasting information can be purchased even though much of it is not in the public domain. European real estate education has been researching and teaching the mechanics of DCF for many years to a level where real estate graduates and students are capable of setting up and discounting cash flows, carrying out risk appraisals and understanding the basis and limitations of property market forecasts. More recently, teaching and research has extended into econometric modelling. Working in the market at the local level, recent graduates should be equipped to adjust regional and town level forecasts to the particular property investment.

(b) Depreciation and obsolescence

Depreciation in property values (in relative terms) may be a function of depreciation in both location and buildings. In the case of location, appreciation is as relevant as depreciation. As discussed above, the location (site value) might be affected by new development at the micro site-specific level (the development of a new shopping mall changing the pedestrian flow within a town centre) or at a regional or national level by changes in the economic prosperity of the town or region. The building will be affected by physical wearing out. More recently, technological changes, which render the use obsolete or the physical characteristics of the building obsolete for the particular use, have become more important. In the office and industrial markets there are numerous examples where changes in practices or space requirements have rendered particular types of building useless for their original purpose (floor to ceiling heights in offices, equipment circulation space in factories), and they have been demolished even though they were physically sound.

Some depreciation, appreciation and obsolescence can be forecasted, for example, wear and tear, but some others, for example, technological change, cannot always be foreseen within an investment time horizon. Forecasts of this kind of change over the life of a new building are particularly difficult but some studies exist of the falling off of rental values over time relative to new property values and the present life cycle of buildings (Baum, 1991). These can be used as a basis for assessing the life of the building and the reduction in rental growth forecasts for particular buildings, always remembering that investment decisions should be based on expectations rather than past performance.

(c) The discount rate

The assessment of the discount rate is usually based on either the nominal or real risk-free rate of return with an additional premium for property risk; in line with the discussions in section 3.3.2. Whether an investor adopts target rates of return in nominal or real terms is related to the objectives, for example, liabilities may be based upon real or nominal changes in wage levels. Although there should be a generalized risk margin for property, each individual property should generate its own particular risk premium, some more and some less than the average market rate. Properties where the cash flow is more certain should have lower risk margins. For example, a heavily over-rented property (let at more than its full rental value) let on a long lease with upwards-only rent reviews to a high quality tenant is a low risk investment, as the level of cash flow is very secure over a long time period. A property let on a short lease with frequent upward and downward market rent reviews to an unstable tenant has uncertainty attached to the cash flow and should attract a higher risk factor.

In an appraisal which adopts the risk-adjusted discount rate approach, even the determination of the risk-free rate is by no means straightforward. The redemption yield on long-dated government bonds is often adopted as a proxy for a risk-free rate as they produce a guaranteed income flow secured on the government plus a guaranteed sum upon redemption. Although risk free in nominal terms, they suffer from inflation risk (the expected real return will be affected by unexpected inflation). In contrast, index-linked government bonds which, if held to maturity, give guaranteed real returns, do not guarantee a nominal return, which depends on the rate of inflation. The life of the bond and the life of the property investment (the proposed holding period) should coincide.

Finally, in discussing appraisals at the individual property level, it is necessary to refer back to section 3.2 on portfolio aspects of property investment. Many of the factors and risks within the appraisal are specific to the property being appraised and, as such, can be substantially diversified away by holding a portfolio.

3.4.3 Property performance measurement

For all strategic property investment decision-making regarding portfolios and individual properties, there is a basic need for information on the past performance of the property, the portfolio and the property market as a whole. This information can be used to compare the individual fund's performance with other similar funds, with the property investment market in general, including different sectors and regions, and with competing assets and to judge the performance of different advisors.

The type of information typically produced at an individual property level is the:

1. total return over a specific time period, often annually but also monthly and quarterly in some circumstances;
2. capital return;
3. income return; and
4. rental value growth.

At a portfolio level, the above measures are usually produced for the total portfolio, the main property sectors of office, retail, industrial, residential, agricultural and leisure, and for a number of regions. Other measures can be provided such as reversionary potential, level of over-renting and equivalent yield.

The total rate of return remains the principal measure. Measuring total returns from property is quite complex and two methods are generally compared. The money-weighted rate of return is the internal rate of return and provides a precise measure over any specific time period. It requires precise knowledge of the timing of all cash flows. It also reflects the amount of money actually invested in each subperiod and produces different performance figures for separate fund mangers who have performed similarly but have had different amounts to invest (for further expansion of this point, see Brown, 1991, pp. 247–55).

The time-weighted rate of return is considered by Hargitay and Yu (1993) to be the preferred approximate method for the purposes of comparing the performance of fund managers as it is not influenced by the amount and timing of capital. The time-weighted rate of return determines return over each subperiod by assessing the market value at the beginning and end, and the income over the period. The return is assessed as:

$$TWRR = \frac{CV_t - CV_{t-1} + I_t}{CV_{t-1}}$$

where I_t is the net income during period t, CV_{t-1} the capital value at the beginning of period t and CV_t the capital value at the end of period t.

Problems arise when capital expenditure occurs during the period of measurement. To be accurate, a valuation ought to be carried out every time expenditure takes place. However, given that in practice valuations occur periodically, often annually, this is unrealistic and an approximation is made. The formula can be adjusted as follows:

$$\frac{CV_t - \left(CV_{t-1} + C_t\right) + I_t}{CV_{t-1} + C_t(1-k)}$$

where C_t is the capital expenditure during time period t and k is the time of expenditure after the beginning of the period as a proportion of time of the whole period.

Brown (1991) suggests that this method provides a money-weighted rate of return which can be used as a proxy for the time-weighted rate of return. In some performance measurement systems, capital expenditure is assumed to take place half-way through the measurement period and therefore k is assumed to be 0.5, therefore $(1-k)$ is also 0.5.

In order to measure the performance over more than one subperiod the returns are chain-linked together. For example, if a property was worth £100 000 at the beginning of period one, £120 000 at the end of period one, had £20 000 spent on it in the middle of period two and was worth £150 000 at the end of period two and generated an income flow of £10 000 in each of the two years, the total rate of return would be:

$$\text{Period 1} = \frac{120\ 000 - 100\ 000 + 10\ 000}{100\ 000} = 30\%$$

$$\text{Period 2} = \frac{150\ 000 - (120\ 000 + 20\ 000) + 10\ 000}{120\ 000 + 20\ 000(1 - 0.5)} = 15.385\%$$

$$\begin{aligned}
\text{Total return over the two periods} &= (1 + R_1)(1 + R_2) - 1 \\
&= (1.3 \times 1.15385) - 1 = 0.5 \text{ or } 50\%
\end{aligned}$$

$$\text{Annual average} = 1.5^{(1/2)} - 1 = 1.224745 - 1 = 22.47\% \text{ pa}$$

The use of market valuations for period beginning and end values arises because the properties are not actually sold and the precision of the returns is a function of the accuracy of the valuations. Returns over short periods are dominated by capital value changes and the uncertainty surrounding valuation accuracy has tended to create suspicion regarding the accuracy of the indices. There is a view that true property market movements are smoothed and lagged by performance measures based upon valuations (see previous discussion in section 3.1.2 for references to this debate).

In order to compare an individual property against similar properties, or a fund against an equivalent or competing investment, it is necessary to have national indices of property market performance. In many countries, governments do not produce this data and property market indices at a national and regional level have been provided by private sector organizations. Indices may be established by the aggregated measurement of individual properties, the aggregation from a number of funds or valuation-based indices using hypothetical properties in actual locations. The availability of indices in each country is outlined in the individual chapters.

3.5. PROPERTY INVESTMENT APPRAISAL – CONCLUDING COMMENTS

Property investment appraisal can be carried out with varying degrees of complexity. In this respect there has been a worldwide movement towards increased sophistication backed by a significant increase in research output. This research covers all aspects of the appraisal; the role, the basis, the methods and each of the variables necessary for each application of technique.

In giving advice, valuers will need to be able to respond with both price and worth in order to satisfy the needs of clients. The individual chapters will provide information on the application of the valuation technique to investment properties in the various countries. Although they will indicate that the use of implicit capitalization rate methods, using comparable transactions as the basis of assessing the level of the capitalization rate, is prevalent in market valuation practice, increasingly valuers are turning to more explicit cash flow techniques to support these valuations.

However, there are problems with the use of explicit DCF as a market valuation (pricing) model. Not only is there difficulty in dealing with some of the more irrational short-term movements in market prices, but there is also a lack of research into the variation in appraisals caused by individual purchasers or sellers applying their own criteria to some of the variables.

For example, owners of portfolios may have a different discount rate choice to one-off purchasers/sellers. Life fund investors may have different objectives to general fund investors and this may lead to different discount rates or holding periods being assessed. There is a view held by some valuers that the subjectivity involved in producing an explicit discounted cash flow makes that type of appraisal inappropriate for assessing market value. This view could be linked to markets which have a brisk turnover of property transactions and do not have substantial multi-occupancy buildings and variety of lease terms, so reducing the need to make major adjustments to the capitalization rate found from comparables.

The contrary view is that comparable-based techniques are backward looking and fail to accurately pick up current trends in value movements. Adjustments to capitalization rates are highly subjective. The more detailed breakdown of variables within an explicit discounted cash flow leads to more rational valuations. In markets which produce irregular transaction information, or where the property assets are highly individual, the capitalization rate comparable approach lacks a supporting information base, making an accurate estimation of the probable exchange price very difficult.

In the absence of comparables, estimating market prices by considering the appraisals carried out by investors when purchasing and selling property assets has much to commend it. Where transactions do exist, they can be tested against the explicit model. Analysis of prices can be carried out in the context of either simple or more complex applications of the investment method. As the more complex, explicit methods are used more often, the price will be increasingly influenced by the appraisal, and the differences between price and worth may reduce. Explicit methods might then dominate the pricing process, supplanting cost-based and capitalization rate approaches.

Although much of the above discussion relates to individual investor preferences and their choice of valuation inputs, all valuations contain variations caused by the inability to determine the precise level of market-based data. The implicit capitalization rate model can create a range of valuations caused by the valuers' difficulties in determining the correct (market-based) capitalization rate. The inability to determine this rate due to lack of information is potentially more dangerous than the subjectivity in an explicit discounted cash flow, because a comparison valuation without a comparable has absolutely no foundation, while the more explicit approach is a logical method. If there are no comparables, the valuer is not able to determine the capitalization rate, except by guesswork.

Other difficulties facing appraisers of property investments include some financial constraints. On the one hand, there is an increasing level of regulation and guidance on good practice and the increasing demands of clients. Set against this is their reluctance to pay adequate fees to underpin the provision of an improved service. Despite this, valuers need to increase their ability to provide a sophisticated service. They need to understand the basis of forecasts even if they do not all have the ability to carry them out. National, regional and local property market forecasts will be provided by specialist consultancies (or in-house research departments) and, having purchased or obtained the forecasts, it is the ability to adjust them to individual properties and use them within the valuation model that is required of valuers.

Most importantly, valuers need to understand the context of property investment within the wider investment market. The technical ability to understand portfolio theories, risk analysis and probabilities, and incorporate them into appraisals is meaningless if it is not coupled with an understanding of the wider investment context. Valuers must understand how property investment links with alternatives and how individual properties fit into this wider perspective. There are examples of good technique compromised by a poor understanding of the market, leading to inappropriate inputs (for example, office properties in London let on long leases at rents which were above open market rental value). Equally, there are examples of inappropriate technique which have influenced price levels leading to some opportunities for abnormal returns (for example, short leasehold property investments in the UK during the 1970s and 1980s).

The quality of appraisals of property investments has taken significant strides forward in both theory and practice in the recent past but there is still a wealth of knowledge to be assimilated and applied.

REFERENCES

Barkham, R. and Geltner, D. (1994) Unsmoothing British valuation based returns without assuming an efficient market. *Journal of Property Research*, **11**, 81–95.

Baum, A. (1991) *Property Investment Depreciation and Obsolescence*, Routledge, London.

Baum, A. and Crosby, N. (1995) *Property Investment Appraisal*, 2nd edn, Routledge, London.

Blundell, G. and Ward, C. (1987) Property portfolio allocation: A multi factor model. *Land Development Studies*, **4**, 145–56.

Brown, G. (1985) Property investment and performance measurement. *Journal of Valuation*, **4**, 33.

Brown, G. (1991) *Property Investment and the Capital Markets*, E & FN Spon, London.

Brown, G. (1992) Valuation accuracy: developing the economic issues. *Journal of Property Research*, **9**, 199–207.

Clapp, J.M., Goldberg, M.A. and Dowell, M. (1994) Crisis in methodology, in *Appraisal, Market Analysis and Public Policy in Real Estate* (eds J.R. DeLisle and J. Sa-Aadu), Kluwer Academic Press, Boston.

Driver Jonas/IPD (1988) *The Variance in Valuations*, Drivers Jonas/Investment Property Databank, London.

Driver Jonas/IPD (1990) *The Variance in Valuations: An Update*, Drivers Jonas/Investment Property Databank, London.

Geltner, D. (1989) Estimating real estate's systematic risk from aggregate level appraisal based returns. *AREUEA Journal*, **17**(4), 463–81.

Hargitay, S. and Yu, S.M. (1993) *Property Investment Decisions: A Quantitative Approach*, E & FN Spon, London.

Lizieri, C. and Venmore-Rowland, P. (1991) Valuation accuracy: a contribution to the debate. *Journal of Property Research*, **8**, 115–22.

Lumby, S. (1991) *Investment Appraisal and Financing Decisions*, 4th edn, Chapman & Hall, London.

MacGregor, B. (1990) Risk and return: constructing a property portfolio. *Journal of Valuation*, **8**, 233–42.

MacGregor, B. and Nanthakumaran, N. (1992) The allocation to property in the multi asset portfolio: the evidence and theory reconsidered. *Journal of Property Research*, **9**, 5–32.

Markowitz, H. (1952) Portfolio selection. *Journal of Finance*, **7**, 77–91.

Markowitz, H. (1959) *Portfolio Selection: Efficient Diversification of Investments*, Yale University Press, New Haven, CT.

Matysiak, G.A. and Wang, P. (1995) Commercial property market prices and valuations: analysing the correspondence. *Journal of Property Research*, **12**, 181–202.

Morley, S. (1988) The analysis of risk in the appraisal of property investments, in *Property Investment Theory*, (eds A. MacLeary and N. Nanthakumaran), E & FN Spon, London.

Rutterford, J. (1993) *An Introduction to Stock Exchange Investment*, Macmillan, Basingstoke.

Sharpe, W. (1970) *Portfolio Theory and Capital Markets*. McGraw-Hill, New York.

Valuation for loan security

4

*Hans-Ulrich Stork and
Colin Humphries*

Throughout Europe, banks are still the main providers of traditional property finance through debt or, very occasionally, equity, although their total exposure is dependent upon the state of the market at any one time. The type of finance available largely depends on the identity of the lender who will offer finance subject to largely predetermined criteria. Borrowers seeking the best deal in the market will consider a number of options, although these are subject to the sums involved, time constraints, the complexity of a deal, the confidentiality required and their knowledge of alternative resources.

4.1 FINANCE MECHANISMS

Traditional sources of property finance from the banking sector typically consist of term loans secured against fixed asset or other forms of security of up to 70–80% of the value of the asset, backed up by a second loan, normally at a higher rate, secured by a guarantee from a borrower's parent company and secured by second mortgage. Equity participation and debt are also widespread, the former being attractive if the borrower's share price is at a discount to net asset value, whilst debt can be tax efficient. Joint ventures are an alternative, spreading the risk of a lender and giving the opportunity of a share in the profits of a project. Savings banks, building societies in the UK and Bausparkasse in Germany, for example, have become more expert in their lending and are now becoming involved in direct funding of much larger projects, although their traditional emphasis has always been non-commercial property.

Insurance companies have, in limited instances, tended either to back up loans with insurance policies for lenders, or have been involved directly in the forward funding arrangements of development projects. The insurance policies that were closed off in the late 1980s have, however, proved less than successful as the downturn in the property markets, which was the risk being insured by the

European Valuation Practice. Edited by Alastair Adair, Mary Lou Downie, Stanley McGreal and Gerjan Vos. Published in 1996 by E & FN Spon, London. ISBN 0 419 20040 1

lender, was far greater than originally foreseen, resulting in losses and the withdrawal from the sector of the few insurers that were involved.

Forward funding arrangements involve the sale of the site to the funder and the provision by them of intermediate development finance. Upon the successful construction and letting of the project, the developer is then paid a fee, or developer's profit. Pension funds are often the providers of long-term finance, with some form of equity participation. This may be in the form of a stake in the special purpose company set up for the project or a share in the profits of a new development, particularly if this is speculative, based on a high loan to value ratio, or where the ability of the borrower to repay is in question. In view of the losses sustained by many banks on speculative developments in the early 1990s, it is expected (Cameron, Markby, Hewitt, 1994) that the institutions will play a greater role in the provision of development finance over the coming five years than during the previous five years.

Major forms of finance, which vary in use between countries, are as follows:

1. The **mortgage** is one form of lending that has at its root the concept of recourse to one, or a number of, specific assets. There may also be recourse to other assets, but a mortgage relies essentially on a charge against property. It is therefore in the interests of the lender to ensure that this retains its income-earning potential in order to support the loan.
2. A **rights issue** is a method of issuing equity, the existing shareholders being invited to take up a pre-emptive 'right' to the additional shares, on for example a 'two for five' basis. Normally only publicly listed companies would be able to generate enough investor confidence to successfully issue this type of paper, but large amounts can be raised. Drawbacks are the greater time commitment of placing the issue and the associated expense, in terms of the underwriters' commissions, advisers' fees, etc.
3. **Debentures** are a form of debt liability, with no pre-emption rights for shareholders, more suitable for medium-sized companies. They are also underwritten, which entails costs, but these are normally lower. Debentures are normally only used for medium- to long-term financing and can be viewed as a back-up facility to the more conventional types of loan, requiring repayment after a fixed period.
4. **Eurobond issues** are similar to debentures and are listed on the London or Luxembourg bourses. This is unsecured long-term (25 year) debt and is redeemable at any time by the company. As it is unsecured it is only available for the most reputable companies.
5. **Unitization** is the division of the rights in a property into units or tradable paper securities. It could be argued that this is not property financing in its purest sense, but it is a way of converting relatively illiquid assets into more readily tradable investments thereby attracting funds which would otherwise not be available (Barter, 1988). The purchaser of the equity in the asset benefits from the property's income receipt and capital growth, but without the management headache of owning property. It involves specific properties rather than a whole managed portfolio, as is the case when investing in property company shares. The advantages for the investor/funder are the liquidity of the asset, the accurate valuation provided by quoted share prices and the potential diversification of the investment with many small lots in various

buildings. The main disadvantages with unitization are the hurdles of tax transparency, legal constraints and the complexity of setting up such a scheme.

6. **Financial leases** involve the long-term right to use developed property subject to the payment of 'rent' which covers the entire cost of the lessor's capital invested in the property, including interest. The title is transferred at the end of the agreement to the tenant, thereby representing a hire-purchase, or the contract may include a purchase option. Whilst in all likelihood benefiting from the same charges over land as a traditional mortgage, financial lease arrangements rely far more heavily on the management expertise of the lessee company directors – the lender has placed all their eggs in one basket, so to speak – the collapse of the borrower also means the disappearance of income from the asset. The financial lease structure is more popular in France and Belgium in view of the different treatment of the interest on the balance sheet. The lessee is able to claim the depreciation of the asset, on a straight-line basis, as well as the investment deduction on the leased asset. UK accounting practice means the lessee must include the property on the balance sheet and is not permitted to buy the asset at the end of the term, thereby reducing the scheme's attractiveness.

7. In a **sale** and **leaseback transaction** the property is sold to a specialist leasing company or investor, the vendor taking back a lease to provide a sufficient return on capital over the period of the lease, normally over a 10 year term. In order to create a marketable product, the purchaser, or effective funder, will be keen for the 'rent' to reflect market rents so as not to impede the income's growth prospects. The vendor tenant will be keen to maximize the capital receipt and will therefore seek a high initial rent. The quality of the tenant vendor is, therefore, of paramount importance in determining the lease terms. The advantage to the vendor tenant is the ability to reinvest the capital receipt and, in Belgium, for example, continue to depreciate on the newly acquired asset, if within five years.

8. **Participating loans** allow the borrower to pay a lower coupon in return for giving the lender a share in any increase in the value of the real estate. To enable a borrower to access funds at a cheaper rate, perhaps in order to bridge the yield gap, a lender may take a share in any profits realized on the disposal of the property.

9. A **convertible loan** or **bond** (less common in the UK) allows the lender to convert a loan into shares, upon which there may be a capital gain for the lender. This is a hybrid form of financing between equity and debt for property companies. The issuer will set the price of the conversion higher than the current price of the underlying ordinary shares. The holder of a convertible loan has greater capital security than a holder of ordinary shares and greater income. Much of the advantage over straight equity is lost, however, in that the issuer has to buy the higher conversion price for their equity, as they typically trade at a premium, with higher service costs before conversion.

10. **Factoring** is a form of finance used in Germany for properties let on long leases to municipalities. Banks will acquire the rent receivable from an investor, by advancing the net present value of a determined future income stream to the investor. Usually, factoring is more widely known in the context of short-term trade receivables/debt management.

Nabarro Nathanson & Arthur Anderson (1993) describe some examples of preferences within Europe as follows:

1. **Belgium** Debt financing is more frequently used by speculative investors and developers, whilst the insurance companies make use of equity or quasi-equity. For debt, financial leases, sale and leaseback and the use of specialist investment funds or SICAFs (which is effectively a form of securitization) are used.

2. **France** Non-recourse lending is very rare, but banks were, in the late 1980s, prepared to lend 100% of cost to developers for speculative projects for the short to medium term, although this level is currently nearer 70%. In addition, many banks lent to *marchands de biens*-trader investors, who would purchase and hope to make a quick sale. Following the fall in French property values after 1990, many lenders were forced to acquire buildings from borrowers and reschedule the debts. Sale and leasebacks, and participating and convertible loans, enable the wide variety of specialist real estate companies to benefit from the specialist tax incentives available in this high tax environment.

3. **Germany** Apart from the fact that many companies tended to build for owner-occupation, the traditional mortgage has always been the most popular way of financing in Germany. Following the increase in investor interest in the late 1980s and early 1990s, German banks have increasingly had to adust their financing to take in limited recourse or equity participation. Interest rates are typically fixed for between 5, 10 or 15 years, or may be variable but capped. Leasing, on a non-full payout basis, is the most popular method where the value of the leased asset is not amortized over the initial lease term; the remaining value is realized through the sale of the real estate at the end of the lease term to the lessee (by an extension of the initial lease term or a sale of shares in the SPV). This enables the funding to occur off balance sheet, and is actually no more than a variation of financial leasing, referred to above.

4. **Netherlands** The market for real estate finance is split between short- and long-term players. Short term debt for up to three years will often be provided by the commercial and merchant banks and a few mortgage banks, for development purposes, whilst long-term financing will typically be made available from institutional investors, like insurance companies and pension funds, on a traditional mortgage basis. This may be for 25–30 years based on fixed, or sometimes floating, interest rates and be up to 70–80% of the value of the property. The main methods of raising finance are through financial lease arrangements, where the lessee takes 10 years to gain full ownership of the real estate, or by the creation of partnership structures, the property owner contributing the real estate and the financier the funds. This structure is largely tax driven. The securitization of assets and the use of deep-discount securities are rare, as the property finance market is relatively conventional in the Netherlands.

5. **Spain** Traditionally, long-term mortgages of 10–15 years have been the preferred method of raising finance by developers and were secured on the property and for 70–80% of its value. There is, however, a distinct shortage of funds available by these means due to the burned-out state of the Spanish property market. There are instances of financial leasing, mortgage-backed

bonds (but still only representing 6% of the market) and, latterly, securitization, which is still in its infancy in Spain.

6. **UK** One of the main differences between the UK and the rest of Europe is the uniquenesss of its market. Its relative transparency, the size of the institutional investment market and the 25 year full repairing lease, have combined to create a favourable environment, where a wide variety of financing options have become available. This is in direct contrast to mainland Europe, where the shorter lease form, smaller institutional market, especially pension funds and insurance companies, and greater illiquidity in the market have led to a concentration of bank financing in only prime locations, where the occupier is of less importance and the location and quality of building are paramount. Coupled to this is the desire for recourse to the borrower or their parent; whereas in the UK much bank finance is non-recourse.

4.2 CHARACTERISTICS OF LOAN REQUIREMENTS

Both lender and borrower will address a number of key areas when considering any new loan.

4.2.1 Domestic or cross-border financing

By lending abroad, lenders and their borrowers may be exposing themselves to unnecessary risk. Cross-border European financing, for instance buying in dollars and borrowing in Deutschmarks, will be considered too risky by many, as property returns in one country cannot be guaranteed to follow interest rate fluctuations in another. Properties that have an international character, or those that have a particular financial or economic significance due to their size or structure, may, however, attract finance from foreign sources, when hedging mechanisms will be adopted.

Domestic borrowers will normally wish to borrow in their local currency in order to avoid the currency risks associated with foreign currency loans. At times of relative stability borrowers may, however, be encouraged to borrow from a foreign lender, although both parties will wish to ensure that their exposure to currency risk is limited.

In the event that European Monetary Union becomes reality, much of the risk in currency fluctuations within Europe will evaporate. Until such time, there will always be a risk of deviating exchange rates, even within strict bands as currently imposed on the remaining participating members of the ERM.

Hedging loans by the use of derivatives, i.e. currency and interest rate swaps, are the alternative means by which the risks for the lender and borrower abroad are typically reduced. However, their cost may be prohibitive if the selected currency is unstable or the degree of hedging sought reduces the risk below market-acceptable norms. Additionally, the importance of the identity of the counter-party should not be underestimated.

Cross-border lending may involve new markets and unfamiliar laws, customs and regulations. The selection of the right valuer – their qualifications and **local** experience – increases in significance when a lender's or borrower's own legal and market knowledge is limited to their home market. The increased reliance on these experts dictates the care that must be taken in their selection.

For a foreign lender to properly compete with local lenders – a central aspect of European Community law – a harmonization of tax allowances and regulatory costs is needed. A recent case highlighted a discrepancy which involved foreign borrowers, holding UK assets, who were not permitted to deduct interest as a cost if the lender was also foreign. This placed foreign banks in an uncompetitive position and hindered the free movement of capital from abroad. Only after substantial lobbying did this situation alter.

4.2.2 Long- and short-term loans

Typically, products with a long economic life will be financed long term, for instance substantial office buildings, whilst the converse is true for short-life properties such as retail warehouses or leisure facilities. However, real estate is always a form of long-term investment and the cyclical nature of the property markets means that any short-term approach carries equal risks and rewards. Short-term lenders will analyse the state of the property market at that time, as many banks did in the UK in the late 1980s, whereas German mortgage banks, often lending for longer terms, will tend to analyse more critically the borrower's ability to pay and the quality of the property. In the UK, over the last eight years, the average length of loan has tended to be around five years (Maxtead, 1993). This exposed many UK banks unnecessarily to the fluctuations in the property cycle and created a niche for a number of German banks which were prepared to lend long term.

Short-term development finance, say up to five years, may have to be weighed up against the ultimate provision of a long-term loan for up to perhaps 25–30 years.

4.2.3 The identity of the borrower

In assessing risk, a view must be taken by the lender as to the nature and success of the business and the level of expertise the borrower has to actively manage the property and to repay the loan, both interest and capital. Research is therefore required into the background of the customer, studying their business record, status, financial position and their abilities in handling the size or type of property being considered.

The borrower may be the owner, purchaser or an owner-occupier. In the event of a sale and leaseback or financial leasing transaction, the covenant of the tenant/borrower will greatly influence the terms offered and a bank's detailed internal assessment and research into the quality of the borrower will form an active part in the decision-making and pricing process. A property company, or less frequently a property fund, may, however, be considering gearing up in order to increase its overall efficiency and performance. Particularly if a loan has recourse to the borrower, a lender will need to form a clear picture, if the information is available, of the nature of third party debt and the degree to which the borrower is exposed to, say, fluctuating interest rates on this. This is all part of the lender's corporate credit analysis of the borrower.

4.2.4   Development risk

Quite apart from the problem of the assessment of the value of a project upon completion, is the risk associated with the development process itself, namely insufficient expertise of the development team (borrower), time and cost over-runs, unforeseen costs or delays and letting voids upon completion. The appointment of a monitor, normally paid for by the borrower, although this may vary between countries, and acting on behalf of the bank, overseeing all aspects of the construction and, optimally, the design of a new project, and acting as the lender's true representative, can reduce this risk.

4.2.5   Legal risk

This can arise from new statutes affecting the rights of the lender or the property owner or poor drafting of loan documentation. The selection of an appropriate firm of lawyers to vet or draft all loan documentation is therefore required and, in view of the sizeable costs involved and the proliferation of firms handling this type of business, references are imperative.

4.2.6   Fixed or floating rate interest

Whether the loan should be on a fixed or floating rate basis is a factor of the length of the term, the product, particularly the length of lease, and the envisaged changes in lending rates over that term. If returns, by way of rent, over the course of the loan are generally level or regular, a fixed rate would be appropriate. Conversely, if a property's income fluctuated widely in the short term, it might be more appropriate to allow the rates to float, with the possibility of a fix at some time in the future. A bank may even insist that an interest rate is fixed at a certain predetermined date, once interest rates reach a threshold: technically a 'reverse drop-lock' arrangement. In the UK, where lease terms are long by European norms, a floating rate has been common. The shorter lease terms on the continent have also indirectly influenced the desire to fix rates, so as to mitigate at least one risk of having no income to service the debt at the end of the lease, which may be before the end of the loan term.

A lender may require straight-line amortization, allow capital repayment holidays with interest only paid or accept a 'bullet' capital repayment at the end of a term.

Swaps, caps, captions, floors and collars are examples of financial instruments, or derivatives, to hedge or reduce the uncertainty of interest rate movements. An interest rate swap can be arranged through the funding bank, or another bank, in order that the borrower, who is being funded on a variable rate basis, may swap its floating rate obligation with another borrower which has access to fixed rate debt, but requires cheaply priced floating rate debt. The bank will act as intermediary between the two borrowers. An interest rate cap sets a maximum limit to the rate of interest a borrower will have to pay. The cost of this cap will depend on the extent to which this limit varies, at the time of purchase, from the floating rate of the day and the period the cap is valid. An interest rate floor is the opposite, in that a borrower will undertake to pay a minimum level of interest and may sell this. A collar is a combination of a cap and a floor and sets a band within which the borrower's interest can fluctuate. A 'no-cost collar' can normally be arranged by sell-

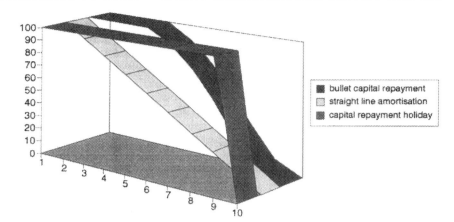

Figure 4.1 Different types of loan amortization.

ing a floor to buy a cap. In the event of default by a borrower on a loan, the risk to a lender may be greatly reduced by being able to rely upon some form of guarantor, be it a parent company or other interested party.

Ways of mitigating the risk to the lender are numerous – by reducing the amount of the loan in relation to the value of the underlying asset, the lender automatically reduces their risk exposure. Similarly, a lender may insist that all, or the majority, of a loan is fixed in the long term, so reducing the borrower's exposure to unnecessary interest rate risks throughout the term. This may have to be balanced with the interest cost which is invariably higher over the longer term. Provided costs are not prohibitive, the lender and borrower may agree to the purchase of a 'cap', perhaps in combination with a 'floor'. The lender may just adjust the margin and this will be dependent upon the type of loan and the lender's perceived risks. This margin would normally be expressed as a percentage over the cost of the lender's funds and will vary in line with competition from other providers of finance. To avoid the loss of valuable time and to give the potential borrower an incentive to pursue an offer of finance, a lender may request an up-front fee, to be paid upon acceptance of the loan. Since the lender's risk is associated with the amount of capital outstanding, reducing this throughout the term by amortization using rental surpluses (over interest costs) to pay off capital, can only be in the interest of the lender.

Specialist properties, such as sewerage plants, may attract a foreign bank that has built up expertise in that type of property; the same way that a particular mortgage bank may specialize in the development of its business in the housing market. Furthermore, banks may specialize in lending to particular sectors, e.g. local government, and their improved credit rating means they are therefore able to obtain funds at cheaper rates.

4.2.7 The requirement for capital security and repayment of capital and interest

Capital security is required by banks in the event of default by the borrower and also by shareholders, but only to the limit of their shareholding. However, this can be distorted in the case of a highly geared property company. Security typically comprises fixed charges over the property, floating charges over all the borrower's assets, especially in the event of a special purpose vehicle which may have no assets other than the property, and personal liability for all claims arising from the credit agreements or corporate guarantees from a parent company. Additionally, documents may agree the ranking of debt with other lenders, or may prohibit it altogether.

The rights of the mortgagee are designed to protect the security, such as the right to obtain possession of the security or to appoint a receiver; to obtain payment, including the right to sue on the personal covenant of the mortgagor; and the right to the security itself, namely the right to foreclose and obtain beneficial title to the property.

The cycle of the property market, and volume of lenders prepared to lend, are some of the greatest influences of loan conditions. Whilst competition varies in intensity, there is a tendency to take on more risk if competition is fierce. However, this is coupled with the fact that competition increases when there are perceived or real upturns in the market and the increased risk is set against a backdrop of potentially reducing risk as values increase. Niches amongst lenders will be created, which will be in terms of size of loan, complexity or type of security. Each lender's desire for new business will also influence the conditions offered, but may be unduly influenced by external factors, such as money market rates and the cost of hedging loans. Historically, lenders have relaxed their lending criteria at times when business has been lean, but it has been those lenders that have not strayed from the basic principles that have had fewer bad loans. This aspect was recently explored in a study relating to the experience of banks in the period 1985–1992 (Maxtead, 1993), which concluded that undue emphasis on 'loan to value (LTV) ratios' caused many lenders to overlook the volatility of 'value'.

During the late 1980s, the LTV ratio was central to many banks' lending policy and was considered to be a good indicator of loan risk. However, the subsequent sharp drop in property values and the failure by many lenders to also dramatically adjust their LTV basis for assessing loans, created a catalogue of losses for many well-known banks in the UK. Only after the property crash of 1990 did many lenders begin to adopt 'income cover' tests to monitor the ability of the rent to service the debt over the term of the loan. The quality of the covenant and the ability of the asset to generate enough income to amortize the debt to a predetermined level, over the loan period, influence the degree of cover required. A mortgage bank, for example, may typically require 120% of rental cover (i.e. 120% of the income required to service the debt) and may adjust the loan amount so that this relationship is maintained.

4.3 OBJECTIVES OF VALUATION

4.3.1 Ability of rental income to cover interest and amortize capital

Irrespective of the type of loan, a number of common factors influence the rental income used to pay off debt: the location of the property will determine supply and demand, thus dictating rental levels; the quality of the building and the speed of its likely obsolescence; the degree of periodic repairs and maintenance; the depreciation of buildings, which may be unduly influenced by the occupier's activity (e.g. tannery, government welfare office); the identity of the tenant, their business prospects, the state of the sector in which they are active and the original tenant's bargaining power; alternative uses for the building, at present or in the future, which may reduce the degree of obsolesence. However, the degree to which the latter is incorporated in a valuer's assessment of rental value remains questionable.

From the lender's viewpoint, some key variables need consideration in assessing security, notably income growth: knowledge of national rental growth rates does not replace the need to estimate the likely income growth for the property in question. Lease breaks and reletting voids require an assumption either that all breaks will be exercised or an assumed average length of stay within the building. A reasoned decision can be reached by identifying the tenant's current space needs, the likely growth of their business and market circumstances at the time their lease was signed. Reletting voids depend on market conditions and a rental void may be assumed at the end of a lease. The question for the lender/investor is the likely period before reletting. A short lease could therefore negatively affect value, although shorter lease terms on mainland Europe enable owners to relet buildings at market rents, freeing them from rent increases linked to a cost of living index. For prime property in a rising or stable market, shorter leases have not had a detrimental effect on value, but have resulted in far higher yields and a lack of institutional interest in secondary property.

It has been argued that inflation favours property, as high inflation tends to persuade investors to switch into real estate. However, it can equally have a negative impact, for example, on properties to be developed, through unquantifiable cost fluctuations. It will also affect maintenance costs for existing buildings.

4.3.2 The value of the asset as security for capital

Consideration of this issue raises questions as to the meaning of 'value'. Ongoing discussions in the UK have highlighted the difference between **worth** and the **price** actually obtainable in the market-place. Whilst many countries have focused on market value for this purpose, mortgage banks in Germany are required to produce their own internal assessments of worth based on market value, depreciated replacement cost and a long-term 'sustainable' value (which is discussed further below). Many banks in the late 1980s overlooked the fact that a valuation is out of date the day it is written, it serves only to provide a snapshot of value and is just an additional tool in assessing the security of a particular investment.

In the UK, in 1994, a committee set up by the Royal Institution of Chartered Surveyors (RICS), under the chairmanship of Michael Mallinson, mooted the idea of a 'stable value' for loan security valuation (RICS, 1994). This was an attempt to consider the long-term view of a property that ignored, or at least flattened out artificially, widely fluctuating property values over the long term. This concept is not new to practitioners in Germany, where such a valuation exercise is carried out as a requirement of mortgage banking law (HBG).

The 'long-term sustainable value' was developed in an era of relatively stable values where increases in property values could be reasonably accurately forecast. Minimum yields are prescribed by the individual mortgage banks for particular classes of property which are regularly monitored by the German Banking Supervisory Authority. In addition, large deductions for outgoings, typically 20–30%, are made from the rental value, which may not be higher than the passing rent, in order to arrive at the net sustainable income. This income is then capitalized for the remaining useful life of the building. The result is invariably lower than the market value of the building, although it is argued that the result could be similar if the bottom of the property cycle has been reached.

Most countries have independently developed a version of market value, for instance OMV as defined by the RICS 'Red Book' (RICS, 1995), in order to determine the value of a property at one particular date. This is the crux of the problem – in boom times the spot value is likely to be considerably above that which would be assessed in the ensuing slump. The concept of a sustainable or stable value as a main basis of valuation was, however, not considered by Mallinson as a serious alternative to OMV as 'the judgements necessary to produce the valuations would be too subjective, and too open to variability between valuers' (RICS, 1994). In the case of the German example, the prescribed method of valuation to some extent reduces this variability.

In terms of the bankers' viewpoint, the concept of a sustainable value, outside Germany, is almost too new to have been properly considered. It seems a panacea is being sought, such as a value that reflects the realizable proceeds at any one time, as well as the downside in the event of a property slump. In order to provide such a spectrum of values, a number of valuations should be carried out and less reliance put on the spot market value. Sustainable value is just one possible solution.

In the case of cross-border lending, where different valuation bases are adopted in each country, it will be for the lender to decide which basis is acceptable. They can either employ a valuer from their own country who will attempt to value on the home-grown basis, or else employ a local valuer in order that the valuation can be taken apart and the core data reassembled for the calculation of a long-term value. The latter is representative of the UK, where German banks lent a significant amount in the early 1990s and local valuers were employed to value to OMV. A discussion between the German banks suggested that *long-term value* was a difficult concept to bring over to UK valuers, and would lead to unreliable and vastly differing values. A few banks have tried to introduce the alternative basis of valuation since, but have met with mixed success.

Irrespective of the method of valuation, its reader must always fully appreciate the underlying assumptions. It is perhaps for this reason that the UK definition of estimated realization price (ERP) has not been unflinchingly taken up by the profession. For lending purposes, the presentation of a single figure on a page is no longer acceptable.

There has been a surge of negligence claims against valuers in the UK following a substantial fall in value in the early 1990s. These prompted disquiet over the use of a single OMV figure as the basis for loan security valuations, to which Mallinson (RICS, 1994) responded with recommendations for the provision of:

1. agreed written instructions;
2. any additional information crucial for the client to understand and benefit from the valuation, given its purpose;

3. 'unattributable form' comparable evidence in support of the valuation;
4. opinion on local economic factors affecting value, with sources;
5. comment on price trends and valuation uncertainty;
6. a second value (ERP): the price at which property would be likely to be sold after an appropriate marketing period starting at the valuation date.

At the time of writing, many of these recommendations are still the subject of controversy, with correspondence suggesting a disinclination on the part of many valuers to state opinion, particularly where it can be construed as forecasting.

Long term, or minimum values over the long term, may be reassuring, but current valuation techniques, which rely on the valuer's experience and market knowledge, are always likely to be too subjective, unless measures are taken to reduce this influence. Valuations, using simple multipliers based on yield, leave many questions unanswered as to the valuer's explicit thought processes. Any valuation will, however, always involve an element of crystal ball gazing and will entail the valuer 'taking a view' of market trends, especially as they move through the spectrum from OMV, to ERP, to appraisal of worth. Through the adoption of 'discounted cash flow' (DCF) techniques, assumptions become explicit, although not necessarily more correct, so that the long-term sustainable value becomes more transparent and can also be more easily adjusted to incorporate, say, long-term rental growth rates or to reflect average property or office yields. Until a universally accepted system exists, this form of sustainable value will, in all probability, be too inconsistent to be reliable, but may form a backup tool for lenders.

The 'prudent' assessment of value and the correct use of discount rates can be eased by undertaking a DCF calculation when many of the risks associated with property will need to be explicitly determined. However, the discount rate to be applied to determine a 'net present value' is an equal partner in this calculation. The traditional approach is to allow the discount rate to reflect the opportunity costs of capital for the particular business being analysed and, as a benchmark, the comparison of long-term rates on government bonds or gilts in the UK. The appropriate margin over the bond rate should take into account the illiquidity of capital and the risk associated with holding property.

As an example of a typical DCF calculation the spreadsheet shown in Figure 4.2 could easily be built up to double check the growth assumptions implicit in a traditional 'all risks yield' valuation. In this instance it is carried out at the end of the cash flow (taking into account the non-annual rent review system in the UK).

The security that comes with real estate is its capacity to generate ever increasing returns in the form of capital or rental increases/gains. A property owner is affected by rises and falls in the property markets; the associated risks for a lender are that a borrower may not always be left in a position to repay the loan. But as the old adage confirms, 'If you owe the bank a thousand, you have a problem, but if you owe the bank a million, the bank has a problem'. The analysis of market surveys to pinpoint potential competing supply and the cycle of occupier demand in the relevant area is therefore a vital part of the lender's, and their valuer's, role. Market surveys are typically provided free of charge by the largest property brokers, to their clients or potential clients.

Tenant covenant affects value, but will be of far less significance in, say Belgium, as retail tenants have the right to quit the premises every three years. Normally, however, the poorer the covenant, the greater degree of cover

Property: 5 Loadsamoney Street.

A. Income Assumptions

Current Gross Income		3,150,000
Outgoings % p.a.	0.00%	0
Current Net Income		**3,150,000**
Current ERV		4,125,000
Outgoings % p.a.	0.00%	0
Current Net ERV		**4,125,000**

Anticipated Income Growth @ 0.00% p.a. for the 1st 4 years up to the Open Review
Anticipated ERV Growth @ 2.00% p.a. before Open Review (See below)
Anticipated ERV Growth @ 4.50% p.a. after Open Review (See below)

n.b.: 4 Years before ERV received

B. Sale Assumptions:

Capitalisation rate (Net initial) 7.75%

GROSS sale proceeds AFTER 20th year. 116,500,000

C. DCF Table

Notes	Year	Income	Voids	Net Flow	Discount Rate (IRR) 12.00%	Discounted Cashflow
	0	3,150,000	0	3,150,000	1.000	3,150,000
	1	3,150,000	0	3,150,000	0.893	2,812,500
	2	3,150,000	0	3,150,000	0.797	2,511,161
	3	3,150,000	0	3,150,000	0.712	2,242,108
	4	3,150,000	0	3,150,000	0.636	2,001,882
	5	4,665,959	0	4,665,959	0.567	2,647,591
	6	4,875,927	0	4,875,927	0.507	2,470,297
	7	5,095,344	0	5,095,344	0.452	2,304,875
	8	5,324,634	0	5,324,634	0.404	2,150,531
	9	5,564,243	0	5,564,243	0.361	2,006,522
	10	5,814,634	0	5,814,634	0.322	1,872,157
	11	6,076,293	0	6,076,293	0.287	1,746,789
	12	6,349,726	0	6,349,726	0.257	1,629,816
	13	6,635,463	0	6,635,463	0.229	1,520,677
	14	6,934,059	0	6,934,059	0.205	1,418,846
	15	7,246,092	0	7,246,092	0.183	1,323,834
	16	7,572,166	0	7,572,166	0.163	1,235,184
	17	7,912,913	0	7,912,913	0.146	1,152,471
	18	8,268,995	0	8,268,995	0.130	1,075,297
	19	8,641,099	0	8,641,099	0.116	1,003,290
	20	9,029,949	0	9,029,949	0.104	936,106
Sale	20	116,500,000	0	116,500,000	0.104	12,077,178

51,289,109 (Gross) Net Present Value

D. Value

Purchase Costs	Transfer Tax	1.00%	
	Agent	1.00%	
	Legal & Notary Fees	0.75%	
		2.75%	−1,369,109
			49,920,000
			(Net) Net Present Value

Implied Growth Rate Calculation
for UK property investments that are let on fixed rents subject to review every n years

Review Pattern (RP)	5 years	(i.e. How often rent is reviewed to OMRV)
All Risks Yield (ARY)	8.00%	(Based on comparables for rack-rented property)
Equated Yield (IRR)	12.00%	(Typically Gilt Yield PLUS 3%)
YP perp @ ARY	12.50	
YP RPyrs @ IRR	3.60	
PV RPyrs @ IRR	0.57	
Implied Rental Growth Rate	**4.63% pa**	

Figure 4.2 Discounted cash flow.

required, expressed in terms of interest rate margins, say 1.50% over LIBOR, instead of 1.25%, a lower LTV ratio, for instance 65% instead of 70%, more rapid repayment of the loan, additional collateral, such as other real estate or cash, or other guarantees from a parent company or interested party.

Risks associated with the fabric of the building, such as inherent defects, poor maintenance, damage through use, depreciation, obsolescence, etc., require assessment. The instruction of a qualified surveyor, with sufficient professional indemnity cover to carry out a building survey, is essential to determine the condition of the premises and the presence of deleterious materials. The latter may have a negative affect on the structural stability and, ultimately, value of the premises.

Of increasing concern over the last 10–15 years have been those risks associated with previously permitted, but contaminative, materials or uses of property. It is the developing nature of this area of law that is cause for concern. Although national laws vary, in general, the current owner is held to be responsible for past contamination, unless the original polluter can be traced. The liability of the mortgagee is also under discussion. This risk can be mitigated to a limited extent by commissioning an environmental audit, which will consider historic uses and actual or potential contamination, including the presence of materials which may be considered hazardous to health.

4.4 RELATIONSHIPS BETWEEN THE VALUER, LENDER AND BORROWER

Partly as a result of the sharp decline in property values in the early 1990s, and subsequent losses suffered by banks, relationships between valuers and lenders have come under scrutiny. Lenders, with the benefit of hindsight, suggest that valuers valued too high and valuers accuse lenders of an overreliance on their valuations without proper scrutiny of the assumptions.

It is of the utmost importance in undertaking a valuation that clear written instructions are issued and subsequently accepted. Accurately drafted instructions ensure that both client and lender are aware of the information to be provided and the extent to which it may be relied upon. A duty of care naturally exists by the valuer to their client, but this is additionally influenced by the valuer's professional standing, qualifications and experience, which will vary from country to country. It is therefore in the lender's interests to be as specific as possible, so that valuations are tailored to their needs and not the valuer's.

It is equally important that a valuer is selected by the lender and not by the borrower, irrespective of the identity of the valuer, who cannot provide the best independent, unbiased advice if their relationship started out with the originator (the borrower). The temptation by a lender to reduce costs, even though these may be borne by the borrower, should therefore be resisted at every opportunity.

In Germany, for example, many mortgage banks are wary of the actual independence of *Immobiliensachverständiger* (property experts) and their ability to consider property in the investment environment rather than merely as bricks and mortar. As a result, most mortgage banks carry out valuations in-house. The independence of their valuer is controlled to a limited extent by the calculation of a number of values, including a DRC-type value and a long-term value, the latter through the use, as previously stated, of minimum yields prescribed by the bank's board of directors.

4.5 REALIZING SECURITY IN CASE OF DEFAULT

In an event of default, the most common remedy for a bank is the sale of the property through foreclosure, or some similar action. If sale proceeds are insufficient to recoup the costs of the outstanding capital, a lender will consider other means of realizing their security and increasing the value of the asset, weigh up the costs of these measures and consider the position of the bank in the event of possession or sale. The most common type of secured lender is the mortgagee who will have as a remedy rights to obtain possession and the right to foreclose. Assuming such rights have been written into the mortgage documentation they may be taken simultaneously once the mortgagee is in possession.

Realization can mean foreclosure and sale, or the appointment of receivers. The main specific advantage of being in possession is the right to receive rents and profits and the right to carry on any business on the premises. However, a mortgagee in possession is also under strict liability to account not just for the sums received but for the sums which ought to be received if the property were managed with due care. Possession, once gained, may well be very difficult to give up again, hence the desire for receivers and the need to carefully weigh up the valuation implications of such an action. The enforcement of collateral warranties are another means by which a lender can realize its security, provided these have been properly set up and the provider of the warranty has the ability to pay.

A forced sale will always cost a bank more than the alternative, which is to be a willing seller, and for that reason is avoided by lenders other than as a means of last resort (*ultima ratio*). To minimize losses, a delayed or postponed sale may be in the lender's best interests. Although a forced sale may not necessarily be the best remedy to realize security, there may be circumstances where this is necessary, for example, to mitigate a much greater future loss. The lender will consider whether they have the required expertise, or even the resources, to manage the property directly or continue to develop an unfinished scheme, and they may therefore sell regardless.

A subjective assessment of the effect on value or, more appropriately, the price expected to be achieved due to the nature of the sale, is greatly influenced by several factors, e.g. marketing period assumed, whether it is three months or a year. The state of the property market and the stage of the property cycle will be crucial, since in a falling market a long sale period could have a negative effect on the net proceeds. The market's knowledge of the health of the mortgagor/vendor can also be material since where they, or the properties, are well-known this may negatively influence the vendor's negotiating position. When assessing the likely receipts from a forced sale it therefore becomes imperative to issue clear instructions to valuers, specifying assumed levels of exposure to the market and marketing period.

4.6 VALUATION OF PROPERTY WITH DEVELOPMENT POTENTIAL

The purpose of a valuation will be influenced by the financing required, be it short-term development finance or 'take-out' finance upon completion, where a developer/investor intends to retain the project. However, if development finance is being provided, short-term risks may become long term, in the event that the developer is unable to dispose of their interest and the development is unable to support the level of rent predicted in initial appraisals. An indication of the value of the end-product, therefore, will be significant. It has not been uncommon, however, for developers to embark on a project with little idea as to the likely end sales price or rental level, relying on the premise that demand will outstrip supply at the time of disposal, based on current market trends. This short-sighted approach is another contributor to the accentuation of the already volatile property cycle. This has certainly been the case in the UK, with a well-developed speculative funding industry, and in the prime sectors of other European markets. However, outside the UK, the ability to fund speculatively in anything other than prime areas is rather more limited and has resulted in a far greater reliance on preletting and owner-occupation and the sharing of the developer's reward and risk with the lender/funder, through participating loans.

Prudence, on behalf of a bank, should involve appraising value in the existing state, assuming no further investment. Residual calculations taking into account the existence of planning permission or any hope value, permitted uses or built volumes on the site, should also be calculated. Investigations should be made into whether the development plans represent the optimal use and, if this is not the case, into any other factors influencing the decision to develop. Conversely, if an analysis of a (re)development initially suggests lower values than that perhaps being paid for the site, external influences affecting the profitability of the development should be researched, such as positive local authority covenants in return for planning permission.

The value of the development upon completion is the second figure to consider and is naturally dependent on the scheme planned. Assessing the value of the completed product, ignoring the development risks, is reliant upon the valuer's preparedness to predict values and to forecast trends. A project that is wholly prelet on a long lease will greatly influence a valuation as the requirement for a great deal of forecasting is removed. Areas that influence future values include changes in supply and demand affecting the development, competing schemes, changes in rental levels and typical letting incentives and changes in market capitalization yields.

A valuation of the finished product can be undertaken in one of two ways; firstly, the cash flow approach, incorporating an allowance for growth, positive or otherwise, in the income and costs, or, secondly, a valuation, assuming a completed development, based on current values and costs. The problem with this approach is that it assumes all values will rise or fall in unison, which is invariably not the case. Forecasting explicit growth rates is, however, not necessarily more reliable.

Lenders have on many occasions lent a far greater proportion of the development costs than would normally be considered prudent. In such instances, by lending say 100% of the project development cost, the lender is effectively placing a far greater reliance on the successful outcome of the scheme than would be the case if only 80% of the costs were lent. As a result, the lender will require a greater return on that top slice of loan. This will be in the form of a percentage share in the developer's profit, or an increased fee upon the scheme's successful completion, letting and/or sale. The level of risk and the appropriate renumeration is a matter of negotiation between the developer and the lender.

On a typical project, a lender monitoring a development would not normally determine the investment value in relation to the stage of the development, but only reflect the changing nature of the property market as it affected the end-product. In the event of a distressed sale, however, the lender will want to know the value of the scheme in its unfinished state. Two methods of assessment are possible; the value of land, in addition to materials used to date and stored on site, or the value of the completed product less the costs required to complete the project as planned.

In any event, it would be appropriate for a lender of development finance to consider both valuations in an attempt to quantify the downside to any loan. Values must be treated with caution as, in the event of a distressed sale, purchasers might not be prepared to take on the existing development team, for example, without some large discount.

4.7 DATABASE MANAGEMENT

4.7.1 Data collection

The type of information collated will be largely dependent upon the use to which it will be put by the collator. For example, the property valuer will wish to collate information regarding economic trends, property trends, property transactions, i.e. lettings and sales, legal developments affecting the industry and historic data of transactions for future reference for internal forecasting. A lender will require a similar database of information, but is likely to more readily accept the detailed knowledge of the valuer and confine themselves to the recording of trends. A borrower, meanwhile, has hopefully undertaken a sufficient amount of research in all fields to enable them to estimate the current worth of the property in question or an appropriate bid price, representing the 'best price' on the market. This judgement is then effectively checked by the valuer and lender.

The source perhaps most relied upon when building up a property database is that information collected in-house using a combination of the various mediums outlined below, most suited to the collator.

Out-of-house research is carried out on a fee basis by organizations such as PMA in the UK, which analyse the raw data produced by other information services. Personal contacts are probably the best source of reliable information, although the analogy of 'Chinese whispers' has connotations here. The vast array of publications available makes a detailed study a very time consuming process so that the use of press services which scan the property publications every week and provide information on call or supply the actual databases themselves are a valuable tool for the property professional; 'To Let' boards can offer access to the real estate brokers and a potential new source of information, although their proliferation can only be a rough indication of the availability of space and not the total supply, since the space may still be occupied.

4.7.2 Property measurement or referencing

It is perceived by some that the physical on-site measurement of buildings, for occupational purposes, is a waste of time and resources. It certainly can be in some instances, but it must not be forgotten that measurement will occur at a number of stages in a building's life; at design stage, for construction purposes, for occupation and ultimately valuation. It is the latter which most concerns lenders.

If the investment value of the building forms the basis of the valuation, the valuer will have to be guided by market practices. If the valuer is to accurately compare rental transactions, they will need to know the basis of floor area measurement. To some extent, therefore, the referencing of buildings will need to take account of local market practices to avoid valuing on a basis that is not practised in the market. As the maxim goes, 'as you analyse, so must you value'.

In Germany, for example, DIN 277 (Deutsche Industrie Norm) sets out a basis of measurement which is generally adopted by the building industry and valuers. However, when it comes to the occupational market, lessors will often manipulate the definitions to present their properties in the most favourable light, a practice that is not uncommon throughout Europe and even leads to different regions adopting different measuring bases for the same type of property. In the Netherlands a general lack of a common standard prompted the formation of the NEPROM (an organization sponsored by various bodies in the property world) code of measuring practice. However, this is still not universally adopted and great care must be taken in determining what is meant by *Brutto* or *Netto* (gross or net) when analysing occupational and investment deals.

In any valuation for loan security, a valuer should always ensure that the property's dimensions are verified by a thorough inspection – either detailed on-site measurement, or by reference to 'as-built' plans using electronic digitizers and comparing this with the check measurements made during inspection. Anything less than this is negligence on the part of the valuer and, regretfully, as the Schneider affair in Germany highlighted, the woefully inadequate property referencing by some banks contributed, to a great extent, to the losses suffered.

The availability of perfectly drawn plans from CAD (computer-aided design) systems and accompanying, often highly detailed, dimensions and areas can easily encourage a false sense of faith in their accuracy. CAD plans are only as good as the information they are fed and may not represent reality.

4.7.3 Market transparency

In northern Europe, the UK and the Netherlands are arguably the most transparent markets where most major sales and lettings are reported in the press and there is a high degree of professionalism in the property industry.

Elsewhere, such as Germany and France and even more so in Mediterranean countries, a general reluctance to disclose any information at all, particularly by the principals involved, has resulted in a heavy reliance on property indices and information published by brokers and estate agents, who theoretically have first-hand knowledge of transactions.

One problem in obtaining information about investment or occupational transactions is the degree to which the parties are, on the one hand, permitted under data protection legislation and are, on the other hand, willing to disclose contract details. In a small market, agents often aim to obtain a greater market share by professing to have greater market knowledge than their competitors and will, in consequence, withold information from other agents, valuers, etc. for fear of losing their competitive edge. The lack of exclusivity in client/broker relationships in mainland Europe, and the general distrust between agents, all stand in the way of the proper distribution of information. In the UK, the view is growing that, due to the institutional nature of property investment and in order for property to be equally regarded alongside other competing forms of investment such as government bonds or equities, there should be even greater transparency. Should this not occur, then fund managers will be deterred from direct property investment. The decision of PGGM, the Netherland's largest pension fund, to invest in property only indirectly is one indicator of the inefficiency, illiquidity and problem of up to the minute valuations in the European property market.

The falling market in the UK in the 1990s resulted in a tendency for lessors to place 'confidentiality clauses' in letting agreements for fear of prejudicing rental levels in other parts of the same building or of losing face in the market, by agreeing rents below the market accepted norms. After much discussion within the property profession of the little merit in such a course of action, these clauses are now actually far fewer in number as a consequence of a slightly rising market and the desire to publicize this fact.

Transparency can be achieved primarily through the cooperation of principals and brokers in the distribution of information on transactions and by the use of independent research houses, such as Investment Property Databank (IPD), which assimilate information on investment property portfolios provided by the major institutional investors and publish indices within a very short timescale which are available without restriction, albeit for a fee. Property companies have traditionally not contributed to such indices, many seeing themselves as entrepreneurial opportunists, who need only prove to their shareholders how they can buck the trends and not necessarily match them.

In France, in recent years, the high exposure by banks to the sector, having become owners after absorbing the assets of collapsed lenders and their general reluctance to sell properties at a loss, resulted in a very illiquid investment market, with little information available. During this period, letting deals were also shrouded in mystery and, until it was realized that values had in fact plummeted, details of deals remained confidential.

An overreliance on a small number of publications can result in a delayed reaction in the market, such as the extension of property booms and a consequent steeper slide in property values on the downward part of the cycle. It had been incorrectly argued in the UK, for example, at a time when indices were a new phenomenon, that their publication only sought to serve the self interest of their publishers, the agents, in order to create a market where there was none. That period is now long past and there is a general acceptance that, despite the plethora of indices, these do serve as a cross-check on each other, although in order to generate new business, each agent's index invariably has a slightly different bias.

The most accurate information on transactions available, though not always publicly, is that from the cadasters and land registries throughout Europe which, at the very least, ease the identification of owners. Supplementary information may include details about building use, plot sizes and rateable values, but rarely presents information about sale prices, the exception being outside Europe – Australia and the USA, for example. This could be a valuable source of information, but would still be historic and would not necessarily present all the relevant facts behind a sale.

4.7.4 Role of information technology (IT)

IT's role is, or at least should be, aiding the transparency of the property market through the management of electronic data. The link, or 'interface', with everyday users is through personal computers (PCs) or a form thereof, as preceded by Mainframes etc., all controlled by any number of operating systems such as Unix, MS-DOS, Windows NT/95, etc., and then linked on a local network (LAN) or a wide area network (WAN) using satellite, fibre optic cable or copper wire. The use of increasingly sophisticated programs, which seem to expand in volume to fill ever-improving hardware, including CD-ROM-based software for word processing, spreadsheets and informational databases, all assist in increasing the analytic and presentational capacity of lenders and players in the property market.

The increasing use of on-line press agency databases, such as Focus in the UK, helps avoid the need to leaf through volumes of print, as information on occupational and investment deals in specific parts of the country are summarized by type and location.

However, IT does not generate information – it only manages it. In any organization it is therefore important at an early stage to ensure that key aspects of data management are addressed, such as the type of information required and by whom, the means of access and the frequency of retrieval and desired speed, although the latter may be subject to hardware limitations. In addition, consideration must be given to whether the right users will obtain the correct information and whether there is a requirement for new IT to be integrated with existing systems. Finally, the users need to understand how to make use of the information. A substantial investment, often overlooked, is in training, particularly for the 'technophobes' who will typically prefer the calculator until shown the simplicity of the spreadsheet.

4.7.5 Data reliability

In many European countries, one or two major publications (such as the *Estates Gazette* in the UK, *Vastgoedmarkt* in the Netherlands, *Expertise* or *L'Événement Immobilier* in Belgium) typically have the upper hand when it comes to the collation of market data. Spurred on by the prospect of some free publicity, most brokers will pass on details of deals, if permitted, to these publishers who, by and large, have a reputation for accuracy and will publish information provided all relevant details are given. However, the press treatment of information is open to abuse. For example, simplistic calculations, in order to produce an eye-catching headline, may distort facts and influence the market and a valuer's overreliance on this one source may lead to inaccuracies. First- or second-hand knowledge of deals takes on a greater significance; external data can never be substituted by personal knowledge.

4.8 FEE LEVELS

A contract normally requires 'consideration' to be binding. This would imply that the lender, who relies on the information, should pay the fee. However, since the borrower normally pays, either through direct recovery of the cost or indirectly through increased up-front costs, contractual liability is often obfuscated.

Both parties have an interest in the results of a valuation: a lender to gain another measure of exposure to risk and the borrower to present a proper case to a lender and secure the best terms for himself. The recovery of valuation fees from a borrower reflects market conditions which favour lenders. In a market with actively competing lenders this situation may reverse. In general, valuation fees represent only a very small part of the overall cost of the arrangement, typically 0.1–0.3% for valuations over £10m, and it is unlikely that borrowers would insist that banks take over these costs, so jeopardizing their financial arrangements by reducing the potential pool of funders.

There will invariably be a commercial discussion amongst valuers about the level of fee and whether this should be related directly to the level of service or to the overall size or profitability of the deal. The relevant factors are highlighted below, but will be highly influenced by the amount of work available and the willingness of lenders to pass on costs to borrowers.

It is naturally enough the valuation figure that exerts the greatest influence on the level of fee. But the level of service required is also of critical importance; for an 'armchair' *re*valuation the duplication of work will rarely warrant another full fee compared with a valuation involving the coordination of other experts (e.g. environmental or building surveyors). The speed of service required will also be considered, as will the complexity of a valuation – multi-tenanted buildings with a wide variation in repairing terms require a great deal more analysis than a single-let building where the tenant is liable for all repairs. Perceived or actual competition with other valuers, at less active times of the market, may also encourage the valuer to lower their fee, although it is hoped that this is not at the expense of quality.

A valuer may additionally increase their fee for the perceived risk in valuing in a sharply rising or falling market and the difficulty, and hence increased potential liability, in accurately forecasting trends. They also increase their risk of claims if a valuation is made public and more than one party comes to rely on it. This determines the appropriate level of professional indemnity (PI) insurance, which many lenders now seek in the UK and is still not properly addressed on the continent. Every valuer should have sufficient PI insurance for each and every valuation and potential claim, to a level commensurate with the value of the subject property. It may, however, ultimately be the borrower who carries the additional costs involved.

4.9 REPORTING

Lenders generally wish valuers to be as specific as possible regarding the assumptions adopted in valuations, but want ever fewer of them. It was the case in the UK that a proliferation of assumptions tended to reduce the validity of valuation reports. This is now being rectified by the implementation of many of the recommendations of the Mallinson report (RICS, 1994). In the Netherlands and France, for example, valuation reports rarely divulge the mechanics of valuations and the quality of valuations generally varies considerably.

4.9.1 Valuers' liability

The quality of information available and the degree of subjectivity to which a method is exposed influence the consistent accuracy of valuations. The valuation of a hotel, for example, has long been regarded as requiring specialist knowledge as the variables involved are all subjective. Residual valuations also tend to be very sensitive to small changes in certain key variables and can vary enormously, so much so that English courts refuse to accept valuations calculated in this way, except in exceptional circumstances. The determination of assumptions and the clear explanation of valuation methods and their significance are therefore vital in informing the client and avoiding claims for poor or negligent advice or valuations.

The degree of error that is deemed reasonable and not negligent was considered by the English courts in the aftermath of the 1974 and early 1990s property market collapses. In Singer and Friedlander v. John D. Wood and Co. (1977) a tolerance of 10–15% either side of the 'correct' figure was held to be reasonable, a view upheld in recent cases such as Private Bank & Trust Co Ltd v. Sallmans (UK) Ltd (1993). However, recent cases, notably Mount Banking Corporation Ltd v. Brian Cooper (1992), have centred more on whether a valuer can demonstrate that they took all reasonable steps to properly determine value at a particular date and exercised a proper duty of care to the client. It should never be forgotten that a valuation is merely the opinion of the valuer.

Of particular interest recently is the role that the courts have had in the UK in assessing the degree to which valuers should be held responsible for the losses suffered by the banks in the property crash of the early 1990s. The Appeal Court judgement in Banque Bruxelles Lambert SA v. Eagle Star Insurance Co. (*Times*, Feb. 21, 1995) held a negligent valuer liable for all a lender's losses, even when a substantial part could be attributed to a fall in the market between the valuation date and the sale of the property following default. Critics of the judgement (Murdoch, 1995) argue that the court has reallocated to the valuer part of the commercial risk of the lender, i.e. that the market securing the loan may fall. The equity of doing so is questionable when the valuer's negligence is unconnected to that particular risk. It remains to be seen whether the case progresses to a higher judgement.

4.10 CONCLUSION

There exists within Europe a multitude of different valuation practices, employed for a wide variety of different purposes. Valuations for loan security are essentially concerned with the process of assessing the quality of the security. The manner in which this is undertaken varies, but will revolve around the determination of a current market value and a view as to the future value, particularly at the end of the loan term. As the latter is invariably impossible to quantify accurately, lenders will carry out alternative internal calculations to reflect investment worth, perhaps using DCFs, or attempt to apply a control mechanism, such as the assessment of reinstatement cost and long-term or sustainable values, or both. Some, more simplisticly, may choose to rely exclusively on current market value and play safe by structuring their loans in a very conservative manner.

As the determination of market value is still of such central importance to lenders in all European countries, it is in the interests of the valuation community at large to agree a common basis of valuation for loan security purposes. However, as recent events in the UK have highlighted, a valuation basis that is universally acceptable is a tough goal. The efforts of the International Asset Valuation Standards Committee have to some extent paid off, as their market value definition is about to be adopted by the RICS, in recognition of its clarity and simplicity. It is hoped that this will lead to a greater feeling of transparency and comfort for investors, especially from other countries.

Alternative methods of valuation, more specifically designed to aid the quantification of risk over the life of a loan facility and beyond (based upon the investment approach to valuation as opposed to replacement cost), do not show any signs of being adopted by countries for which they are not part of the valuation tradition. A reference in the Mallinson report (RICS, 1994) rejected the sustainable value concept on the basis that it is unreliable due to its subjectivity. However, independent research on historic yield and rental growth patterns for all types of property, available as a point of reference for valuers for loan security, could enhance this method's credibility. Market valuation is the only method which can be relied upon to be accurate, if only at one point in time, and so it is this basis alone which, in all probability, will continue to predominate as the basis of valuation for lenders throughout Europe for the immediate future. Lenders, at the end of the day, will understandably adopt home-grown property analysis techniques. The increased availability of vocational real estate education in many EU countries, however, and the greater appreciation of other countries' valuation techniques will no doubt set the scene for greater market transparency and associated cross-border lending.

REFERENCES

Barter, S. (ed.) (1988) *Real Estate Finance*, Butterworths, London.
Cameron, Markby, Hewitt (1994) *The Cameron, Markby, Hewitt Property Survey, November 1994*, Cameron, Markby, Hewitt, London.
Maxtead, W. (1993) *Project Finance Secured on Non-Recourse Loans*, Jones Lang Wootton Educational Trust, London.
Murdoch, J. (1995) Damages and BBL: a better way? *Estates Gazette*, **9510**, 115.
Nabarro Nathanson & Arthur Anderson (1993) *Real Estate Financing in Europe*, Nabarro Nathanson and Arthur Anderson, London.

RICS (1994) *The Mallinson Report: Commercial Property Valuations*, Royal Institution of Chartered Surveyors, London.

RICS (1995) *Appraisal and Valuation Manual*, Royal Institution of Chartered Surveyors Books, London.

CASE LAW

Singer and Friedlander Ltd v. John D. Wood and Co. (1977) 243 EG 212 and 295.

Mount Banking Corporation Ltd. v. Brian Cooper & Co. (1992) 35 EG 123.

Bank Bruxelles Lambert S.A. v. Eagle Star Insurance Co. (1995) 12 EG 144.

Private Bank and Trust Co. Ltd v. Sallmans (UK) Ltd (1993) 09 EG 112.

LEGISLATION

Hypothekenbankgesetz (HBG) BGBl 1 S 81.

Valuation practice in Europe

PART 2

Belgium | 5

Jan de Graeve

This chapter explores valuation practice in Belgium. Initially, the contextual background is set in relation to the property market and data sources. This is followed by a consideration of property rights providing the institutional context of valuation. The basis of valuation is further reviewed from a theoretical perspective and is supported by an example relating to valuation for investment purposes.

5.1 GENERAL BACKGROUND

5.1.1 Introduction

Belgium is a small country between powerful neighbours, from whom it has inherited many influences. For example, the basis of law is the 'Code Napoleon' which has evolved in parallel with French legislation. This is an important consideration regarding property valuation as the legal system exerts a strong influence. Politically, Belgium is a federal construction of three entities: Flanders (speaking Flemish), Brussels (French and Flemish) and Wallonia (speaking French). In the latter there is a small entity of a German-speaking population which was incorporated (Eupen–Malmedy) as a compensation from the First World War. Each of these entities has its own government and prepares their own laws, so legal differences do arise, for instance, in relation to property rights, urbanization and pollution. Clearly, these matters are relevant for appraisals as seemingly comparable pieces of land give rise to different property values in cases where pollution or redevelopment rights differ between regions. In addition, the European policy of open borders means that a large proportion (10%) of the population is non-Belgian. Currently one million inhabitants are not of Belgian origin, but through property ownership integration is achieved.

5.1.2 Property market development

In Belgium property rights are held in very high esteem. Nearly 70% of Belgians own their home, although a very large part of this is achieved through financing

European Valuation Practice. Edited by Alastair Adair, Mary Lou Downie, Stanley McGreal and Gerjan Vos. Published in 1996 by E & FN Spon, London. ISBN 0 419 20040 1

and mortgage. Indeed, accessibility to housing has been a political target since the early part of the century and 'social housing' has been heavily subsidized. In the retail sector it is estimated that some 50% of total space is still family owned, in content the larger shopping centres are found in the rental sector. The majority of offices are rented in Brussels, 7.4 million m² (c. 70% of the national office stock; 1993 figure). The impression is that occupiers such as the EU offices and foreign companies are mostly tenants, whereas a large portion of the offices of indigeneous Belgian companies are still owner-occupied, for instance, the headquarters of the banks. Commonly, owner-occupiers prevail in the industrial sector, with the exception of rental premises for firms working in the light industrial and distributive sectors.

The owner-occupied housing and retail markets are reasonably buoyant with an upward trend in prices over a considerable time period, although recently severe price fluctuations have occurred. A recent trend in the retail sector is the regulation by government to reduce the expansion of new retail developments with the aim of protecting small retailers. In comparison the office market development is more cyclical, for instance, rental prices of office space per m² doubled from 1986 to 1992 in Brussels' EU quarters. Since then the market has experienced a downturn due to the economic recession and an increased supply of prime office space. The industrial market has many problems and is difficult to appraise due to restructuring over a considerable period of time. Ownership of commercial business property is increasingly in the hands of institutional and foreign investors, in part due to the relatively unfavourable property tax situation for the small private investor. Property accounts for c. 8% of the investment portfolio of the large domestic investors, being built up mainly of offices, followed by large shopping centres and small retail properties with residental occupation on the upper floors of the building. These institutions maintain a buy-and-hold policy and after some 15 years the property is sold to private investors and dealers.

5.1.3 Market data

As a general rule, in Belgium transactions are secret and the land registry considers the information of the notarial acts as protected and not publicly available. Therefore, in Belgium most data, if available, are unreliable, difficult to verify and subject to interpretation as all conditions to match market value are not provided. Another reason for this is the tax environment. As a result of the very high taxation policy, tax avoidance measures are frequently used. For example, some transactions have part of the price which is not mentioned in the notarial deeds but when real estate is incorporated in a company or investment society its value is often inflated above the market value to increase the depreciation possibilities and thereby lower the taxation. Even the results of the relatively important public auction market in Belgium are subject to interpretation. Furthermore, the main notarial procedures to sell in cases of forced sale auctions do not reflect the assumptions of the market value definition set up by international organizations such as TEGOVEFA, TIAVSC and EUROVAL.

Market changes have varied considerably due to external pressures such as expansion of the European Union, the influence of Scandinavian investment and other factors. Also local markets vary considerably between cities, notably differences between Brussels and the rest of the country. As a consequence considerable differences exist in yields and rents. In Brussels price differences between offices will be in the order of 25%, whereas in other regions with small office markets often a variation of 75% can be found.

Thus, as a result of the data problem, valuers have to rely on their personal database of market evidence or, sometimes, a database provided by the local professional body. Other sources include a major mortgage company (Anhyp) which sells data from its databank but this information is not controlled. The Brussels' professional body of land surveyors studies the market for residential properties and publishes yearly reports. In addition an internal databank is available based on analysis of public auction prices over a longer period.

Due to problems of data transparency, the application of the comparative method is particularly difficult in Belgium. Thus, regarding valuations, each property type needs to be appraised by the most appropriate method and checked and controlled by at least one other method. Data relating to asking prices are available through the larger estate agencies, especially for professional use and commerce, however, transaction data (realizations) remain difficult to accces although some specialized firms do publish their results.

5.2   PROPERTY RIGHTS

5.2.1   Freehold and ground leasehold

Valuation practice is concerned with valuing rights on property, in Belgium this is commonly owned freehold. In cases of succession of a deceased person it often happens that the freehold property right goes to the children and the usufruct right remains with the other partner in marriage. The usufruct is the right to use someone else's property for a period of time not exceeding 30 years for judicial entities, for a fixed period or for a lifetime for a private person. However, some exceptions on freehold possession can be found concerning the right to use property when land is developed, of which the following categories are relevant.

1. Problems may arise if development takes place on land in third-party ownership. If the legal steps necessary (*recht van natrekking or droit d'accession*) are not adhered to there can be a loss of property rights in a third-party ownership. The courts will adjudicate on the matter only for some form of compensation.
2. Ground leasehold (*erfpacht or droit d'emphythéose*) is regulated by a special law. This is of more relevance to public authorities and cities in need of long-term projects. This form of tenure can be no shorter than 27 years but does not exceed 99 years, although a renewal is possible.
3. For ports, canals and mineral rights there are concession rights to use land (and buildings) for specific purposes in a regulatory manner, though the ownership generally remains with a public agency regarding the commercial exploitation of the resources.

5.2.2   Rights on property regarding the rental agreement

Commonly a rental agreement is granted, this being a personal right. Legally tenants are afforded a high level of protection in the residential, agriculture and retail sectors, in turn this exerts an important influence on valuation. For example in the case of commercial leases, protected by the law of 30 April 1952, the rental agreement is of either three, six or nine years duration, or longer for a first period. In the retail sector the tenant can claim for up to three further periods of nine years totalling 36 years, but has the right to leave every three years (break options). In the case of industrial property the duration of the contract depends on the terms agreed on. Furthermore, subletting is normally not allowed and there is no privity of contract on assignment of the lease.

Rents are initially fixed at open market level based on **gross** floor size and subject to annual indexing by inflation (CPI). Every three years there will be an open market level rent review. In the case of retail property this has to be proven according to law by market evidence with valuers acting as court witnesses. Liabilities, such as repairs, services and insurance are normally paid by the tenant, with the exception of large structural repairs which are paid by the landlord.

All rents received by the landlord are subject to taxation referred to as *précompte immobilier*. In the rented housing sector the basis of taxation is the *Revenu Cadastral*, or the normal net income, which is 60% of gross rents of a property as valued on the date of 1.1.1975. Regarding rents from commercial or professionally occupied properties, in addition to the *précompte immobilier* the normal net rental income is added to the personal income of the landlord for direct taxation purposes. In the case of companies corporation tax on profits is levied at a rate of 39%.

Stamp duty in Belgium is very high (12.5%), with the exception of social housing and first-time buyers of small properties. Notary fees are a percentage of the market value but decrease with value. For example, fee plus registration (14.15%) for selling a house of BF5 million, or fee plus registration (12.77%) for a building of BF50 million. The fee of an estate agent is around 3% (plus VAT) of the selling price, while the cost of a simple valuation is around 2–3% per thousand BF of the value of the property, with a minimum of BF15 000.

5.3 EDUCATION AND THE VALUATION PROFESSION

From as early as the 16th century laws have regulated the areas of competence for land surveyors–valuers in Belgium. The most recent legislation of 6 August 1993 updates the law of 1825 and a royal decree published on 7 March 1995 establishes, by charter, an institution for land surveyors and valuers of real estate which will regulate the practice of valuers and surveyors.

Regarding the education of land surveyors, a diploma is obtained after a full-time four year academic course at the faculty of Geography (Topography) in the Universities of Ghent (in Flemish) or Liege (in French). Before 1990 this course included two years of theoretical study and two years of practice at the office of a private land surveyor. A similar and parallel study is available at polytechnic level (Department of Building Technology) for which four institutions in each linguistic part of Belgium have been founded. However, the total amount of time spent on formal valuation training in these courses is rather small.

These training courses are the minimum requirements to work in private practice and an additional one year training is necessary to join the institution for land surveyors and valuers. However the profession has been regulated in

Brussels since 1876, through an organization known as the UBG (*Union Belge des Géomètres-Experts – Belgische Unie der Landmeters Experts*) and its local affiliated associations. Currently there are 600 members. The UBG represents Belgium in a number of international organizations relevant to real estate including: FIG, the International Federation of Surveyors (1878); EUROVAL, the European Valuers Association; TEGOVOFA, the European Group of Valuers of Fixed Assets. For fixed asset valuation the UBG has created a body (TEGOBEX) to run a two year seminar course on valuation for their members.

However, it should be stressed that in Belgium the practice of valuation is not exclusive to surveyors–valuers but involves other individuals and professionals. Furthermore, the title of a valuer is not yet legally protected. For example, civil servants in registration offices control notarial acts, control the market value and basis for taxation; estate agents give free estimations to client vendors; mortgage companies generally employ their own internal valuer and architects are involved in the costing of buildings. In total there are some 10 000 persons employed in brokerage activities without any specific valuation education, of which the more experienced persons (*c.* 1200) belong to the professional body UPSI–CIB (*Union Professionnelle du Secteur Immobilier – Confédération des Immobiliers de Belgique*). The valuation and brokerage of offices and large shopping centres for investment purposes is mainly in the hands of international surveying firms, whereas other types of property are mainly served by domestic land surveyors and estate agents.

Valuation is generally an opinion given by the valuer and is rarely in the form of a valuation certificate, except in the case of fixed assets valued by chartered surveyors. For the latter the valuer needs to use their academic background, experience, appropriate methodology and techniques. The highest standards of professionalism, as guided by a Code of Ethics complemented by local regulations, must be adhered to. The valuer is liable to their client and Belgian law regulates good practice. In a case of incompetence or bad behaviour the professional body may even exclude the valuer from the professional practice. Valuation takes one of three reported forms:

1. a simple advice: generally a statement of the appraised value;
2. a valuation report: this is a description of a few pages about the building including photographic material and a statement of value;
3. a certificate: this is an extensive report describing precisely the building, definitions of applied values and applied valuation methodology, and a statement of the property value based on a survey of circumstances and market evidence.

Regarding mortgage valuations, banks and financial institutions use both in-house and external valuers. In the case of the former advantages include availability, standardization of information and cost considerations, although there is the disadvantage that the valuer is no longer independent of the commercial, financial and administrative considerations of the organization. In contrast, the external valuer has wider experience, potentially has more up-to-date knowledge and is perceived as being independent. However, regarding housing, as this is considered to be a safe investment lenders do not weight the appraisal of the property so much in their lending decision. In the housing sector mortgages of 80–100% of the property value are given. In the commercial sector mortgage loans to business are mainly based on the creditability of the debtors, hence, in those circumstances in which the borrower is financially sound, the property value as a guarantee for the mortgage loan is of less importance.

5.4 PURPOSE OF VALUATION AND VALUATION METHODOLOGY

The main purpose of valuation is to arrive at an 'open market value' (*valuer venale* or *verkoopwaarde*) to buy or sell property. This value represents the price which one could reasonably expect to obtain at the date of valuation, under conditions of a willing seller and a willing buyer, and a reasonable period to market the property, with stable prices during the period considered and where a bid of a special purchaser is excluded. Due to the unfavourable tax environment very often the 'average' market value is stated in the valuation report, in contrast to the highest possible value which could be received in the market. In such cases an average yield, not reflecting the future, is used in estimating the capital value of rental property. As a consequence, the open market value is known as the 'normal market value'.

Other valuation purposes include valuation for tax reasons, as a basis for inheritance taxes, for claims and damages in civil law, depreciation and damages to the building caused by tenants, depreciation in property value due to urban planning, fixing a forced sale value for financing purposes and mortgages ('auction value'), fixing indemnities in forced sale and compulsory purchase.

In Belgium the following three methods of valuation are generally applied, namely the cost, comparison and income approaches.

5.4.1 Cost approach for investment

The cost approach includes a value for both construction and land. The estimate of 'construction value' is based on the new construction costs of the elements of a new building, including fees. To this value the land, or 'ground price', is added, which is the price which could be obtained on the open market of the building to be constructed. For older buildings a correction is applied to the new construction value for age and obsolescence, ending up with a 'depreciated replacement value' of the property. Corrections vary according to quality of the construction, depreciation of the building and maintenance quality. For industrial buildings obsolescence can correct the above value by 80% or more and the total value can become negative. This method is not only used for estimating the market value of the property, but is frequently used for owner-occupied business property in cases of valuation for tax purposes and balance sheet valuations. Also, for insurance purposes, reconstruction value, depreciated reconstruction cost and depreciations for accidents (fires, other damages) are determined. In these cases the cost approach value is not related to either the demand/supply conditions of the market or the locational situation of the property.

5.4.2 The comparison approach

Open market value of property and rental value is often based on market evidence of comparable transactions. Comparable evidence is based on measurement of land surface, analysis of building elements (surface, age, facilities, location, standing), income-producing capacity and tax income. A minimum of five comparable transactions is required, but this is not always easy to achieve due to data problems, though if applicable the results of recent auctions are taken into account. In this context the rental value for commercial leases, housing and residential leases, administrative and cadastral purposes is determined.

5.4.3 The income approach

This method is mostly used for estimating market value for income-producing properties, capitalizing estimated rental value with an estimated yield; it encompasses a range of techniques:

1. The actual rent multiplied with the average yield. From the capital value received, stamp duty and corrections for not leased parts or disputes are deducted.
2. The potential rent multiplied with the average normal yield. From the received capital value a correction for non-occupation and stamp duty is deducted.
3. Discounted cash flow calculation, though this is used more for financial programming (calculating a subjective value for an investor) than for a calculation of actual market value. As changes in law and taxation and the market happen frequently in Belgium, this technique is highly unreliable for a period longer than five years.

5.5 APPLICATION OF VALUATION

Normally, two methods of valuation are used for any particular property, with a third method being used as a control on the valuation. This process is considered to be good practice. The valuer personally visits the property and meets the occupants. The building is measured and notes are taken of construction quality and defects. The valuer examines the leases, titles, planning applications and local rules.

5.5.1 Housing

In the case of residential properties and small condominiums valuation needs to be undertaken for forced sale value, mortgage purposes and market value, and for sales, auctions and acquisitions. The cost approach gives the total cost of the investment, this is compared with the open market value by the comparison method which indicates the normal acquisition cost. The income approach is not relevant in Belgium for this type of property. For the area, construction costs are valued and depreciated as a percentage of costs and repairs.

5.5.2 Offices

The cost approach gives the depreciated replacement cost for land and buildings, while the income approach gives the open market value. For this use type the comparative method is used as a control.

5.5.3 Retail shops

For retail premises the study of the lease contract is essential as are the implications arising from it. Comparison is difficult and the yield (income approach) depends upon situation, local taxation and the quality of the tenant. Again, the cost approach can serve as a control.

5.5.4 Industrial property

For industrial buildings a capital value and rental value are fixed. The comparison method is very difficult to apply and in going concern valuations the cost approach is adjusted according to age and obsolescence.

5.5.5 Mortgages on property

Valuations for mortgages encompass the cost method and are compared with the estimate by the comparison method. Forced sale values of auctions are compared with actual market value.

5.6 CASE VALUATION FOR INVESTMENT PURPOSES

5.6.1 Preamble

This valuation of a hypothetical office property is being undertaken to provide a comparative example of a valuation for investment purposes. We are instructed by a client, the owner of the freehold interest, to carry out an 'open market valuation for sale purposes' of the subject property detailed below.

1. Date of valuation: April 1995.
2. Location: prime city centre Brussels – near the new European parliament.
3. Size: new building (1990) of 2000 m² net lettable floorspace on four floors, 2300 m² gross area, with good specification and air-conditioning, two passenger lifts to all floors. No car-parking.
4. Construction: standard construction for a property of this type in this location.
5. Condition: good state of repair.
6. Tenure: freehold. Good title to the property can be shown and the property is not subject to any unusual or especially onerous restrictions, encumbrances or outgoings.
7. Lease: let to a 'blue chip' tenant on a modern standard rental agreement for a three/six/nine years period with break options every three years.
8. Annual indexation to CPI.
9. Estimated gross rental value is BF9000 per m² per year.
10. Inducements: rent free periods assuming 5% of gross rent.
11. Effective gross rent per m² (after taking into account inducements): BF8550 m²
12. Level of costs for landlord:
    (a) management fee of rents is 5% of gross rent;
    (b) cost of insurance.
13. Costs for tenant:
    (a) cost of general maintenance;
    (b) cost of local taxes;
    (c) costs of precompte immobilier (BF1 million per year);
    (d) cost of insurance;

(e) running costs: water, heating, electricity.
14. Sale transfer costs: stamp duty 12.5%, notary 0.057%.
15. Initial yield: 7.25%.

5.6.2   Valuation

(a) Income approach (rental capitalization technique)

Gross rental value per year (2000 × BF9000)	BF18 000 000
Less: inducements 5%	BF9 000 000
Effective gross rental value per year	BF17 100 000
Less: landlord costs	BF855 000
Net rental value	BF16 245 000
Multiplier (at 7.25% in perpetuity)	13.793
Capital value	BF224 068 965
Less: stamp duty 12.5% and notary costs 0.057%	BF24 997 415
Market value	BF199 071 550

(b) Costs approach

Costs of this building with total gross area constructed 2300 m²:
Ground price:

BF15 000 per m² gross floor area (15 000 × 2300)	BF34 500 000
Plus: stamp duty	BF4 502 700
	BF38 002 700
Building costs: 2300 × 45 000 per m²	BF103 500 000
Plus: architect's fee 6%	BF6 210 000
Less: penalty for no parkings (40 parkings × BF75 0000)	BF3 000 000
	BF151 712 000
Financing project costs	
Three years on land acquisition cost at 8%	BF9 760 500
Two years on building in progress at 8%	BF9 016 800
	BF170 490 000
Developer's profit and risk 15%	BF26 250 000
Sale value	BF197 000 000

(c) 'Balanced value' by averaging (a) and (b)

Average appraised open market value   **BF198 000 000**

It should, however, be noted that under actual market conditions in Brussels the above property could not be sold at the appraised price, except if rented and occupied. Currently (1995) the investment market is weak with few transactions, but this situation is expected to improve in the short term. Indeed, if this property was currently for sale no price higher than BF175 000 000 would be achieved if not occupied. Consequently the above method is more applicable for a balance sheet for fixed asset valuation.

5.7 CONCLUSION

In Belgium there is a problem of data availability and reliability, even public auctions are subject to interpretation. Furthermore, the main notarial procedures to sell, in cases of forced sales, do not reflect the assumptions of the market value definition set up by TIAVSC and adapted by TEGOVOFA and EUROVAL. Market changes vary considerably due to external pressures such as expansion of the European Union and foreign investors. Also, local markets vary considerably between cities, notably differences between Brussels and the rest of the country. There are, as a consequence, considerable differences in yields and rents. Regarding valuations, each property type needs to be appraised by the most appropriate method and checked or controlled by at least one other method.

FURTHER READING

Anhyp (1995) *Yearly report for Belgium on housing and land.*

Association Belge du Crédit Immobilier (1992) *Le crédit hypothécaire de l'independence de la Belgique à la Communauté Européene.*

Commission de l'evaluation foncière (1994) *La loi du 30.6.1994 modifiant et complétant les dispositions du Code Civil relatives a la Copropriété.*

De Graeve, J. (1993) *Report Fédération Hypothécaire auprés de la Communauté Européenne – Assemblée Générale du 25.6.1993,* Bruxelles.

Deschrijver (1970) *Schatten van onroerende goederen,* Simon Slevin uitgeverij.

Gabele, F. (1981) *Les expertises immobilières.*

Lurquin, P. (1985) *Traité de l'Expertise en toutes matières.*

Souris, P. (1994) *L'Expertise judiciaire en droit de la construction.*

Union des Géomètres–Experts de Bruxelles (1926–1995) *Market Reports for Brussels' Residential Market* (yearly).

Finland | 6

*Kari I. Leväinen and
Tero Lahdes*

Towards the end of the 1980s the Finnish property market saw a tremendous upswing, followed by a consequential sharp downswing in the early 1990s. The collapse of the property market caused enormous problems, especially to the banks that had allowed credit to a property market which previously was so stable. Whilst the banks have recovered with support from the State, many small and medium-sized firms have gone bankrupt as the value of their real estate assets, constituting the securities for loans, declined. Currently, in the balance sheets of many firms, banks, insurance companies and pension funds, real estate valuation is very problematic, indeed, there is a vigorous discussion as to how property should be valued.

As a consequence greater consideration is being given to valuation reports and the skill of the valuer than formerly. Efforts to develop the valuer's expertise are being undertaken, including new valuation methods and information systems to assist real estate valuation. Indeed, in autumn 1995, a new system is to be launched for the authorization of real estate valuers in order to ensure the expertise of the valuers and to promote public confidence in professional real estate valuation.

6.1 THE VALUATION PROFESSION IN FINLAND

Finnish valuers can be members of two associations, namely the Association of Finnish Surveyors or the Finnish Association for Real Estate Valuation. The former which was established in 1890 has about 1150 members with an employment profile across a number of bodies:

the National Board of Survey	43%
other state officials	5%
cities and other municipalities	17%
education and research	5%
private enterprises	23%
others	7%

European Valuation Practice. Edited by Alastair Adair, Mary Lou Downie, Stanley McGreal and Gerjan Vos. Published in 1996 by E & FN Spon, London. ISBN 0 419 20040 1

The members must hold, as a minimum qualification, an MSc degree in surveying from the Helsinki University of Technology or other comparable academic degrees. Those employed by the National Board of Survey are involved in statutory valuation work while those in private enterprises are involved in other areas of valuation.

In comparison, the Finnish Association for Real Estate Valuation is a more recent body, established in 1978. Its members are drawn widely from professionals working in the valuation sector and has been influential in the establishment of official authorization procedures for valuation. The aims of the association are to promote the development of valuation methods and their utilization in practice; to promote research on real estate valuation; to provide training for members; and to ensure high-quality and equitable valuation services.

The Association has about 260 members, for admission new members must fulfil one of the following criteria:

1. surveyors with an MSc degree from the Helsinki University of Technology and at least two years experience;
2. agronomists or foresters with an MSc degree from the Faculty of Agriculture and Forestry, University of Helsinki, and at least two years experience;
3. hold other university degrees with at least 3–5 years experience;
4. those without university degrees need at least 10 years experience.

Almost half of the members are surveyors, the rest being lawyers, economists, construction engineers, foresters or agronomists. Two-thirds are working in the private sector and one-third in the public sector. However, the number of full-time valuers is only about 20% of the membership.

Advanced level education of valuers (MSc Degree) is provided by the Department of Surveying at the Helsinki University of Technology which trains graduate engineers for real estate valuation. There are currently three professorships in real estate studies and one professor in real estate law, though training in agriculture and forestry valuation is also provided by the University of Helsinki. In addition, four polytechnics (Espoo-Vantaa, Mikkeli, Vaasa and Rovaniemi) offer programmes in surveying.

6.2 LEGISLATION AND REGULATORY PROVISION

Statutory valuation is based mainly on acts and decrees concerning expropriation, cadastral surveys, land-use planning, construction and taxation. For example, the National Land Survey issues orders and regulations for statutory valuation, and the National Board of Taxation lays down new rules concerning property valuation for taxation purposes every year. Furthermore, the Ministry for Social Affairs and Health has issued general guidelines for insurance companies including the appraisal of property investments. Thus, for residential estates an initial yield of 4%, for commercial and office estates 7% and for industrial estates 8% should be used unless a more justifiable valuation method is utilized.

According to the Property Tax Act (1993), the assessed property value is about 70% of the market value which is obtained from the value of the site and the value of the buildings. The former is based on directives using the normal real estate valuation principles and land value maps are produced for each urban area. Regarding taxation, the assessed value of agricultural land is determined by calculation which has no real connection with the actual capital value (market value). In practice the taxable value of agricultural land is much lower than the market value.

The first Finnish book on valuation the *Kiinteistöarvioinnin käsikirja* ('Handbook of Real Estate Valuation') was produced in 1976. The Finnish Association for Real Estate Valuation published *Kiinteistöarviointisanasto* ('Real Estate Valuation Terminology') in 1986, in an attempt to clarify the definition of terms. The latest book published by the Association (1991), *Kiinteistöjen arviointikäsikirja* ('Handbook of Real Estate Valuation, 1991'), is currently the basic manual for Finnish valuers dealing with economic and legal questions related to real estate valuation, different valuation techniques and their applications, and various appraisal examples.

The Finnish Association for Real Estate Valuation has published a valuers' code of honour. Under present practice the liability of the valuer is governed by a general Damages Act, although if a real estate agency is involved in valuation, liability for damages may also be imposed by the Consumer Protection Act. In accordance with the Damages Act any damage arising from a deliberate or negligent act shall be compensated, the liability for damages in full but the amount of compensation may be adjusted. The employer has the primary liability for damages caused by an employee to a third party, however, the employee has to compensate for the damages caused by them to the employer only where the employee is guilty of serious neglect or deliberately causes the damage. The liability for damages may be defined in the written contract of a commissioned valuation report, though written contracts have rarely been used in the field of valuation.

In valuation practice, liability for damages caused to a third party may also arise. This kind of damage shall only be compensated where it has been caused by an act prescribed in law as punishable, or where other serious reasons provide for the liability. Cases of damages in real estate valuation are unusual and thus there is no legal precedent.

There is a high degree of variation in the educational background and experience of real estate valuers. Indeed, the real estate and banking crisis indicated that not all valuers possessed sufficient skills. Hence, the development of a system of authorization for valuers has been a major goal. The first authorizations will be granted in autumn 1995. The granting and supervision of authorizations will be the responsibility of the Association for Real Estate Valuer Authorization, whose members include the different institutions of the real estate profession. Indeed, the composition of the Committee of the Association for the Real Estate Valuer Authorization consists of the representatives of the Finnish Association for Real Estate Valuers, the Finnish Real Estate Owner Association, the Central Chamber of Commerce, the Ministry for Social Affairs and Health, and Authorised Public Accountants and is intended to take into account the different interest groups involved with real estate valuation.

An authorized real estate valuer should meet the following requirements:

1. an authorization test;
2. 10 years suitable work experience, or five years work experience and an acceptable training, or three years work experience and a suitable academic degree;

3. practical involvement in real estate valuation;
4. integrity and good reputation;
5. full legal capacity;
6. and be aged under 65 years.

The Association for Real Estate Valuer Authorization will supervise the operations of authorized real estate valuers, keep a public register of authorized valuers, express opinions on matters under its auspices, and promote and develop the expertise of real estate valuers (Määräykset kiinteistöarvioijien auktorisoinnista, 1995).

6.3 CONTEXTUAL INFLUENCE

The majority of full-time valuers work in real estate agencies, some of which, particularly in the Helsinki area, exclusively concentrate on real estate valuation. The two largest companies (HK Property Advisors and Huoneistomarkkinointi) are nationwide real estate practices owned by commercial banks which merged together in autumn 1995 to form the Merita Bank. As these two agencies are larger than the others, they have better resources regarding both personnel and market data. In Finland there is little exchange of information about, for instance, rent or sale contracts, every agency has to maintain their own files and supplement these with rather meagre public sources of information.

Banks normally need one valuation report to support a financing decision, but in more difficult cases two reports are required. The valuation report is usually commissioned from one of the two major agencies, or another agency with special expertise either local to the area or specializing in the nature of the valuation object. Branch offices are under no obligation to commission valuations from the agency owned by their own bank group. Institutional investors usually undertake their own appraisals using their in-house experts and data, although an outside opinion may be requested to facilitate decision-making. Another major real estate owner, the state asset management company Omaisuudenhoitoyhtiö Arsenal Oy, formed during the banking crisis to take possession of property from banks in liquidity difficulties, usually orders two valuation reports when selling or purchasing. Although direct foreign investment in the Finnish real estate market became possible in the beginning of 1993, to date (1995) no foreign real estate and valuation agencies have been established in Finland.

It is important to note that banks or clients cannot influence estate value assessment, but they can affect the information content of the valuation report. For example, banks and clients may request a certain valuation technique as additional information or, for example, a more extensive evaluation of the present real estate market situation and especially its future development.

6.4 PROPERTY TENURE

As a legal and technical concept, real estate in Finland is a parcel of land which has boundaries and has been registered in the cadastre. Real estate has a wide meaning including land, buildings and the flora. Usually the owner of the land parcel also owns the building, but real estate can be leased completely or in part.

Normally apartment and office buildings are formed as joint-stock housing companies (*asunto-osakeyhtiö, kiinteistöyhtiö*). The joint-stock company owns both the site and the building(s) or has the site on leasehold and owns the building(s). An individual or an organization can buy shares in a housing company, entitling the owner to possess and occupy specified flat(s) in the building and to take part in decision-making as one of the owners. The owner of a flat (the owner of property shares) may lease the flat to a tenant.

All deeds of real estate purchase must be ratified by an official authority. Concerning the purchase of a flat (housing company shares) the only formality required is that signatures of the seller and the buyer must be confirmed by two witnesses. Regulations for leasing offices, flats and other commercial premises are similar, though a lease agreement on land must be made in writing. If the leased land lies in an area which is covered by a detailed plan the lease agreement can be written as a special site leasehold. Other valuation services are bound by various legislative regulations. For example, the legislation on site leaseholds specifies the maximum growth in permissible rent normally up to 50% of the cost-of-living index, during the first five years.

The major landlord in urban areas is usually the city. For instance, the City of Helsinki dominates the renting of land for commercial premises in its metropolitan area. The term of a lease is normally for a period of 30–60 years with the annual rent 5% of the market value of the site. Rents are adjusted according to the cost-of-living index. The annual rent per gross floor area of industrial sites is currently FIM20–75, and for office and shop sites FIM100–250. As the cities are independent, rental policies and other terms of land lease vary locally (Statistical Yearbook of Finland, 1994).

If the lease agreement concerns a flat, a part or the whole of a building, the contract has to be concluded according to the Tenancy Act, which is the subject of reform. The reformed Act will consist of two laws, one concerning commercial properties and the other residential estates. It is likely that the new tenancy legislation may become the most liberal in the EU, since it will impose no restrictions on lease terms or rents. Leases may be made for a specified period or until further notice.

Leases on residential properties are usually made until further notice or for a period of one to three years. For example, in the Helsinki region in 1994 more than half of all commercial property leases were made until further notice and about one-third for a period of over five years (Olkkonen and Salo, 1994). In an until-further-notice lease both parties have the right to terminate the lease at three or six months notice, thereby allowing for prompt reaction to market changes. Rents in until-further-notice leases and fixed-term leases are revised annually according to the contract, with increases usually bound to the cost-of-living index. Longer lease terms have recently become more common along with the increased demand and higher rents. The duration of a lease usually also depends on the size of the estate. Large estates of over 5000 m² are leased for 10 years on average and head office-size premises (over 10 000 m²) for 10–20 years. Under certain conditions, the tenant's rights remain in force in the case of ownership changes. Furthermore, a lease cannot be transferred to another tenant without the consent of the landlord; nevertheless, a lease on commercial premises may be transferred in connection with business sales on certain conditions.

Lease inducements and graded rents have become more frequent in the 1990s. In the sale of real estate, on the other hand, an arrangement has become common in which the retailer guarantees the purchaser a fixed rental return for the whole lease period. Rents cannot be reduced during the lease period without the approval of the landlord. Lease agreements remain valid and recession, for instance, is not a legitimate reason for reducing the rent of commercial premises during a long-term lease [Supreme Court precedent (KKO, 1994)]. The distribution of the costs arising from the maintenance of commercial property is agreed upon on a case-by-case basis. Nevertheless, it is usually the owner who is responsible for the following expenses: heating and electricity; water and sewage; fire insurance; maintenance and repairs; waste management and cleaning; real estate tax and other taxes.

The rate of owner-occupation in all property sectors is high in Finland with many companies owning their own premises and while some financial institutions have concluded sale and leaseback contracts, interest in these has not been sustained in the bearish real estate markets of the early 1990s. Furthermore, such contracts do not provide any particular taxation or other indirect advantages.

Since 1993 and the Act on the Supervision of Property Acquisitions by Foreigners there are no more restrictions on a foreigner wishing to buy real estate in Finland. The only exceptions relate to holiday property and real estate in frontier zones and special conservation areas which still require a permit. Foreign companies and foundations, and Finnish companies controlled by people living abroad, need permission from the relevant provincial department of the state.

6.5 VALUATION METHODS

Real estate is divided differently in rural and urban areas. In the former real estate is agrarian and forest land, including some buildings, whereas in the latter, the subdivision is into unbuilt and built real estate. Examples of unbuilt land are urban fringe areas (raw land), streets and parks, development areas and sites while built real estate consists of single unit housing, flats, commercial and industrial premises.

The most commonly used valuation methods are the comparative method, cost approach, income approach and development value method. Valuers of commercial property make use of the profit-based method, the comparative method and the cost-based method, according to which technique is best suited for the valuation. Cash-flow methods were not commonly utilized until the 1990s, with the profit-based method and the comparative method being the more usual forms of valuation. However, the final value of the property is determined at the valuer's discretion, with the valuer relying not only on the calculations but also upon experience and expertise.

As the property registers (section 6.6) are very reliable, the comparative method is extremely popular in real estate valuation. However, the problem with this method is finding enough comparable transactions, especially as the market has recently been in recession. Collecting information on commercial property transactions, which usually are transactions of shares (joint-stock housing companies) can also be problematic. Since there is no public database for this kind of information, valuers have to use their own databases and there is seldom exchange of information between valuers.

Mathematical-econometric models are especially useful in statutory valuation (for example, in expropriation). The technique, which is mainly utilized for calculating land prices, especially for determining the influence of different predictors, is regression or covariance analysis. It is also used to investigate the impact of real estate prices and other factors on property markets. Other comparative methods in use are case studies and comparisons based upon experience.

The replacement cost method is used in those circumstances where there are no comparable sales available, particularly in cases where properties are infrequently or never traded and which are occupied by a user who is not generating a profit. This approach is the basis of valuation for insurance purposes and sometimes for expropriation. It is also used in the valuation of public sector property assets such as schools, libraries, sports centres and other public buildings. In this context the valuation adds a site value to the cost of replacing the building, depreciated on the basis of age and obsolescence. The cost-based method is mainly used as supplementary to other methods and suffers from the disadvantage that it does not take into account differences between regional markets. Hence, two similar commercial buildings in different regions may have the same cost-based value, but the market value may be very different.

In contrast, the income approach is often combined with a cash-flow analysis and is based on capitalizing the net income per year. Deductions of taxes, municipal rates, insurance and maintenance are made before discounting.

The capitalization method is perhaps the most popular technique used in the valuation of commercial property in Finland. Based upon the rental yield, the method determines the capitalized yield value that an investor–buyer is willing to pay as expressed by the following equation:

$$\text{Value} = \frac{\text{Rental yield}}{\text{Yield requirement}}$$

The difficulty of the method lies mainly in the use of a number of uncertain, discretionary factors. Hence, its application requires high expertise. These uncertainty factors include rental yield capacity, maintenance costs and the applicable interest rate/investor's yield requirement. The capitalization method resembles the comparative method in that the determination of applicable rental levels and capitalization rate is based on comparative data on sales of lease targets in the market. In the event that the target is leased, it is necessary to examine the lease contract conditions, the most essential factors being rent, rental revision procedure and the duration of the lease. Furthermore, it should be made clear whether the rent corresponds to the market level or if it is higher or lower. For example, in the current market situation in Finland rents specified by old, but still valid, contracts are higher than the market rental level set by new contracts. However, the most difficult stage in the capitalization method is the determination of yield requirement, which varies strongly according to the quality and location of the target. The requirements are also affected by the market situation and interest rate but due to the long-term nature of property investments the rental yield requirement varies less than the general interest rate.

Example 6.1
Office/shop building, constructed 1985, good state of repair, city centre (A–B), empty

−1 floor	store 600 m²
0 floor	shop 800 m²
2–3 floor	office 2000 m²

1. According to comparative transactions

office	2000 m² × FIM5000m²
shop	800 m² × FIM5500/m²
store	600 m² × FIM1000/m²

total value FIM 15 000 000.

2. Capitalization method

Gross rents
office	FIM55/m²/month
shop	FIM60/m²/month
store	FIM15/m²/month

Costs: FIM15/m²/month floors 0–2 (includes all normal costs + yearly maintenance/repair, no bigger renovations)

Yield   9–10%
Renting time 1 year, so 0.5 years rent will be lost.
After that vacancy risk is included in the yield.

Gross rent income/year FIM16 700 × 12	= FIM2 004 000
costs/year FIM15 × 3400 × 12	= FIM 504 200

Net income/year	FIM 1 500 000
capitalization 9%	FIM 16 700 000
capitalization 10%	FIM 15 000 000
Lost rent (6 months)	FIM − 1 000 000
Value	**FIM14–15 700 000**

In valuation the yield requirement may also be approached via sales of comparable leased targets. In a normal (stable) market situation, and especially with regard to standard type targets, this approach will succeed; but special targets and a changing market situation can complicate matters. Currently (1995) the market is more illiquid and thinner than normally, adding to valuation problems.

Theoretically, the yield requirement may be approached using the following equation:

$$K = p + i + r - g + d$$

where K is the initial yield (= initial rental yield requirement), p is the real yield level of a safe investment, i is inflation, r the risk premium, g the gearing (= value rise expected) and d is depreciation.

In selecting the final yield requirement in practice, it is necessary to take into account the market situation, the investors' interests and objectives together with the valuation target. In other words, the final yield requirement should be derived from the market and mathematical models are only tools which help formulate the structure of yield requirement.

The following factors (plus others) affect the yield requirement.

1. The development of a locality affects expectations, rental yield development and thus values. In vibrant localities rents usually increase more rapidly and have a reducing effect on rental yield requirements.
2. Regional appreciation factors affect yield requirements even within one locality. In the highest appreciated areas the demand is heavier and the lease risk smaller thereby reducing yield requirements.

On rented plots the investors' yield requirements have traditionally been higher than on freehold plots. Institutional investors favour freehold plots, so there is less demand for rented plots. However, rented plots involve a factual risk with regard to the continuation of the lease at the end of the lease period, unless the tenant has a right to redeem the plot at a fixed price. Attitudes towards rented plots have, however, changed during the current recession. Indeed, the importance of the tenant and the lease contract have become a more significant factor than plot ownership.

The purpose of use has a impact on, among other things, the depreciation period and, hence, on yield requirements. The yield requirements for manufacturing and storage premises are higher than those for commercial and office premises. This is due to, apart from the shorter usage period caused by technical– functional wear-out and outdatedness, the distant location which, with regard to scarcity, does not involve an effect that would positively generate the rental level.

The problem with the capitalization method is that it does not give sufficient consideration to the fact that the initial flow of the valuation target may not be steady in the years to come. This is due to, for example, the varying market situation, changes in the property lease situation and the possible reparation costs. The risk of changes in initial yield is theoretically taken into account by selecting the capitalization interest rate, whereas in the cash-flow methods the examination of yield and cost is prolonged over a longer period.

The basis of these cash-flow methods is that the value of the target is perceived as equal to the sum of the initial yields due from the target in the future, discounted to the present time. Applicable factors include yields, maintenance and other rental costs, inflation, the prospects for value development and discount rate. An individual investor usually adds the investment costs and financing to these factors. Furthermore, the cash-flow analysis is usually made for a period shorter than the life cycle of the target, as it is 'absurd' to make development forecasts for longer terms. Typically, the analysis will cover a period of 10 years, and discounting and evaluation of the terminal value of the target will be included in the value examination. (Kujanpää, 1994).

Table 6.1 DCF appraisal model

Discount Rate 14%
Vacancy Rate 10%

	1995	1996	1997	1998	1999	2000	2001	2002	2003	2004
Potential gross income	2004	2094	2188	2287	2390	2497	2610	2727	2850	2978
Annual growth	4.5%	4.5%	4.5%	4.5%	4.5%	4.5%	4.5%	4.5%	4.5%	4.5%
Less vacancies	(200)	(209)	(219)	(229)	(239)	(250)	(261)	(273)	(285)	(298)
Effective gross income	1804	1885	1970	2058	2151	2248	2349	2454	2565	2680
Less operating expenses	(504)	(524)	(545)	(567)	(590)	(613)	(638)	(663)	(690)	(717)
Annual growth	4.0%	4.0%	4.0%	4.0%	4.0%	4.0%	4.0%	4.0%	4.0%	4.0%
Less replacements	0	0	(300)	0	0	0	(1000)	0	0	0
Net operating income	1300	1361	1124	1491	1561	1634	711	1791	1875	1963
Discounted NOI	1217	1118	810	943	866	795	303	670	616	565
Present value 1	7904									

	1996	1997	1999
Net market rent	FIM1500/year		
Period: 10 years			
Average rent growth	3.0%	4.5%	6.0%
Net market rent end of the period	2 016	2 329	2 686
Terminal car rate	10.5%	10.5%	10.5%
Capitalized value end of the period	19 199	22 185	25 584
Discount rate	14.0%	14.0%	14.0%
Present value 2	5 179	5 984	6 901
Present value 1	7 904	7 904	7 904
Present value 2	5 179	5 984	6 901
Total present value	13 083	13 888	14 085

6.6 PROPERTY DATA

This section deals with public property data and registers, which in Finland possess a high degree of reliability. However, public registers do not provide data about the latest transactions with a time lag of between one to six months.

The Real Estate Register (*Kiinteistörekisteri*) contains information about every real estate parcel in Finland. The register, which includes information about parcel size, location, easements, plans, titles and mortgages, is maintained by the National Land Survey and the local courts. The register is computerized and open to public scrutiny with all basic information available (in principle).

The National Land Survey in Finland began to maintain the Official Market Price Register at the end of 1981 and contains over one million real property transactions. The register includes data about purchase price, area, location and land use regulations and publishes annual statistics on land purchases in Finland. The purpose of the register, as set forth in the Act, is to promote the valuation of real estate in surveys for redemption, for land-use planning, for taxation, for the granting of credit and for other valuation and research purposes. The deed of a purchase is the point of data collection for the register. All deeds of real estate purchase must be ratified by an official authority, once ratified it is reported to the Provincial Survey Office within seven days. The report includes data on the purchased real estate, the names of the seller and purchaser, social security codes, occupations, home addresses and a description of the location and boundaries of the purchased land. After receiving a transaction report, the Provincial Survey Office checks that the information about purchased real estate is correctly given in the report. They also supplement the data, indicating, for instance, whether there is a detailed plan for the area, whether a shore line is included and the coordinates of the real estate. The National Land Survey has carried out several studies based on data extracted from the Register, for example, prices of cultivated land, building sites in rural and urban areas, and leisure building sites.

In addition, several cities now maintain their own municipal real estate purchase registers, which are more detailed than the Official Market Price Register and essentially cover the area of the city. Also cities and other municipalities maintain real estate registers including information on detailed land-use plans, buildings and flats. One example is the data register of Helsinki Metropolitan Area (*Pääkaupunkiseudun tietorekisteri*).

On the basis of transactions Statistics Finland publishes quarterly reviews of flat prices. However, this information is statistical in nature and it is not possible to get details about any particular transaction. Statistics Finland also publishes dwelling rent statistics annually, including information on flat size, location, age and form of financing.

The KTI Institute of Real Estate Economics, affiliated with the Turku School of Economics, maintains a database consisting of leases of over 20 000 commercial premises. The institute publishes market reviews, research reports, rental indexes and yield data on the Helsinki area.

Real estate agents and companies have knowledge of transactions of joint stock companies. Some of these publish their own market reports and some real estate agents also publish rent, price, yield and return information.

6.7 VALUATION REPORTS

The Finnish Association for Real Estate Valuers has issued general instructions on the content of valuation reports, and these are followed in practice by nearly all valuers. According to the instructions, the valuation report should include at least the following information (Kiinteistöjen arviointikäsikirja, 1991):

1. on whose request and for what purpose the report has been made;
2. object of valuation, with details of location and ownership;
3. current use;
4. information about the area and the buildings;
5. rights and easements;
6. plan details, prohibitions and restrictions on construction;
7. building permit data;
8. municipal infrastructure and its charges;
9. details of current leases;
10. costs imposed on the real estate;
11. other factors affecting the value (market situation, factors which may essentially alter it);
12. target value and the basis for its assessment (selling price, taxation value);
13. valuation techniques;
14. supply of basic information for valuation calculations;
15. analysis of basic information;
16. determination of target value with appropriate justification;
17. assessment of the reliability of the result;
18. date and signature.

In addition to the above information the valuation report usually contains photographs of the object, maps, floor plans of the building and other documents that may be necessary for the valuation. It depends on the valuer to what extent comparative price and rental data are presented to support the valuation and how extensively the present market situation and its future development are appraised. Differences also occur in the application of valuation techniques and the degree of detail in the presentation.

The valuation report should not be handed over to parties other than the client, unless otherwise agreed. Moreover, the valuer is under obligation to observe secrecy concerning any information about the client's internal circumstances and operations that is acquired while carrying out the task. The charge of the valuation report and the basis on which the price is determined are usually made known when the assignment is agreed on. The charged sum usually depends on valuation time and costs, property type and value, and the level of expertise of the valuer. There are no listed prices for valuation reports, but the prices are competitive. As a rule, the smaller agencies charge somewhat lower rates than the large ones, which tend to charge for the advantages of their larger organization. The normal cost of a valuation report on commercial property amounts approximately to FIM 4000–15 000. The comparatively low cost of a valuation report reflects the fact that indemnity insurance is not used in Finnish real estate valuation, since the definition of liabilities has been found to be problematic.

6.8 CONCLUSION

The general expertise of the Finnish full-time valuers is very good. Advanced level education of valuers is provided by the Department of Surveying at the Helsinki University of Technology, which trains graduate professionals for real estate valuation. Finnish valuers can be members of two associations, namely the Association of Finnish Surveyors or the Finnish Association for Real Estate Valuation. New members have to meet tight criteria.

In autumn 1995 a new system is to be launched for the authorization of real estate valuers, in order to ensure the expertise of the valuers and to promote public confidence in professional real estate valuation. The committee of the Association for Real Estate Valuer Authorization consists of the representatives of the different interest groups involved with real estate valuation.

The Finnish Association for Real Estate has published a 'Handbook of Real Estate Valuation', which is currently the basic manual for Finnish valuers dealing with economic and legal questions related to real estate valuation, different valuation techniques and their applications, and various appraisal examples. Valuation of investment property is usually done by valuers who work in real estate agencies. The two largest agencies HK Property Advisors and Huoneistomarkkinointi merged during the spring of 1995, creating an agency which has much better resources regarding both personnel and market data than any of its competitors.

The most commonly used valuation methods are the comparative method, cost approach, income approach and development value method, according to whichever technique is best suited for the valuation. The most popular profit-based method seems to be the capitalization method. Detailed cash-flow analyses were not commonly utilized until the 1990s. However, the final value of the property is determined at the valuer's discretion, with the valuer relying on calculations, experience and expertise.

REFERENCES

Kanerva, V., Palmu, J. and Ridell, H. (1991) *Kiinteistön arviointi*, Vammala.

Kiinteistöjen arviointikäsikirja (1991) *Suomen kiinteistöarviointiyhdistys*, Rakennustieto Oy.

Korkeimman oikeuden ratkaisu (1994) 10.10.94. KKO 1994:96.

Kujanpää (1994) Kassavirta-Tuottoperusteiset arviointimenetelmät, AEL-INSKO R3363L/94 III Helsinki.

Myhrberg Olavi (1994) Arviointimenetelmät ja niiden muuttuneet lähtökohdat, AEL-INSKO R3363L/94 I Helsinki.

Määräykset kiinteistöarvioijien auktorisoinnista (1995) Kiinteistoarvioinnin Auktorisointiyhdistys (KA) r.y. Helsinki.

Olkkonen, O. and Salo, M. (1994) Toimitilamarkkinat Helsingissä 1994. *Helsingin kaupungin tietokeskuksen tutkimuksia*, **2**.

France | 7

Sandrine Bardouil and
Philippe Malaquin

Property valuers were originally employed in France as arbitrators or expert witnesses in law courts. This role was expanded in the middle of the nineteenth century as mortgage lending increased. In 1848, the *Comptoir des Entrepreneurs* was founded to finance development projects and in 1852 the *Crédit Foncier de France* was established as a mortgage bank specializing in the long-term financing of all types of properties. After 1945, post-war reconstruction stimulated property development throughout the country, particularly in the residential sector. The French government subsidized and controlled most of these developments and in the process boosted demand for valuations from the banking sector. By this stage, the valuation services of mortgage banks were also in demand in cases of divorce and inheritance as well as in company mergers and acquisitions.

The profession only began to expand outside the banking sector following the law of 1971 on judicial valuers. This legislation standardized the selection of valuers by judges, following consultation with the Society of Judicial Valuers. Post-war legal developments on planning, residential financing, housing rent controls, commercial leases and compulsory purchase further widened the role of the valuer in France (Table 7.1).

7.1 OVERVIEW OF VALUATIONS

7.1.1 Mortgage valuations

Mortgage valuations are not compulsory unless the loan is financed by property bonds (obligations foncières), as in the German Pfannbriefe system. Mortgage valuations are based on the open market value. In practice, the lending institutions require full valuation reports when substantial loans are involved but, generally, little more than a valuation figure for small loans. The large mortgage banks instruct their own valuation service. For instance, Crédit Foncier relies on Foncier Expertise to carry out such valuations.

European Valuation Practice. Edited by Alastair Adair, Mary Lou Downie, Stanley McGreal and Gerjan Vos. Published in 1996 by E & FN Spon, London. ISBN 0 419 20040 1

Table 7.1 Valuation purposes and bases

Valuation purposes	Valuation basis
Purchase/sale/letting of property	Open market value/open market rental value
Leasing finance/leasebacks	Open market value
Loans	Mortgage value
Repossession	Open market value/forced sale value less legal costs
Successions/gifts	Open market value
Mergers	Open market value/depreciated replacement cost
Portfolio of an investor	Worth to investor
Revaluations	Open market value/depreciated replacement cost
Insurance companies' fixed assets	Open market value – Decree of 5 November 1990
Sociétés Civiles de Placement Immobilier (SCPIs) – a form of property unit trust	Open market value – Law of 31 December 1993
Development sites	Open market value

Valuation practices have also developed out of associations between property consultants and the banking sector. Expertim, for example, is a valuation practice which combines the valuers of property consultants, Auguste-Thouard, together with banks Crédit National and the Banque La Hénin.

7.1.2 Investment valuations

By law, the fixed assets of insurance companies as well as those of property unit trusts, *Sociétés Civiles de Placement Immobilier (SCPIs)*, have to be valued. There is no such obligation on the property assets of other property investment companies, except in the case of company mergers and/or acquisitions. Therefore, the *Sociétés Immobilières pour le Commerce et l'Industrie (SICOMIs)*, which specialize in leasing finance, and the *Sociétés Immobilières d'Investissement (SIIs)*, which have to place the majority of their funds in residential properties, do not require valuations by law. However, in practice the *SICOMIs* and the *SIIs* request portfolio or individual property valuations regularly, especially when they want to purchase, sell or swap some of their properties. This is an important market for valuers and is currently (1995) worth about 120 million fr. (French).

The portfolio valuation of insurance companies is governed by Decree No. 90–981 of 5 November 1990. This was a market worth about 300 billion fr. (French) in 1994 and, in accordance with the Decree, the assets of insurance companies need to be valued every five years. To achieve this requirement, a fifth of the portfolio is valued each year and the previous year valuations are updated annually. As a result, the portfolio is valued in its entirety every five years. Article 15 states that the portfolio of insurance companies must be valued on two valuation bases. The first valuation is the depreciated purchase price, or construction price together with the cost of improvements. The second valuation assesses the *valeur de réalisation*, which is the open market value assessed by an independent valuer. The choice of valuers must be accepted by the Commission de Contrôle des Assurances.

The portfolio valuation of the *SCPIs* is governed by Decree No. 94–483 of 9 June 1994. The valuers of *SCPIs* are instructed for a period of four years. Accordingly, the whole portfolio must be entirely valued in the first year, with annual revaluations in the following four years as the portfolio must be valued in its entirety every five years. Article 8 of the Decree states that the portfolio valuation of *SCPIs* must be based on the open market value by independent valuers. This instruction takes place following the acceptance of the valuers by the Commission to the Stock Exchange (*Commission des Opérations de Bourse* or *COB*). The *COB* regulates the format of valuation reports which include detailed information on the valuer. Below are some of the key elements of such a report.

1. Identification of the person who takes responsibility for the valuation with references, curriculum vitae detailing the valuers' professional experience, information on the valuation practice, such as geographical expertise, number of persons employed, annual accounts and turnover.
2. Detailed description of valuation methods and definitions. If valuers are members of a professional organization, reference to its code of ethics and professional regulations.
3. Terms of instruction with the valuer such as fee levels. In addition, valuers must confirm to the *COB* that they are independent.
4. Annual report on the valuation of the property portfolio. There must be a full valuation report of each property at least once every five years. In the interim, the valuer must update the previous year's valuations. The valuer must list the revaluations separately from the full valuation reports. Valuations are based on the open market value inclusive and exclusive of purchaser's costs. In addition, the reports must be clear and in a language which lay people can understand, including a glossary of property terms in the appendix.

7.2 VALUATION STANDARDS

Valuation standards in France have largely arisen from valuation practices and property organizations keen to project the image of the valuer as a professional, not dissimilar from the chartered surveyor in the UK. In fact, the standards which now exist are largely inspired from the 'Red Book' and *Code of Ethics* published by the Royal Institution of Chartered Surveyors.

In addition to the British influence, and in view of the decrees relating to the valuation of the fixed assets of insurance companies and of the *SCPIs*, auditors and accountants in France have put pressure on valuers to define their legal status more clearly. As a consequence, the government is currently drafting a law to regulate the activities of valuers and protect their clients. The new law should also cover the educational and practical training of valuers.

The key document on valuation practice in France is the Methodological Guide and Charter of Property Valuation (*Guide Méthodologique relatif à l'Evaluation des Actifs Immobiliers* and the *Charte de l'Expertise en Evaluation Immobilière*) which the *Institut Français de l'Expertise Immobilière* (*IFEI*) last published in June 1993. This document is the result of a 1991 conference organized by the Council of Chartered Accountants (*Conseil Supérieur de l'Ordre des Experts Comptables*) and the National Property Federation (*Fédération*

Nationale de l'Immobilier). The advice and guidance in the guide and in the charter are not compulsory. This 45 page document, to be updated every three years, simply encapsulates the key definitions and methods which valuers in France are expected to adopt (section 7.5).

7.2.1 Who are the valuers?

In theory, anyone can be a valuer (*expert*) in France except under the title of agricultural and forestry valuer (*expert agricole et foncier*) or judicial valuer (*expert agréé par les tribunaux*). These two fields are strictly governed by legislation, namely the law of 1977 which regulates the role of the *expert agréé par les tribunaux* and the law of 5 July 1972 No. 72565 which regulates the *expert agricole et foncier*. The title of *expert* is therefore loosely defined and valuers come under a wide range of titles including the following.

1. *Experts fonciers et agricoles* Valuers listed by the Ministry of Agriculture with their status enshrined in law.
2. *Experts agréés par les tribunaux* or *experts judiciaires* Valuers appointed by magistrates who are qualified to present evidence in front of the courts. Their appointment is based on reputation.
3. *Inspecteurs de la fiscalité immobilière, inspecteurs des domaines* Valuers in tax administration.
4. *Experts de crédit foncier* Valuers in the lending institutions or in the banks.
5. *Experts d'entreprise* Valuers in private practices comparable to chartered surveying firms.
6. *Experts de l'Administration des Domaines* Valuers who are also civil servants and who work exclusively for their government department.
7. *Experts indépendants* Sole practitioners who tend to carry out valuations locally.

In addition, other professionals may be involved in property valuations from time to time.

1. *Agents immobiliers* Estate agents who advise on sales, purchases and lettings which entail some sort of valuation knowledge. In this capacity, they are known as *évaluateurs* rather than *experts*.
2. *Commerciaux* Property agents in private practices comparable to the chartered surveying firms and who mainly advise owners on market values and/or rental values of their properties prior to marketing.
3. *Géomètres-experts* Essentially land suveyors but may be called upon to undertake valuations, particularly if based in the provinces.
4. *Notaires, avocats-conseils, gestionnaires de patrimoine* Notaries, solicitors and property managers, respectively, who may be involved in the more straightforward valuations.

The above list is not, and cannot be, exhaustive. Moreover, there is no reference book which records all valuers in France. However, it is estimated that in 1992 there were between 1250 and 1350 valuers (Etude, 1992).

7.2.2 Professional education

There is no compulsory university course or professional qualification to become a valuer in France, despite the existence of about 250 property-related courses. Among other courses, the most popular are the evening courses for property professionals who want to specialize, for example at the Institut des Etudes Economiques et Juridiques Appliquées à la Construction et à l'Habitat (ICH) which offers a valuation course. There are also post-graduate diplomas, Diplômes d'Etudes Supérieures Spécialisées (DESS) which mainly cover property law and where property practitioners are invited to lecture on valuation. At the Ecole Supérieure des Professions Immobilières (ESPI), post-Baccalauréat students can enrol on a three-year day course which covers valuation in the second and third years. Currently, however, most valuers have either a university degree or a diploma from one of the élite university level schools, the grandes écoles. In addition, they may have gained some professional qualification in engineering, law or land surveying.

Upon entering the property market, prospective valuers are trained in the companies they have joined. However, the training system is not as organized as in the UK where surveying firms compete to recruit graduates onto their two to three year training programmes. The training system in France is more *ad hoc* and there is no final examination like the UK's Assessment of Professional Competence (APC) to become a chartered surveyor. Instead, in its Charter of Property Valuation, the IFEI states that valuers must either have obtained a property diploma at university level or gained seven years professional experience in property and, at least, four years in a valuation practice. In addition, valuers must continually develop their skills to keep up-to-date with changes in the property market.

7.2.3   Code of ethics

The charter of property valuation produced by the IFEI includes a code of ethics which is no more than a 'code of common sense' for the members of this organization. For instance, the section on the valuer's duties states that the valuer is entitled to refuse an instruction and that, when carrying out a valuation, they must do so with honour, dignity and correctness. This includes being absolutely impartial, keeping deadlines, respecting professional confidentiality and rejecting outside pressure. The duties of the valuer towards their clients are to prepare clear and precise reports which do not lead to misinterpretation and to be prepared to justify the conclusions reached. Somewhat amusingly, the code also makes it clear that the valuer must be courteous with other valuers. More seriously though, the valuer is also invited to share their professional experience and skills if the information is not confidential and does not threaten the interests of their clients. This is interesting as, in practice, exchange of information between valuers from different practices is far from systematic. The assessment of the professional responsibility of the valuer to their clients and third parties is based on whether they exercised due diligence in their work rather than on the correctness of the valuation figure. The code also touches on advertising which must be discreet and must not rely on comparative claims.

7.2.4   Sanctions

Valuers may be pursued for negligence through the courts but this has rarely happened. In the case of the Caisse Autonome de Retraite des Sages Femmes

Françaises v. Mr Georges Nobilet, 1971, the valuer was proved to be negligent as he had not inspected two of the properties he had valued for mortgage purposes. The valuer was required to pay the difference between the loan and the value of the two properties which were sold under forced sale conditions.

In negligence cases, the courts do not attempt to assess whether or not the valuation figure is correct. They accept that valuation is an art as much as a science and that there is a certain degree of uncertainty. However, their role is to find out whether the valuer acted with due diligence. Indeed, valuers have to assess all the elements which may influence a valuation such as location, property specifications, state of repair, leases, planning issues and market evidence. In addition, part of due diligence in site valuations now requires valuers to be more explicit about the assessment of contamination. If some key information is missing, it is the duty of the valuers to inform their clients and to include caveats to this effect in their valuations.

The majority of valuers in France are insured and all the valuers who are members of professional associations have to take out insurance. However, their professional liability insurance premiums do not always cover their valuation figures.

7.3   CONTEXTUAL INFLUENCES

Compulsory valuations are governed by law. For example, the Commission de Contrôle des Assurances and the Commission des Opérations de Bourse control the choice of valuers for insurance companies and *SCPIs*, respectively. They have also standardized the format and content of valuation reports (as highlighted in section 7.1.2).

Other valuations originate from owner-occupiers such as the large industrial groups which have developed substantial and diversified property portfolios as their companies grew. Similarly, the Army, the Church and public bodies have acquired substantial property portfolios over the years. On a different scale, small businesses are often faced with property questions. The common strategy of these owner-occupiers is to actively manage their portfolio and valuers are called upon to advise on the relative merits of purchasing versus renting, relocating, building, investing or selling. These decisions are often based on valuation advice.

Other sources of valuation instructions originate from a variety of persons or entities. These include notaries, solicitors and barristers who call upon valuers in inheritance or divorce cases as well as property transactions. In divorce cases, it is not unusual to find two or three valuers together with an arbitrator instructed to resolve a dispute. Judges also rely on judicial valuers to produce expert evidence in court, in particular in cases where valuations for the assessment of inheritance tax have been conservative. The tax officer has four years to contest such valuations in which case, three judicial valuers may be called upon to arbitrate. Also, developers often request valuations when assessing the feasibility of development projects.

International valuation instructions have a tendency to be directed to chartered surveying firms. Often, clients are familiar with valuations in the UK and welcome the opportunity to obtain the same service from a subsidiary of these firms based in Paris. The reports are prepared in accordance with the same tried and tested formula and some clients prefer reports written in English.

7.3.1 Fee levels

Fee levels are negotiable. They largely depend on the number of instructions from the same client, the format of the valuation reports and the number and types of properties. The charter of property valuation of the *IFEI* summarizes the aims of the valuation report as follows:

1. it must respond to the client's instructions;
2. it must be short and to the point – supporting documents must not form part of the report but be attached in the appendices;
3. it must be clear and use a minimum of jargon;
4. it must be precise and answer what is being asked.

Valuation reports are not to be confused with audits (*audits des méthodes* or *audits de cohérence*) or feasibility studies which tend to use the valuation to advise a client on investment or development strategy. Desktop valuations (*avis de valeur* or *estimations sur dossier*) are also different from valuation reports as they are carried out without an inspection of the property. The *IFEI* in its valuation guide specifies that there can be no valuation report without a physical inspection of the property. In addition, there can be no valuation at a future date or valuations based on assumptions which do not correspond to the legal and physical characteristics of the actual properties.

Valuation reports can consist of a valuation certificate which, in France, is essentially a summary valuation report. Alternatively, valuers produce longer reports covering all the physical, legal, financial, market and planning aspects of a property. Valuers are able to issue valuation certificates without the support of a full valuation report. The certificate is a two to three page summary of the key points together with the valuation figure. It includes the main physical characteristics, income flows and valuation figures and assumptions. Such certificates are used to support straightforward valuations. They are also used for property revaluations, such as the annual revaluations required by law of the property portfolios of insurance companies and *SCPIs*. These types of certificates are called *actualisations* or *certifications d'une expertise initiale*. When the property has not materially changed, valuers do not usually reinspect it and their revaluation is based on the updated information.

Full valuation reports are very different. As a rule, they would start with confirming the terms of instruction. After stating the valuation purpose, address and type of property being valued, as well as the valuation and inspection dates, the valuer will state the valuation assumptions and list the documents which have been relied upon. In addition, some of the key definitions, such as open market value, rental value and the main terms of the 1953 Decree regulating commercial leases, will appear before detailing the characteristics of the property. In the second part of the report, the valuer describes the property providing a short summary on its location, situation, general characteristics and state of repair. When stating floor areas, the report usually includes the corresponding definitions such as *surface utile brute* (*SUB*) or *surface hors oeuvre nette* (*SHON*). Furthermore, the description recaps and comments on the tenure, leases and easements. The valuer researches the planning situation and confirms whether or not the property conforms to planning regulations. This section of the report is usually closed by a summary of the advantages and disadvantages of the property. The valuation and a justification of the methods used follow a market study on supply and demand as well as specific transactions and recent market trends. The valuer has to justify the variables used for the calculation of value. Calculations may be included in the report but this is not systematic. The report also contains appendices which may give a breakdown of the purchaser's costs, floor plans, photographs, leases, planning documents, glossary of terms and the parties' financial liabilities under the lease.

Clients usually request that fees are agreed before the valuation. As a general guideline, valuers charged 1% of the approximate value in 1993/94 plus expenses and VAT for full valuation reports. This scale was reduced to 0.7–0.9% in 1994/95. For certificates, valuers charge between 0.15 and 0.35%, plus expenses and VAT. Revaluations, which are required by law for insurance companies and *SCPIs*, command fees of about 20% (before VAT) of the original valuation. Furthermore, as the revaluations take place for four years after the original full valuation, the revaluation fees are generally indexed to the construction cost index of *INSEE*. In addition, valuers usually request 50% of the bill plus VAT before embarking on the valuation. The outstanding bill is sent to the client with the report.

7.4 PROPERTY TENURE

The ownership of property can be freehold or leasehold. A freehold can, however, be *en toute propriété* which is equivalent to the English freehold tenure, i.e. full ownership, or *en copropriété*, which is the equivalent of the US condominium, i.e. coownership. In the case of coownership, the division of ownership may be vertical or horizontal. As such, flats and office floors, for example, may be owned freehold. In addition, under this regime, a proportionate amount of the common parts of the property belong to the coowner.

The leasehold structure is generally similar to the UK. The most common form of lease is the commercial lease (*bail commercial*) which is governed by the Decree of 30 September 1953 (as amended). In addition, financial leases (*crédit-bail*) are a frequent method of purchasing property in France and are subject to the provisions of the law of 2 July 1966. Building leases (*baux à construction*) are governed by the law of 16 December 1964, which limits such leases to terms of between 18 and 99 years. Finally, long leases (*baux emphytéotiques*), which confer to tenants almost the same rights as the freeholder, are less common.

The most typical lease is the commercial lease, regulated by Decree No. 53–960 of 30 September 1953, which has been regularly amended. The decree applies to retailers (*commerçants*) who are registered in the *Registre du Commerce et des Sociétés*. It also applies, among others, to craftsmen (*artisans*) if their business is registered in the *Répertoire des Métiers* and to teaching institutions. As a generalization, the decree applies to shops, offices and their auxiliary premises as well as industrial properties.

The decree does not apply to long leases (minimum 18 years) which confer on tenants nearly all the rights of a freeholder (*baux emphythéotiques*), nor does it apply to short leases (less than two years), concessions on public land (e.g. newspaper kiosks) and leases to tenants such as dentists, doctors and lawyers. As the decree deals in great detail with the relationships between landlords and tenants, commercial leases tend to be shorter than in the UK. For example, the decree contains specific provisions on lease duration, renewals, assignments, sublettings, usage and rent reviews. In addition, the French Civil Code covers maintenance and repairs obligations separately under articles 605–606.

Key aspects of commercial leases under the 1953 Decree are as follows.

1. **Typical lease length** Leases must be for a minimum of nine years. In addition, they often contain triennial break options and nine years leases have become known as the three-six-nine leases (*baux trois-six-neuf*). Leases of more than 12 years must take the form of a notorial deed. Twelve year terms are exempt from rent limitation under the decree and are typical of retail properties, especially in shopping centres. Longer terms are possible but tenants are reluctant to accept them. Parties may contract outside the decree if the agreed lease is less than two years (*bail précaire*).

2. **Rent reviews by indexation** During the term of the lease, rents are reviewed by indexation and, usually, the construction cost index of the *Institut National de la Statistique et des Etudes Economiques* (*INSEE*) is used. However, other indices may appear in the lease. For example, the indexation of the rent on a bakery could be based on a 'wheat index' as long as it did not result in a higher rent than a market-based rent. The use of an index based on the cost of living is, however, forbidden. Most often, indexation takes place annually but the parties are free to agree on the appropriate frequency. In addition, the impact on rental values of tenant's improvements or mismanagement are never taken into account.

3. **Rent reviews to market levels** Retail properties, which are often on 12 year leases to avoid the rent limitation at reviews, are able to use a hybrid system of indexation and turnover rents. Under this system, the parties agree to a low base rent at the beginning of the lease which is indexed annually or as agreed. On top of this rent, the parties agree to a percentage of the tenant's turnover to form part of the total rent payable. When indexation results in an increase or decrease in rent exceeding 25% since the previous revision, either party may apply to the courts to have the rent reviewed to open market value. If rental values have not moved, upwards or downwards, by more than 10% since the last review (Law No. 56–245 of 12 March 1956), rent reviews are indexed (e.g. *INSEE* index). Therefore, if one of the parties can prove a 'material' change of rental levels of at least 10% the grounds for review will be based on five elements: characteristics of the subject property, usage, parties' covenants, local factors and comparable evidence. In practice, the 10% rule has been difficult to prove, especially if it goes against the tenant. Furthermore, there are two exceptions to the 10% rule. If the landlord has agreed to extend/change the user clause of the lease or if the premises are sublet at a higher rent than that paid by the tenant, rent reviews can be based on open market rental levels.

4. **Rents on renewals** Generally, the rent on the renewed nine year lease will be based on the initial rent at the beginning of the previous lease multiplied by the construction index of *INSEE*. This system is known as *plafonnement* because it sets a ceiling limit upon the new rent. However, it is sometimes possible to avoid this ceiling, known as *déplafonnement* of which applies in the following circumstances:

   (a) When premises with exclusive office use are let on renewal at an open market level.

   (b) If the original term of the lease was 12 years or more, the rent on the new lease is based on the open market rental. For this reason, many retail leases are of 12 years.

   (c) When 'material' changes occur in one of the five elements which form the basis of rent review negotiations: i.e. characteristics of the subject property, usage, parties' covenants, local factors and comparable evidence.

5. **Options to determine** Unless specified to the contrary in the lease, tenants can terminate their lease at the end of each three year period by giving six months' notice to their landlords (Law No. 85–1408 of 30 December 1985). However, in many cases, tenants agree to forgo this option in exchange for fitting out works paid for by their landlords. Landlords can also determine leases every three years for building, rebuilding, extending or restoring the property.

6. **Lease renewal** Tenants have an automatic right to renew if they have carried on their business for a minimum period of three years but they need to request renewal six months before the lease expires. Should none of the parties notify their intention to renew or terminate the lease six months before expiry, the law assumes that the lease has been tacitly renewed for an indefinite period until one of the parties terminates or renews (article 1738 of the French Civil Code).

   Compensation is payable to the tenant if the landlord refuses renewal. This can prove to be very expensive with the compensation based on the loss and damage suffered as a result of eviction. It takes into consideration the value of the business as well as the costs of removal and of acquisition if applicable. However, if the landlord wishes to demolish/redevelop, or if the tenant has breached the covenants of the lease, the landlord does not have to compensate the tenant.

7. **Repairs and decoration (articles 605–606 of the French Civil Code)** These articles define the responsibility of the landlord for all maintenance, structural and external repairs. The tenant often carries out internal repairs and decorations. If the lease does not cover the responsibilities of the parties for substantial repairs, article 606 of the code assumes that it is the landlord's responsibility. Sometimes the landlord can successfully pass on all repairing obligations to the tenant, through the service charge provisions. The service charge may also include the landlord's property tax (*impôt foncier*) and/or the landlord's insurance premiums.

8. **Assignment and sublettings** Assignment is allowed subject to the landlord's consent. In addition, clauses in leases under the 1953 Decree forbidding assignment are void (article 35–1). However, in cases where the assignee requires a change of use, the landlord may request payment of a capital sum.

The 1953 Decree forbids subletting unless specified otherwise in a lease. In a subletting situation, if a subtenant pays more than the tenant, the landlord is entitled to demand an increase in rent equal to that figure.

7.5 BASES OF VALUATION

7.5.1 Open market value

The key basis of valuation is the open market value. In France, this concept arises under various labels such as *valeur vénale, valeur de marché, valeur marchande, prix de marché, valeur de réalisation* or *valeur de reconstitution*, which all mean 'open market value'. However, the confusion does not stop there. There is also a variety of definitions which attempt to clarify the concept of 'market value'. The various decrees and laws on the valuation of fixed assets for certain companies, such as insurance companies, spell out their understanding of market value. In addition, the *IFEI* in its charter of property valuation uses a definition which differs in one important respect to the open market value definition found in the '*Red Book*' as it defines the market value as being the 'price' rather than the 'best price'. However, some of the larger valuation practices adopt the direct translation of the '*Red Book*' definition of open market value. As such, they assess the 'best price' rather than the 'price' of a property. This implies that, in theory, valuations based on the *IFEI* definition should be more conservative than those based on the '*Red Book*' definition, but, in practice, the two definitions appear to be interchangeable.

Generally, valuation reports give a definition of their understanding of open market value. Some small variations occur in the definitions and it is therefore important to link the valuation figure to the chosen definition. The *IFEI* definition reads as follows:

> Open market value is the price at which an interest in property can reasonably and amicably be sold on the market as at the valuation date, under the following assumptions:
>
> a) a willing seller,
> b) a reasonable period of time for negotiations, with regard to the type of property and the state of the market,
> c) that values are stable throughout this period of time,
> d) that the property interest is offered on the open market, without reticence and with reasonable advertising conditions,
> e) that no account is taken of any additional bid by a purchaser with a special interest.

In addition, the open market value is reported net of transfer costs (*hors droits de mutation* or *HD*) and VAT.

Another label for the same concept appears in the Decree No. 94–483 of 9 June 1994 on the *SCPIs*, which refers to *valeur de réalisation* and *valeur de reconstitution* (article 14). Decree No. 90–981 of 5 November 1990 on insurance companies also uses the notion of *valeur de réalisation*. To summarize, the *valeur de réalisation* is in fact an open market value (*valeur vénale*) assessed by an independent valuer whereas the *valeur de reconstitution* is essentially an open market value inclusive of acquisition costs.

7.5.2 Going-concern value

The going-concern value, or *valeur d'utilité*, applies to those properties designed and adapted for particular uses and which change hands in the open market at prices based directly on trading potential for a strictly limited use. Such properties include hotels, bars, cinemas, theatres, petrol stations and specialized leisure and sporting facilities. The guide to property valuation produced by *IFEI* defines going-concern value as:

> The *valeur d'utilité* is that corresponding to the amount of money (or total investment) which a prudent and knowledgeable company director would accept to pay to acquire a property which is necessary for the performance of his business activity.

The *IFEI* specifies that, for standard properties, the going-concern value is based on the open market value inclusive of taxes, acquisition costs and potential works on the property to adapt it to its use. If the type of property does not change hands very often, the going-concern value is based on a replacement cost approach.

7.6 VALUATION METHODS

Valuation methods are not set in law – they have evolved empirically, though the courts have attempted to give guidance. In the Tribunal of Moulins case of 30 January 1951, the Court stated that:

> The absolute value does not exist, nor does the intrinsic value or reasonable value of a property; the value has to be determined with reference to the market, showing market evidence of comparable properties (...) this method is perhaps empirical but it is the one which arises from facts and must consequently be used.

In practice, the main methods are the comparative, capitalization, residual and reinstatement cost methods.

7.6.1 Comparative method (*Méthode par comparaison*)

This method is used to assess the open market value of a property. The unit of comparison is the square metre and is based on the *surface utile brute (SUB)* or *surface hors oeuvre nette (SHON)* (section 7.8) when dealing with commercial properties and the living area (*surface habitable*) when dealing with residential properties. In the case of garages, the unit of comparison is the number of parking spaces. The unit of comparison for hotels is bedrooms and for clinics and hospitals it is the number of beds. In an active market, valuers can find evidence of comparable properties relatively easily but the French market is not as transparent as that in the UK. As a rule, valuers do not tend to contact their competitors to discuss their valuation, however, they may pretend to be interested in a property on behalf of a client and thereby find out more about the local market.

Generally, valuers who work in the larger valuation practices use their own agency department to identify comparable transactions. Most practices have detailed databases of market activity which speeds up the search process. As in the UK, the search for comparable evidence depends on the type of property being valued. The valuation of castles and luxurious hotels is based on a national or even international market and evidence from another part of the country becomes relevant for this type of property.

Example 7.1

Say 4000 Frs/m² and *SUB* (section 7.8) area 1000 m². Therefore:
4000 × 1000 = 4 000 000 Frs *droits inclus* (inclusive of purchaser's costs)
4 000 000/1.195 = 3 347 280 Frs rounded to 3 347 000 Frs *Hors Droits* (exclusive of purchaser's costs).

7.6.2 Capitalization method (*Méthode par le revenu*)

This method is often used together with the comparative method of valuation. However, this is the first choice for the valuation of investment properties.

(a) Determination of rent

Valuers often debate whether the gross or net rental income should be capitalized. In France, full repairing and insuring leases are rare and landlords are often responsible for major or structural repairs as well as for the property tax (*taxe foncière*). In some cases, landlords are able to pass on these liabilities to the tenant via the service charge. Jacques Boulez (1993) argues that in most leases net rental incomes vary greatly from year to year due to the landlord's liabilities under the 1953 Decree on commercial leases. The fluctuations in the landlord's costs imply fluctuating net rental incomes which, in turn, lead to wild swings in capital values from year to year.

However, valuers do not always take the gross rent as stated in the lease at face value. Indeed, certain charges paid for by the tenants (for example, maintenance charges) are sometimes viewed as an 'additional' rent. If this is the case, some valuers will recalculate the 'actual' rent before capitalizing it. There is no standard practice and it is for valuers to use and justify their approach with each valuation. In cases when no adjustments are required, valuers capitalize the gross rent, exclusive of taxes and service charge (*loyer hors taxes/hors charges*).

(b) Determination of yield

The choice of yield is influenced by the property market as well as the financial markets. Valuers will relate their choice of yield to rates of return on traditionally safe investments such as bonds. If available, valuers analyse transactions on comparable properties which help them select the appropriate level of yield. Such yields are influenced by the location, type and characteristics of the property as well as its rental prospects and lease covenants. In most valuations, all the risks inherent in the property are reflected in the yield rather than quantified separately.

During this process, it is particularly important to assess whether the yields analysed are inclusive or exclusive of transfer taxes. Indeed, as such taxes may amount to 19.5% in many cases, the impact on yields is considerable. For instance, assuming that a valuer comes across a straightforward comparable property based on a rack-rented income of £10 000 and a capital value of £100 000 the net initial yield to the purchaser is 10%. However, if the capital value did not reflect transfer taxes at, say, 19.5%, the actual purchase cost becomes £119 500 which reflects a net initial yield of 8.37%.

The key is to correctly label yields. The exact terminology is sometimes cumbersome but, in practice, valuers tend to use net yields (*taux de rendement*). As market evidence is based on net yields, the main valuation practices prefer to use such yields (*taux de rendement net effectif*) to capitalize rents.

Table 7.2 Table of yields

Gross initial yield (GIY) on gross passing rent (*Taux de rendement brut effectif* or *taux de capitalisation effectif*)

> GIY = gross rent passing/CV
> If gross rent passing = £8000 and CV = £100 000; GIY = 8%

Net initial yield (NIY) on gross passing rent (*Taux de rendement net effectif*)

> NIY = gross rent passing/(CV + purchaser's costs)
> If gross rent passing = £8000; CV = £100 000 and purchaser's costs = 19.5%;
> NIY = 6.69%

Net initial yield on net passing rent (*Taux de rendement net sur le revenu net*)

> NIY = net rent passing/(CV + purchaser's costs)
> If net rent passing = £7200; CV = £100 000 and purchaser's costs = 19.5%; NIY
> = 6.03%

Net initial yield on ERV (*Taux de rendement net théorique* or *taux de placement*)

> NIY = ERV/(CV + purchaser's costs)
> If ERV = £10 000; CV = £100 000 and purchaser's costs = 19.5%; NIY = 8.36%

ERV, estimated rental value; CV, capital value.

Example 7.2
Assumptions

Valuation date is May 1995
SUB area (section 7.8) is 2000 m²
Lease three–six–nine from 5/94 in accordance with the Decree of 30 September 1953. Major repairs are the landlord's responsibility.
Rent = 320 000 Frs/pa
ERV = 400 000 Frs/pa
Capitalization yield (*taux de rendement net effectif*) say 7% (cf. Table 7.2).
Purchaser's costs, say 19.5%

$$NIY = \frac{NOI}{CV + PC}$$

$$NIY \times CV + NIY \times PC = NOI$$

$$CV = \frac{NOI - NIY \times PC}{NIY}$$

$$= \frac{7200 - 1176}{6.03\%}$$

$$= 100,000$$

$$PC = 19,500$$

$$CV = \frac{7200}{6.03\%} = \frac{119.402}{1 + PC}$$

$$= 100.000$$

Valuation

(a) Valuation of gross rent in perpetuity:

Gross rent	320 000	
YP perp at 7%	÷ 0.07	
Less purchaser's costs	÷ 1.195	
		3 825 000 Frs HD

(b) Valuation of uplite in perpetuity:

Uplift	−80 000	
YP perp at, say, 8% (higher risk)	÷ 0.08	
Less purchaser's costs	÷ 1.195	
		837 000 Frs HD

(c) Less uplite deferred 8 years:

Uplift	−80 000	
YP 8 years at borrowing rate of, say, 9%	× 5.5348	
Less purchaser's costs	÷ 1.195	
		370 000 Frs HD
	Total CV	4 300 000 Frs HD

(d) Recap:

Capital value		3 825 000 Frs HD
	Add	837 000 Frs HD
	Less	370 000 Frs HD
	CV	4 292 000 Frs HD
	CV say	4 300 000 Frs HD

7.6.3 Residual method (*Méthode dite du bilan-promoteur* or *méthode de récupération foncière* or *méthode de compte à rebours opérateur*)

This method follows the same rules as in the UK. The site value is derived by deducting from the market value of the completed property the various development costs. These include costs of construction, costs of finance, fees and profit margins.

7.6.4 Profits method (*Méthode dite professionnelle*)

This method also follows the same rules as in the UK and is usually applied to hotels, cinemas, hospitals and clinics. Valuers also use it for leisure properties and certain commercial centres. Generally, valuers assess the notional rental levels from sustainable turnover. For instance, notional rents on restaurants would be of the order of 5–10% of turnover; hotels at around 20–30% of turnover and food retailers in the region of 1.5–5% of turnover.

7.6.5 Reinstatement cost (*Méthode par le coût de remplacement*)

The guide of property valuation reviews three methods to assess the replacement cost of a property.

1. **Replacement cost of an identical building** This is the market value of the site (*valeur vénale*) plus cost of reconstruction of identical buildings together with existing installations, ancillary costs and non-recoverable VAT. This method is rarely used when calculating the *valeur d'utilité*. However, it is the most used method when dealing with fire insurance valuations.
2. **Replacement cost of an equivalent building** This is the market value of the site (*valeur vénale*) plus costs of reconstruction of equivalent properties built at the valuation date. As such, the valuer has to take account of current regulations on floor areas, construction materials and installations.
3. **Market value** (*valeur vénale*) of a property plus purchaser' costs and necessary works to adapt the property to the business. This method is used to value those properties which may be adapted to be comparable to existing properties.

Although the depreciated replacement cost (DRC) method is not mentioned in the guide on property valuation it is used in practice. It follows the same rules as in the UK by using the reinstatement method as a starting point and making allowances for depreciation and obsolescence.

7.6.6 Indexation method (*Méthode indiciaire*)

This method consists of updating a previous valuation by indexing it. The guide specifies that this method is rarely used as there is no general index which can quantify growth for specific properties. The indices used may be based on inflation (*INSEE*) or construction costs (*ICC*).

7.6.7 Discounted cash flows (DCF)

Valuers do not tend to use this method very often, reflecting the fact that, on the whole, valuation assumptions are implicit rather than explicit in France. However, chartered surveyors working in France would use the DCF approach more frequently. The method applies to properties in need of periodic refurbishment such as hotels and cinemas. In addition, as in the UK, valuers use this method to calculate the 'worth' of a property to a particular investor and the historical performance of a property fund.

7.7 TRANSACTION COSTS

Whichever method is selected, valuers have to be clear about whether the reported value is inclusive or exclusive of transfer costs, which are among the highest in the European Union. Transaction costs depend on the date of sale after the property is completed and, under certain circumstances, on whether the previous buyer was a *marchand de biens* (property trader).

If the property is sold for the first time within the five-year period following its development, and provided the property had not previously been sold after its completion to a property trading company (*marchand de biens*) the purchaser is liable to pay VAT at a current rate of 18.6%. If the property is sold prior to its completion (*en état d'achèvement*), it also attracts VAT payable upon the higher of the purchase price or the open market value. Under this regime, however, the purchaser may be able to reclaim VAT as long as it is charged on rents and the purchaser operates within the VAT regime. In addition, the purchaser incurs other costs under the VAT regime (Table 7.3).

Table 7.3 Purchase costs

VAT at	18.60%
Tax of property advertising (*taxe de publicité foncière*) at	0.60%
Legal fees 0.825% + VAT	1.16%
Mortgage bureau fees 0.10% + VAT	1.14%
Total purchaser's costs under VAT regime	**20.50%** and VAT amounts to 18.804%

However, if the property is sold after the five year period following its completion, or for at least the second time within the five year period, the purchaser is liable to pay transfer duties (*droits de mutation*). Unlike VAT, these costs cannot be recovered by the purchaser. As under the VAT regime, the duty is levied on the higher of the purchase price or the open market value of the asset. Purchaser's costs, such as agency fees, are included within this figure. In addition, the purchaser attracts other costs under the transfer regime (Table 7.4).

Table 7.4 Stamp duty costs

Property	Commercial	Residential
Droit d'enregistrement: Departmental tax *Droit départmental* (e.g. Ile-de-France)	For most departments at 15.4%. Exceptions: Corse du Sud at 8.5%, Haute Corse at 9.5%, Guyana at 10% and Lozère at 13%.	4.2%
State tax at 2.5% of departmental tax	0.385%	0.105%
Local tax *Taxe communale* (e.g. Région Ile-de-France)	1.2%	1.2%
Regional tax	1.6%	1.6%
Legal fees for sales above 110 000 French Francs	0.825% + VAT	0.825% + VAT
Mortgage fee *Salaire du converseur des hypothèques*	0.1% + VAT	0.1 + VAT
Total	**19.51% + 0.172% (VAT)**	**8.03% + 0.172% (VAT)**

7.8 DATABASE MANAGEMENT

7.8.1 Property inspections

The list of documents required prior to inspection usually includes title deeds (*titres de propriété*) which consist of a certificate of conformity to prove that the building conforms to the original plans submitted for planning permission. The valuer also requires a copy of the land registry (*service foncier du cadastre*) which is the 'identity card' of the site. It specifies the name of the owner and the exact site area. The information is regularly updated. In addition, the valuer studies the leases (*baux*), floor plans and planning information.

Site inspection consists of photographing the property, taking notes of the general condition, state of repair and services. In addition, the valuer checks that there is consistency between the floor plans and the property. In the majority of cases, clients communicate floor areas to the valuers who rely on this information for valuing. As valuers do not tend to measure floor areas, their valuation reports include a clause stating that the floor areas are subject to confirmation by a *géomètre-expert*.

In order to value, however, valuers need to be familiar with the different assessments of floor areas which are defined. The site areas (*surface cadastrale*) are contained in the land registry. The measurement of sites by land surveyors (*géomètres*) forms the basis of land taxation and valuers rely on them for their valuation report. Such measurements are rarely disputed.

The definitions of floor areas are outlined in the Code of Planning (*Code de l'Urbanisme*). In addition, Circular No. 90/80 of 12 November 1990 from the *Ministère de l'Equipement* clarifies which elements form part of the floor area definitions. The most commonly used floor areas for the valuation are the *surface hors oeuvre nette (SHON)*, and the *surface utile brute (SUB)* for commercial properties and the *surface habitable* for residential properties.

The *SHON* roughly corresponds to the gross internal areas and forms the basis of measurement for the valuation of industrial properties. This is also the basis of measurement when assessing the authorized planning density. The *SHON* is the *surface hors oeuvre brute (SHOB)* less the floor areas which cannot be used for residential or commercial purposes. There are four types of floor areas to be excluded:

1. floor to ceiling height below 1.80 m (5.9 ft);
2. plant and machinery basement areas;
3. areas which cannot be easily used are excluded; for example, floor areas with insufficient floor loading capacity for the proposed use;
4. balconies, roof terraces and uncovered extensions at ground floor level, such as car-parking.

The *SHOB* includes all floor areas together with internal and external walls as well as external projections such as balconies. The *SHOB* excludes ground floor terraces which are not covered and vertical voids such as lifts, access ramps and staircases. However, the *SHOB* includes the base of the staircase, lift or access ramp.

The *SUB* roughly corresponds to the net internal areas and forms the basis of measurement for the valuation of offices and shops. The *SUB* is the *SHON* less structural walls and those vertical circulations which were not already deducted.

In summary, the *SUB* includes horizontal circulations, toilets, changing rooms and staff rooms, as well as floor areas used for work purposes such as offices, workshops and laboratories.

In the case of retail properties, valuers often use the concept of *surface pondérée*, which is a form of zoning. However, there are no rigid rules to decide the depth of the zones or the percentages to apply to such zones. Valuers reassess these factors with each property and refer to the local practice of the letting market.

The *surface habitable* is used as the basis of valuation for residential properties. It is defined in article R111–2 of the Code of Construction and Housing as the floor areas less walls, partitions, stairs and staircases as well as window and door splays.

7.8.2 Practical application of techniques

The thrust of the valuers' market analysis centres on the search for direct comparable evidence. However, outside the major centres, market activity is limited and valuers rely more on market reports and trends. The larger valuation practices often have a department specializing in strategic advice (*conseil*) and valuers are able to draw from this research. These departments carry out in-depth market research to advise their clients on portfolio strategy, buying/selling options or market trends.

Comparison for rental levels is based on a price per square metre per annum, usually exclusive of VAT and service charge. This translates into FF/m²/an/*Hors taxes/Hors charges* or FF/m²/*HT/HC*. As full repairing and insuring leases are rare, valuers are careful to compare leases on the same basis. Generally, the basis of comparison is standard leases under the 1953 Decree, whereby the landlord is responsible for maintenance, structural and major repairs. However, if these costs or any other of the landlord's expenses are recovered under the service charge, the analysis must take it into account in order to compare like with like.

In addition, over recent years, tenant's incentives have become common in terms of rent free periods or capital contributions from the landlord. This also needs to be reflected in the analysis which, in practice, does not take account of the time value of the incentive. Such incentive is usually discounted on a straight line basis until the determination date of the lease. Other considerations include the basis of future rent reviews, whether indexed or reviewed to open market levels. In some instances, to counterbalance poor rental growth prospects, landlords are able to obtain rents which are above market levels. In addition, in the case of retail properties, 'key money' (*pas-de-porte*) is often paid and valuers sometimes assess this as an advance payment on the rent.

Investment transactions are often broken down to a price per square metre exclusive of purchaser's costs (FF/m²/*Hors droits* or FF/m²/*HD*); if such costs are included, the term used is *droits inclus*. The valuer needs to know whether such costs are included. If the VAT regime applies, transfer costs are substantially reduced for purchasers who are able to reclaim VAT. But under the transfer costs regime, such costs can amount to almost 20% of the purchase price. This obviously impacts substantially on the reliability of the evidence which the valuer collects.

Another factor to consider is the loan/value ratio. Since loans are usually a maximum of 80% of the value of a property, prices are occasionally artificially inflated to enable the purchaser to borrow a greater percentage. Conversely, when no loan is required the reported sale price may be below the market level. However, these unorthodox practices are becoming less and less common.

Valuers also rely, to a large extent, on their in-house market information. The large valuation practices hold vast amounts of market evidence from their agency arms. In addition, companies produce regular market reports and statistics. *Crédit Foncier* publishes annual reports covering all markets and property advisory firms, such as Auguste-Thouard, Bourdais and Jones Lang Wootton, publish statistical information particularly in the commercial sector. The Chamber of Solicitors (*Chambre des Notaires*) publishes statistics twice a year on the Parisian residential market. In addition, all sale prices on commercial and residential properties, as well as sites, agricultural land and forests, are held by the Mortgage Bureau (*Conservation des Hypothèques*).

Other sources of information are private or confidential. For example, solicitors hold a databank of transactions which is particularly strong in the residential sector in the Paris region. Lending institutions, such as Crédit Foncier, also compile a comprehensive databank of site values at the national level. Otherwise, in the absence of specific comparable evidence, valuers rely on market reports and market trends published by the larger French property practices and chartered surveying firms, as well as making contact with local Chambers of Commerce.

7.9 CONCLUSION

Property valuation in France has developed at a fast pace, particularly in the 1980s as the property profession started to take steps to recognize and regulate the status of the valuer. In relation to the valuation of insurance company portfolios from 1990 and for *SCPI* from 1993, the Minister of Finance (*Direction du Trésor*) and the accountancy profession have been actively involved in promoting procedures and valuation standards. The *IFEI* has been instrumental in producing the Charter of Property Valuation and Code of Conduct whereas the government is now taking steps to enshrine the role and responsibility of the valuer in law. However, this new found authority of the valuation profession goes hand in hand with additional responsibility and inevitably it is expected that valuation practice will have to become more sophisticated to meet the challenges of the 1990s.

FURTHER READING

Fergos, J. (1990) *L'expropriation et l'évaluation des biens*, Moniteur, Paris.
Achour, D. (1992) *Evaluation immobilière* Agence d'Arc, Quebec.
Boulez, J. (1993) *L'expertise immobilière*, Masson, Paris.
Etude (1992) *L'Expertise Immobilière en France en 1992*, Alain Dumat.
FNAIM (undated) *L'Expertise vue par les experts*, FNAIM, Paris.

IFEI (1993) *Charte de l'Expertise en Evaluation Immobilière.*

IFEI (1993) *Guide Méthodologique relatif à l'Evaluation des Actifs Immobiliers.*

Lefebvre, F. (1991) *Memento Pratique Urbanisme, Construction, Gestion,* Francis Lefebvre, Levallios.

Paulhac, F. (1990) *L'évaluation des Actifs Immobiliers*, Eyrolles, Paris.

Germany 8

Mary Lou Downie,
Karl-Werner Schulte and
Matthias Thomas

On 3 October 1990 the German Democratic Republic (GDR) acceded to the Federal Republic of Germany (FRG), creating a federation of Länder or states with an area of 357 000 km² and a population of 80.6 million (1992 estimate). The economy of the FRG ranks third in the world, with exports typically accounting for a high level of 31% of GDP. Manufacturing dominates the economy, based on traditional engineering skills, and the structural shift to the private service sector has been smaller than for other OECD countries (OECD, 1994). Unification accompanied a period of economic growth and optimism, followed by realization of the massive costs of rejuvenating the Neue Bundesländer's (ex GDR) infrastructure and economy. Inflationary pressure followed, interest rates rose in 1992, and recession resulted as the Deutsche Mark's strength reduced export competitiveness. The economy is now growing again, although future growth for the FRG is forecast to be lower than in previous recoveries. This will probably be partly compensated for by high growth rates in the Neue Bundesländer (OECD, 1994).

The unification of Germany created opportunities for new property markets in the Neue Bundesländer in terms of speculation, development and trade. The creation of a market in land rights, where previously there was none, has been complicated by uncertainty over landownership and intense speculation in locations such as central Berlin. Because market evidence based methods of valuation do not function in the absence of prior market activity, the German Government, through the agency of the Treuhandanstalt, instituted a system of property valuation based on economic fundamentals in the local area and on a comparison with locations in West Germany.

This state of affairs is transitional and already shows signs of being replaced by the normal functioning of the market and the accompanying methods of valuation (Dieterich and Joeris, 1995). For this reason, and lack of space, this chapter deals with the traditional methods of valuation associated with the FRG and its legislation.

European Valuation Practice. Edited by Alastair Adair, Mary Lou Downie, Stanley McGreal and Gerjan Vos. Published in 1996 by E & FN Spon, London. ISBN 0 419 20040 1

8.1 VALUATION FOR INVESTMENT

The turnover of the German freehold property market in 1991 is estimated to be DM205 billion (N.N., 1992) excluding the turnover in the Neue Bundesländer. Due to changes in taxation law, this sum can be estimated for the first time from the amount of Grunderwerbsteuer (property transfer tax) paid. There were roughly 86 000 property sales (excluding the GDR) of qualified building land and prospective building land zoned within local plans. This figure excludes agricultural land transactions, agricultural land surrounding settlement areas which could eventually be used for other purposes and land for which intended uses are known and a preparatory land-use plan exists. The average price for all these types was DM90.71/m², which equals a turnover of DM94 billion for these specific land types. The average price for building land was DM125.41/m² and the average price for prospective building land was DM54.36/m² (Statistisches Bundesamt, 1993).

The Münchner Institut estimates institutional investment for 1993 as follows (Bulwien, 1994):

	DM
closed-end real estate funds	9.5 billion
open-end real estate funds	7.25
insurance companies and pension funds	6.5
real estate investments in the form of part ownerships	5
foreign investors	1.25

Certainly, many investors seek the advice of agents, brokers or surveyors before purchasing or selling land. (The terms 'surveyor' and 'valuer' are used synonymously and represent persons in Germany effecting property valuations. This does not suggest any relationship with a professional body.)

8.2 LOAN SECURITY VALUATION

The *Hypothekenbankgesetz HBG* 1990 (Morgage Bank Act) (BGBL, 1990) governs lending by a Hypothekenbank on the security of property. Under section 13 HBG each Hypothekenbank must publish its own instructions for carrying out valuations which have to be approved by the Bundesaufsichamt für das Kreditwesen (BAK), the Banking Supervisory Authority. The amount of loans in Germany secured by mortgages in 1992 was DM975.3 billion. Creditors are banks with DM778.5 billion, building societies with DM99.1 billion and insurance companies with DM97.7 billion (Statistisches Bundesamt). The Deutsche Bundesbank (German Federal Reserve Bank) differentiates the German banks as shown in Figure 8.1.

There are *Universalbanken* (universal banks) and *Spezialbanken* (specialised banks). The universal banks are active in all kinds of banking business and can furthermore be divided into:

1. *Kreditbanken* (commercial banks, e.g. Deutsche Bank AG; Dresdner Bank AG, Bayerische Vereinsbank AG; Commerzbank AG);

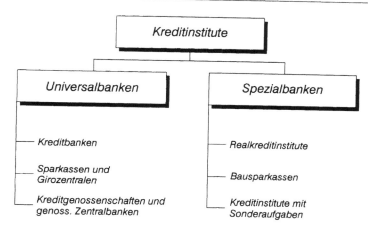

Figure 8.1 The structure of the German banking system.

2. *Sparkassen und Girozentralen* (saving associations and state banks, e.g. Westdeutsche Landesbank Girozentrale; Bayerische Landesbank Girozentrale; Norddeutsche Landesbank Girozentrale; Landesbank Hessen-Thüringen Girozentrale); and
3. *Kreditgenossenschaften und genossenschaftliche Zentralbanken* (cooperative banks, e.g. DG Bank Deutsche Genossenschaftsbank; Westdeutsche Genossenschafts-Zentralbank eG; Südwestdeutsche Genossenschafts-Zentralbank AG).

These banks usually do not themselves engage in long-term property financing, as they generally own a mortgage bank as a subsidiary, but are willing to engage in short-term bridge financing. The specialized banks can be divided into:

1. *Realkreditinstitut* (mortgage banks, e.g. DePfa-Bank Deutsche Pfandbrief-und Hypothekenbank AG; Deutsche Hypothekenbank Frankfurt AG; RHEINHYP Rheinische Hypothekenbank AG);
2. *Bausparkassen* (building societies, e.g. Bausparkasse Wüstenrot, Deutsche Bank Bauspar AG); and
3. *Kreditinstitut mit Sonderaufgaben* (banks which fulfill special duties, e.g. Kreditanstalt für Wiederaufbau; Deutsche Ausgleichsbank).

Within this group of specialized banks only the mortgage banks and building societies are of importance for real estate finance. The mortgage banks, governed by the HBG, are licensed to provide mortgage loans and issue *Pfandbriefe* (mortgage bonds) as a way of refinancing as well as granting loans either to, or guaranteed by, domestic public law institutions and to issue *Kommunalschuldverschreibungen* (communal bonds) for refinancing purposes.

The building societies are governed by the *Gesetz über Bausparkassen* (Building Society Act) and grant loans under a savings plan scheme. Before being granted a loan the debtor has to pay their saving instalments which normally yield a low rate of return until a certain predetermined amount has been accumulated and a given minimum period has elapsed. The debtor then receives their savings and may take up a loan with a low interest rate, usually significantly below market rates. Building society loans usually occupy a place behind the mortgage banks in section III of the *Grundbuch* (land register), which lists mortgages and land charges. Insurance companies engage in the financing of property in some instances, if the loan is combined with life-insurance contracts (von Schenck, 1991, p. 74).

8.3   THE OPEN-END INVESTMENT FUNDS

A major group of institutional investors in the German real estate market is the open-end real estate funds. In 1992 there were 12 such funds in Germany with assets of DM22.7 billion invested in 505 different properties. Prices for participation rights are quoted daily and can be bought from about DM80 onwards from the investment company. The investment company is obliged to buy back participation rights at the intrinsic value (von Schenck, 1991). Figures by the Münchner Institut suggest that these funds invested DM7.25 billion in 1993 (Bulwien, 1994). Open-end funds are exempt from corporate taxes, thus avoiding double taxation. Each fund has to value its assets annually and publish the values. The valuation process is controlled by the *Gesetz über Kapitalanlagegesellschaften* (KAGG) 1977 (Law Concerning Capital Investment Companies) and supervised by the BAK in order to secure the interests of the investors against fraudulent valuations. The details of the legislation are given in section 8.12.

8.4   CLOSED-END FUNDS

The open- and closed-end real estate funds serve different needs and objectives of investors. Closed funds usually invest in only one, occasionally in up to five properties, whereas open funds must have a diversified portfolio of at least 10 different properties. The construction of a closed fund is usually in the form of a limited partnership; holdings in such a partnership are available from DM20 000 onwards. After the placement of the participation notes, no additional notes will be issued. Due to their legal construction there is no liquid secondary market for participation rights in closed-end real estate funds. Due to the interest payable on loan capital, these closed-end funds are only profitable if financed by a considerable percentage of equity capital, which has a lower yield (von Schenck, 1991).

8.5   VALUERS

Generally, German valuers are not a homogeneous profession but fall into categories according to the client groups they serve and the valuation function they fulfil. In order to analyse the relationship between valuers and financiers it is essential to distinguish between self-employed valuers and those employed by a larger valuation organization. Most valuers are self-employed and carry out valuations only in the region of their office. Until recently larger valuation companies in Germany have up to now usually been subsidiaries of British organizations. Local valuers will often also practice as architects or engineers. The Chamber of Commerce for each locality nominates a limited number of valuers for appointment by the courts as expert witnesses. These appointments are sought after among the self-employed valuers.

Banks are highly influential in all areas of commercial activity in Germany (Smith, 1994), property valuation being no exception. Mortgage banks normally have their own valuation departments, since their guidelines for the estimation of collateral value have to be approved by the BAK. Some have now begun to outsource their valuation departments and operate them as separate legal entities, in order to carry out valuations for third parties. Mortgage banks do use external valuers, adhering to the bank's specific guidelines, as their in-house departments sometimes lack knowledge regarding individual property markets.

Valuation by external valuers has been criticized in the case of the collapse of Dr Jürgen Schneider's development companies. In this case the 'Zeil-Galerie', the first vertically designed shopping mall in Europe, was valued on the basis of construction plans at the same date (January 1989) by two different external valuers, one at DM225 million and the other at DM311 million. In September 1991 the value was estimated at DM726 million by the same valuer who had arrived at the higher of the two previous figures. Under the leadership of a major German bank, Schneider received a loan of DM415 million (Licher, 1994) based on the external valuer's figure. It is self-evident that if the investor or developer him/herself acts as principal to the valuer, he/she may try, out of self-interest, to influence the outcome of the valuation when it forms a basis for negotiations with financiers.

An increasing number of offices of the larger international property consultants, many with UK chartered surveyor origins and orientation, have been opened in Germany during the last 20 years. Some of these provide predominantly agency services, but others also provide valuations carried out in the UK/international tradition, rather than the German. Clients are largely international in their property activity.

8.6 AGENCY AND BROKERAGE

Many local valuers operate in practices providing a spectrum of architectural, engineering and valuation services. These and the widespread self-employed valuers do not practice as agents. Property transactions do not traditionally involve an agent acting for the vendor or purchaser and seeking to achieve the best possible price for the client. Instead, a *Makler* or broker (Dieterich *et al.*, 1993) introduces the parties, taking a fee from one or both, without liability to either. This activity is perceived as non-professional and unsuitable for valuers. However, the divorce of agency and valuation functions leaves valuers, in many cases, without experience of current market prices and the forces shaping them. In some circumstances, for instance where a valuer works in-house for a bank which is party to many commercial transactions, a supply of current data will be available. Valuers without alternative sources must rely on the Gutachterausschuß, newspaper reports and the market reports of the larger property brokers.

8.7 EDUCATION

Valuers' education is normally at undergraduate level as part of an engineering, town and country planning, land surveying or architectural training. Until recently it has centred on the statutory system of valuation. The Royal Institution of Chartered Surveyors (RICS) in 1992 awarded exemption from its examinations to successful students on the postgraduate course at the Immobilienakademie at the European Business School at Oestrich-Winkel and Berlin. They are post-graduates from the business, banking and investment community who study part-time. The course provides education in both the traditional German methods of valuation and the UK/international approach. Bank valuers receive in-house training in their speciality.

8.8 PROFESSIONAL BODIES

Valuers have the following professional associations which are affiliated to the international organizations shown:

1. *(BVS) Bundesverband der Öffentlich Bestellten und Vereidigten Sachverständigen* (EUROVAL, TEGOVOFA);
2. *(BVDI) Bund der Öffentlich Bestellten Vermessungs – Ingenieure* (EUROVAL, TEGOVOFA);
3. *(DVW) Deutscher Verein für Vermessungswesen* (EUROVAL, TEGOVOFA);
4. *(RDM) Ring Deutsche Makler Bundesverband* (CEPI, CEAB, EPAG, EUROVAL);
5. *(BDGS) Bundesverband Deutscher Grundstückssachverständiger*
6. *(DVCS) Deutsche Verband Chartered Surveyors* (EUROVAL, TEGOVOFA) (the *DVCS* is a relative newcomer to this list and differs from the others in its function as a qualification awarding body).

Currently, the influence of professional bodies on legislation and changes of the *WertV* is insignificant. Problems arising when valuing property in the ex GDR soon after reunification have been dealt with within the *Treuhand-Anstalt*. As these problems decrease there are no legal changes to be expected in the near future.

8.9 VALUER'S LIABILITY

8.9.1 Private claims for compensation

Private claims for compensation arise where a client makes a loss as a result of inadequacies in the valuer's report, for instance selling at below market value. Liability may arise under the *Bürgerliche Gesetzbuch* (*BGB*) or Citizens' Law, due to the contractual nature of the valuer–client relationship and is actionable for 30 years. Alternatively, the claim may be based on the law of criminal neglect, being actionable for three years from the time the principal knew of the damage and the person liable for compensation.

German law recognizes that valuations are often the basis of a transaction involving a third party, for instance, a lender to the client on the security of the property valued. The BGB section 328, therefore gives the third party the same protection as the client and they can also claim under the criminal law. Claims for damages can only be made if the valuer has acted culpably (section 276 BGB). The claimant must prove intention or negligence. Negligence occurs when the valuer has not exercised due care in producing a report. Agreements to limit liability fall into two categories: private agreements and agreements for general use in all contracts, following a prescribed formula. The latter are subject to the General Business Conditions Law, which renders the condition ineffective if it unduly disadvantages the contractual partner of the user. Therefore, a clause which might be acceptable in a one-off agreement may be ineffective if automatically used in all of the valuer's contracts.

8.9.2 Claims against a court-sworn valuer

The position is different if the valuer is an expert appointed by a court – they then have court law obligations, under section 402 *Zivilprozeßordnung* (*ZPO*). The valuer is sworn in to the effect that he/she has reported objectively and in good faith and is subject to *öffentlich rechtlich* (public law). They are not a member of the court but an adviser to it; the judge must decide what weight to attach to their evidence. Litigants disadvantaged by an incorrect valuation have no contractual relationship with the valuer and can only bring criminal actions, for instance, for perjury, subject to a three year limitation period.

Federal law and individual Land regulations lay down similar specifications for basic minimum standards expected of persons providing expert advice (*Sachverständige*). They should be unbiased, objective, personally thorough and conscientious, have ability in the relevant subject to a basic level of expertise, with regular personal retraining and practice as an expert. Case law has also evolved some principles (Zimmermann, 1993).

1. Thorough preparation of the report, including selection of appropriate data sources whose contribution must be clearly stated. Nevertheless, the valuer retains overall responsibility.
2. Assembling all necessary data, including land registration, location, constitution, legal restrictions and impositions, materially insured third party rights, building charges, actual use, use allowed under the planning and building control system, existing development, legal tax requirements, etc.
3. Local property market information, data from the *Gutachterausschuß* on comparative prices, average site values, property investment capitalization rates, rental details and any others relevant. Only if the court or client presents the valuer with a clear dossier of facts can he/she rely on that instead of investigating all details him/herself. If he/she notices obvious inaccuracies they must point them out and take instructions on which facts to use.
4. Following the correct procedure and method of valuation and explaining why it is relied on.
5. Giving reasons for all opinions to enable the client to understand and verify them – particularly the choice of valuation method, e.g. *Sachwert, Vergleichswert, Ertragswert.*

8.10 VALUER'S FEE LEVELS

The fees for engineers and architects effecting a valuation are dealt with in section 34 of the *Honorarordnung für Architekten und Ingenieure (HOAI)* (BGBL, 1991) or Fee Regulations for Architects and Engineers. The fees depend on the value of the real estate involved. If the value is below DM50 000 the valuation fee can be determined through hourly rates between DM77 and DM155 but may not exceed DM810 in total. If an architect or engineer negotiates a higher valuation fee this is a violation of the maximum fee concept of the *HOAI* (Volze, 1990). Fees for values over DM50 million can be negotiated freely. The regulations of the *HOAI* are valid for architects and engineers only, valuing on behalf of non-government clients.

For valuations on behalf of private persons carried out by valuers other than architects or engineers the fee can be negotiated freely. An hourly rate of up to DM300 is common. If a surveyor carries out a valuation for judicial purposes they are remunerated within the fees set by the *Zeugen- und Entschädigungsgesetz* (Witness and Compensation Law).

8.11 PROPERTY TENURE IN GERMANY

8.11.1 Prevailing forms of tenure

Although information is available from the *Statistische Bundesamt* (National Statistical Office) concerning residential owner-occupation rates in both West Germany and the former German Democratic Republic, no such information is available for commercial or industrial property. Dieterich *et al.* (1993) suggest that levels of owner-occupation are high, particularly in the industrial sector, but have decreased over the last 20 years.

8.11.2 Letting formats

Commercial tenancies usually run for periods of five, 10 or, less often, 20 years and are in written form. The initial negotiation may lead to inclusion of a tenant's option to extend or automatic extension in the absence of any purposeful action to terminate the lease by either party. There is no statutory security of tenure for business occupiers (Volhard *et al.*, 1991).

8.11.3 Rent adjustment mechanisms

Leases containing standard clauses are subject to the *Allgemeine Geschäftsbedingungen* (Act on General Terms and Conditions of Trade) which nullifies any standard clause imposing an unfair disadvantage on either party to the contract. The effect is that rent adjustment clauses must allow for upwards and downwards rent adjustment to avoid unfairly disadvantaging the tenant. The predominant method of adjustment is by indexation to the *Lebenshaltungskostenindex* (the cost of living index). An adjustment would automatically follow a specified change in the index in either direction, e.g. a 10 point rise or fall since the rent was set or last adjusted. Automatic rent adjustment clauses can be rendered void if approval for them is witheld by the *Landeszentralbank* of the relevant state.

Approval can be expected when the lease contract is for at least 10 years and the clause operates to adjust rent upwards and downwards. Adjustment of rent to the market level has become more common but is not the norm.

8.11.4 Income growth pattern

A major feature of the German economy in recent years has been successful implementation of the *Bundesbank*'s statutory duty to maintain the value of the Deutsche Mark, so suppressing inflation. In contrast, the effect of supply and demand imbalances in specific submarkets, such as the Frankfurt office market, has at times accelerated rental growth well beyond the low inflation level. As a result, indexed rents may lag well behind current market rental value during the course of a typical 10 year lease, giving rise to significant reversionary potential. However, this is vulnerable to subsequent falls in the letting market, as experienced in Frankfurt offices in recent years and illustrated in Figure 8.8.

A criticism sometimes levelled at the German valuation system is that values are based solely on current rental income, ignoring reversionary value (Barnett, 1994). The classic response is that the reversionary income is too uncertain to rely on, due to the illegality of ratchet clauses. There is no doubt, however, that in competitive situations, such as valuation for acquisition by an open fund, the reversionary potential is sometimes allowed for, and may even be included, in valuations for annual reports where the reversion is close and the market shows no signs of oversupply.

The valuation literature reveals differences of opinion on this issue. The *WertR* 91 Tz. 3.5.1 requires the *Ertragswert* (investment value: see section 8.13) to be based on current rental value. Some valuers suggest that if the rent received differs from the rental value and is based on a contractual agreement which cannot be cancelled in the near future, this should be considered as one of the 'other factors influencing value'. Other sources do not follow this view but require valuation on current rental value.

8.11.5 Income risk and gross to net income adjustment

Under German law, leases are contracts rather than interests in land and as such cannot be assigned to a third party. Subletting may be permitted at the lessee's discretion.

Generally, lessors in Germany expect to take an active role in the management and physical upkeep of their property. It is not normal for the tenant to undertake liability for structural repairs although they will customarily undertake to decorate the premises during their occupation. Common areas and facilities, such as entrances and lifts, will normally be maintained by the lessor and the expenses may be charged to the occupiers. Operating costs will normally be paid by the lessee although not necessarily the lessor's insurance premiums, land tax (*Grundsteuer*) and management costs.

8.12 GERMAN LEGISLATION

Property valuation in Germany has a long history of state involvement. The current legislation was introduced in the post-war period when the concept of a social market economy was implemented as the basis for economic reconstruction of the Federal Republic of Germany. Since the concept relied on market price as the mechanism for achieving efficient resource allocation, land prices needed to be transparent and free to find their market level.

8.12.1 The *Gutachterausschuß*

Federal legislation, the *Bundesbaugesetz*, subsequently replaced by the *Baugesetzbuch* (*BauGB*) 1986, included provisions to realize this aim. It allowed for the *Kreisfreie Städte* (county-free towns) and *Landkreise* (counties) to create a system of Boards of Expert Valuers, the *Gutachterausschuß*, commissioned to collect and publish data on land values and carry out valuations for the public, thereby enhancing property market transparency.

The Federal legislation allows for the establishment of the *Gutachterausschuß* at local level, their actual duties being set out by legislation of each land or state: the *Gutachterausschußverordnung* (*GAVO*), or State Order for the Board of Experts. Thus, the duties of the boards vary slightly from state to state.

Certain of the boards' duties are, however, common, being allowed for in the Federal legislation (section 193 BauGB).

1. The *Kaufpreisammlung* (collection of sales prices) (section 195 BauGB) This is analogous to the 'particulars delivered' system of the Inland Revenue in the UK. The relevant *Gutachterausschuß* is informed of every capital transaction in real estate when it is notarized. Because the detail of individual transactions is covered by data protection legislation, this data can subsequently only be released publicly in aggregate form.
2. Analysis of sale prices to produce *Bodenrichtwerte* or land values (section 196 BauGB) Each board publishes a plan of the geographical area for which it is responsible, showing land values derived from actual transactions. Particularly in densely-developed urban areas where transactions in bare land are infrequent, the *Gutachterausschuß* computes a price for a m² of bare land by deducting their estimate of the value of the building from the price paid for the real estate. Normally, the plan is published annually. However, the time taken to assemble, analyse and publish the data means that values are often dated. This is more of a problem in times of fast changing property values and may not be so severe for markets set in the low inflation economy which Germany has enjoyed until recently. These values are widely used in valuations carried out under the influential statutory Valuation Order, the *Wertermittlungsverordnung* (*WertV*) 1988, since this requires all valuations to be an aggregate of land value and building value. The *WertV* is described in detail below. A typical example of data provided by the plan is shown in Figure 8.2.
3. The collection, analysis and publication of other necessary data The extent and nature of the data analysis will be set out in the *GAVO*, so that this is the main area of the boards' duties in which there is variation between *Lander*. The annual report should at least contain information about bare and developed land zoned for housing purposes, developed commercial real estate, condominiums and agricultural land. In addition, there should be information about turnover in space, the average and range of value in each group.

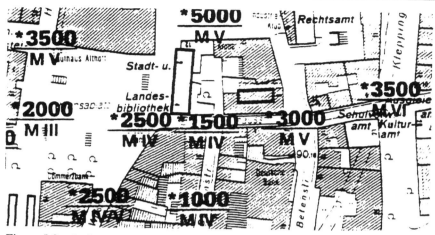

Figure 8.2 *Bodenrichtwerteplan (extract).*

4. The *Gutachterauschuß* is intended to contribute further to market transparency by carrying out valuations at the request of property owners within its area. However, this function has declined in usage and is usually only applied to residential property.

The *Gutachterauschuß* is generally perceived as part of the local government structure, because it invariably shares offices, property records and officials with the local authority property department. However, legally it is distinct and independent.

8.12.2 The *Wertermittlungsverordnung* (*WertV*) 1988 (The Federal Order for Valuation)

The *WertV* provides a detailed code of valuation concepts which are the foundation of traditional valuation practice. The *Wertermittlungsrichtlinien* (*WertR*, 1991), provides guidance and data for valuers in interpreting and using the *WertV*, including formal mathematical models expressing its concepts of value. Official commentaries are available on each by Kleiber *et al.*, (1993) and Kleiber (1991), respectively.

Certain valuation functions rely heavily on the *WertV* concepts and procedures, since they are approved by the *BAK*, the role of which is outlined in the following section. This legislation is therefore extremely influential.

8.12.3 The *Hypothekenbankgesetz* (*HBG*) 1990 (The Mortgage Bank Law)

The *HBG* provides a specialized and conservative definition of value for loan security and limits the loan to 60% of this value. The definition is explained in section 8.13. The *HBG* also allows for regulation of loan security valuation practice by the *BAK*. This control over valuations, both methodologically and in regard to values, is exercised strictly and in detail, extending even to agreement on minimum capitalization rates (European Community Mortgage Federation, 1989). Spot checks on valuation files ensure each bank adheres to its approved valuation regulations and to the methodology of the *WertV* and the *WertR*.

8.12.4 The *Gesetz über Kapitalanlagegesellschaften (KAGG)* 1970 (The Law Concerning Capital Investment Companies)

This law, subsequently amended, governs the operation of the open property investment funds. Under section 34 *KAGG*, each fund has to value its real estate assets at least annually, for published accounts, through a *Sachverständigenausschuß* (valuation committee). This consists of at least three independent, reliable and professional surveyors with outstanding experience in the field of surveying. Their appointment has to be approved by the *BAK*, which will also order replacement of any member it deems unsuitable. The *Sachverständigenausschuß* has to value assets before acquisition, section 27(3), and prior to disposal, section 37(1) and any transaction may only proceed at a price not, 'or only insignificantly' different from, its valuation.

These valuations are carried out in line with the *WertV* in order to satisfy the *BAK*. The funds would not be able to function in the highly competitive prime commercial property markets they favour unless the panel valuers were highly market-aware. In effect, this means that the investment purposes of the funds are reflected in the panel's interpretation and usage of the *WertV*. The valuer will typically provide both a *Sachwert* and *Ertragswert* and conclude that the *Verkehrswert* is best represented by the *Ertragswert*.

The valuer will, in this application of the legislation, be a market-orientated professional, specializing in an urban commercial and retail property market. They will be closely in touch with the investment thinking of their client and have available data provided by the open fund and possibly its banking parent. Rather than relying on aggregated data, such as investment yields and gross to net income adjustments, provided by the *WertR* and other texts, they will use current information originating from their experience and from the portfolio history of the fund client.

In effect, this is a 'market' application of the German valuation system and the high level of activity of these funds in competitive prime markets refutes the suggestion that the statutory German system of valuation is non-viable (Barnett, 1994).

8.13 DEFINITIONS OF VALUE

8.13.1 *Verkehrswert* (Market Value)

The Federal legislation establishing the Boards of Expert Valuers also establishes a definition of the *Verkehrswert* (section 194 BauGB), or market value

> The *Verkehrswert* is defined as the price which, at the time to which the assessment refers, would be attainable in normal business dealings, in accordance with the legal circumstances and actual characteristics, the particular state and situation of the property or other object for valuation, without regard to unusual or personal circumstances.

At first glance this appears to coincide with the RICS '*Red Book*' definition of open market value (OMV), but one aspect of the definition's interpretation is significantly different. It is made clear in the consultation draft new '*Red Book*',

(RICS, 1994, VAS 4.2) that OMV represents 'the best price which could reasonably be expected to have been obtained in the market on the date of valuation' (subject to exclusion of a special purchaser bid), 'not a "fair" price, nor an average price ...' The *Verkehrswert*, in contrast to this, is conceptualized as exactly that which is rejected by the RICS, an average price which could be offered by the average bidder in the market 'in normal business dealings'.

According to Kleiber *et al.* (1993), the following normative principles also apply to the interpretation of the *Verkehrswert* definition:

1. it is determined on the basis of all the physical and legal characteristics of the property, which influence its value to all bidders within the relevant submarket;
2. it is determined by the perceptions of the free market economy, without considering unusual or personal circumstances;
3. it is dependent on the conditions prevailing in the relevant property submarket on the specified valuation date and is valid for this date alone.

The *Verkehrswert* is an objective exchange value, without consideration of fairness entering into the issue. As it is defined as a price determined under specified normative principles, it may not coincide with the price in a particular transaction, which is influenced by the subjective considerations of the parties involved. As the *Verkehrswert* is distinguished by several imprecise legal terms, it is only ever an estimate rather than a precise mathematical calculation.

8.13.2 *Beleihungswert* (loan security, lending or collateral value)

Section 11 *HBG* defines the *Beleihungswert*, or lending value of the property upon which a mortgage is secured, and section 12 states that the lending value may not exceed 60% of the *Verkaufswert* or 'prudently assessed market value'. In arriving at this 'only the permanent characteristics of the property and the income, which any tenant can always ensure by proper management, shall be taken into account'. In addition, any assessment of the *Verkehrswert* arrived at under the definition of sections 192–199 *BauGB* must be taken into consideration.

The concept of 'prudently assessed market value' set out in section 12 *HBG* has been characterized as the 'sustainable market value' (European Mortgage Federation, 1989). This definition excludes any value attributable to the individual occupier of the property, or for which purchasers other than the occupier would not be prepared to pay. In addition, the valuer must ask how the current level of exchange value relates to worth. This involves considering the balance of supply and demand and whether the market is at a period of volatility, where values are likely to be inflated or deflated by temporary excess demand or excess supply. Where values are considered to be at a peak due to such an excess of demand, the value will be reduced to the level considered to be sustainable in the long term. This concept would seem to be more easily operated in a low inflation economy with property markets which do not show large cyclical movements.

The concept of sustainable value provides an interesting contrast with UK valuation for loan security which has been based on open market value, forced sale value or estimated realization price. Property's investment worth and the question of possible overpricing has been outside the UK valuer's remit when valuing for loan security but it is required by the statutory German concept of the

Beleihungswert. [The outcome of *The Mallinson Report* (RICS, 1994b) may change UK practice in this respect.]

It is possible to argue that the UK valuation system, following market movements intimately, will provide an inflationary impetus in a competitive development and investment market, and that the German concept of sustainable value will tend to dampen property price rises by restricting the size of mortgage funding for development, investment and occupation.

8.13.3 Methods of valuation: The *Wertermittlungsverordnung* 1988 (*WertV*) (The Federal Order for Valuation)

Section 7 *WertV*, augmented by the *Wertermittlungsrichtlinien*, 1991 (*WertR*), sets out three conceptual models for arriving at the *Verkehrswert* (market value) namely the:

1. *Vergleichswert* (sections 13, 14 *WertV* 1988) (capital comparison method);
2. *Ertragswert* (sections 15–20 *WertV* 1988) (investment income method); and
3. *Sachwert* (sections 21–25, *WertV* 1988) (depreciated replacement cost method).

The valuer is instructed to use at least two of these methods, depending on whether the type of property is usually held for owner-occupation or letting, for example *Vergleichswert* and *Sachwert* when the property type is usually held for owner-occupation, *Ertragswert* and *Sachwert* when it is usually held for income from letting. The *Verkehrswert* is then a considered compromise between the two outcomes.

The *Sachwert* was formerly favoured by banks and, since valuations for banks dominated other purposes, the *Sachwert* was pre-eminent among the three methods. Within recent years the expansion of commercial property's role as an investment has prompted a wider application of the *Ertragswert*. This was formerly confined to valuation of let residential property; industrial, office and retail property being predominantly owner-occupied and relatively illiquid. The move to an active investment and letting market is more marked in cities which have attracted speculative office and retail development and international investment, as opposed to centres so far relatively untouched. All three methods are conceptually equivalent to methods used in the UK, but differ fundamentally in their application.

8.13.4 *Bodenrichtwert* (land value)

Before considering each method individually it is worth noting that each of them conceptualizes value as consisting of two elements; namely the value of the land which is perpetual and is taken from comparable transactions, or in their absence from the *Bodenrichtwert* Plan produced by the *Gutachterausschuß*, and secondly the value of the building, including external works, which is a wasting asset with a finite life and is valued as such. The split into perpetual land value and the value of a building with a limited life contrasts strongly with the UK practice which, apart from depreciated replacement cost, applied to value properties for which there is no active market, deals with land and buildings as a unit.

8.13.5 The *Vergleichswert* sections 13 and 14 WertV

The value is built up from the usual two elements, land value and the capital value of the buildings, derived from comparable transactions, devalued on both a price per m^2 and per m^3 as illustrated in Figure 8.3. Several issues arise.

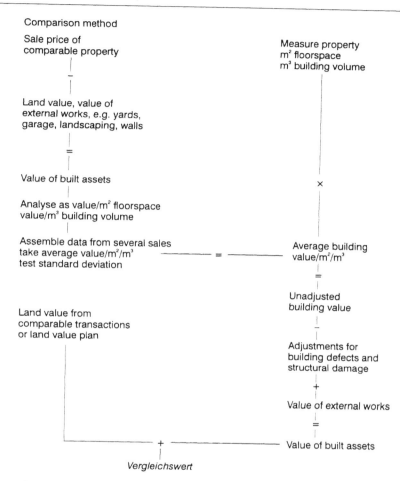

Figure 8.3 *Vergleichswert* (sections 13 and 14 *WertV*).

The **transactional data** are analysed by deducting the land value from the transaction price, to arrive at a comparative building price which can then be devalued to a unit building price. Error in land price will lead to error in the devalued building price. Two potential sources of error arise: firstly, the land value may be in doubt since it is sometimes derived from a residual analysis of the sale price of developed land. Secondly, delay in publishing the plan means that its values may be out of date. This is less of a problem when inflation and land price movement is low as is the cultural expectation in Germany. However, in locations affected by volatile international investment and over- or undersupply of space, price movements have recently been dramatic. Such effects are illustrated in Figures 8.7 and 8.8, which show prime office yields and rents for Frankfurt driving price increases in the period to 1991, followed by falls in 1991–1993.

The **devalued building price** will usually be taken from the aggregate data published by the *Gutachterausschuß*. Traditional German valuation favours a statistical approach to data in contrast to the UK valuer's search for individuality. For instance, the German valuer would look at the mean and standard deviation of sale prices, whereas a UK valuer would seek details of the individual properties involved and weight their evidence of price according to their degree of similarity with the property to be valued.

Individual attributes of the property, such as outbuildings, landscaping and yards are sometimes added as a supplement to the building price, taken from published average prices (Ross et al., 1991) and ignoring locational variations in value.

8.13.6 The *Ertragswert* sections 15–20 *WertV* 1988

Once again, the value is built up from two elements, land value taken from comparable transactions, or the land value plan, and the capitalized net income attributable to the building, as illustrated in Figure 8.4. The model depends on the following inputs: I_T is the total net annual income, I_B is $I_T - (p \times V_L)$; where I_B is the net income attributable to the building, V_L is the land value from the land value plan, p is the real property interest rate, or *Liegenschaftszinssatz*, expressed as a decimal and n is the remaining useful life of the building, or *Restnutzungsdauer*, in years.

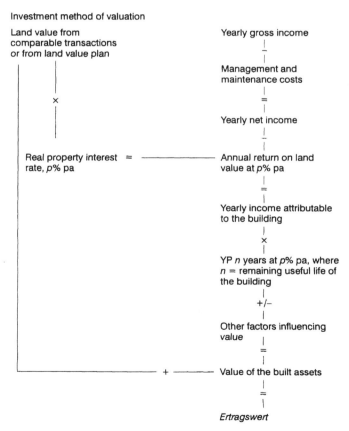

Figure 8.4 *Ertragswert (sections 15–20 WertV).*

The *Ertragswert* can be modelled in two ways:

1. EW = Yearly income attributable to the building,   + land value
   capitalized for its useful life at $p\%$

$$= \left(I_T - p V_L\right)\frac{(1+p)^n - 1}{(1+p)^n\, p} + V_L$$

2. EW = Total yearly income capitalized for the useful   + land value
   life of the building at $p\%$ deferred n
                                                              years at $p\%$

$$= I_T \frac{(1+p)^n - 1}{(1+p)^n\, p} + \frac{V_L}{(1+p)^n}$$

Example 8.1: *Ertragswert*

Type of building	Apartment building
Land value	DM480 000
Floorspace	1200 m²
Monthly gross income	DM10/m²
Management and maintenance costs	22%
Remaining useful life of the building	60 years
Real property interest rate	5%

Determination of the income value according to sections 15–19 *WertV*:

Yearly gross income:	
DM10/m² × 1200 m² × 12 months	DM144 000
− Management and maintenance costs (22%)	DM31 680
= Yearly net income	DM112 320
− Annual return on land value at 5% p.a.	DM24 000
= Yearly income attributable to the building	DM88 320
Income value attributable to the building	
(YP: 18.93)	DM1 671 897
+ land value	DM480 000
= income value	DM2 151 897

Liegenschaftszinssatz (capitalization rate)
In order to calculate the net income attributable to the building, the real property interest rate, $p\%$, is required. This is arrived at by analysis of sales of let property or by aggregate data on such sales produced by the *Gutachterausschuß*.

Rewriting the expression for the *Ertragswert*:

$p \times EW$ = total income −   annual sinking fund to replace the income
                                 attributable to the building after n years at $p\%$

$$p = \frac{I_T}{EW} - \left[\frac{p}{(1+p)^n - 1} \times \frac{(EW - V_L)}{EW}\right]$$

Applying this to analyse the sale price of a let property:

Real property interest rate	$p\%$		
Yearly net income	I_T	=	DM30 000
Remaining useful life	n	=	30 years
Sale price	EW	=	DM500 000
Land value	V_L	=	DM200 000
Value attributable to the building			DM300 000
Approximate yield	$p \times 100\%$	=	6%
'Correction factor'	$\dfrac{p}{(1+p)^n - 1}$		

$$\frac{0.06}{(1.06)^{30} - 1} = 1.26$$

$$p = \text{approximate yield} - \left(\text{correction factor} \times \frac{\text{building value}}{\text{sale price}} \right)$$

$$= 6\% - \left(1.26 \times \frac{300\ 000}{500\ 000} \right)$$

$$= 5.24\%$$

Comparing the German *Liegenschaftszinssatz* and the UK initial yield
According to Kleiber (1990), the expression for the *Ertragswert* can be rewritten as:

$p \times EW$ = total income $-$ *ASF* to replace income attributable to the
building after n years at $p\%$

$$p = \frac{I_T}{EW} - \left[\frac{p}{(1+p)^n - 1} \times \frac{(EW - V_L)}{EW} \right]$$

where p is the real property interest rate as a decimal, I_T the total annual net income, EW the *Ertragswert* and V_L the value of the land.
As

$$n \to \infty,\ p \to \frac{I_T}{EW} \times 100$$

i.e. $p_G \to p_{UK}$

For small n (i.e. a short-life building):

$p_G < p_{UK}$

where p_G is the real property interest rate used in Germany and p_{UK} is the all-risks yield or investment yield used in the UK.

Research suggests (Downie, 1993) that some valuers prefer to use standard values for p rather than attempting to follow market movements. These may be derived from past experience or from publications such as

Ross *et al.* (1991). In valuation for loan security the *BAK* will agree a generally applicable floor for capitalization rates with the bank valuer (European Community Mortgage Federation, 1989).

Error may potentially arise from the nature of the process giving rise to the land value and resulting error in the analysis of transactions aimed at finding p, the real property interest rate. Harrop (1990) suggests that the use of standard deductions from gross income to arrive at net income may not be tailored to individual contractual liabilities. The method also suffers from the difficulty of assessing the remaining useful life of a building which may be complicated by extension of its life by refurbishment. Standard figures are used, from the *WertR* (Kleiber, 1991) and texts such as Ross *et al.* (1991).

8.13.7 The *Sachwert* sections 21–25 *WertV* 1988

This translates as the 'real value' but corresponds most closely to depreciated replacement cost, as defined in the RICS '*Red Book*' (RICS, 1990) and investigated by Britton *et al.* (1991). Essentially, the *Sachwert* equals the land value plus the value of the built assets, depreciated according to age and obsolescence, as illustrated in Figure 8.5.

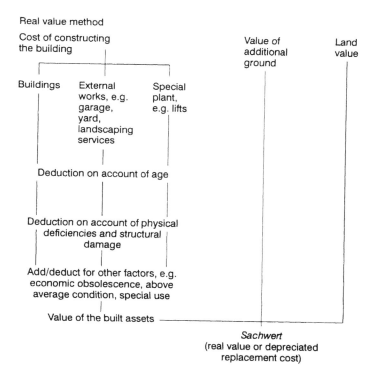

Figure 8.5 *Sachwert* (sections 21–25 *WertV* 1988).

(a) Depreciation

As in the assessment of *Ertragswert*, the valuer must consider depreciation of the building due to age. In this case it is expressed not as the 'remaining useful life' but as the '*Alterswertminderung*', the percentage reduction in value due to age. Figures for various building uses and construction types can be found in Ross and Brachman (1991).

For instance, the normal useful life of various building types is recorded as follows, depending on construction type:

houses	100 years
office buildings	70–80 years
shopping centres	60 years
inner-city commercial building	35 years

The normal useful life is adjusted to allow for 'modernization'. For example, the reduction in value, due to age, of an unmodernized 70 year old building may be 59.5%. After modernization it has a fictional age of 50 years, giving a reduction in value of only 37.5%

Example 8.2: *Sachwert*

Freestanding bank/insurance building in good condition

Year of construction	1985
Building volume according to DIN 277/1950	2400 m³
site area	950 m
Valuation date	1992
Net cost of construction per m³	DM555
Additional cost of construction	15%
Cost of construction index 1988	106.6
Cost of construction index 1992	130.5
Land value for developed land according to the land value plan 1992	DM1800

Cost of constructing the building at 1988 prices:

2400 m³ × DM555/m³	= DM1 332 000
Additional cost of construction (15%)	+ DM199 800
Total cost of construction	= DM1 531 800

Cost of constructing the building at 1992 prices:
Index 1988: 106.6
Index 1992: 130.5

(130.5/106.6) × 1 531 800	= DM1 875 233

Deduction on account of age:
Total useful life of the building: 80 years
Remaining useful life of the building: 73 years

Deduction on account of age: 8.75%	− DM164 082
Value of the built assets	= DM1 711 151

Land value:

950 m² at DM1800	+ DM1 710 000
Sachwert	= DM3 421 151

Britton *et al.* (1991) point out the problems of assessing quantitative allowances for depreciation and obsolescence, even after the research of Salway (1986) and Baum (1991). These difficulties apply to any application of this method. In Germany, more detailed figures are available, but they run the risk of being used routinely without querying the many factors influencing levels of depreciation, such as location and the point in the economic cycle, identified as important by Salway (1986).

8.14 CULTURAL DIFFERENCES (VALUATION UK VERSUS FRG)

8.14.1 The *Sachwert*

Within the German tradition of valuation stress is placed on the depreciated replacement cost (DRC) approach, which is used to value all types of mainly owner-occupied buildings like detached housing, schools, hospitals, market halls, factories, etc. One explanation for this is probably the method's inclusion in the *WertV*. Normally, the *Verkehrswert* is derived by using either the comparable, the investment or the DRC approach or by using results of more than one of these methods and deducing the *Verkehrswert* from them. This differs fundamentally from the view taken by British surveyors, where the DRC approach is only used to value properties which are infrequently traded and for which no market value can be determined.

8.14.2 Valuations for company accounts

In Germany the idea of historic cost resembling market value still exists for certain property types and furthermore can be found in German accounting laws, which require corporations to balance property at the historic costs of acquisition or construction (if self-constructed). Therefore, there is no need for annual revaluations. German accounting principles only require valuations to be effected before properties are transferred to a newly established subsidiary company, which are normally launched with assets valued at market value.

8.14.3 Valuation in a low inflation economy

There are some differences between the UK and the German property market, arising from the fact that Germany is a country with low inflation (Figure 8.6). Between 1983 and 1989 there was negligible inflation, the rate being around 2.5%. As a consequence of German reunification, inflation has now risen to 4%.

Yields for high quality property are due to low inflation, traditionally very stable in Germany as is illustrated by prime office yields in Frankfurt (Figure 8.7). Due to the surplus of office space and general recessionary trends in the German economy, yields are now moving slightly upwards, whereas rents are falling (Figure 8.8).

8.14.4 Methodological differences between Germany and the UK

Whereas the structure of the DRC and comparable methods are similar in the UK and Germany, there are some differences between the investment method

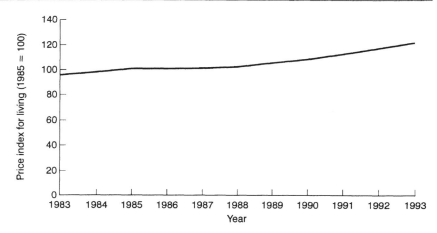

Figure 8.6 Cost of living index (1985 = 100). *Source*: National Statistical Office, 'Preise', Fachserie 17, Reihe 7, Preise und Preisindizes für die Lebenshaltung, August 1994, p. 4.

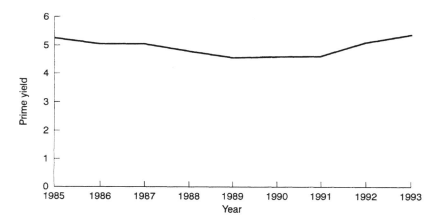

Figure 8.7 Prime office yields in Frankfurt (%). *Source*: Jones Lang Wootton, *City Report Frankfurt, Update February 1994*, p. 3.

and the *Ertragswertverfahren*. The major difference lies in the separation of the land value and the capital value of the building. The capital value of the building is estimated by multiplying the net income received by the years purchase, calculated for its remaining useful life. This method is criticized in British valuation literature as it is argued that it is nearly impossible to estimate the useful life of a building. Valuations in the UK usually assume that the net income will be received into perpetuity. The UK literature suggests that if the building has a terminable life – assuming a reversion to site value at the end of the lease – the portion of the present rent that will continue will be discounted for the building's remaining lifetime, at the all-risk yield attributable to properties similar in nature, in a similar location and whose structural life is estimated to be 75 years or more. The remainder of the rent will be discounted for the remaining lifetime

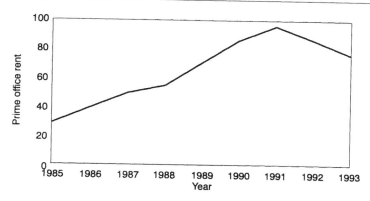

Figure 8.8 Prime office rents in Frankfurt. *Source*: Jones Lang Wootton, *City Report Frankfurt, Update February 1994*, p. 2.

at a dual rate to allow for a sinking fund to cover rebuilding costs as well as taxation. The site value today will be discounted at a rate below the all risks yield (Britton *et al.*, 1989). Undoubtedly, in this case, the British approach approximates to the German *Ertragswert*. From the German point of view the British method has several shortcomings. Firstly, concerning the sinking fund, as it is very difficult to predict the future costs of rebuilding as well as to determine the correct tax adjustment and dual rate. Further, it is not logical to discount current land value at a lower rate than the all-risk yield, as the latter allows for implied growth of value. Using a lower rate suggests a less risky investment opportunity and clearly there is no reason why a site with an obsolescent building should be less risky than an investment in property with an up-to-date building. Market evidence for the lower rate may be difficult to obtain.

8.15 DATABASE MANAGEMENT: DATA COLLECTION, RELIABILITY AND METHODS OF MEASUREMENT

Data collection, reliability and the method of measurement depend on the valuation method.

8.15.1 The *Vergleichswert*

The approach differs, according to whether a bare or developed site is to be valued. The usual sources are either the valuer's own knowledge or an application to the *Gutachterausschuß* for an extract from the collection of sale prices. Valuers accredited by the local chamber of commerce can obtain, in anonymized form, comparable sales from the *Gutachterausschuß*. For other valuers or third parties the possibility of doing so depends on the country regulations. *Bodenrichtwert* plans from the *Gutachterausschuß* can be of assistance, but they show average prices for certain value zones which have to be adjusted to reflect differences in the nature of the individual property. As they are published yearly or two yearly, adjustments have to be made to reflect changes in market supply and demand.

Some *Gutachterausschüsse* publish statistical data in order to enable a comparable valuation, e.g. regressions between the size of a flat and the price per m² achieved in certain housing districts. Although this data is highly reliable, being based on every notarized transaction, sometimes not enough recent data is available to obtain good valuation results.

8.15.2 The *Ertragswert*

The land value is estimated by applying the *Vergleichswert*. The yields to be applied, reflecting the property's specific use and location, are normally published in market reports, either from the *Gutachterausschuß* or property agents and consultants. Usually a yield range is published, so the valuer has to take into account market changes since the publication of the report, as well as specific characteristics of the property to be valued.

The yearly gross income has to be derived from the market in case the rent paid differs from the market rent. The *Ertragswert*'s gross income relies on the sustainable rent. If the rent, e.g. for diplomat housing, is higher than the market rent, this overage may not be taken into account, as it is not sustainable. If the difference between rent received and market rent cannot be broken up within a reasonable period of time the *Ertragswert* has to be adjusted to reflect these differences in order to determine the *Verkehrswert* (Kleiber, 1991). To date, German valuation literature has not dealt with this problem, yet there are some publications dealing with the valuation of buildings with *Staffelmietverträgen*, i.e. rental agreements with upwards only rental changes of a certain percentage within a given period of time, suggesting that the rising income, which is secured by the rental agreements, is to be capitalized at the real property interest rate (Kleiber *et al.*, 1993, p. 227).

The outgoings are determined by analysing the rental agreement as well as by empirically determined averages appropriate to the use, site and construction time of the building (Rössler *et al.*, 1990).

8.15.3 The *Sachwert*

The land value is estimated as in the *Vergleichswert*. The value of the building is derived by multiplying the gross floor area or gross building volume by the appropriate construction cost. The *umbauter Raum* (gross volume) and its measurement method (Rössler *et al.*, 1990, pp. 222–39) is defined in the DIN 277 (German Industrial Norm). For valuation uses, DIN 277 in the version of 1950 is applied, although several changes were made in 1973 and 1987. There can be a difference of up to 50% between gross space measurements made according to the 1950 and 1973/87 versions, e.g. when measuring a building with an uncompleted attic. Therefore, for valuation purposes only the 1950 version should be used, as the published normal construction costs relate to this measurement.

The statistical normal construction cost has to be indexed up to the valuation date. In order to avoid flaws resulting from indexation it is advisable to use the most recent normal construction cost. Many valuers in Germany still rely on normal construction costs on a price basis of 1913/14 which are then indexed up to the valuation date. Further adjustments have to be made for regional building price differences, e.g. it is more expensive to build identical structures in Berlin than in a town of Lower Saxonia. Information regarding normal construction costs are not collected nationally, but locally. The chamber of architects of Baden-Württemberg, for example, publishes building cost information. These costs do not include architects and other fees, insurance, interest, etc., further adjustments for these are usually approximate, being a percentage range of the normal construction costs.

Deductions for age can follow different patterns (e.g. the depreciation of Ross follows the ballistical curve of a bullet, further depreciation methods are linear, parabolic or rely on statistical evidence of certain regions). There are different systems of depreciation and it is impossible to generalize which method best reflects the obsolescence of the property being valued. Therefore, a wide range of valuation outcomes is possible, depending on the chosen approach to depreciation. Further deductions for physical deficiencies can normally only be quantified by external experts.

The accuracy of the input data is of course, dependent upon the source and no generalization on data reliability can be made. In applying the depreciated replacement cost approach, it is very much at the discretion of the valuer to achieve acceptable results or not.

8.16 MARKET TRANSPARENCY

Despite the establishment of the *Gutachterauschuß*, the German property market is usually considered to be intransparent.

8.16.1 Market indices

Transparency is improved by the publication of indices. The 'Prices of Building Land' published by the Statistische Bundesamt only deals with building land; there is no official index monitoring the performance of real estate. There are, however, some indices, of differing quality, published by estate agents or consultants. The Kempers Index describes the market value of fictitious, ideal buildings used for commercial purposes in prime locations across 103 different cities and is published every three years. The changes in value are derived from factors like rental value, pedestrian frequency, zoning factors, etc.

Aengevelt Immobilien KG publishes an index of yield changes achieved for office space in the Düsseldorf area. It is based on contracts agreed before a notary under the advice of Aengevelt. The yields are calculated by dividing the net income of the property by the price of the building, including transaction costs. The annual Müller International index compares the office markets of 11 cities by analysing supply, demand and price.

In Germany there is no institution comparable with IPD, offering a performance index compiled by a neutral institution. As all indices are published by estate agents and consultants their accuracy cannot be verified, as the database is not accessible to third parties. All major property advisers and to a certain degree developers publish their own market reports which focus on the office markets of the major cities such as Berlin, Frankfurt, Munich, Hamburg, Düsseldorf, etc. The problem here is that they concentrate only on prime locations and can be suspected of inaccuracy, being designed to function as a marketing instrument.

In 1993 the *Gesellschaft für immobilienwirtschaftliche Forschung e.V.* (Society of Property Researchers, Germany) was founded. One of its aims is to enhance the transparency of the German property market by defining standards in the measurement of rents, supply and demand, etc.

8.16.2 The role of information technology

Several software packages have been developed on the German market to assist the valuer in effecting valuations. The market can be divided into three segments (Tillmann, 1993): word-processing, integrated software packages and commercial valuation software, although the latter do not cover the whole variety of valuation methods. Commercial valuation software has the inherent danger of high standardization and can give the undesirable impression that a valuation is the result of computer calculations instead of an individual appraisal.

Two types of commercial valuation software can be differentiated: firstly, the solution preferred by beginners, where the user is guided completely through the program, at the cost of flexibility and scope for individuality. Secondly, those in which the valuer can use single components of the software with the effect that these programs are more demanding.

Increasingly, insurance companies are developing expert systems to derive fire insurance and collateral values of property, seeking to enhance valuation efficiency in the strong belief that expert systems can assist valuers (Burghard and Hartmann, 1990).

8.17 CONCLUSION

Germany has a clearly conceived system of property valuation with considerable support at Federal level through legislation and published guidelines on its application. It incorporates the three classic methods of valuation and has definitions of market value and of sustainable value orientated towards different valuation purposes. The system is implemented by valuers with an engineering or architectural background, mainly practising within their local area and has apparently operated satisfactorily in the low inflation economy of the past 40 years, during which owner-occupation of commercial and industrial property has been the norm. It remains to be seen how it will adapt to the volatility in property markets introduced by increased levels of speculative development and cross-border investment, and whether clients will favour the traditional methods and their exponents, or a more international system of valuation introduced by consultants operating on a pan-European scale.

REFERENCES

Barnett, A. (1994) Valued opinion. *Estates Europe*, **3** (1), 6.
Baum, A. (1991) *Property Investment Depreciation and Obsolescence*, Routledge, London.
Britton, W., Connellan, O.P. and Crofts, M.K. (1991) *The Cost Approach to Valuation*. RICS/Kingston Polytechnic, London.

Britton, W., Davies, K. and Johnson, T. (1989) *Modern Methods of Valuation*, 8th edn, Estates Gazette, London.

Bulwien, H. (1994) Der Markt für Gewerbe- und Wohnimmobilien in Deutschland. Lecture at the ebs Real Estate Academy, Oestrich-Winkel, 20.8.94.

Burghard, P. and Hartmann, S. (1990) Expertensysteme in der Versicherungswirtschaft. *Handbuch der modernen Datenverarbeitung*, **153**, Mai 1990, Vol. 27, 83–99.

Dieterich, H., Dransfeld, E. and Voß, W. (1993) *Urban Land and Property Markets in Germany*, UCL Press Ltd, London.

Dieterich, H. and Joeris, D. (1995) Bodenwertermittlung in Gebieten ohne Funktionierenden Bodenmarkt, in De Leeuw, A. and Sayce, S. (eds), *Theorie un Praxis der Wertermittlung von Ge äuden, Grund und Boden*, Travaux Scientifiques de la Faculté Européenne des Sciences du Foncier, Strasbourg, Peter Lang, Frankfurt.

Downie, M.L. (1993) Property Valuation in Germany: a Different Tradition. Paper given at European Real Estate Conference: an Agenda for Research, Reading.

European Community Mortgage Federation (ed.) (1989) *Study on the Valuation of Property in the EC Countries*, Grenz-Echo, Eupen.

Kleiber, W. (1990) Theorie and Praxis der Ermittlung von Grundstückswerten in Großbritannien, in *WertV '88 auf dem Prüfstand*, Bundesanzeiger, Köln.

Kleiber, W. (1991) Sammlung amtlicher Texte zur Wertermittlung von Grundstücken in den alten und neuen Bundeslander (WertR 91/WaldR 91), Bundesanzeiger, Köln.

Kleiber, W., Simon, J. and Weyers, G. (1993) *WertV '88*, 3rd edn, Bundesanzeiger, Köln.

Licher, T. (1994) *Wundersamer Mehrwert*, Capital, Heft 6, pp. 8 and 9.

N.N. (1992) Erstmals Hochrechnung zum Immobilienmarkt, *Der Langfristige Kredit*, **10**, 1992, 339.

OECD (1994) *Economic Surveys, Germany 1994*. Organisation for Economic Co-operation and Development, Paris.

Ross, F.W., Brachman, R. and Holzner, P. (1991) *Ermittlung des Bauwertes von Gebäuden und des Verkehrswertes von Grundstücken*, 26 edn, Theodor Oppermann Verlag, Salzgitter.

RICS (1990) *Statements of Asset Valuation Practice and Guidance Notes* ('Red Book'), Royal Institution Of Chartered Surveyors Books, London.

RICS (1992) *Manual of Valuation Guidance Notes* ('White Book'), Royal Institution Of Chartered Surveyors Books, London.

RICS (1994) *Consultation Draft of Statements of Valuation and Appraisal Practice and Guidance Notes*, Royal Institution of Chartered Surveyors Books, London.

RICS (1994b), *The Mallinson Report: Commercial Property Valuations*, Royal Institution Of Chartered Surveyors, London.

Rössler, R., Langner, J., Simon, J. and Kleiber, W. (1990) *Schätzung und Ermittlung von Grundstückswerten*, 6th edn, Hermann Luchterhand, Neuwied.

Salway, F. (1986) *Depreciation of Commercial Property*, College of Estate Management, Reading.

Statistisches Bundesamt (ed.) (1993) *Statistisches Jahrbuch 1993*, Wiesbaden.

von Schenck, Kersten (1991) in *Real Property in Germany* (eds R. Volhard, D. Weber and W. Usinger), 4th edn, Fritz Knapp, Frankfurt am Main.

Smith, E.O. (1994) *The German Economy*, Routledge, London.

Tillmann, H.-G. (1993) Auswahl und Anwendung von EDV-Programmen zur Verkehrswertermittlung. *GuG*, **1**, 1993, 1–16.

Volze, H. (1990) section 33 HOAI – Honorarregelung für Gutachten. *Der Sachverständige*, Juni 1990, **6**, 135.

Zimmermann, P. (1993) *Haftungsrechtliche Folgen einer schuldhaften Falschbegutachtung für den Grundstückssachverstandigen* (The Property Expert's Legal Liability Resulting from an Incorrect Valuation.) Der Sachverständige, März 1993, **3**, 15–25.

LEGISLATION

Baugesetzbuch (1986) BGBL.1 S 2253.

Gesetz über Kapitalanlagegesellschaften (KAGG), BGBL 1 S.127.

Honorarordnung für Architekten und Ingenieure (1991) BGBL 1 S. 533.

Hypothekenbankgesetz (HBG) BGBL 1 S 81.

Richtlinien für die Ermittlung der Verkehrswerte von Grundstücken (Wertermittlungs Richtlinien 1991 – WertR 91), Beil. BAnz 182 a.

Verordnung über Grundsätze für die Ermittlung der Verkehrswerte von Grundstücken (Wertermittlungsverordnung – WertV) 1988, BGBL III 213-1-5.

Italy 9

Manfredo Montagnana,
Franco Prizzon and
Ferruccio Zorzi

Traditionally, real estate valuation in Italy has been characterized by a lack of advanced training and practice in the appraisal of property investments, both in the private sector and, in particular, the public sector. However, there is a long tradition of appraisal connected with the valuation of domestic property and land. In addition, there are few dedicated professional bodies and specialized journals dealing with property. Indeed, the public sector has not even addressed the issue of acquiring professional competence in the field of commercial real estate appraisal.

This divergence from other western countries is primarily due to the low risks which have characterized real estate investment in Italy, although this difference has lessened in recent years. Indeed, real estate investment performance, until the 1980s, produced relatively high returns. Consequently, it is not surprising that the major focus of investors has been on identifying investment opportunities through development activity rather than assessing property investment performance. Consequently, valuation practice is largely based on the investors' subjective experience without any objective input. For the private sector this situation is changing, due to structural changes in the real estate market at the beginning of the 1980s. Price trends for both residential and non-residential property are now more volatile than in the past due to the effect of economic cycles. The risk level has increased, with the consequence that instructions to valuers for forced sale valuations of investment properties have increased.

These changes have, in effect, defined a new point of reference for valuers. Property no longer represents the only medium in which to protect investments from inflation. Greater knowledge of the real estate market, new investment instruments and returns on government bonds have had the effect of diversifying investments by directing them towards the financial markets. Long-run price trends show market variations in both the residential and non-residential markets and no longer guarantee returns greater than the inflation rate, as was the case prior to the 1980s. Currently, the volume of investment valuations is increasing

European Valuation Practice. Edited by Alastair Adair, Mary Lou Downie, Stanley McGreal and Gerjan Vos. Published in 1996 by E & FN Spon, London. ISBN 0 419 20040 1

and the principal client groups are banks and insurance companies, investment companies and private individuals.

9.1 LEGISLATIVE AND REGULATORY CONTEXT

Generally, there are no laws covering property valuation in Italy except in cases of the compulsory purchase of land and buildings. Furthermore, there are no generally accepted valuation methods although many developers have their own preferred formats. Each bank, for example, uses different valuers for loan security valuations, requiring a valuation outline which comprises size of lettable space, details on location, external and internal characteristics. While broadly similar in structure and content, the valuation reports requested by the banks are not identical.

The same is true for investors and real estate developers. While discounted cash-flow appraisal for investment valuations, is becoming more widespread, there is no single approach. In addition, no specific valuation bases, standards or methods have been defined by the professional bodies. Data interpretation and its use in a valuation is a professional responsibility and sanctions, such as admonition or suspension, can be imposed by the valuer's professional body. Sworn appraisals for legal cases carry greater responsibility due to the official nature of the appraisal. Specific legal complaints can be taken up by the clients in the courts.

In the property and construction sectors in Italy three kinds of professional are officially recognized, namely architects, engineers and design technicians/surveyors (*geometri*), each with their own professional body. The surveyors (*geometri*) undertake real estate valuations, certify development projects and may request building permits for property owners. The professional bodies (*ordini*) are associations instituted by Royal Decree in 1925. Membership is mandatory for professionals involved in property and construction activity that requires certain competencies and carries specific responsibilities. Professional bodies have a limited range of control, usually corresponding to the provincial territory. There is also a central body, the National Council, based in Rome which represents the profession as a whole and has advisory and deliberative functions. In 1991, the professional institutions had the following membership: architects, 50 000; engineers, 90 000; design technicians (*geometri*), 80 000.

The use of professional brokers, or firms that deal with real estate transactions, is less developed in Italy than in other European countries. There are no detailed statistics, but it is estimated that in the smaller towns around 70% of transactions are undertaken without recourse to brokers, while in the main cities a larger percentage of sales are executed with the help of real estate agents. Another specific feature of the Italian market is the presence of a high number of brokers, (estimated at approximately 60 000–70 000 active broker firms in 1986). The number of firms increases or decreases according to real estate market cycles.

The development of professional bodies has led to improved standards and the offering of guarantees to clients. A law has been passed (L. 39/1989) to regularize broker activities requiring the deposit of standard contract forms at the local Chamber of Commerce (assignments, sale proposals). Furthermore, the law requires brokers to be licensed and failure to comply negates the right to commission. Brokers' costs vary around 4–8% of the estate value and are usually evenly charged to buyer and seller. In recent years larger brokers have broadened and diversified their activity, including the promotion of complex development ventures.

The training and qualification of valuers is at an embryonic stage in Italy. There are a number of valuation courses at undergraduate and post-graduate levels with one Masters program offered at Turin Polytechnic. A law of 1989 (39/1989) requires six months attendance at a course including real estate valuation techniques in order to perform the activities of a real estate agent. However, across most courses it is only in recent years that appraisal has evolved from the traditional valuation of individual properties to the valuation of investment properties as assets.

9.2 CONTEXUAL INFLUENCE

An overview of the property market in Italy can be obtained from an analysis of investment activity in the various sectors of the construction industry. In 1992 investment in housing was 48% of the total (26% new construction, 22% refurbishment), 27% was directed to non-residential building and 25% to public works (Table 9.1).

Table 9.1 Fixed investments in the construction sector

Period	Residential constructions			Non-residential constructions and public works			
	New construction	Restoration	Total	Construction	Public works	Total	Total fixed investment
Billions of lire – current values							
1986	26 761	23 410	50 171	24 953	27 784	52 737	102 908
1987	26 568	24 437	51 005	25 797	29 228	55 025	106 030
1988	29 204	26 487	55 691	31 033	31 747	62 780	118 471
1989	32 099	27 945	60 044	35 247	34 905	70 152	130 196
1990	36 525	31 673	68 198	41 322	36 858	78 179	146 377
1991	40 264	35 476	75 740	45 473	39 487	84 959	160 699
1992	43 547	38 184	81 731	46 783	41 629	88 412	170 143
Year variations – constant values							
1986	−4.6%	1.1%	−2.1%	7.8%	7.2%	7.5%	2.6%
1987	−4.7%	0.2%	−2.4%	−1.8%	1.0%	−0.3%	−1.3%
1988	1.9%	0.5%	1.3%	12.1%	1.9%	6.6%	4.0%
1989	4.4%	0.2%	2.4%	6.3%	3.7%	4.9%	3.7%
1990	2.9%	2.5%	2.7%	6.4%	−3.3%	1.5%	2.1%
1991	1.0%	2.7%	1.8%	2.6%	−0.7%	1.0%	1.4%
1992	3.5%	3.0%	3.3%	2.3%	0.5%	−0.9%	1.0%
1993*	−0.7%	1.2%	0.2%	−6.5%	−14.3%	−10.3%	−5.3%
1994*	−4.0%	−1.4%	−2.1%	−0.8%	−4.2%	−2.4%	−2.2%

Source: CRESME (on constant values) from ministry data supplied by the treasury.
*Estimate.

When considering public works it is interesting to subdivide investments according to the promoting authority. In Italy the responsibility for the public works falls on local authorities. Spending for public investment in 1993 shows that provinces and municipalities were the main spenders (41%), followed by central state companies (21%).

In the non-domestic sector the most significant development components are service–executive–commercial centres and industrial buildings. The former is the focus of the main developers: financial companies, building firms, insurance companies. They usually assemble the operation and negotiate with local authorities. In practice, the development is handled by smaller developers and design professionals. In the mid- and small-sized towns, design professionals often have a role of 'expert–developers', both in housing and industrial developments, due to their knowledge of local real estate markets.

In 1992 the rent control law was changed (L. 359/1992, Art. 11 Contracts in derogation) allowing rents agreed by owners and tenants to be applied to new properties and for the renewal of expired contracts. This is a first step towards liberating the market and has produced a substantial increase in new rental contracts (3% in 1993 and 10% in 1994). The duration of lease contracts for residential dwellings is four years (or more) and renewable for another four years. The duration for offices or other commercial premises is six years and renewable for another six years. Residential dwelling contracts, in general, provide for an annual increase equal to 75% of the inflation rate.

Rented housing is considered to be an important private investment opportunity in Italy. However, macro-economic variables, such as inflation, financial market trends and income distribution influence the number of houses available for renting. Figure 9.1 shows the annual variation in rates of alternative returns (R) (calculated as a weighted average of government bonds, share funds, shares) and housing prices (P) (three year moving average), all net of inflation. It is evident that while R and P followed similar trends in the 1970s, the two diverged in

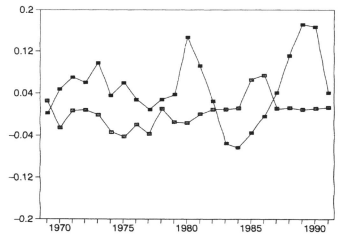

Figure 9.1 Annual variation in rates of alternative returns (R) and housing prices (P) (all net of inflation). ■, P, mobile mean; □, R, weighted average.

the early 1980s: where R increases, P decreases and vice versa. This divergence is the result of the inflow of large amounts of savings to the financial markets which previously had been invested in housing. The changed attitude can be ascribed to new options (e.g. investment funds), high interest rates on government bonds (due to the public debt) and to more widespread economic performance information.

9.3 GROSS TO NET ADJUSTMENT

The following sections relate to expenses connected with investment in residential property which is an important sector of the real estate market in Italy.

9.3.1 Insurance and management costs

The premium for building insurance currently varies from 0.40 to 0.80 per thousand of the insured value (400–800 lire per million insured) for a 'comprehensive building' policy. (There are obviously different types of policies, from those that cover only fire–explosion to 'comprehensive building' policies that also cover wider claims and the 'civil liability' of the building. In general, managers are oriented towards the latter type. It is also necessary to take into account that buildings are separated into four categories based on the type of material used in the construction of the vertical support structure, the floors/ceilings, external walls and the roof. For example, Class 1, which is a lower risk, requires fireproof materials to be used for the above-mentioned elements in the buildings.) The cost to the user, however, almost doubles when additional expenses and taxes are taken into account. As an indication, annual expenses can be 2–2.5% of the total rents. Management expenses involve the services paid for management of the building. There are no precise tariffs for management expenses, which are awaiting approval by the register of real property managers. In general, total annual expenses amount to approximately 0.4–0.6% of total rents.

9.3.2 Maintenance costs

There are often many difficulties in defining and quantifying maintenance costs due to the lack of systematic information on expenses sustained by managers of real property assets. Seventy years is normally considered to be the economic life of the building. Data on maintenance costs for residential buildings are obtained from IACP of Milan. An evaluation of the increase in maintenance costs over time (Pollo and Prizzon, 1993) identified an annual cost equal to 0.7% of the initial construction costs, with the following exponential increase over time:

$$m = 8884e^{0.0166t}$$

where m is the increase in maintenance costs and t is the number of years.

In the case of newly constructed property, maintenance costs are usually considered constant around 0.4–0.7% of the construction costs. For existing buildings, the rate takes into account the age of the building, using a formula similar to the one above.

9.3.3 Vacancy rate (*la quota di sfitto*)

The vacancy rate must be included in the cost of management in order to account for the absence of income due to tenant turnover. For example, this rate can be fixed at 3.3% of the rental pool. This means that, in practice, one out of 30 units would not be producing any income.

In other countries the vacancy rate percentage is estimated to be much higher, equal to 5–8% of the rental pool (Ferguson and Heizer, 1990). This depends, in the first place, on the high mobility that is recorded in the rental market, producing frequent changes in tenants, resulting in non-income generating periods. In addition, there are situations of scarce demand (or excess supply), prolonging the period. Both of these elements are not found to the same degree in Italy where the absence of a free tenancy market and high demand produce a vacancy rate of 2–4%.

9.4 THEORETICAL BASIS OF VALUATION TECHNIQUES

'Valuation practice is strictly tied to usage and customs related to the economic activity of different countries and therefore arises from and is developed in national contexts in relation to legislative, administrative and fiscal regulations and in general to the economic and social situation.'

Simonotti, 1990

This quotation amply describes the practice of valuation in Italy today. The new Italian appraisal school, established in the early 1900s through the work of Serpieri (1917), set the assumptions for theoretical in-depth studies. Subsequent contributions by Medici (1937), Famularo (1947), Di Cocco (1960) and Forte (1968) developed a structure for valuation theory. The fundamental principles of valuation can be summarized as: firstly, that value is an estimate of price; secondly, that a valuation is essentially a forecast of future benefits from the property. Further, the appropriate value definition is dictated by the purpose of the valuation and the data on which it is based are of primarily comparable market transactions which represent the current, normal market situation.

9.4.1 Concepts of value

Classical authors define a number of bases of value depending on the purpose of the valuation. For example, market value, construction value, development value, complementary value, replacement value and, for some, capitalization value. Famularo (1947) considered only market value and cost value (or construction value) as fundamental values, defining the others as exceptional ones.

Market value means the value, often coinciding with price, that a property would realize in a hypothetical sale. Construction value or cost is defined as the total cost to construct the property including all ancillary costs. Development value is used to reflect the value of the property when altered technically, legally or economically in such a way as to transform its nature. Development value is given by:

$$Vt = Vm - Kt$$

where Vt is the development value to be estimated, Vm the market value of the asset after development and Kt are the costs required to produce the development.

Complementary value is estimated when an asset is an integral part of a larger group of assets and the value of the property can be defined only in relation to the entire group. Complementary value is used when a property, which would have little value on its own, is married with other assets. This basis of value is often used in compulsory purchase to take into account damages that the removal of a property could cause the owner. Therefore:

$$Vc = Vm - Vm'$$

where Vc is the complementary value of the property to be valued, Vm is the market value of the entire group of assets and Vm' is the market value of the group of assets less the property to be valued.

Replacement value corresponds to the price (or cost) of replacing the property to be valued with a similar property. Capitalization value (or income value) corresponds to the present value of future income produced by the property. Current practice is to consider only market value and construction value as effectively autonomous values (Grillenzoni and Grittani, 1990), relating them to classical and neoclassical economic theories of exchange value and construction value.

The valuation of public property, for which there is no normal market, deserves a separate discussion. Generally, the value of the property relates to its importance in terms of conservation and protection or its use for public utility. In this case a social use value is used, whereby the valuation is expressed in monetary terms, or of total economic value (Pearce *et al.*, 1991) or total social use value (Fusco Girard, 1993) when the valuation is expressed in nominal form.

Before considering the valuation procedures, it is necessary to consider a further characteristic which influences the type of valuation utilized. When the valuation arises from a legal dispute requiring an explicit super partes judgement the valuer must comply with all precepts of objectivity and up-to-date values. On the other hand, when the valuation is required for defining profitability the valuer must take into account any exceptional aspects of the purchaser and of the property (e.g. special capabilities for constructing at lower than average costs, knowledge of probable zoning, development potential, etc.).

9.4.2 Valuation methods

In terms of methodology, the preferred approach is the comparative method. Different procedures can be identified for arriving at the valuation of the property. The valuation can be classified as direct (synthetic) or indirect (analytical), depending on the way the comparative method is applied. [Originally, a distinction was made between empirical procedures (based on direct comparisons with the market) and rational procedures (based on analyses of the accounts book of the agrarian enterprise and then on the capitalisation of income).] In brief, the valuation procedure for direct comparison is based on the assumption that the value of a property must be compared to that of a known similar property.

Variations in the valuation will therefore reflect different attributes across the comparable properties.

Analytical (or indirect) valuation procedures are related to the income capitalization system for the assessment of market value and to the computation of unit prices for the cost value. In the former, having estimated rental income and capitalization rate, financial formulas are used for the calculation. In a simplified case of constant, deferred, unlimited annual income, the following is the formula:

$$Vx = \frac{R}{r}$$

where Vx is the value to be estimated, R is the net capitalizable income and r is the capitalization rate.

9.4.3 Comparison

Generally, the unit of comparison is related to similar properties in terms of floor area, age, condition, etc. Other comparative indicators, e.g. value of the business or rental contracts, are rarely used due to difficulties in recognizing a direct connection between property value variations and variations in the indicators. In estimating the market value of commercial buildings, the most utilized parameter is floor area. The two most utilized definitions are net floor surface, which includes external and internal walls plus specified parts of the external appartenances (commercial surface), and conventional surface which comprises the net surface plus a percentage of common areas. In industrial and hotel buildings volume parameters such as number of rooms can be used. The choice of the parameter, when it is not dictated by specific regulations (in the case of public buildings), is generally tied to local usage and custom. Comparative data are published by the Chambers of Commerce, Industry, Agriculture and Crafts.

9.4.4 Cost-based methods

Cost-based methods for calculating market value are often not very practicable in Italy, primarily due to the influence of two factors which may distort the valuation. Firstly, difficulties in calculating the land and building costs, especially in large urban areas, makes the application of internationally recognized procedures complicated. For example, there are difficulties in estimating the value of the land in its highest and best use, and the value of the building, depreciated to take account of age. Such methods are extremely problematic largely due to the lack of transparency in the Italian real estate market. Secondly, development rights in Italy are tied to landownership, except for relatively limited cases of projects supported by public financing. However, this situation may change as development activity becomes more sophisticated.

A consequence is that development value outside of ownership is absent in the Italian context. The price is therefore determined through negotiations which may favour the property owner or the purchaser, but which often exclude the highest and best use for the land.

Valuations for market value related to construction cost remain confined to special cases. For example, a person interested in purchasing a large complex for manufacturing or service industry could evaluate the profitability of the operation by comparing, as an alternative, the price of the land and construction of the required buildings. This scenario involves the utilization of data from the market with profitability valuations of individual operators in order to determine the balance between respective profit margins (Zorzi, 1994). In contrast, the practice of using replacement value is fairly widespread for defining indemnities for insurance companies in the event of total or partial damage to property. In this case, the insured value is not the market value but the replacement value (or depreciated cost) of a property which is considered separate from the site.

9.4.5 Sources of cost information

The difficulty in applying valuation procedures based on cost arise from the paucity of public information on the value of building land. Consequently, it is not possible to quantify increases in value resulting from development activity. At most, only average values of agricultural land can be obtained, conventionally defined by fiscal officers for registering real estate, or analysed for certain territorial precincts by university study centres. The large difference in value between agricultural and building land makes such information of little significance in assessing the value of land and buildings.

Information related to construction costs is generally easier to obtain. Studies conducted by the Central Institute of Statistics (ISTAT) on a provincial basis are available, although in aggregate form and in indexes. Price lists are issued periodically within territorial precincts (although not for all provinces) which itemize unit prices (from the Chambers of Commerce or other entrepreneurial and professional organizations) to be applied to building elements.

9.4.6 Treatment of depreciation

In order to estimate depreciated cost value, the economic and physical life of the building must first be identified. In this context it is assumed that the cost value becomes close to zero at the end of the useful life of the building (except for any residual value attributable to the recovery of reusable materials). The residual value, at time t_i, is obtained through interpolation of the value of the initial cost and the final cost (verging on zero), then adding the market value of the land to produce a final valuation.

9.4.7 Income/investment method

Valuations based on the capitalization of income represent a classical approach to determining market value. Key aspects include the determination of the capitalizable income and the discount rate. The income to be capitalized is estimated through an analysis of rental income, whereas the net income would be compared with similar properties.

When the rental contract is to be considered, the following formula is used:

$$C - (Q + Sf + In + Amm + I + Tr)$$

where C is the annual gross rent, Q is the amortization, maintenance and insurance rates, Sf is a percentage related to the risk of not being able to rent the property for a certain period, In is a percentage related to the risk of not being able to collect the rent from the tenant, Amm is the management expenses, I is the interest on ownership expenses, distributed evenly throughout the year and *Tr* is taxes.

The capitalization rate is estimated through direct market comparison or with similar investments. When there is sufficient market data the capitalization rate is estimated as a ratio between income and the value of similar property using the following formula:

$$r = \frac{\sum R}{\sum V}$$

where *r* is the rate required, *R* is the income of property similar to the one being evaluated and *V* is the market value of similar property.

When market data are not available the same formula can be used, related to assets that represent similar investments for duration, degree of security and interchangeability on the market. In the absence of such information, analyses of investments on the financial market may be used (e.g. returns from public debt bonds), especially when the valuation is used for assessing profitability. Once the capitalizable income and the capitalization rate have been defined the valuer must also consider the time element which is related to the degree of utilization of the asset.

9.5 DATABASE MANAGEMENT – SOURCES OF DATA

In general, there are few sources of prices of land and buildings, and as these are not highly reliable there is, therefore, a lack of market transparency. There is an official source, the Real Property Registry Office, where details of individual transactions are recorded. The Registry Offices are at a provincial level but, unfortunately, do not furnish printouts on registered deeds. The checking of deeds and prices is therefore a laborious task since not all offices have been computerized. Information on prices is consequently not drawn from data from the deeds but from interviews with brokers in the sector.

Il Consulente Immobiliare ('*The Real Estate Consultant*'), a magazine for real estate agents, provides a quarterly review of prices for new and second-hand residential properties in the provincial capital cities since 1964. Another source is the report by Nomisma, a research centre in Bologna, in which data on prices and rents of residential dwellings, shops, offices and indicators on demand and supply are published on a six month basis for the principal cities. CRESME, a research centre in Rome, provides information on prices and rents. Sources that involve specific local markets can also be found.

There are no sources for management costs. However, it is possible to obtain information on maintenance costs from some public building management agencies (IACP, Institute of Public Housing). There is an official source for construction costs, i.e. the *Annuario* (annual book) on building activity and public works compiled by ISTAT (National Institute of Statistics). Unfortunately, this source suffers from long delays before publication. At a regional level, updated data on costs are available on a monthly or quarterly basis on the price of building materials, transportation and labour costs from the Regional Commissions.

With regard to planning permission for land or buildings, inquiries can be made at the Municipal Technical Office in which the land or building is located. There are no sources relative to investment yields in the real estate sector. Traditionally, the results of an investment valuation (e.g. IRR) are commonly compared to the yields from government bonds (at no risk) for a similar period of time.

9.6 PRACTICAL APPLICATION OF TECHNIQUES

From a practical point of view, the assembly of comparable data requires careful attention to detail depending on the type of valuation. When evaluating property values of similar properties with updated prices must be researched. Ideally, they should differ from the subject property by only one parameter, for example, floor size. Valuations of large properties, other than by the comparison-based method, use in addition the capitalization method. The two values are then reconciled. Investment valuations, which are less common, utilize discounted cash flow analysis.

Current practice for commercial property investment valuations utilize indirect procedures based on the capitalization of the net income. The risk factor is considered by incorporating a risk premium in the valuation, for example the discount rate applied in DCF may indicate zero risk by using the yield from government bonds for a similar period. Once the IRR has been determined, the difference between this and the discount rate indicates the investment risk premium and, consequently, the profit threshold for the investor. In more detailed analyses a probability analysis would identify the most significant variables.

There is no defined standard for the final report, although it usually contains a description of the property, development potential subject to planning regulations, the method of valuation; sources of data; the outcome of the valuation and additional considerations. Unfortunately, especially in the evaluation of investments, there is often an exceedingly optimistic attitude on the part of the valuer often wishing to meet investors' expectations. However, a more professional approach would emphasize greater caution with a view to protecting the client's interest.

9.7 CONCLUSION

Italian real estate markets present a number of peculiarities that have been outlined in this chapter; in particular, the lack of market transparency due to difficulty in obtaining reliable information regarding prices, the tax system and to the low risk level that is typical of real estate investments, at least until the 1980s. These elements have influenced the valuation context and from a regulatory point of view have contributed to the specific valuation approach.

Today the situation is changing both as a consequence of the evolution of the real estate market in which a number of structural factors have increased the risk level and as a consequence of the investors' behaviour. However, the demand for valuations of projects for investment purposes is now increasing, together with greater accountability and sophistication in the valuation process.

REFERENCES

Di Cocco, E. (1960) *La valutazione dei beni economici*, Edagricole, Bologna.

Famularo, N. (ed.) (1947) *La stima dei fabbricati*, Calderini, Bologna.

Ferguson, J. and Heizer, J. (1990) *Real Estate Investment Analysis*, Allyn and Bacon, Needham Heights, p. 187.

Forte, C. (1968) *Elementi di estimo urbano*, Etas Kompass, Milano.

Fusco Girard, L. (1987) *Risorse architettoniche e culturali: valutazioni e strategie di conservazione*, F. Angeli, Milano.

Fusco Girard, L. (ed.) (1993) *Estimo ed economia ambientale: le nuove frontiere nel campo della valutazione*, F. Angeli, Milano.

Grillenzoni, M. and Grittani, G. (1990) *Estimo. Teoria, procedure di valutazione e casi applicativi*, Edagricole, Bologna.

Medici, G. (1937) *Lezioni di Estimo*, Zanichelli, Bologna.

Pearce, D., Markandya, A. and Barbier, E. (1991) *Progetto per un'economia verde*, Il Mulino, Bologna.

Pollo, R. and Prizzon, F. (1993) Economic life evaluation and maintenance technology, in Papers W55 CIB International Symposium on Economic Evaluation and the Built Environment, Lisbon.

Serpieri, A. (1917) *Il metodo di stima dei beni fondiari*, Ricci, Firenze.

Simonotti, M. (1990) L'evoluzione della metodologia estimativa tradizionale. *Genio Rurale*, **2**, 11.

Zorzi, F. (1994) I beni immobili non residenziali. *Genio Rurale*, **5**.

The Netherlands 10

Gerjan Vos and
George ten Have

This chapter examines valuation theory and techniques as utilized in the Netherlands with particular emphasis upon application for investment and loan security purposes. Initially the market structure of brokerage is considered, as it provides the institutional context within which valuation practice is set. Consideration of market data and sources available in the Netherlands are evaluated, followed by a discussion on tenure forms, property rights and rental agreements. The basis of valuation is reviewed from a theoretical perspective and is supported by examples relating to investment and loan security.

10.1 MARKET STRUCTURE FOR BROKERAGE ACTIVITIES

10.1.1 Property market

As in many other countries, over the last 35 years there has been a fundamental change in the ownership of commercial property in the Netherlands. Institutional investors have for the greater part taken over the ownership of prime property which formerly was in the hands of owner-occupiers or small private investors. Little research was undertaken in this market sector until the 1970s and, as a consequence, valuation techniques were similarly neglected. Since then research into both markets and techniques has taken place, at the same time as the growing wealth and influence of institutional investors in society and on the economy. However, as a result of poor domestic and foreign property market returns over the last decade, valuation methods and property as an investment vehicle are being reappraised. Several issues are now on the agenda of the institutional investor. Certainly, investors are only willing to invest in property assets if both return and performance are sound. According to Kohnstamm (1995) more reliable data are required, thereby permitting better insight in relation to true market value and reliable valuations of individual properties, diversification benefits (risk reduction) of property portfolios; renewed questioning concerning the share

European Valuation Practice. Edited by Alastair Adair, Mary Lou Downie, Stanley McGreal and Gerjan Vos. Published in 1996 by E & FN Spon, London. ISBN 0 419 20040 1

of real estate in a mixed portfolio; revising the property risk/return profile and taking into account market inefficiency; and reappraising internal strategies regarding illiquidity of direct property, currency hedging, political/legal aspects of property, outsourcing market expertise and capacity.

Moreover, as property cycles recur at varying intervals, caused by the general economic cycle and the sentiment of players in the property sector, much more attention is currently focused on the direct income element of property. Education of property agents in the Netherlands has traditionally concentrated on vocational training, but investors now are championing the need for specialized property people.

10.1.2 Institutional framework and guidelines

In the Netherlands the title of a valuer and the execution of valuations is not legally protected, whereas, in comparison, the title of a sworn broker (who can also be a valuer) is protected by court law. Several requirements are demanded to become a sworn broker in real estate and the activities of professional bodies are directed, amongst others, to the improvement of the quality of professional practice. The largest institutional body representing agents in the Netherlands is the 'Dutch association of sworn property brokers' (the NVM), which produces reports and vocational training on a regular basis, including the discussion of many aspects of valuation. Indeed, the way in which valuations are produced is guided, in a limited way, by the NVM and by (case) law. The NVM has, for example, established some rules regarding the relation between the valuation report, the type of valuation and the fee. Until February 1994 conditions and rates for NVM agents were standardized, currently there is free competition within general NVM guidelines. However, it should be noted that as there is no legal framework with respect to valuation methods, the value of property is considered to be a matter of professional judgement. Valuations account for, on average, 10% of the annual turnover of property agents though there is a clear demand for higher quality appraisals for both investment and legal reasons. NVM agents take *c*. 75% of the housing market and *c*. 60% of the commercial market.

10.1.3 Training

A professional examination is required to become a sworn property broker. This consists of a theoretical component (a one year written course providing the SVM diploma) and a practical component (test of competence). The theoretical examination is legally supervised by state representatives and the examination for the practical element is supervised by a committee of the Chamber of Commerce (de Kousemaeker, 1994). A weakness of this basic course is the low level of emphasis given to valuation and therefore new members of the NVM have to follow another two year seminar course. Thereafter these agents acquire full NVM membership. A further two year seminar program offers specialization in areas (called sections) such as: property management, mortgage finance, commercial and industrial property, and agricultural property. These courses, which are to a relatively high level, include extensive consideration of valuation and are designed for brokers working in these specialized areas. NVM agents who complete the course relating to the above specified sections, acquire membership of the NVM/BOG-Section. Since 1989, the University of Amsterdam together with the NVM and the Dutch Society of Property Developers have offered a part-time post-graduate course in investment and property studies. This academic course, which is an extensive training programme of two years duration (comparable with a one year full-time academic course), received professional recognition by the Royal Institution of Charted Surveyors (RICS) (UK) in 1994.

10.1.4 Legal responsibility

In conditions relating to a valuation, the NVM requires that the agent is liable for the correct information in the report and for a correct methodology in determining the value estimate. A deviation of 10% of the fair market price is accepted in practice, depending on the marketability of the property. The valuation report for dwellings normally consists of a few pages, describing the building, the relevant real estate market, a photograph of the building and statement of value. For commercial property the economic scenario for the specific property and the property market are included, together with zoning and planning considerations. Only for special purposes will a client require a large, extensive market report and valuation.

10.1.5 Bases of valuation

In practice there are many value definitions used for different purposes. The estimate used in many cases for property is *de onderhandse verkoopwaarde in verhuurde staat*, translated as 'the actual market value on the date of valuation'. This value is the price which could be achieved by a willing seller offering the fully rented property, after best preparation, to the highest bid of willing buyers (not being the tenant) (ten Have, 1992).

10.1.6 Application of valuation methods

The appropriate method depends on the availability of information, the purpose of the valuation, use and type of the property. For income-producing real estate the sales comparison method is commonly used. The gross or net initial yield is used as a capitalization factor for the initial rental income, with determination of the yield and rental income based on market evidence of comparable transactions. As these comparable figures are not published, or may not be readily available, the justification of a certain yield is therefore difficult and the argument is commonly not presented in the valuation report. The discounted cash flow method is sometimes used by property agents using specialized software applications, but is more commonly used by institutional investors to calculate the internal rate of return of an investment proposition.

10.2 MARKET DATA

In general, reliable data on property transactions (prices, rents, yields) are not publicly available. Data on ownership and transaction price of property is available at the state controlled Property Register (*Kadaster*) but these data are not considered to be particularly useful for valuations or for investment purposes. As a consequence the NVM, the larger agencies and consultants, and investors gather data on an in-house basis. Nevertheless some indices are published on a regular basis, for example for owner-occupied housing and the prime commercial property market. Information on the stock, supply, absorption and vacancy in the commercial market is also limited though some financial papers publish data annually for the office, retail and industrial market. Similarly, the level of property data on a regional or local scale is also variable, only partly complete and not publicly available.

The owner-occupied housing market is an exception in that very good data are available for members of the NVM organization, as every NVM broker is obliged to directly report through a central computer system any properties offered for sale or for letting. The system includes a comprehensive operator guidance service containing the history of nearly one million houses, including information on any previous transaction for a specific property. The availability of sufficient reliable data on the housing market enables agents to estimate accurate values by computer, suitable for individual valuations and mass appraisals, including the use of advanced statistical techniques.

The application of mass appraisal techniques was stimulated by the decision of the Dutch government in 1994 that valuations for tax purposes should be made in a uniform manner. The enabling legislation included a new instruction which provided rules for the valuation of every type of property. In this context the NVM multiple listing system is extremely useful, although currently the information for commercial property and owner-occupied business property is not yet of the same quality level as that relating to residential property. In addition, some large cities are building up their own database suitable for mass appraisals, thereby enhancing the capabilities for the application of statistical modelling techniques (Francke, 1995; ten Have, 1994).

Another recent stimulus for valuation has been the creation of the so called ROZ – IPD property index, established in 1994, of which the first results will be available in 1995. The index measures, in a uniform way, the return and performance of property portfolios held by Dutch institutional investors and is constructed in a similar fashion to the IPD index for the UK. In constructing the index the same range of data has to be gathered for each property and valued in a uniform way either by an in-house expert or by an external appraiser. It is considered that the valuation instructions for the index will create more homogeneity in the market (more reliable data) and, in particular, the way in which valuations are carried out. Research in this field pointed out that valuation estimates for comparable properties, executed by different agents, showed an indefensible spread of outcomes, however, after setting a uniform valuation instruction the distribution of appraisal estimates came into an acceptable range of variation (Hordijk, 1994).

The type of information which is available for the commercial property market in Amsterdam is similar in nature to that available for major urban areas in the UK. For example, rental levels and yield information are available for the office market and prime retailing locations in Amsterdam such as the Kalverstraat (Figures 10.1 and 10.2).

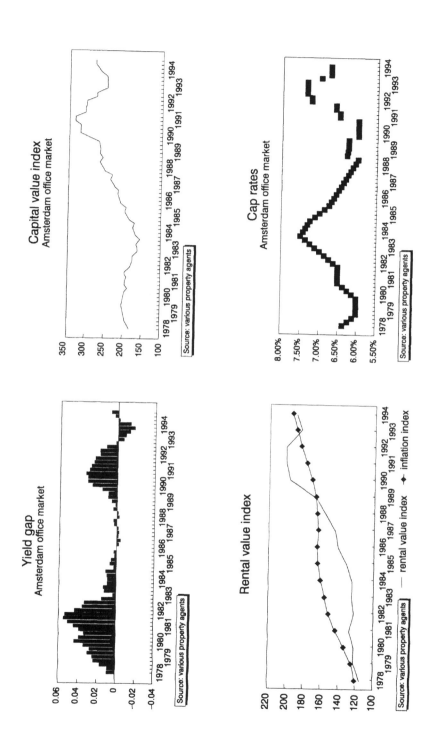

Figure 10.1 Amsterdam office market; rents, yields, capital value, yield gap.

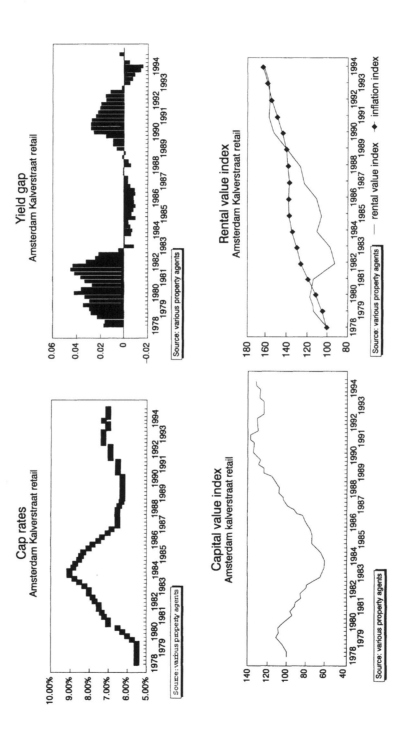

Figure 10.2 Amsterdam high street retail, Kalverstraat; rents, yields, capital value, yield gap.

10.3 THE RENTAL AGREEMENT

10.3.1 Types of ownership

Real estate in the Netherlands is commonly owned freehold, though a form of condominium ownership also exists. In some cities long-term leasehold owner-ship (ground leases) is common. Leases can be for terms of 50 or 90 years, or longer, and the leaseholder either pays a ground rent (reviewable) or a fixed cap-ital sum which covers the entire term of ownership, or ownership in infinity. It is possible for landowners to put restrictions on the future use of the land and also for rights over the property to be created. The distinction between legal and equi-table ownership is unknown under Dutch law, a system based on the Code Napoleon from the nineteenth century. Almost identical arrangements to those in the UK are however achievable, by making a distinction between legal and eco-nomic ownership. However, these so called leasing contracts (not to be confused with the entirely different concept of leasehold real rights) are relatively new and the market is still limited (Arthur Andersen, 1994).

10.3.2 Renting

The most common method of letting commercial property is by a rental agree-ment (a contractual right) between the landlord and the tenant (see Figure 10.3). The provisions are subject to general rules, for example the rental contract can-not be traded or transferred without consent of both owner and tenant. In the case of non-retail property the rental contract is subject to a limited number of formal requirements and rules. Tenant protection exists for short contracts with long-term agreements negotiable, after the rental term expires (commonly a five years term), the tenant has limited protection for one to three years. In comparison rental contracts, with respect to retail and restaurants, are subject to more mandatory provisions, the agreement covers a period of at least five years and is automatically extended to 10 years. If the agreement has not been terminated after the 10 year period it will continue for an indefinite period, unless parties have agreed otherwise. In the residential sector a high level of tenant protection exists.

10.3.3 Rents and rent reviews

Regarding floorspace calculation, commonly the valuation is reduced to a unit of comparable information based on value per size unit. The '*Dutch normalisatie instituut*' has developed a standard on 'Areas and volumes of buildings; terms definitions and methods of determination' (NEN 2580) in which the standard units of value are priced per m^2 net internal area (net lettable floor surface). Concerning the basis of rents, the rental level will be set at open market level per m^2 per annum. The rent review frequency and the basis of review for non-retail property will be open market level review yearly or otherwise depending on the content of the agreement. For retail the review is every five years, based on average rental market level during the last five years (the legal adjusted rental value), with an annual rental indexation, for every type of property, based on the consumer price index.

10.3.4 Deregulation

As in many other countries in Europe, governmental deregulation has been a policy to encourage the operation of the property market. New liberalized policies are being formulated regarding the brokerage of property, the rental agreements and rent reviews; the freeing of opening hours for retail premises; policies for the establishment of new retail activities, especially the opening of large-scale shopping malls. In relation to rental contracts there will be more protection for the tenant for all property types: moving to a five year duration of the agreement with an option for a further five years, and protection for an indefinite period after 10 years (Figure 10.3). For the retail sector the change will be more freedom to determine the basis of rents set at open market level.

10.4 THE BASIS OF VALUATION METHODS

10.4.1 Valuation methods

Valuation is at the heart of any transaction where property is traded, such as a purchase for investment purposes or where a mortgage loan is granted in exchange for a guarantee on property. The value of an asset can be seen as a reflection of both the quantity and quality of information. This is in accordance with one of the most important ideas in modern economics, namely that prices reflect all knowable information. Property agents fulfil the role of interpreting the information set which is relevant to the valuation.

Moreover, the concept of value is a purpose concept with different concepts for different purposes. As a result, value concepts vary between each other and appraisals can cover a number of different requirements in the field of accounting, taxation, insurance, mortgage, performance management and development. Thus, there are different terms available and in common usage, namely actual market value, current use value, redevelopment value, insurance value, mortgage value and going-concern value. Arguably the most important, the actual market value, may be required in different situations and for several purposes. It presents the property exchange value at a single point in time.

Valuers apply several methods and techniques to arrive at a certain value. Using information type as a criterion, valuation methods can be divided into three categories, namely methods which use historic information (such as book value or historic investment prices), actual information (such as replacement value or current prices) and future information (such as future gross or net income).

In considering only actual market value five well-known methods can be identified, based on whether actual or future information is applied. Furthermore, each is used as a basis for different purposes and a specific technique is applied to arrive at a calculated value, ranging from a simple assessment of value to a detailed assessment using sophisticated statistical analysis. In the Netherlands the comparative method, which includes the rental capitalization technique, is the most frequently used approach while the other methods are applied less often.

1. Rental agreement

Duration

Non retail: mostly 5 yrs, continuing for further 1–5 yrs unless terminated
Retail: minimum of 5 yrs, automatically continued for a further 5 yrs

Right to renew

Non-retail: no automatic right; commonly option to renew for 1–5 yrs. Tenant can be evicted after 1–3 yrs, but not easy.
Retail: lease continues unless terminated in prescribed form by landlord, high security of tenure (break option for tenant after first 10 yrs).

Assignability, subletting

No rights unless agreed in lease (no leaseholds). Retail tenant is entitled to assign lease to buyer of his business.

Grant of lease

Generally drawn up by landlord or agent. A verbal offer can constitute a binding contract.

Privity of contract: No privity of contract on assignment of lease

2. Rents and reviews

Determination or basis of rents

Rent will be set at open market level per m^2 per annum.

Floor space calculation excludes

Non-retail: structural walls, stairs/lifts. Use net rental floor area (NEN 2580; definition set by the Dutch normalisation institute)
Retail: use *net* rental area.

Payable quarterly in advance: commonly quarterly in advance

Review frequency, basis of review

Non-retail: open market level review every year, depending on contract
Retail: every 5 years, based on *average* market level during the last 5 years (law valuation criterion)

Indexation frequency, basis of indexation: Annually based on CPI

3. Liabilities tenant/landlord

Landlord responsible for structural and external repairs, insurance and a proportion of property tax.

4. Property law system, procedures and restrictions

Arbitrators, court, registration
Court proceedings for non-payment of rent. Use of arbitrators in retail; little use in non-retail sector. Registration in public register and notarial instruments are not required for a rental agreement.

Planning law: yes

Investment restrictions (foreign investors): no
Rent control: no
Rental contract reforms: yes

5. Transaction costs for investors (taxes, fees)

Valuation: agent's fee: 1.25–2.00% per thousand guilders, depending on property value
Purchase: costs (7%) plus agent's fee (1.5–2%) related to a sale are usually paid by a purchaser.

Figure 10.3 The standard rental agreement (landlord–tenant relationship in the Netherlands for business property).

Information basis of valuation methods for actual market value

Actual information   *Future information*
Comparative method   Income method (DCF)
Cost method   Profits method
Residual method

(a) Comparison of capital values and rental values

The estimated value of property is based on market evidence of comparable transactions. The comparative method requires a representative number of examples of recent sales of property and takes a common measure between these comparable properties and the one to be valued. The method is usually applied to property types for which market evidence is available in the form of transactions (such as the housing market). However, it is also used for an estimate of value in rental transactions and for yield estimate in investment transactions, thereby capitalizing the initial net rental income. As a consequence the capitalization technique is considered to belong to the family of comparative methods.

(b) Cost-based methodology

This method approaches an estimate based on the expenses of newly-built property, taking into account the state of repair and depreciation. In its simplest form it requires taking the actual cost of replacing the property for the existing use and deducting the cost of renovating the building to be valued. Often certain depreciation factors are applied based on the future life expectancy of the different construction elements of the building taking into account the technical, economical and functional degree of obsolescence. The actual market value received using this method is also referred to as the adjusted replacement value. The method is used as a basis of last resort, where there is no transaction market in the property asset to be valued. The replacement value and cost method are also applied for balance sheet valuations when a firm is the owner-occupier of the property.

(c) Residual method

This method uses actual information on prices and cost elements of new buildings for the appraisal of a property (or a piece of land) with development potential. It is a residual approach in that the solution is a residue of income after expenditure. The income element is represented by the expected selling price of the redeveloped property on the basis of comparison. Deducting from this price the actual expenses for construction results in the market value of the existing property (or existing site). The method is considered to belong to the family of the cost methods.

(d) Income method

In this case the valuation estimate is based on the income-producing characteristics of the property. The property is seen as an investment good and the method involves a discounted cash-flow calculation (DCF) of expected future net income. The procedure takes the form of either an explicative DCF or a reduced

DCF. The former explicitly determines the current value of future net rental income streams, discounted at an interest rate which compensates for the riskiness of the property. The cash flow will be assessed after a detailed survey of the property and its location and will reflect the valuer's expectations concerning the future potential use of the property. In contrast, the reduced DCF method is the all-risk yield approach, involving the capitalization of the initial net income. The multiplier (the reciprocal of the all-risk yield) is often obtained by comparison of similar property transactions, thus this reduced DCF technique is also considered to belong to the family of the comparison methods.

(e) Profits method

Profits-based methods are often used for speciality property (for instance in the leisure sector: e.g. hotels, cinemas) and is based on the future income element of the activity housed in the building. These buildings are designed for a particular use with price reflecting the trading potential for that particular use. When the market value for existing use is required and recent comparable transactions are not available, as is frequently the case, these properties are usually valued by a profits method. The method first assesses the net profit from the business operations (excluding housing expenses). The profit assessment is the product of information from the actual accounts and the valuer's expertise in the business sector. This profit can be split into a rental value attached to the property and a premium (goodwill) for the running of the business. In the end the rental value is capitalized as an investment representing the market value of the property.

10.4.2 Theoretical background of the capitalization technique

As property may not always be traded in an open market, or because access to information in an open market is often limited, the professional valuer needs to fill the information gap by developing knowledge of individual properties and market transactions. Only with an assessment of true market value or investment value is it possible to tell whether a property is under or overpriced relative to its market price. The framework in which the investment decision takes place is not principally different from other investment markets. Indeed, the most common types of valuation methods to assess market value are commensurate with the dividend discount models. Under the capitalization technique the conventional method of calculating the actual price of a property with an adjusted cash flow received annually in arrears is expressed as:

$$P_O = R_O / p \qquad (10.1)$$

where $p = k - g$, and P_O is the actual market value (capital value), R_O the initial net rental market value, p the initial net yield or all-risk yield, k the discount rate (required average rate of return) and g the annual expected average growth rate in rental income.

Although valuers are aware of the required rate of return and growth rates, for simplicity they prefer to make use of initial rental yields, which is the difference between the required rate of return and the growth rate.

In practice, rental contracts sometimes appear to be fixed for a certain number of years with periodic rent reviews. Thus, rents are not adjusted on a yearly basis but a periodic rent review pattern is included. If the period between two rent adjustments is n years then, using the DCF model and after elimination, the market value can be calculated as follows:

$$P_O = \frac{R_O}{k - k\left[(1+g)^n - 1/(1+k)^n - 1\right]} \qquad (10.2)$$

where n is the period between rent reviews.

The initial yield being $p = R_O / P_O$ (Equation 10.1) substitution will give:

$$p = k - k\frac{(1+g)^n - 1}{(1+k)^n - 1} \qquad (10.3)$$

These general formulae express the mathematical relationship between the initial yield, the rental and capital growth, and the average total return of the property with the value of property estimated by capitalizing the net initial rental value with the help of the all-risk yield (in the Netherlands called the *NAR*). It can be seen that, with annual rent review periods ($n = 1$), Equation 10.2 reduces to Equation 10.1.

In Equation 10.3 the initial net yield implies a certain rate of rental growth for a given required rate of return at a given moment in time. If, for instance, with annual rent reviews, $p = 7\%$ is known from market evidence and the discount rate $k = 10\%$, then the implied rate of expected average rental growth is $g = 3\%$. Similarly, given the required total return $k = 10\%$ and the rental growth rate $g = 3\%$, then the yield (and the capital value) of the property can be calculated for differing circumstances. For instance, if the rent review period is five years, p will be 7.39%; if the rent review period is one year then p will be 7.0%; and if the yearly expected growth rate is zero, p will be 10.0% (equal to k).

In practice the two-period model is frequently used in those cases where the tenant is not paying the full rental market value. Hence, the valuation contains two income levels. The first is the contractual rent payable until the next renewal of the rental agreement and the second is the current market rent. The contractual rental income can be below or above the level which could be expected at the time of reversion, showing, respectively, a marginal deficit or a surplus for the remainder of the current term. In the Netherlands the term and reversion technique is applied to this type of problem. The marginal income stream is discounted back by using the opportunity cost of money, normally the long-term bond rate plus a risk premium of 2%, as illustrated by the following example.

Example 10.1: Property with rent renewal within three years

1. Underrented property (current market rent 50 000; contractual rent 41 000):

Current market rent	50 000	
Multiplier, or YP perpetuity at 5%	20.0	
		1 000 000
Less deficit (50 000 – 41 000)	9 000	
Multiplier, or YP 3 years at 10%	2.486	
		22 374
Capital value		977 626

2. Overrented property (current market rent 41 000; contractual rent 50 000):

Current market rent	41 000	
Multiplier or YP perpetuity at 8%	12.5	
		512 500
Plus surplus (50 000 – 41 000)	9 000	
Multiplier or YP 3 years at 10%	2.846	22 374
Capital value		534 874

The time period to reversion must be short (say three years), otherwise uncertainty with respect to the rental market level at the time of reversion is too large.

10.4.3 Investment value versus actual market value

Computerized discounted cash-flow models are utilized by individual investors, and a minority of the agents, to estimate the investment value or true market value of properties relative to their market prices or actual market value. These models can deal with irregular rent reviews, different annual discount rates, finance options, tax problems and transaction costs. The advantage of the full DCF models is that they produce an investment value based on *ex-ante* information reflecting the expected underlying economic processes. A disadvantage is the increased number of unknown variables which diminishes the practical value of the model.

The advantage of the simple multiplier model, using only a few variables, is that it is based on market evidence: initial yields are chosen by reference to comparable market transactions and are combined with comparable actual rent levels. However, a potential disadvantage is that it is basically an ex-post approach reflecting the expected actual market price on the date of valuation, assuming that in an efficient market all relevant information is embedded in the variables of the model. Investors will compare the investment value (based on the explicative DCF approach) with the actual market value (based on the simple multiplier model) and draw a conclusion as to whether the property is under or overpriced. Hence, they apply both value estimates and methods in a purchase/ sale model to allocate their funds as illustrated in the example below.

In addition, the calculated investment value of the property is often compared with the return on an investment purchase in a state bond (a fixed loan). The outcome of such a comparison is the maximum purchase price of the property to be paid by the investor measured against the return characteristics of an alternative investment in a riskless bond. It is a maximum price because the comparison does not take into account that investment in property is risky and, as a consequence, the calculated value is in fact too high.

Example 10.2: Valuation of a shop

Comparison/rental capitalization method
The date of valuation is 31/12/94 with all prices in Dutch guilders (Dfl). The valuation is carried out for a possible buyer of the shop in a medium to large city. The property is fully rented and owned by a pension fund.

Zoning of high street shop units is frequently carried out using a zoning measure of 10 m, with a depreciation factor of 50%. Assuming the shop is 6 m wide and 36 m deep, this gives 109.5 m² of net lettable surface.

$$
\begin{array}{llll}
\text{Zone A} & 6\ m \times 10\ m \times 100\% & = & 60\ m^2\ \text{ITZA} \\
\text{Zone B} & 6\ m \times 10\ m \times 50\% & = & 30\ m^2\ \text{ITZA} \\
\text{Zone C} & 6\ m \times 10\ m \times 25\% & = & 15\ m^2\ \text{ITZA} \\
\text{Zone D} & 6\ m \times 6\ m \times 12.5\% & = & \underline{4.5 m^2}\ \text{ITZA}
\end{array}
$$

Total 109.5 m² ITZA

Sales comparison analysis shows that the market rent is Dfl1500/m² in terms of zone A (ITZA), which is the legal adjusted rental value for the shop being the average comparable market rent during the last five years. This legal rent level, which must be proven, will incur some costs for the landlord. The rental contract will end on 31/12/97, thus the valuation is three years away from the renewal and rent review. The standard duration of agreement is five years.

Input data	31/12/1994
Contract rent/m²	1386
Market rent/m²	1500
Net lettable surface ITZA	109 m²
Duration lease (standard five years)	3 years
Average annual indexation CPI	2.5%
Landlord's rental outgoings (local tax, insurance, management, maintenance, reservation structural repairs, etc.)	16 021
No vacancy	

Starting with the net market rent, the shop is capitalized on a net yield basis and comparison indicates a net initial yield of 7.5% for this property. The rental deficit, being the difference between the market rent and the contract rent, will be discounted back for three years (payments received quarterly in advance) against a rate of 9%, being the long-term capital market rate of 7% to which a risk premium of 2% is added.

Current market rent (109 m² ITZA × Dfl1500)	163 500	
Less actual outgoings (10.75%)	16 021	
Net market rent	147 479	
Multiplier or YP perpetuity at 7.5%	13.33	
		1 966 387
Less deficit	12 426	
Multiplier or YP 3 years at 9%		
(Q in advance)	2.657	
		33 016
Less cost fee for adaptation rent differential		10 000
Less immediate repairs		15 000
Capital value		1 908 371
Less transfer costs (tax, notary) at 8%		141 361
Property sale value for purchaser		**1 767 010**

DCF method

In additional to the information already given concerning the shop premises, the following is specified for the DCF calculation:

Input data	31/12/1994
Average indexation outgoings	3.75%
Ground value	1 200 000
Depreciation period building	40 years
Required discount rate DCF	9%

The discounted cash flow produces an explicit cash flow output of all items calculated over a period of 40 years, including the depreciation costs of the building (Table 10.1). On this basis an investment value can be estimated for every required holding period of the property. The investment value at the date of valuation (year 0) reflects a holding period of 40 years. Similarly, year 10 reflects an investment value of Dfl2 769 000 being the net present value of the property with a future cash flow of 30 years from that date.

Table 10.1 DCF cash flow and investment value (in Dfl1000)

Year	Gross c.f.	Outgoings	Net c.f	Investment value
0				2.231
1	151	16	135	2.289
2	155	17	138	2.349
3	159	17	142	2.410
4	175	18	157	2.461
5	180	19	162	2.512
10	204	22	182	2.769
11	209	23	187	2.821
20	261	31	231	3.268
21	268	32	236	3.312
30	335	43	292	3.577
31	343	44	298	3.584
38	408	57	351	3.387
39	418	59	359	3.312
40	428	61	367	3.222

Similarly to the comparison method, the estimated property sale value for the purchaser will be established as follows:

Investment value (DCF)	2 230 821
Less cost fee for adaptation rent differential	10 000
Less immediate repairs	15 000
Capital value	2 205 821
Less transfer costs (tax, notary) at 8%	163 395
Property sale value for purchaser	2 042 426

The output of the DCF results in a capital value of Dfl2 205 821 on the date of valuation, implying a surplus of Dfl297 450 relative to the capital value of the comparison method of Dfl 908 371 (both before transfer costs). Hence, the investor will conclude that the property can be purchased in the market at a lower price relative to its expected investment value and will probably take such a course of action. In such circumstances the internal rate of return will be well above the required rate of 9% if the property can be purchased against the price based on the comparison method, confirmation of which is shown by comparing initial yields (Table 10.2). The DCF net yield is 6.69% relative to the comparison net yield of 7.73%

Table 10.2 Comparing property's investment value and market value

	Comparison method	DCF method
Capital value	1 908 371	2 205 821
Gross rental market value	163 500	163 500
Net rental market value	147 479	147 479
Gross initial yield	8.57%	7.41%
Net initial yield	7.73%	6.69%

10.5 VALUATION FOR MORTGAGE LOANS

10.5.1 Financing

Mortgage financing is usually provided by banks, insurance companies and pension funds. Valuation is an important element of financing, specifically the value (execution value) in the event of a forced sale. This value should protect the lender against risk of advancing the loan. The lender will require the loan to be secured by a mortgage on the property and may also require additional security such as personal guarantees. The mortgage interest rates can be either variable or fixed and normally amount to 1–3% above either the published money market or capital market rates, depending on property type and mortgage design. Lenders charge an origination fee of 1–2% of the loan amount.

A long-term lender on non-residential property will usually be prepared to lend up 70% of the execution value, the latter being 75–90% of the actual market value of the property. Effectively this results in a range of a loan:market value lying between 55 and 65%. A higher loan:value ratio is possible but must be compensated by extra interest or guarantees. For dwellings loans of up to 100% of the execution value (90% of market value) are possible though loan conditions can vary depending on the terms agreed. For example, the loan can be paid in instalments or at the end of the loan period, annual accelerated prepayments also are permitted.

10.5.2 Valuations of property for mortgage loan

The actual market value of property is normally appraised when the loan decision is made. In the case of dwellings this is frequently carried out by an independent valuer though on occasions an in-house expert of the lending institution will be used. Business property appraisals are normally carried out by an external valuer. The property will be valued again in case of default of the borrower, when the lender has the right to foreclosure and beneficial title to the property.

In many cases the lender will not sell on the auction market, but will purchase the property and sell it privately, usually in a more profitable way. Only in-house directives of the lender exist concerning the valuation of property.

10.5.3 Housing

In originating a loan several risks are analysed, such as default risk, the degree of affordability and the market timing element. For default risk the loan:value-ratio (LTV) is used as the criterion. For affordability risk the payment:income ratio (PTI) is used, which measures the mortgage burden for a specific borrower. The higher the LTV and the PTI, the higher the probability of default. For market timing risk the market affordability index can be used which measures mortgage payments:income in time, based on market averages per year of mortgage rates, housing prices (calculated from transactions) and family incomes. For example, a relatively high index point means that the average dwelling at that time is not particularly affordable for an average family (Figure 10.4). The index combines macro-developments in the housing market, the mortgage capital market and the family income together, while the market timing element can be traced from this index for years with high, low or stable affordability. It is known that for default risk the year of granting the loan is very important. For example, a year with a combination of a high market index and a high LTV ratio for borrowers will result in a higher chance of default for these mortgages and under such circumstances the LTV ratios will be lowered by the institutions and vice versa.

10.5.4 Business property

The credit worthiness of the debtor (owner-occupier) is the most important consideration when making a mortgage loan to a company or organization rather than the value of the property. However, when the debtor is running a property business (and therefore is not the owner-occupier) the situation is different and credit worthiness is dependent on the quality of the property portfolio which the company exploits. In this situation both the short- and long-term trend in

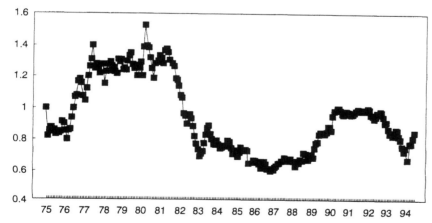

Figure 10.4 The affordability index of housing markets in the Netherlands. ■, Based on figures from NVM and the Central Bureau of Statistics.

property prices is important. Over the short term the strength of the property market is determining the value of a property though over the longer time period market prices are highly correlated with the increase in construction prices.

If a property is of good quality, having market potential and is highly liquid, the LTV ratio may be higher than normally allowed. In this context the future property market value, for instance in five years time, is also appraised and the LTV ratio after five years is compared with the outstanding loan at that time. Two other coverage ratios are also tested: the debt-coverage ratio and the *break-even:cash-flow ratio* (for default risk). The debt-coverage ratio compares the net rental income stream of a property to the annual debt (interest and repayment). Hence, this ratio must preferably be much greater than one; a low ratio means high risk. The break-even ratio considers the annual debt and annual gross property expenses of the borrower relative to the gross rental income stream. This ratio needs to be break-even or preferably lower than one; a high ratio means high risk. In both cases the rental value and its development have to be appraised. Therefore, the rental values and capital values achieved by a property receive considerable attention in the valuation report.

Example 10.3: Valuation of leisure property for mortgage purposes

The leisure activity in this example is a party centre with camping facilities (caravans). The property consists of a main building with rental facilities for parties, a small theatre, a rental dwelling for the leaseholder, land for recreation (camping) and other facilities (such as infrastructure). Mortgage finance is required for a purchaser of the property and therefore a valuation is carried out. The valuation for the main building is based on a gross yield capitalization while the other capital elements are based on a costs method. From the accounts and balance sheets of the business the net cash flow is calculated to provide an indication of the affordability of mortgage payments. Finance capacity is calculated by splitting the total appraised capital value into a depreciated value and a residual value. Financing the depreciated value is based on annuity payment (interest and repayment) taking into account the depreciated life of these capital elements. The residual value of the capital is financed only with interest payments (annuity to infinity). Finally, the margin between net profit and mortgage payments is considered as goodwill. When the capitalized value of goodwill is added to the appraised sale value of the property the going-concern value of the business is derived. (In this valuation example the going-concern value excludes the short-term liabilities and short-term assets of the balance sheet). Finally the loan application is evaluated.

Valuation real property

	Dfl
Rental value main building	238 600
Capital value (YP perpetuity gross yield at 12.5%)	1 908 800
Other capital elements (costs method):	
Theatre	98 900
Dwelling	50 000
Land (playground, camping)	374 000

Caravans	198 000
Infrastructure	237 000
Camping facilities	160 000
Inventory antique, curiosa	552 690
Inventory general	853 376
Inventory games	178 257
Inventory kitchen	361 732
Capital value	**4 972 755**
Less transfer costs (6.5%/1.065 of 4 972 755)	303 501
Property sale value for purchaser	**4 669 254**
Plus goodwill (capitalized excess return: 27 792 × 5)	138 960
Going-concern value business	**4 808 214**

Net cash flow calculation of activity

Cash inflow:	Dfl
Turnover rental facilities	302 961
Gross profit restaurant	1 643 859
Turnover camping	203 382
Rents dwelling	5 280
Total income	**2 155 482**

Cash outflow:	
Personnel	793 812
Housing costs	199 973
General costs	173 711
Travelling costs	35 008
Lease costs current assets	17 018
Maintenance costs	2 945
Rental cost real property	11 786
Insurance	31 601
Turnover costs	42 688
Finance costs	10 777
Taxes and other legal costs	4 846
Other	291
Total costs	**1 324 456**
Net cash flow	**831 026**

Finance capacity and goodwill

	Dfl	
Net cash flow	831 026	
Entrepreneurs' salary	125 000	
Available for finance		**706 026**

Less finance costs

	Depreciation value	Residual value	Appraised value
Main building	870 050	1 038 750	1 908 800
Theatre	98 900	0	98 900

Dwelling	10 000	40 000	50 000
Land (camping)	34 000	340 000	374 000
Caravans	198 000	0	198 000
Infrastructure	237 000	0	237 000
Camping facilities	135 000	25 000	160 000
Inventory antique	52 690	500 000	552 690
Inventory general	768 376	85 000	853 376
Inventory games	148 257	30 000	178 257
Inventory kitchen	326 732	35 000	361 732

Finance costs: depreciation value (annuity at 8% for n years)

	Depreciation value	n	i (%)	Annuity
Main building	870 050	30	8	77 284
Theatre	98 900	15	8	11 554
Dwelling	10 000	30	8	888
Land (camping)	34 000	p.m.		0
Caravans	198 000	10	8	29 508
Infrastructure	237 000	10	8	35 320
Camping facilities	135 000	15	8	15 772
Inventory antique	52 690	25	8	4 937
Inventory general	768 376	8	8	133 709
Inventory games	148 257	5	8	37 132
Inventory kitchen	326 732	8	8	56 856
Total				**402 960**

Finance cost: residual value (annuity at 8% in perpetuity)

	Residual value	i (%)	Annuity
Main building	1 038 750	8	83 100
Theatre	0		0
Dwelling	40 000	8	3 200
Land (camping)	340 000	8	27 200
Caravans	0		0
Infrastructure	0		0
Camping facilities	25 000	8	2 000
Inventory antique	500 000	8	40 000
Inventory general	85 000	8	6 800
Inventory games	30 000	8	2 400
Inventory kitchen	35 000	8	2 800
Total			**167 500**

Available for goodwill, risk and profit	**135 566**
Risk and profit (5% of total income)	107 774
Excess profit available for goodwill	**27 792**

Mortgage loan
On the basis of the above valuation the lender will consider the loan

capacity on the basis of the appraised going-concern value of the business and the coverage of finance cost in the profit/loss accounts. The affordable finance costs on the basis of the above statement of appraised assets are Dfl570 460 (402 960 + 167 500).

Going-concern value of the business   **4 808 214**
Affordable finance costs   **570 460**

For business property the lender will normally be prepared to lend up to 75% of the execution value, the latter being 90% of the appraised market value. Effectively this results in a LTV ratio of 67.5%. Therefore, the maximum loan capacity will be Dfl3 245 545 (0.675 × 4 808 214). If the loan is made (for instance an annuity at 8% for 30 years on a loan of 3 245 545), it means a mortgage payment of Dfl288 293 per year which is well below the affordable finance costs of Dfl570 460 covered in the profit/loss accounts.

10.6 CONCLUSION

Institutional ownership of property has been an important characteristic of the market in the Netherlands over the last two to three decades. It is therefore important that reliable data sources and expertise are available. Regarding the former while information sources relating to residential property are highly developed the situation is somewhat different for commercial property. However, the ROZ-IPD index is likely to set new standards and create more homogeneity in the market, particularly in the way in which valuations are carried out. Similarly, progress is being made with respect to education and training with greater specialization in valuation.

In the Netherlands different valuation terms are in common usage, the most important of which, actual market value, is required for different situations and purposes. In arriving at actual market value various techniques are applied. The comparative, cost and residual methods are based upon actual information while the income and profits methods utilize assessments of future information. The most commonly used method in the Netherlands is the comparative method including the rental capitalization technique. Also, within the Netherlands increasing use is being made of computerized discounted cash-flow models to estimate the investment value of property relative to actual market value. The latter is usually compared against the return characteristics of an investment in a riskless bond. Regarding valuations for mortgage purposes considerable emphasis is placed upon different ratios, in particular loan:market value and, for commercial property, the debt coverage ratio and break-even:cash-flow ratio.

REFERENCES

Arthur Andersen (1994) *Investment in Netherlands Real Estate*, Arthur Andersen, Amsterdam.

de Kousemaeker, F.J.M. (1994) *Praktijkaspecten onroerend goed*, Samson Tjeenk Willink, Alphen aan de Rijn.

Francke, M.K. (1995) *De waarde van woningen, een modelmatige aanpak*, Uitgave gemeente belastingen Amsterdam, Stadsdrukkerij.

Hordijk, A. (1994) Will a detailed and uniform set of valuation instructions have a positive impact on real estate risk? Paper presented at the ERES conference, Amsterdam.

Kohnstamm, P.P. (1995) Trends in European investment, performance and real estate education. *Journal of Property Valuation & Investment*, **13** (2), 51–8.

ten Have, G.M. (1992) *Taxatieleer onroerende zaken*, Educatieve Partners, Houten.

ten Have, G.M. (1994) Taxes, a computer assisted mass appraisal. Presented at the International Conference on Property Taxation, Mass Appraisal and Geographic Information Systems, Dublin.

Norway 11

Erik H. Larsen

In Norway valuation is carried out extensively in connection with the sale and financing of real estate property. In this context three principal groups, namely property owners, investors and financiers, utilize the services of valuers. Previously, valuation services were mainly requisitioned by financiers requiring a valuation document as verification of value but also serving as a description of the property's technical condition. With respect to investment in real estate the key actors are property developers, private companies, public authorities (though this is mainly for the disposal of property), property managers and property companies.

The practice of valuation in Norway has a long tradition with the basic duties of a valuer defined by law in 1821. However, there is evidence of valuations having been conducted prior to this. Indeed, a document dated 14 November 1769, mentions the effectuation of a valuation process of farmland property. In 1907 the first laws regulating transactions carried out by financial institutions were passed and subsequent to this a series of by-laws required valuations to be carried out.

The types of property most commonly valued include residential (apartments, semi-detached houses and single-family homes), commercial buildings (office blocks, trading centres, warehouses, hotels), industrial property (manufacturing, research and processing), agricultural property (farmland, forests) and property for specialized use (sports facilities, recreational facilities). In addition to preparing valuation reports for the above property types, the Norwegian valuer is frequently required to give advice on matters such as repair reports; appraisal of planned building projects; valuations in connection with indemnity insurance; preparation of repair and maintenance budgets; in-court and out-of-court settlements between parties in conflict, and valuation for taxation purposes.

Due to the nature of the profession in Norway, the valuer has the standing of being an arbitrator who is completely impartial as to the outcome of the case. Therefore, the valuer is often called upon to mediate in controversial situations requiring a qualified 'common sense' approach for its solution. Such matters are

European Valuation Practice. Edited by Alastair Adair, Mary Lou Downie, Stanley McGreal and Gerjan Vos. Published in 1996 by E & FN Spon, London. ISBN 0 419 20040 1

often settled 'out of court'. Although lawyers frequently encourage such a means of settlement, the valuer may be called as an expert witness in court and, thus, professional integrity is a necessity.

Valuation for both investment and loan security purposes are currently two areas of considerable significance, as during the period of declining property values, from the beginning of 1988 until mid-1993 (Figure 11.1), many financial institutions, especially banks, experienced great losses. These circumstances arose due to general optimism and a willingness to grant loans for the financing of projects, some of which were rather risky. The strategy is now both for greater care and increased security regarding lending transactions, and as a consequence valuation has become one of the most important factors to consider. Insurance companies and other institutions did not experience the same degree of loss, partly because of internal regulations regarding the security required and also possibly due to a more careful approach in general.

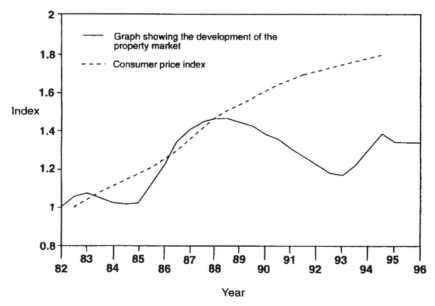

Figure 11.1 Property market and consumer price indices.

11.1 THE VALUATION PROFESSION

The Norwegian Surveyors Association is a nationwide organization consisting of members drawn from all categories of professionals working within the subject of valuation. However, there is no formal recognition or official authorization governing valuation in Norway, though the association is at present engaged in efforts to obtain some form of official recognition, possibly through state licensing or a certification system of valuers. It should nevertheless be emphasized that the lending companies give preference to the services of members of the Norwegian Surveyors Association in the assessment of value concerning both sales and loans.

Members are approved in the following main categories: real estate, industrial property, financial evaluations, agricultural property, vehicles, machinery and construction equipment, vessels and boats, and specialist areas such as fisheries and data equipment. Membership of the association is dominated by those involved in real estate, in total there are approximately 700 members of which some 150 are full-time valuers. The association has its own by-laws, ethical rules and instructions for the completion of valuation documents, all of which the members are obliged to follow.

The aims of the association are:

1. to encourage reliable and objective valuation in accordance with existing laws and by-laws;
2. to further the valuer's proficiency;
3. to further the utilization of experienced valuers;
4. to ensure adequate recruitment to the profession in accordance with the demand for valuation services;
5. to further members' interests and affiliation;
6. to preserve the profession's ethical obligations in accordance with the association's code of ethics.

However, as valuation is not a 'protected' profession, there is a limited number of persons (non-members of the association) who undertake valuation work on a small scale, often without relevant education and, at times, with adverse consequences for the profession.

As there is at present no form of general public educational facility for valuers in Norway, the Surveyors Association runs its own combined correspondence and seminar school for this purpose. The school was originally established in 1981 with the objectives of improving the profession's standing in society; striving towards standardized terminology and standardized valuation certificates; ensuring recruitment of qualified valuers throughout the country; and forming the basis for official authorization.

11.2 LEGISLATION AND REGULATORY PROVISIONS

A number of laws, by-laws and regulations govern valuation in Norway. Many of the legislative regulations are directly related to various valuation objects and therefore bear a direct influence on the value of the property. For example, a law applying to maximum yearly rent payable for flats in apartment blocks built prior to 9 April 1940 in the towns of Oslo and Trondheim. Also, legal regulations regarding land leasing for domiciles specifies the maximum amount to which the yearly rates can be adjusted. Regulations concerning selling prices for flats in building society complexes exist for the first seven years after completion. However, the most important restrictions for the valuer is the law governing land lease, various cost-control directives relating to rental levels and parts of the legislation concerning the building and zoning of areas.

There are no standards for valuation on a national basis and this tends to cause some confusion with regard to the definition of terms. However, the Norwegian Surveyors Association has laid down a set of ground rules which its members are bound to follow. The *Handbook For Valuers*, first published in 1993, contains all the basic rules of valuation and has been distributed to all major users of valuation services. The rules are to some extent also incorporated in the limited liability insurance schemes, compulsory to its members. This initiative plays an important role in setting standards for all who practice valuation, both members and non-members of the recognized association.

The Association also has its own directives for area measurement, correlated with the relevant Norwegian Standard (NS 3940, last revision June 1986). Instructions/guidelines exist for the valuation of residential homes, offices and shops, and industrial property. However, for hotels and leisure/recreational property no guidelines exist.

In Norway no single office or partnership provides for all the services encompassed by financing, estate agency and valuation. Relationships are thus purely on a professional basis with the valuer acting in an advisory role to other professional groups. For example, most financing companies have the requirement that a third-party valuation must be carried out before a loan is granted. In this capacity, the commissioning of a valuer ensures that the property undergoes a thorough inspection with regard to state of repair, usefulness, technical installations and building materials. The valuer's report not only contains a conclusive value, but also gives a number of facts of relevance to various potential users concerning the property. However, the valuer faces a challenge in that increasingly there is the tendency for the nature of valuation work to be biased towards an economic analysis of income and costs using capitalization interest rates, arguably an area of expertise in which financiers claim that they are equally qualified to assess property values. Consequently there is a need for greater sophistication of methodology and reporting practice on the part of the valuer.

Valuers are normally commissioned on a case to case basis with financiers selecting from a short list of potential valuers, with long-standing business relationships important. In geographical areas where the market operates in an efficient manner in terms of both demand and availability, valuation is carried out prior to selling. In other areas where demand is rather more limited, valuation services are requested after the sales transaction is completed. Under these circumstances the valuation provides verification of the 'correctness' of the selling price.

A number of organizations are engaged in the collection and handling of different forms of statistical material used in the prediction of future trends within the real estate market. There is a requirement for analysis to become more sophisticated providing improved and more accurate predictions than in the past. In particular, the need to understand market behaviour is increasingly apparent following the dramatic decline in property values in the period from the late 1980s up until mid-1993, after which prices started to rise as a function of the rather sudden drop in the lending interest rate and a sustained period of low inflation (Figure 11.2). Combined with a high level of demand, outstripping supply, the result has been buoyant market conditions during 1994.

Most of the finance companies require at least the participation of two valuers for the valuation of commercial buildings, though for special cases, such as industrial complexes and hotels, the normal procedure is for three valuers to be involved in the valuation process, often with cooperation between valuers from

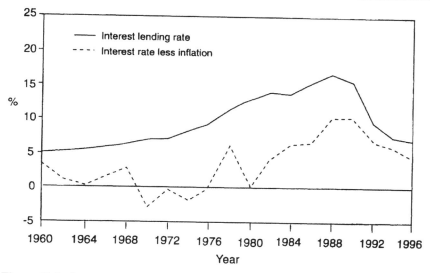

Figure 11.2 Interest rate movement.

different practices to ensure impartiality. Such working relationships are seen to be beneficial both from a point of view of developing expertise and also from the perspective of strengthening the profession's standing in general.

The last decade has shown a marked increase in the number of libel suits filed against valuers and, because of the greater risk and exposure, personal liability insurance has become a necessity. This is not necessarily as a result of bad workmanship but reflects the public's increased use of the courts for trying minor disputes. The situation must also be seen in the light of the general decline in market prices in the early 1990s, resulting in persons and lending institutions losing money. Under such conditions, it has been easier to prove economic loss. However, the present situation (1994–1995) is the reverse, with a rise in market prices and a marked decline in libel suits.

Valuers' fee levels vary from object to object. Normally fees are based on payment per hour, fixed rates or tendered prices (mostly in the case of public offices).

11.3 PROPERTY TENURE

Commercial and residential real estate is normally let to tenants under fairly standardized forms of agreement. Length of agreement/contracts are normally for periods of either three, five or 10 years for commercial buildings. In the case of residential property, normally one to three years for single-family homes, while flats in apartment buildings usually have no time limitation.

With specific reference to commercial property, there is no special regulatory legislation regarding rent adjustment mechanisms. Normally this is linked to statistical indices reflecting growth in consumer expenditure with a consequent annual adjustment of rent. Income growth pattern is fairly predictable and normally related to consumer price indices for all types of contract. Indeed, there is no legal mechanism for the renegotiation of the rental level within a contract period, in that contracts once entered into between two, presumably, professional undertakings can normally not be changed during the contract period.

The tenant will normally pay a service charge for part of a building's public area, computed on the basis of the actual areas rented and total area. In addition, the tenant is normally charged for the costs of refuse disposal, lighting of public areas and must also bear the cost of maintenance of the rented areas. Costs for insurance, administration and caretaker functions, landlease fees, taxes and external maintenance of the property are normally borne by the landlord.

Landlease is a form of tenure with special legislative controls which is available across a range of property types, including commercial buildings. The length of contract must be more than 10 years and, in addition, the tenant must be allowed to renegotiate the contract to a total of 80 years, a period which is frequently the norm.

11.4 THEORETICAL BASIS OF VALUATION TECHNIQUES

This section considers some of the most commonly used valuation methods in Norway. Specific terms are defined and examples of valuations are provided.

Teknisk verdi (the technical value – depreciated replacement cost including the value of the land) of a property is the land value plus the replacement cost of a new building today, with the same construction and use of materials as the existing building, with a deduction made for age, untimeliness, usage and other physical deterioration, and, if applicable, also for work still to be completed. The land value will, as a rule, include the following elements: virgin land price; municipal costs for roads, water and sewage mains; on-site costs for access, water and sewage lines; connection charges (municipal) for water and sewerage; costs necessary for preparatory building works; site costs of a permanent value.

A property's normal market value or *normal salgsverdi* is that value which it is presumed the property can be sold for, on the day of the valuation. In contrast the *låneverdi*, or the property's lending value, is assessed in terms of the capitalized net income value and the normal market value. Thus, the lending value should reflect a carefully estimated market value as a basis for long-term loans.

In connection with going-concern valuations, the terms *verdi I* (value I) and *verdi II* (value II) are introduced. The valuer arrives at *verdi I* by comparing the technical value as defined above, the capitalized net income value and the capitalized working surplus or trading profit of the company. *Verdi I* is the fixed asset's total value (including plant and accessories) assuming the present usage, expressed as what an imaginary purchaser would be thought to pay under conditions of free sale, assuming continuing production under the present conditions, also taking into account the manufacturing plant's income potential. *Verdi I* is used as a basis for loans to the company. Clearance value (*verdi II*) is commonly referred to as the 'slaughter' value, and reflects the value assuming the termination of the business and possible alternative utilization. This value is also assessed by the valuer.

There is an official register, named the *Grunnboka* ('*Ground Book*'), in which all individual pieces of land are given an exclusive registration number. The register also contains information about ownership, mortgages and easements of the property. Extracting information from this register, which is open for inspection, is essential to all valuations and a prerequisite for sales transactions.

The Norwegian Surveyors Association has instituted a permanent committee, the Expert Committee, which continuously monitors the fluctuations in interest rate and inflation rate, and publishes recommended values for the capitalization rent to be used for various valuation objects. The capitalization rent (the inverse of the income multiplier expressed in per cent) is defined as the difference between the nominal interest rate and the rate of inflation plus a risk factor depending upon the type of property in question. Additional risk percentage is added at the surveyor's own discretion depending on such factors as 'merchantability' and other elements affecting the value. Minimum values for the capitalization rent are given for residential homes and ranges of values for commercial buildings, industrial properties and hotels. The values relate to the lending value and, at present (1995), they range from 7.5 to 22.5% for the various categories. Hotels lie in the highest part of the scale. The Expert Committee concerns itself only with percentages to be used in connection with the assessment of lending values, thus for assessing sales values the capitalization rent to be used must normally be 1.5–2.0% lower, i.e. the multiplication factor must be increased.

The definition of end value is often simplified by assuming that the future value is based upon the same multiplication factor (related to net income) as the present multiplication factor. This is the case when the time span is short (10–20 years) and there is no reason to believe that it will change. Otherwise the economic lifespan for buildings (without investment costs) is 60–70 years (end value 0). However, this value can be greatly affected by external factors such as the building of a new motorway or airport in the vicinity, or the introduction of new zoning regulations. Such factors can be both beneficial and detrimental to the property. The values arrived at in the various valuations are gross values and no deductions are made for transaction expenses.

11.5 VALUATION METHODS

Comparative price information is normally gathered from the valuer's own acquired knowledge and supplemented by statistical series. Since the valuer usually works in a limited geographical area, knowledge of the sales prices and the rental market is generally good. However, for commercial buildings, valuation on a nationwide basis is often carried out, necessitating liaison with local valuers on such projects. This system is considered to work well and is increasingly becoming the established method.

The depreciated replacement cost method is commonly used as one of the factors considered as part of the final valuation. However, the method is seldom used on its own, except in the case of the valuation of public buildings in remote areas where there is little market evidence. In this method land value and state of repair are the key parameters which indicate fluctuation in market value, normally cost of construction only shows a small variation from place to place. The various organizations in the construction industry provide statistical data regarding construction costs. The calculation of depreciation is to a large extent left to the valuer's judgement. Normal lifespans of 70–100 years are assumed and corrections are made for the type of building materials used, the usage and the state of repair of the building.

For commercial buildings the income approach method is the most commonly used valuation technique with considerable reliance placed upon it in assessing final value. It is often combined with cash-flow analysis and is based upon capitalizing the net yearly income, after deductions have been made for taxes and other municipal rates, insurance, administration, maintenance and, possibly, land lease (if this is applicable). Often a deduction is made for an assumed amount of vacant space (present and assumed permanently without tenants) mostly for the purpose of clarification. This element is often included as a risk factor in the chosen capitalization rent, though it is advisable to mention the amount included for this specific risk element in the valuation certificate. Letting contracts are entered into for rather a short length of time. The valuer must assess the 'normal' income for the property, taking into account the present market conditions. The effect on valuation, caused by higher or lower than normal incomes, and the period over which these abnormal conditions will lapse must also be considered.

The assessment of risk is generally incorporated in the chosen capitalization rent. It is the practice of the financial institutions to add their own risk factor, over and above that allowed for by the valuer, according to their own statutes and lending interest rates. The risk of vacancy is often deducted directly from the gross annual income as a fixed annual cost. At present the total risk percentage generally varies from 2.0 to 8.0% over and above the actual (net) rate of interest and currently (1995) is at 5.5% for commercial buildings. Somewhat higher risk percentages are used for industrial property and hotels while for residential property the risk factor is normally 3% and upwards.

The going-concern method is basically a valuation of a company's fixed assets, based on that company's results, past and predicted, as the main factor of influence. As a valuation technique it is mostly used in areas with limited market potential and where the use of the buildings and plant are developed for the purpose of a specialized type of production. For the financier it is of utmost importance that the company shows results of such a magnitude that it is able to meet its obligations. Thus, the going-concern method is based upon an analysis of the net income before depreciation of plant and buildings. The assumed value thus obtained is capitalized and the result is compared with the maximum and minimum values obtained under the definitions of market value and *verdi II*. The higher the capitalized income value the more the value (*verdi I*) tends towards the market value, whereas the lower the capitalized income value the more the value tends towards *verdi II* (clearance value). If it is lower than *verdi II*, the business should (in theory) be terminated and the property put to the usage under which *verdi II* is determined.

Regarding cash-flow methods, two lines of application prevail. In the first method the expected net income for the property concerned is listed over the period for which contracts are running. Consideration is given to the ability of 'survival' for the contract period for each of the tenants and their chances of upholding rental payments. Normally a 10 year period is analysed. For contracts ending within the period, the valuer estimates the market rental rate and uses this for the remaining period. The end value of the property is calculated as a function of the 'final plus one' year's net income, using the capitalization rent chosen for the project. A cash-flow calculation is carried out with chosen values for lending interest rates, assumed distribution of foreign and private capital, capital yield and inflation rates. The initial value of the cash-flow series can thus be calculated and is used as a value indicator.

The second approach is a more simplified version where the valuer asserts the normal net market value of the income and capitalizes this with the chosen rate. The net present value of the cash flow for the difference in the factual net income and the asserted net income is then calculated to give a positive or negative value to the previously calculated figure.

The annual cost approach is mostly used by property developers. It is based upon an estimate of all costs incurred during the lifetime of the building. The present value of the cost of construction, annual costs for maintenance, taxes, municipal rates, insurance, administration and improvement costs are calculated. These costs are then reallocated and presented as an annuity and are used as a basis for determining letting prices after the capital return requirement has been added.

The following is an example of the technique used for the valuation of an office block with the given floor areas, tenants and usage. The extract includes the income approach with correction for a limited term higher than market price and the cost replacement value together with the valuer's conclusion.

Example 11.1: Valuation of an office block

Floor	Area (m^2)	Tenants and usage
Ground	1000	Tenant pays what was market rent in 1990. Good tenant. Rent review each year. Contract can be renegotiated in 1995
1st	1000	As above.
2nd	1000	Tenant pays what was market rent in 1993. Poor tenant. No rent review. Contract can be renegotiated in 1996.
3rd	1000	Tenant pays peak market price from 1988. Good tenant. Rent review each year. Contract can be renegotiated in 1998.
4th	1000	As above.
5th	1000	Vacant for the last nine months.

The official registration number for the property e.g. gnr 20 bnr 183 municipality of Oslo.

Review of actual and assessed rental income

Building (ABC etc)	Floor No.	Rentable gross area	Present actual annual income	The valuer's assessed normal annual income		
				pr.m^2	pr.annum	Remarks
		Ca.				
A	Ground	1.000	850.000	900	900.000	
	1 st	1.000	850.000	850	850.000	
	2 nd	1.000	850.000	850	850.000	

3 rd	1.000	1.050.000	800	800.000	
4 th	1.000	1.050.000	800	800.000	
5 th	1.000	0	800	800.000	Vacant
				0	
				0	
Correction for interest free deposits				0	

Total kr.		4.650.000	Total kr.	5.000.000

) : kr 416.667 monthly

Deductions to be made to gross annual income			
Annual ground rent (if any)		kr	
Municipal rates and taxes	kr		
Insurance premiums	kr		
Administration and misc. all costs	kr	600.000	
Assessed maintenance costs	kr		
Other expenses	kr		600.000
The property's net annual income		kr	4.400.000

Capitalized value

Capitalized value using __12.5__ % capitalisation of net rental income

The use of the chosen rent figure is to be commented upon   kr. 35.200.000

The chosen capitalisation interest rate includes kr. 400.000 annual loss in income. This is taken into account by increasing the rent from 11%. The excess income for the 3rd and 4th floors will presumably last for another 3 years. The effect of this is calculated on the basis of the value corresponding to the extra cashflow generated by these kr. 500.000, – each year for three years. 8% interest is used and the value becomes kr. 1.288.548. For the sake of being conservative kr. 1.000.000, – is added. The lending value thus becomes kr. 36.200.000, –.

Cost replacement value

Normal building costs as if a new construction:

A	kr	48.000.000
B	kr	
C	kr	
D	kr	
Sum normal building costs	kr	48.000.000
Deductions for usage, age, deterioration, remaining works etc.	kr	5.750.000
Normal building costs after deductions	kr	42.250.000
Normal ground (land value) costs	kr	3.500.000
Cost replacement value	kr	45.750.000

Conclusion based on the above factors and comparative price information:

☒ Free land ☐ Leased land

The property's normal selling value   kr 42.500.000,–
Market value at the time of the valuation

The property's lending value   kr 36.200.000,–
If the land is leased, this is taken into account in the valuation

As a supplement to this example, Table 11.1 shows an extract from the cash-flow analysis of the same property. This analysis gives the valuer additional input to the decision-making process, final choice and conclusions drawn.

Table 11.1 Extract from cash-flow analysis

Liquidity	1995	1996	1997	1998	1999	2000	2001	2002	2003	2004
Income	4650	5562	5646	5720	5244	5307	5371	5435	5501	5567
Normal costs	600	612	624	637	649	662	676	689	703	717
Special costs	0	0	0	0	0	0	0	0	0	0
Assumed vacancy	400	406	412	418	425	431	437	444	451	457
Landlease	0	0	0	0	0	0	0	0	0	0
Surplus	3650	4544	4609	4665	4170	4214	4258	4302	4347	4392
Cost of borrowed capital	2080	2080	2080	2080	2080	2080	2080	2080	2080	2080
Liquidity	1570	2464	2529	2584	2090	2133	2177	2222	2267	2312

	IRR	Invest.	1995	1996	1997	1998	1999	2000	2001	2002	2003	2004
Private funds	14.0%	–14937	1570	2464	2529	2584	2090	2133	2177	2222	2267	14916
Total funds	9.7%	–42676	3650	4544	4609	4665	4170	4214	4258	4302	4347	44736

Key figures in this analysis are:

Assumed increase in annual income	1.5%
Assumed increase in annual costs	2.0%
Borrowed capital assumed to be (of total)	65.0%
Interest rate	7.5%
Rate for capitalization – sales	11.0%
Rate for capitalization – lending	12.5%
Sales value – year 10	40 340 000
Yield – private funds including risk	14.0%
Private funds	14 940 000
Borrowed funds	27 740 000
IRR – private funds	14.0%
IRR – total capital	9.7%

This produces a slightly higher value than the above approach and in this case the valuer may conclude at a sales value of possibly kroner 42.5 million with a corresponding lending value of kroner 36.5 million.

11.6 DATABASE MANAGEMENT

There is no official systematic handling of data regarding sale prices in Norway, normally information is collected from searching public records, newspaper advertisements and estate agents' records. However, the market is generally open with information being accessible to the public, though often with a time lapse of three to six months before the data is recorded. Statistics from these records will therefore always be somewhat historic.

Information regarding sale prices is usually reliable, but the records include both forced sales as well as negotiated prices between agreeing parties. Thus, selective and critical consideration is necessary when using the data from these sources. All values are converted to a price per m^2 of floor area, though the varying understanding of the definition of floor area makes some of the data questionable, particularly as not all area measurements comply with the Norwegian Standard for area measurement in buildings. For the rental market all statistics are based on sales prices per m^2 or rentals per m^2 per year. Sometimes monthly rates are the basis and other times yearly rent per office employee is the parameter used.

The assembly of comparable evidence is mostly carried out on an individual valuer basis. However, all sale transactions are registered with other information particular to the property, such as ownership, registration numbers for allocation, mortgages and information regarding easements accessed by personal computers and modem linkages. Data from the *Eiendomsregisteret* is published on a private basis for some of the major municipalities, but only for residential property.

11.7 VALUATION REPORTS

All valuation reports follow a more or less standardized layout. Uniformity arises from the reporting of factual information concerning the property. This is normally:

1. a description of the assignment and directives including the purpose of the valuation, also information regarding the client's position;
2. a description of all the underlying documents with reference dates and a short commentary on each;
3. a description of the area where the object is situated;
4. a description of the actual site of the object and a description of the buildings on the property, together with a schedule of actual floor areas;
5. a brief account of the official regulations regarding the property and the surrounding area, together with reference to any future planned developments for the area;
6. a summary of the various valuation methods employed;
7. a listing of limitations and conditions under which the value is given;

8. various enclosures such as photographs, extracts from the *Grunnboka*, maps, drawings, official injunctions and development plans.

For residential homes and some commercial buildings extensive use is made of standard forms. These forms, of which there are two types, have been in use for a number of years and are virtually unchanged. The layout follows a number of logical steps including the reporting of all relevant facts and descriptions of the property. A specific page of the report contains elements of the calculation of capitalized income and depreciated replacement costs, and the valuer's conclusion. Both market value and lending value is reported. Comparable market prices are not mentioned in the form, but there is an increasing tendency for the valuers to report any such figures under the item of miscellaneous information.

11.8 CONCLUSION

The valuation profession in Norway is undergoing a gradual change in the direction of increased proficiency. This is in keeping with the ever increasing demand for a professional approach to the various problems concerned with modern day property transactions and financing. There are, however, other professions entering the field of valuation, for example economists, but there is still a basic requirement that a valuer must possess a sound knowledge of building materials, the construction process and the various technical installations in modern day buildings.

FURTHER READING

The Norwegian Surveyors Association (1981) *Takstmannsskolen trinn I og trinn II*.
Takseringshåndboken ('The Valuers Handbook').
Statistisk Sentralbyrå ('Bureau of Statistics').

PROFESSIONAL BODIES

The Norwegian Surveyors Association (*Norges Takseringsforbund*), Fyrstikkalleen 20, 0661 Oslo, Norway
Norges Eiendomsmeglerforbund, Inkognitogt. 12, 258 Oslo, Norway
Den norske Advokatforening, Kr. Augustsgt. 9, 0164 Oslo, Norway

Portugal 12

Maria dos Anjos Ramos

12.1 INTRODUCTION

Valuation is a process which varies with the object to be evaluated, its physical, social and economic environment, and the valuer's expertise. Therefore, in describing the evolution of valuation in Portugal, it is important to consider all these elements in order to understand better the rules and methodology used.

The main clients for valuation services used to be those banks engaging in mortgage business, insurance companies, investment funds, accountants, stockholders and investors. Even though their aims differ, except for special users such as the fiscal authorities and the courts whose specific purposes are defined by law, their common objective was to establish the value of an asset within a given market, in order to guarantee the success of a business transaction whether it be finance, investment or insurance.

12.2 GEOGRAPHICAL AND HISTORICAL BACKGROUND

Nowadays, with close to 11 million inhabitants, continental Portugal's geography can easily be classified into a few characteristic areas. The North/Coastal area is picturesque and more densely populated; the Northeast has inland problems which are slowly being resolved; the Central/Coastal area is very similar to the Northern area; the Central/Inland area is devoted to farming and less populated; the area of greater Lisbon encompasses all the neighbouring districts and grows at a rate practically proportional to the depopulation of the other areas; the South/Inland area is predominantly agricultural and increasingly depopulated; and the South/Coastal area is mostly tourist oriented. These areas have their own definite markets as far as real estate is concerned, but there is obvious pressure on densely populated areas such as Lisbon, Oporto and Setúbal.

As time went by, people built themselves homes and stores or offices from which to conduct business and other activities. Such real estate was valued by

European Valuation Practice. Edited by Alastair Adair, Mary Lou Downie, Stanley McGreal and Gerjan Vos. Published in 1996 by E & FN Spon, London. ISBN 0 419 20040 1

the benefits it brought to the owners. This benefit could present different aspects: palaces were built not only to give shelter and comfort to their owners but also as a display of power and riches. Transfers of property were usually made through inheritance, as payment of debts or as simple exchanges, and the market for buying and selling was reduced to those situations where a sale was unavoidable. We do not know when the *mercado de arrendamento*, or rental market, really started. We know that it was common, in the case of rural properties, for the tenant farmer to pay the owner all or part of the rent with the product of their harvests.

As is natural within any kind of society, the structure of things changed, the systems evolved and valuation forms and techniques adjusted to each particular situation.

12.3 VALUATION PRACTICE AND TECHNIQUES 1950–1973

For historical and political reasons, both domestic and international, from 1951 until 1973 economic growth was secure and economic indicators showed unreserved optimism. Living within a closed political system with an economy upon which external influences were practically non-existent, the first petroleum shock was received with the utmost surprise. On a real estate level we should point out that these two decades were important in altering the public's and market operators' behaviour.

12.3.1 Urban growth and property market development

This period registered a considerable growth in the economy with parallel expansion and development of the most important urban centres. From the 1950s the cities grew and spread out towards the neighbouring towns, which became dormitories. These subsequently started developing their own life, a few nowadays being quite important urban centres in their own right. The farms, which were considered in the old days as places of leisure and recreation, became urbanized, more or less densely populated and, at times, almost inhuman. Large houses surrounded by gardens located in the central avenues were torn down and replaced by buildings several stories high, which house banks, insurance companies and big national and multi-national companies. In the smaller urban centres, the needs of the individual governed what was built and usually it was they who instigated the construction of a house or workshop, for which the land had to be purchased if it was not inherited. In the big cities, buildings were developed for sale and, as inflation and speculation were almost non-existent, their price reflected mainly their construction costs together with the price of the land, taxes and the promoter's fees.

From 1961 to 1973 many new projects were developed and around 1970 the most important urban centres, Lisbon, Oporto, Setúbal, etc., grew towards the suburbs. In the Algarve, tourist villages and time-shares were developed, under British and German management without the nationals participating. Peripheral residential dormitory settlements proliferated along the railways connecting Lisbon to Sintra and to Estoril, taking advantage of the fastest means of transportation – the train. The first shopping centres and the first office space appeared and the concept of a 'condominium' became well established.

In the rest of the country, homesick or returning emigrants developed small clusters of houses, usually quite substantial, their styles copied from the countries where they were working. This kind of development had disastrous effects with consequent environmental loss of character, from an aesthetic as well as historical point of view. In such cases valuers were almost always faced with a problem since these large houses, with very expensive architecture and finishings, were located in areas with no real estate market for the type of building. Their commercial value was therefore inevitably well below their real cost. This period ended with a favourable stock market, delivering swift and easy profits, and a simultaneous boom in the real estate market, pertaining mainly to apartments located near the urban centres or near transport networks giving easy access to them.

12.3.2 Property investment

Effective demand from investors wishing to invest their savings or their income was usually determined by the way payment was made – in full or deferred. The return required was usually related to the rate of interest on deposit bank accounts. The income from the investment, by way of rents paid by the tenants, should at least equal the interest on money in a bank deposit account or on any other banking application which, being both secure and attractive, could substitute for the investment. The substantial sum required for such investments was enough to limit the effective number of potentially interested investors. Nevertheless, the idea that real property was a secure investment created an attractive market (Dornbusch and Fischer, 1984).

Although buildings could legally be divided into autonomous parts, traditionally very few bought them in this way. As a result only substantial investors could place their savings or income in buildings bought for investment. Beyond a few individuals with means, most were institutional investors such as the Social Security Services, the pension funds and the insurance or mutual companies, buying to obtain a revenue. This revenue remained constant and, even though theoretically there was no inflation, the investors started seeing their objectives undermined by a leasing law disadvantageous to them. The idea that real estate was a safe investment still prevailed however, and even when very rarely it was seen in practice to be otherwise, this psychological factor was able to maintain stability within the sector. In reality, investing in land, particularly well located land, has always been safe and profitable on a long-term basis. In the 1960s, due to the war in the colonies and to a violent flux of emigration, there were social changes. New rents were high compared to incomes and the supply in this segment of the market decreased substantially. To overcome such difficulties it became normal to sell residential buildings as 'horizontal property', i.e. apartments or flats. Thus, the purchase of subdivisions of fixed assets became a reality and access to finance through bank loans stabilized the market. This started a new system of purchasing a house for owner-occupation with bank finance. In the case of emigrants, the access to finance to purchase apartments as an income-producing investment, with special open credit, served to attract their savings to Portugal's weakened economy. Most investors bought houses for their own permanent use but emigrants, taking advantage of these legal facilities, bought apartments to let. Even though the system was initially aimed at the upper classes with healthy incomes, and only three Banks were allowed to grant credit, it turned out to be a success and opened up a portion of the almost unknown real estate market – the selling of residential buildings as 'horizontal property'. Meanwhile a hoard of foreign investors took over the southern tourist areas. Prices sky-rocketed amid widespread speculation. Mistakes were made by nationals as well as by foreigners on such a scale that they could hardly ever be remedied. Finance on the basis of mortgage guarantees became an everyday occurrence necessitating valuations by the financing banks. The banks allowed by law to engage in this business were the Caixa Geral de Depósitos, the Crédito Predial Português and the Montepio Geral.

There was practically no buying or selling of new buildings for retail or offices. Only the big companies, usually banks and insurance companies, put up buildings, with the sole purpose of housing their operations. Any other need for this kind of space was covered by modifying buildings initially planned for housing, the first choice being those located in central areas. Commercial space was much more difficult to find: the old market was consolidated and new premises were obtained only through transfers or subletting. This led to the uncontrolled transfer of old coffee houses and restaurants located in strategic points within the city and, in their place, bank branches opened up. Since the rents were unchanged, or suffered only minor adjustment, the transfers were highly profitable for the tenants while the owners were mere spectators throughout the whole transaction, with no share in the profits (Harvey and Johnson, 1971).

12.3.3 Value concepts

The concept of valuation as an engineer's technique, agricultural, civil or mechanical, according to the type of asset under valuation, be it rural or urban property or equipment, was developed during the 1950s and 1960s (Ariel). Assets were valued for the revenue they brought or the investment that was needed to create them. The notion of market value was mainly a theoretical one since markets hardly existed. Only in the urban areas, and especially in the suburbs, could demand and bidding be found, on a level which would now be characterized as a very restricted market. In the less important urban centres and in rural areas things continued to be valued for the benefits they brought or on the basis of their construction costs (Amling, 1984). Therefore, there were three concepts of value which everybody understood.

(a) Valor do investimento/custo de reposição (Replacement Cost Value)

This is calculated as the sum of the direct and indirect costs of development to which the probable or acceptable promoter's net profit is added. The principal factors that establish this value are:

1. building costs, including the contractor's fees and all the expenses involved in construction; general liabilities, such as licences and inspection fees;

2. financial liabilities, encompassing interest on all the costs incurred, except for the land, at the bank's normal rate for this kind of operation, during the construction period. This item was interpreted differently by valuers, some thought that the investment was deferred in time, so lowering the rate; others simplified the issue and estimated a fixed rate for a shorter period of time, on the basis that as soon as sales started the construction financed itself. Others took none of this into account;
3. the value of the land by comparison to local practice, taking its potential into account;
4. the promoter's net profit.

(b) The value derived from income or investment income value

In this case the value was established on the basis of its actual or probable income, capitalized at a competitive rate based, as described above, on the returns from other investments, always taking into account the building's characteristics, its maintenance costs and the operator's risks.

(c) Valor venal (Value Derived by Capital Comparison)

At the time, even when transaction comparisons were made, they were limited to a few comparables which were not always trustworthy, the alliance between buyer and seller being such that it was normal for nobody ever to know the real price obtained from the sale. This situation arose not only from the widespread belief that 'secrecy is the soul of business' but also because open knowledge of the values in any transaction could incur taxation which both buyer and seller wanted to avoid.

Under these conditions, the need for someone capable of working with the relevant factors, e.g. an engineer, to calculate the value of such assets was acknowledged. However, in those areas where an engineer could not be found, there were so-called *Louvados*, a kind of valuer who, with or without payment, established the fair value for a sale or exchange of property, in a simple and swift way, with no written reports nor large estimates. They were usually mature men whose moral integrity was above all suspicion, good judges of the asset, its usefulness and its location, and who probably had inside knowledge and were entrusted with the values involved in any other business transactions in the area. They can still be found making valuations for tributary purposes or to apportion inheritances.

12.4 VALUATION FOR COMMERCIAL PURPOSES 1973–1990

12.4.1 Political shocks and property values

As of September 1973 the first big fall in the real estate market took place, triggered by the world oil crisis. In April 1974 the old political system fell and brought a socialist revolution. Inflation, an opening to foreign influence, democracy, socialism and several other almost unknown concepts, brought along swift and profound changes within society. This radical change caused the sale, at almost symbolic prices, of assets of the best quality. The valuer's role was so complicated that it became an inconsistent profession with almost no reason for existing. Ironically this was a time when occasional valuers proliferated.

The move of Portuguese political and economic life towards socialism opened up new finance possibilities for the lower classes and another phenomenon emerged, no less interesting but outside the valuer's scope: the construction of illegal housing on parcels of land without substructures and without the necessary municipal council's authorization. On the other hand, the independence of the colonies brought home almost a million Portuguese settlers and refugees. The need to shelter all these people was pressing and, after an emergency situation where whole families were housed in hotels for a number of years, things slowly started adjusting to the new reality.

The Government took over all the big companies and the entrepreneurial network suffered a complete change at all levels. Following a socialist ideal, the Government sponsored the construction of cost-controlled housing, with both successes and failures, and the real estate market in housing began anew, supported by grants to assist housing finance from banks. In this case, finance and bonuses were given according to several factors dictated by legislation. These were briefly:

1. the family's income and size;
2. the unitary index which varied according to the house's site and represented the price asked for 1 m² of gross built area. This area was defined in a Government regulation as being the space circumscribed by the house's outside walls and, in the case of condominiums, by the centre wall separating the apartments to which the corresponding share of the area to access the floor level is added. Balconies, garages, storage rooms and common rooms were considered accessory areas;
3. the total value of the construction.

Such a system restricted valuers' work while making the financing bank's evaluation important, since it had to guarantee the enforcement of the law and, at the same time, confirm that the values put into practice represented reliable security for the loan. The system, notwithstanding this negative aspect, within market limitations and despite the inevitable leaks, was effective because it sustained speculation during a very important period. Throughout this sometimes confusing time, the only seemingly consistent value was the *custo de reposição*, itself not easy to calculate due to strikes and other union demands which impacted heavily on construction costs.

12.5 THE DEVELOPMENT OF A MARKET FOR COMMERCIAL VALUATIONS

Around 1982, although it is hard to pinpoint the exact moment, talk of 'sales value' or 'commercial value' or 'market value' started (Ariel). Definitions copied from other countries started appearing, which could only in a somewhat artificial way be adjusted to our reality. The banks, besieged by a great number of requests for finance, started setting standards for their valuation reports to facilitate the valuer's work. A great number of outside valuers trained for this type of operation appeared at this time and simultaneously more engineers were hired to join the banks' staff, the financing banks being still the same initial three. The application forms issued by the banks were very similar and in almost all of them the valuer was asked to determine the asset's value with estimates of the following:

Buildings	value on the basis of *custo de reposição*
	value on the basis of *valor venal*
	value on the basis of investment income
Apartments etc.	value on the basis of *valor venal*
	value on the basis of investment income

Under these circumstances, the estimate of investment income value was totally inconsistent, since the rents were outdated and nobody wanted to let their property since the law protected tenants to such an extent that the owner looked like society's benefactor.

Similarly, in the areas with the most sales – the environs of the large cities – the sales price was fixed by law. Potential buyers were usually dependant on other interest to be able to obtain and enjoy bank finance, which was closely related to the family's income. The highest valued properties were usually bought by foreigners, either private or official such as the embassies, or by more daring people almost always under the protection of strong political alliances. Business was always conducted with the utmost secrecy.

The process preparing Portugal to join the European Community started and was completed in 1986. This relatively calm period, with its opening to outside influence, induced the construction of retail and open-plan office buildings in the big cities. It was hoped that the market would rapidly absorb the supply, since the sales rate was good, but such was not the case and, after a period of great excitement where inflation justified speculation and vice versa, a period of crisis settled in which did not end until 1987.

It was then that the first real estate investment funds appeared in Portugal, instigated by banks linked to this area of business, together with insurance companies and real estate offices. The real estate market took on a new life with buildings offered to let, but only for commercial space and offices. The attempt to relaunch residential leasing was not successful, because legislation was still hard on owners and the funds were not capable of turning any profit on their investments. The spirit of these funds changed due to this hard reality: the stock exchange rose, real estate prices rocketed and easy money sprouted everywhere. From 1987 the presence of foreign investors was becoming evident, especially where office buildings located in fashionable areas were concerned. Their financial capacity was definitely higher than that of their Portuguese counterparts and they bought everything, no matter what the price. A few of these buying operations were launched from countries known as 'fiscal paradises', but the main buyers were the Spaniards, the Swedes and the French. Notwithstanding the euphoria, certain aspects were difficult to understand. Market value dictated the rules and there was no evident reason for the price rises nor for the basis on which they were negotiated. This seemed doubly strange in a country with a practically non-existent market, limited as it was to a few business transactions in assets which, more often than not, had no direct basis of comparison. This phase of Portugal's property market can be explained by the profound changes in society and the many business deals transacted in Portugal which had their origin abroad. Eventually it would be interesting to study the foreign market's influence within this sector to reveal its effects. These, which on first analysis seemed advantageous, since they underpinned values amidst really extraordinary dealings, can now be seen only to have served the interests of the few and started the confusion which gave way to the current crisis.

For valuation purposes, the correct value seemed to be that based on comparison to the prices achieved in market transactions. This comparison sometimes defied belief, since one can only compare on the basis of characteristics and values previously identified as significant by the valuer. Possibly the only criteria at this time was to consider yesterday's value outdated today. This situation worsened with the appearance of foreign valuers. These had an interest in the sale as intermediaries the commission for which was higher than the valuer's fees, but being ignorant of local practices and customs, legislation and the market's capacity, they promoted the unsupported rise of prices and collected the respective profits. Nowadays we can prove that the biggest errors were the consequence sometimes of greed, otherwise of naïvety, but for the most part they happened through ignorance of a few fundamental factors which no valuer, working in a geographical area and in an economy such as ours, can ever ignore, such as urban planning, legislation, sociology, economy, engineering and marketing.

Nevertheless, it was found that location, area and the quality of construction weigh heavily in the balance and can act together or separately. Another factor regulating the market is the balance between the amount of supply and demand which should be supplemented by the quality of supply and the demand's financial capacity. To define this balance, which dictates the market's true value, it is necessary to possess a profound knowledge of the asset and the significant circumstances. In a Portuguese 'market', which does not even exist for certain assets, one must not confuse a single business deal with a market. The market explains itself statistically; a business deal is usually influenced only by subjective factors or reflects the private interests of just one person or company, but cannot be replicated.

12.6 CURRENT PRACTICE

12.6.1 Assessing market value

This apparently negative experience did in fact have a positive effect on the practice of valuation, for although well-intentioned, but badly prepared, valuers can still be found, a capable élite is already at work. The process of publicizing valuation expertise and methodology is now well under way and there are permanent debating groups whose objective is to dignify the profession of valuation. Generally speaking, even though there is no legal obligation, most valuers follow the criteria and methodology of TEGOVOFA's *Guide Bleu* (GNI). This has come about more as a consequence of their practicality and good sense rather than as a result of them being promoted. We should nevertheless gratefully acknowledge the participation of a few of TEGOVOFA/EUROVAL's associates in training courses, given at the Instituto Superior Técnico (Technical College) and coordinated by the Building Materials Centre, a fundamental step towards publicizing the valuer's work. The interest shown by an ever increasing attendance at these seminars and courses indicates their success.

Even when the uses of the valuation differ, for instance appraisals may be for a mortgage, for insurance, for the apportioning of inheritances, for business and tax purposes, for the courts, etc., the valuer's practical objective is to find the asset's sale price: i.e. in normal circumstances, within a reasonable period of time, the buyer being anyone without a special personal interest. The way the asset is advertised, its price and the form of payment are also taken into consideration. 'Normal circumstances' are considered to mean that the seller, although wishing to sell, is not under any kind of pressure to do so, nor is the buyer forced to buy that specific asset, but can freely choose it among others. In addition, the asset, as well as its owner, should be able to meet the conditions necessary for the transaction to be made within the normal requirements of the law or, that not being the case, the buyer should be fully aware of the circumstances of the asset.

On the other hand, the valuer can only use feasible plans which have legal support, unless they are so constricted by their client, in which case it should be mentioned in their report. Any valuer's report should fulfil all the client's requirements, especially when they provide the forms to be filled out, but the valuer is always free to add anything they might deem indispensable. The report should be written in a comprehensible way, explaining all the criteria, methods and concepts used and always following the principle that it is meant for people who know nothing about valuations and do not know the asset.

To elucidate our explanation we can categorize fixed-asset valuations into three groups (below) depending on the asset type. The chosen criteria and methodology appear in almost every book about valuations.

(a) Group I: subdivisions of buildings and whole buildings

This applies to residential or commercial buildings or those providing a mix of these uses, and to both rural and urban land (Ariel).

1. *Valor venal* (the market value, assessed by comparison with market transactions) This method is the most widely used in every valuation; requiring an exhaustive analysis of the property's relevant attributes, such as location, type of construction, condition of maintenance and a comparison of these parameters with those of the comparable properties. The subsequent synthesis of the parameters determining value should be carried out on a statistical basis. If we had at our disposal a reliable database, this procedure could be replaced by the application of inferential statistics and multiple regression, using suitable software. However, in the current depressed property market, there are too few transactions to develop these methods.
2. Market value assessed by the investment income method This can be a direct or a comparison method. The direct method can be used if the property is already leased, when the value is arrived at by capitalizing the annual rent. The comparison method will be used when the property is not let, when the valuer will research the rents agreed within the area for similar assets and capitalize the probable annual rent. This actual or probable income can be gross or net and the capitalization rate has to relate to whichever is chosen.

In the case of buildings or land this method needs careful study of alternative investments to evaluate the appropriate capitalization rate.

3. *Valor do investimento/custo de reposição* (market value on the basis of the replacement cost) As mentioned above, these costs are estimated as the sum of the construction costs of the building, general liabilities and the value of the land estimated by comparison. Following this method the value to be finally proposed is obtained after the promoter's gross profit is added to the costs.

When the construction is not new, depreciation takes place due to processes of physical, functional and economic obsolescence which may act together or separately. Physical obsolescence means the deterioration suffered by the structure due to its function, the quality of materials utilized in its construction, the action of physical or chemical agents and even to the absence of adequate maintenance. This type of obsolescence requires heavier costs to be incurred in maintaining the building's use. Functional obsolescence depends in part on physical obsolescence, but often the cause rests in aesthetics and social change, new customs or fashions, or in the advent of new productive processes unfitted to the type of construction and to which it cannot be adapted. Connected with this process is something termed the building's 'useful life', meaning the period from the beginning till the end of a building's operational usefulness. Economic obsolescence concerns the real or probable profitability of the property, either let or in owner-occupation, and it may be more significant than its physical or functional deterioration. There is a consensus that physical and functional obsolescence should be considered together with economic obsolescence. This position can be justified by two simplifying hypotheses:

1. The first is that the property is let at a current rent which is lower than the increased costs of maintaining it; therefore its income diminishes, lowering its value.
2. The second is that the building is vacant and its standing value is nil, i.e. its demolition will be funded by the sale of the products of demolition and the property value is equal to the site value, taking into account its realistic potential uses.

These scenarios will be considered whenever relevant to the property being valued.

In valuing land, even though the basic methodology is the same, the fact that there are two types of land has to be taken into consideration: urban land and rural land. There is still an intermediate legal status which is land with 'urban capacity' or which is potentially urban. To assess which type of land is being valued, the first thing a valuer must do is to enquire from the competent authorities, which are the Municipal Councils, as to the land's legal situation and its intended use. Urban land is valued taking into account its development potential. Rural or agricultural land has to be valued by agricultural engineers and its value is estimated according to its actual or probable yield. In intermediate situations, the valuer's judgement has to prevail, taking into account the land's practical potential and assessing the risks involved and the delay before a final decision will be made on its use. Hence the need for a sound knowledge of the law and its implementation as well as of the town planning regulations.

(b) Group II: industrial buildings, hotels and leisure areas or buildings

This includes such properties as golf courses and casinos: assets which can be valued on the basis of the income they generate, by their buildings' potential and versatility or simply the potential of the land on which they are situated (Rushmore, 1992). Market value for this group can be estimated using the methodology followed in Group I, but the valuer must know the area's development plan, since the value for alternate use may have to be calculated; the building's characteristics, its structure and versatility, whether it can be easily adapted to any other kind of occupancy or to other industries requiring a different layout, its state of preservation; the market demand, the characteristics of any alternative supply. In addition, the valuer must be aware of the state of the stock market, and social and political, scientific and technological circumstances such as war, technology transfers, fashion, cultural events and so on (Butler and Richmond, 1990).

Even though some authors hold that fixed assets in this group are worth only the income they create, it is the author's opinion that this is not entirely accurate, because they may be valued for their inherent characteristics such as land and construction. Value may be attached to the physically, legally and financially justifiable possibility of an alternative use, for example, where an obsolete use is located in an area covered by an Urban Plan which introduces change. To estimate the value of the property attention must paid to both the financial situation presented by the current or last management – bearing in mind that profitability is dependent, in many cases, exclusively on the quality of the management – and also to the situation of similar companies located in the neighbourhood, or even in distant areas with comparable characteristics.

(c) Group III: historical patrimony, ecological reserves, easement and rights of surface access, etc.

This group includes special cases whose valuation requires a specialist knowledge (Moreira Filho).

Example 12.1: The valuation of a National Monument

We are instructed to carry out a valuation of The Insua Fortress Convent which stands on a rocky islet by the Minho riverside, 200 m off the coast, equidistant from Portugal and Spain, in front of Moledo and close by Caminha. Only two valuation bases are recognized for buildings and land: market value and *custo de reposição*. This area in Minho is provided with substantial roads to Spain and to important cities within the country, including other historic and tourist destinations. Agriculture, viniculture and small industries form the main economic resources in this micro-countryside. Tourism is an interesting development with evident potential, just beginning to become economically important.

The buildings
In the fourteenth century a group of Franciscan friars commenced building the Holy Mary Insua Convent. In the seventeenth century the fortress was built and the convent was restored to serve both as a clerical and a military establishment, and in 1910 it became a National Monument. Its

walls still stand as a witness to the history of architecture, containing elements from different periods: notched stones from the sixteenth century, a medieval façade, a cloister from the seventeenth century, a cross from the eighteenth century and a barrel vault, in baroque style, whose origins are medieval. Restoration of the entire property would be very expensive.

Areas:
The land area included within the battlements totals 4569 m^2, consisting of the cesspool at 4432 m^2 and land at the fountain 137 m^2.

The built area, including the church, consists of 913 m^2 on the ground floor and 324 m^2 on the first floor, totalling 1237 m^2.

Battlements varying between 5 and 10 m in height cover an area of 525 m^2.

Accommodation
The military installations:
    10 compartments and storehouse.

The convent:
Ground floor: kitchen, buttery, pantry, refectory, chapter, sacristy, church, chapel, cloister, pigeon house, 11 unidentified compartments;
First floor: choir and five unidentified compartments.

Valuation
The estimate of market value is normally obtained by two methods: the valor venal, or comparison of market transactions, and the income capitalization method based on the estimated rent.

Valor Venal
Despite a lack of comparable data, we tried to identify the market for properties like this one, looking for the most similar properties and restricting the search to the immediate region. This indicates that there are neither any other islands to sell nor properties classified as National Monuments. We found land with ancient mansions advertised for sale, some of them almost in ruins. Although we are apparently trying to compare the incomparable, in fact all property has a price depending on the advantages it offers, and in this case the State may transfer the fortress at market price, retaining its status as a National Monument.

The prices of the sites with derelict buildings suitable for restoration vary from Esc6 000 000/m^2 to Esc20 000 000/m^2, according to the individual characteristics of the property. Ignoring for the present the fact that this is a National Monument, we propose that the sale value on the basis of these comparables, for existing use is:[1]

Market value: 4569 m^2 × 20 contos/m^2 = **91 380 contos Esc**

---

1. Conto denotes Esc 1000. Numbers are given according to the UK convention; for example, 1000.50 means one 'thousand and five-tenths'. According to Portuguese convention this would be written as 1.000,50.

The income capitalization method

This method has no practical application in the case of the fortress, since in its current condition it would not yield a rental income. However, while avoiding speculation, we should consider the concept of alternative use value and the likely use to which the property could be put, such as an inn.

Some valuers use a quick method, called the 'North Atlantic Theory', to calculate the value as a lodging house. This theory holds that any lodging house will only be profitable for the operator if its price or value does not exceed 1000 times the daily receipts, the valuer having a record of average receipts by unit, and also for bars, restaurants and other sources of revenue. Employing this approach, we are going to use in comparison the D. Dinis Inn, situated at Vila Nova de Cerveira, which is located in the same neighbourhood and is also within a National Monument, its facilities we estimate being similar to those which could be provided in the fortress, according to the proposed plans. The normal room prices vary in accordance with the season of the year and with the room type, as shown below. However, the current crisis in the hotel sector has affected inns. Their management is being adapted accordingly and, as part of this, pricing practice is more aggressive, producing 'packages' for families, honeymoons or meetings and business conventions. Taking this into account, we start with the assumption that the mean yearly occupation would be 60% and the normal accommodation charges for the night would be augmented by other receipts amounting to an extra 50%.

For a development with five suites and 10 bedrooms, the market value based on 1994 season revenues can be estimated thus:

	Low season	Mid-season	High season
5 suites at	20 = 100 contos	20 = 102 contos	32 = 160 contos
10 bedrooms at	16.4 = 164	25.5 = 255	26.2 = 262
Total	264	357	422
Add 50% for other receipts	132	178.50	211
	396	535.50	633
Occupancy at 60%	0.60	0.60	0.60
	237.60	321.30	379.80
Multiplier to give market value	1 000	1 000	1 000
Market value	**237 600** contos	**321 300** contos	**379 800** contos

Normally, the best occupation rate is in the high season when it may well be 100%. However, we will take the most prudent value, corresponding to the three seasons average:

Appraised market value: 313 000 contos

In fact, only some stone walls remain standing which will cost a lot to improve, representing more or less site value only. To reflect this, we depreciate the market value of the improved property by 60–70%. Therefore, the **depreciated comparative alternative use value** varies from:

0.30 × 313 000 contos = **93 900 contos** to
0.40 × 313 200 contos = **125 200 contos**.

Custo de Reposição
This is essentially a comparative method because we simulate the expected reconstruction cost on the basis of the costs normally incurred in the locality for similar buildings. Although the costs of this type of construction are not hard to calculate in normal situations, here we are costing construction to be carried out on an island with difficult access and all the associated problems, so that defining the costs becomes more complicated. Although it may be debatable, we estimate that these costs will be twice the usual level.

The construction cost, including developer's reward will be:

Battlements 525 m² × 150 contos/m²	78 750	contos
Construction 1 237 m² × 150 contos/m²	185 550	contos
General taxes 12% construction costs	32 700	contos
Site 4 569 m² × 12 000 contos/m²	54 830	contos
Unadjusted restoration cost	350 000	contos

Net replacement cost
Following the argument used previously, that the value after allowing for depreciation varies from 30 to 40% of the replacement cost, we have:

0.30 × 350 000 contos = 105 000 contos
0.40 × 350 000 contos = 140 000 contos

Conclusion
Following the reasoning above, and on the basis of the plans provided, we verify that the value of the fortress lies within the following range, according to the basis of valuation applied:

Market Value
by the valor venal method:
market value for existing use is 91 000 contos

income method:
market value for alternative use as an inn is between 94 000 and 125 000 contos

custo de reposição method:
market value for existing use or as an inn is between 105 000 and 140 000 contos

These values are compatible, though based on different assumptions. As expected, the *custo de reposição* basis gives higher values, because of the extra costs associated with the inaccessible location and the onerous nature of the existing construction. Discounting the fact that the fortress–convent has historical significance, being classified as a National Monument, we propose the following.

Appraised market value: 110 000 contos,

This is on the basis of the mean of the values arrived at, varying from 90 000 to 140 000 contos. In addition, an historic value may be considered. Having consulted various papers about the valuation of historic properties, we have come to the conclusion that the most appropriate method of valuation for this kind of property is formulated by Eng. C. Sousa Alves in his work *The Valuation of Romantic and Historical Properties*. This method propounds the principle that an historic property's value has three components: site value, construction value and historic value. The land and construction values are already calculated by the methods described, leaving the historic value to be calculated as a function of the age, quality and rarity of the property. In fact, location and quality are already implicit in the calculation of the site and construction values; it remains to reflect the building's age from the historic value definition. If we adopt this method we are able to increase the value by 68.05%. Therefore, where CRH is the *custo de reposição* with allowance for historic value, *HVA* the historic value addition, *S* the site value and *C* the construction value, depreciated for dereliction:

$$HVA = 0.6805C$$

As we define the property value by the sum of the three component parts, we get:

$$CRH = S + C + HVA$$
$$CRH = S + C + 0.6805C$$

Applying a depreciation allowance of between 30 and 40% of the whole construction cost to allow for the fact that the buildings are derelict, and taking the costs as before:

Battlements	78 750	contos
Construction	185 550	
General taxes	32 700	
Total	= 297 020	contos
$C_1 = 0.30 \times 297\,020$ contos	= 89 100	contos
$C_2 = 0.40 \times 297\,020$ contos	= 119 000	contos

Since

$$S = 4569 \text{ m}^2 \text{ at } 12\,000 \text{ contos/m}^2 \quad = \quad 54\,830 \text{ contos}$$

the historic value will be:

$$CRH_1 = 54\,830 + (297\,020 \times 1.6805) = 205\,000 \text{ contos}$$
$$CRH_2 = 54\,830 + (119\,000 \times 1.6805) = 255\,000 \text{ contos}$$

The values arrived at, although debatable, reflect the bases of the valuation. The choice of these bases was not random, but proceeded from a well-considered search to as great a degree of accuracy as possible. It is not only theoretically sound but also practical, in that it reflects market values.

The methodologies adopted are recognized internationally and the choice of the valuation method for historic property developed by C. Sousa Alves was made after finding the alternatives less adequate to the situation. Decisions on the future improvement of the fortress remain with the owner, in this case the Portuguese State. The fact that we propose a range of values rather than a single figure has been justified already, it is clear that for such ancient buildings value is difficult to determine even during or after restoration.

12.7 VALUATION APPRAISALS

Most valuations are made for mortgages, privatisation, real estate investment funds, insurance, fiscal purposes, or dispossession.

The last three cases, valuations for insurance, taxation and dispossession, warrant special treatment. The insurance companies' concern is to insure real estate and guarantee that the insured value is securely covered by the real estate value in case of an accident. In the case of dispossession, there is a specific code, which has been updated, allowing for the payment of indemnities to dispossessed owners up to a value very close or even equal to the asset's market value. Valuations made for taxation purposes are carried out by commissions, appointed by the Financial Services, consisting of at least three valuers who use very specific criteria outside the scope of this book (Boulez).

12.7.1 Mortgage valuations

These usually follow the criteria and methods described above. The valuer has to understand that the value proposed will have to serve as a financial guarantee and might even be called upon to pay the corresponding debt. When there is a crisis and the borrower does not meet their obligations, the final debt may exceed the value agreed for the mortgage due to interest accrued on deferred payments, or other liabilities. The market value may then be insufficient to cover the debt. The financing banks usually have specific report forms which valuers have to fill out and which will subsequently be studied by the bank in determining the size of the loan. The loan is usually 20–25% lower than the value of the real estate, but each case is studied on its merits. Even though the bank provides the forms, and their format depends on the type of property involved – for instance, whether it is an apartment or an entire building – almost all require the valuer to observe the following steps:

1. identification of the valuer;
2. identification of the property and its location;
3. site characteristics;
4. general description of the state of construction;
5. valuation by the valor venal method;
6. valuation by the *custo de reposição* method;
7. valuation by the income capitalization method;

8. valuer's final opinion of value;
9. insurance value;
10. additional comments and information;
11. photograph.

12.7.2 Valuation for privatization

From any point of view, be it legal, economic, social or political, the privatization of a collective asset is a complex undertaking. The types of company chosen for privatization are usually large industrial, transportation, telecommunications, banking or insurance companies. The property assets they own often represent a considerable proportion of the company's value and also provide the premises from which they operate. In most cases, when these premises are being valued, the valuer has to decide whether the company will be able to continue an activity generating sufficient income to enable it to pay a rent equivalent to the asset's value. In other cases the premises may be old, in bad repair and obsolete, and fitted only for their current use. In such cases, the value for alternative use would be required. However, it is necessary to consider the legal situation and verify whether the company, as a social entity, can or ought not to stay on in the premises. In determining the value in such cases, overriding any mathematical calculations, it is important to have a good legal and social understanding of the situation, for each case is unique.

12.7.3 Valuation for real estate investment funds

The objective of these funds is to make profits which will be distributed between the fund's participants. Therefore, it is important to maximize revenue and minimize both expenses and vacancy rates. To estimate the value for acquisition purposes, on the basis of the income received, it must be capitalized at a rate which can be reconciled with the fund's objectives. With rental legislation giving tenants unequivocal protection and allowing no updating of rents in line with inflation, the valuer's attention must be turned to any factor which may affect the stability of this revenue. Such factors may concern the premise's versatility, their size, the quality of construction, age and the volume of existing competition.

The funds' assets are valued by the same methods employed by the banks, on the basis of market value, these valuations being supervised by the Bank of Portugal. However, valuers studying any fund's investment potential, are conditioned by the following factors:

1. the gross or net capitalization rate required by the fund; this rate is governed by the return available on alternative possible investments and the financial market in general;
2. the rental value which depends on the state of the market and is negotiable;
3. the price set by the vendor.

Example 12.2: Investment income valuation

Consider the following scenario. A fund aims to obtain a 10% net return on an investment of 500 million Esc (escudos) and an opportunity has arisen to invest the sum in a well-located building in a downtown area with 1250 m² usable space to be let as offices. No lessees are lined up as yet and the price tag of the property is exactly 500 million Esc or 400 thousand per m². The asking price conforms with market practice on the basis of comparison with other similar buildings.

Knowing that the required initial yield is 10% the net rental value should be 10% of the capital investment of 500 million Esc, which is 50 000 000 Escs per annum or 4 167 000 Esc per month.

Allowing for security, two elevators, maintenance being the responsibility of the owner when substantial repairs are concerned and of the lessee when they are small, we come to an estimate of outgoings which will amount to 30% of the owner's income; therefore, the gross rent should be:

4 167 000 Esc × 1.30 = 5 420 000 Esc/month

As there are still no tenants, a real estate agency will probably have to be commissioned to undertake letting at a fee equivalent to a month's rent. On the other hand, there could be a *vacância*, or time lapse, before the first rents are due, for which we allow 10% of gross rent. Thus, we reach the desired amount for the gross asking rent:

5 420 000 × 1.10 = 5 965 000 Esc per month

This amounts to:

5 965 000/1250 m² = 4772 Esc per m² per month

This is a comfortable value for a market with good financial prospects such as banks, insurance companies or higher public services, but is hardly within the general market sphere. It has an element of risk which merits careful deliberation.

If a tenant were already interested in renting the space and willing to pay this price, a terminable lease contract should be made to guarantee the investment's amortization.

Example 12.3: Market valuation of an office property
We are instructed by a client, the owner of the freehold interest in a property in Lisbon, to carry out a market valuation for sale purposes of the property detailed below.

Date of valuation: April 1995
Location: prime city centre
Size: new building (1990) of 2000 m² net lettable floorspace on four floors with good specification and air-conditioning, two passenger lifts to all floors; no car-parking
Construction: standard construction for a property of this type in this location
Condition: good state of repair
Tenure: freehold. Good title to the property can be shown and the property is not subject to any unusual or especially onerous restrictions, encumbrances or outgoings.

Lease: let to several 'blue-chip' tenants on a modern standard rental agreement.

Annual indexation to CPI

Estimated rental value is $3750 per m^2 per year

Inducements and rent free periods: assume 15% of gross rents

Effective gross rent after taking into account inducements: $3190 per m^2 per year

Level of landlord's costs, outgoings, maintenance, etc.: 20% of effective rent

Initial gross yield: 11% (net yield 8%)

Valuation

The real estate market in Portugal at the date of valuation is bearish. Due to the very good location of the property its market value is estimated on the basis of the investment income capitalization approach only. The net yield applied is 8% which is estimated by comparison. Gross yields in the commercial office market are nowadays at 11%.

	$ per m^2	
Gross rental value	3750	
Less inducements at 15%	563	
Effective gross rental value	3187	
Less landlord's costs at 20%		637
Net rental value	2550	
Total net rental value: 2000 m^2 at 2550 per m^2		$5 100 000
Multiplier at 8% in perpetuity		12.50
Market value		**$63 750 000**

12.8 CONCLUSION

I believe that the valuation techniques and forms used in Portugal do not differ from those used all over the world. Despite our market's peculiarities and the nature of the economy being that of a small country which, for decades, lived within its own borders and was subject to very strong state intervention, traditionally real estate has been both attractive and respected. That is to say 'to own real estate gave one a certain status'. After 1974, alongside internal conflict and ever-growing state intervention, aided by a constitution which envisaged development along a socialist route, came the country's opening to the outside world. Subsequently, in 1986, accession to the EEC brought about a complete reversal in the country's politics with a return to privatization, almost total exposure to foreign influences and resulting dependency on the models and economic and financial influence of our most significant partners, such as Spain, Germany and the UK. The property boom and collapse were imported. Legislation applying to this sector has been progressively adapted in order to rectify past mistakes without incurring new social injustices. However, its relative transience has deterred me from referring to any particular cases for fear that they might be considered out of date tomorrow.

The property system has adapted to each of the periods described above and, notwithstanding the recent property crisis, real estate retains a lively interest within Portuguese society and is still a secure and profitable operation whether let or owner-occupied and is the subject of well defined laws. The approval of the Municipal Director Plans has helped to clear some uncertainty and the Portuguese citizens, true to their nature, love to own real estate. It is important to continually be aware of current events. An exchange of knowledge between valuers and real estate operators is fundamental. The property system is evolving at such a speed that increasingly sophisticated methods are necessary. At the moment data banks are being assembled and, whenever it is needed, inferential statistics and multiple regression methods are used with the help of the appropriate software. These programs are inexpensive and easy to access, thus reducing the time needed to obtain a result, time being an important feature especially in the mortgage market which is now extended to all the banks. Nevertheless, all results should be quality controlled, whenever the user has no experience of the traditional valuation system (Amling, 1984).

REFERENCES

Amling, F. (1984) *Investments: An Introduction to Analyses and Management,* 5th edn, Prentice Hall, Englewood Cliffs, New Jersey.

Ariel, A. (ed.) *Manual de Valoraciones Inmobiliárias,* Josep Roca Cladera, SA, Barcelona.

Boulez, J. *L'expertise Immobilière,* Masson.

Butler, D. and Richmond, D. (1990) *Advanced Valuation,* Macmillan, London.

Dornbusch, R. and Fischer, S. (1984) *Macro-economics,* 3rd edn, McGraw-Hill, New York.

Harvey, J. and Johnson, M. (1971) *An Introduction to Macro-economics,* MacMillan, London.

Moreira Filho, I.I. *Avaliações de Bens por Estatistica Inferencial & Regressões Múltiplas,* Avalien-Porto Alegre (RG), Brazil.

Rushmore, S. (1992) *Hotels and Motels: A guide to market analysis, investment analysis and valuation,* Appraisal Institute, Chicago.

Spain 13

Sandrine Bardouil and
José de Pablo Méndez

The greater part of valuation work in Spain is carried out by Spanish valuation companies, whose valuers are called *tasadores* and are required to follow the rules set out in the Royal Decree on valuations of 30 November 1994. Valuation companies are also bound by legislation, in particular they are not allowed to have any agency involvement. Furthermore, the law is stated in such a way that Spanish financial institutions rely on *tasadores* for their valuation work. As a consequence, valuers in international surveying firms and property consultancies focus on valuations required by foreign companies, and the needs of local owner-occupiers and investors who may request advice on their properties regarding potential sale, relocation, diversification or other matters. In this chapter attention is specifically focused upon the Royal Decree and the way in which *tasadores* carry out valuations.

13.1 VALUATION PRACTICE

The practice of valuation according to Spanish law is undertaken by *tasadores* who are architects or engineers by profession. In contrast with estate agents, *tasadores* are valuers recognized by law. Although the term *tasador* is not defined in the law, their work is clearly identified in the Decree on valuations of November 1994. Usually, *tasadores* work for a registered valuation company (*sociedad de tasación*) or for the valuation arm of a lending institution such as a bank. Traditionally the principal area of valuation work for *tasadores* relates to mortgages. However, they can carry out other valuations such as the asset reserve of insurance companies and portfolio valuations of property funds. Estate agents (*agentes de propiedad inmobiliaria*) and chartered surveyors may also carry out valuations for certain purposes such as advice on sale/purchase prices. In addition, chartered surveyors value for international clients such as investors or foreign banks following procedures laid down by the Royal Institution of Chartered Surveyors (RICS).

European Valuation Practice. Edited by Alastair Adair, Mary Lou Downie, Stanley McGreal and Gerjan Vos. Published in 1996 by E & FN Spon, London. ISBN 0 419 20040 1

As a rule, the valuation market in Spain is divided between these two groups. *Tasadores* are not legally allowed to take part in other fee-producing work except valuations and as such they do not advise on property purchases, sales or management. They must be totally independent. Chartered surveyors and estate agents are not bound by legislation affecting *tasadores* and can combine valuation advice with other fee-producing property work, but are not qualified to value for the purposes described in the 1994 Decree on valuations. The main difference between *tasadores* and chartered surveyors is illustrated below:

Tasadores	Chartered surveyors
Bound by Royal decree 30/11/94	Bound by RICS guidance notes
Work for valuation companies or valuation arm of lending institutions	Work for surveying firms, property companies and foreign banks

Law 2/1981, followed by Decree 685 of 17 March 1982, saw the introduction of regulations concerning the mortgage market in Spain and the creation of specialized valuation companies. Article 38 of Law 2/1981 of 25 March 1982 stated that mortgage valuations could only be carried out by 'the financial entities which have access to the financial markets or by specialist entities created for that purpose', namely the valuation arm of the lending institutions such as banks and related financial companies. The first valuation company was created in 1982 under the name of Sociedad de Tasación S.A.; by 30 November 1994 there were 160 such valuation companies.

Under the state publication Boletín oficial del Estato (BOE) of 10 August 1991 the current requirements to become a valuation company are set out as follows. Some are currently being reassessed.

1. to be a limited company (*sociedad anónima*) based on national territory;
2. to confine its corporate business to property valuations;
3. to have a minimum capital of 25 000 000 ptas and hold at least 50% of this capital.
4. to have a minimum of 10 qualified professionals as either part of the staff or in a contracted capacity;
5. to be registered on the official registry of Banco de España, the procedure for registration being explained in Article 40 of BOE No. 83 of 7 April 1982.

Although the law does not define a *tasador* it nevertheless does refer to the persons who are authorized to sign valuation certificates and valuation reports. Mortgage valuation reports have to be signed by an architect in the case of urban property, urban land or residential property. In all other cases, the valuation report must be signed by an engineer specializing in the valuation of the type of property being considered. In addition the decree of 30 November 1994 specifies that only registered valuation companies and the valuation arm of the mortgage institutions can carry out mortgage valuations, valuations of property investment funds and valuations of the reserve assets of insurance companies.

Qualification as a *tasador* is achieved by undertaking an academic degree course of five to six years duration followed by practical training in a bank on a full-time basis. Others, who usually run their own practice as architects, may enter into exclusivity contracts with registered valuation companies to carry out valuations on an *ad hoc* basis. Normally they would join valuation companies through recommendation and/or interview and undergo regular in-house training courses to become recognized valuers.

Since 1986 the Banco de España has been empowered to investigate and sanction the work of *tasadores*. Current sanctions are described in Law 3/1994 of 14 April. The law grades the professional breaches of valuation companies and valuation arms of mortgage institutions as 'very serious', 'serious' and 'minor', and for which various sanctions are laid down. Examples of breaches and sanctions are:

1. Very serious (a sanction of 50 000 000 ptas)
   (a) deceitful valuation report;
   (b) resisting or obstructing the investigation of Banco de España.
2. Serious (a sanction of 25 000 000 ptas)
   (a) discrepancy between valuation certificates and valuation reports;
   (b) valuation figure which does not fit in with the evidence collected;
   (c) breaching professional confidentiality.
3. Minor
   (a) other non-compliance with the legislation on property valuation.

APIs (the *Agentes de Propiedad Inmobiliaria*) are essentially estate agents. They have to take an entrance examination to become a member of the Council for Estate Agents (the Consejo General de los Colegios Oficiales de Agentes de la Propiedad Inmobiliaria). The council, which is organized on a federal basis, was founded by decree in 1948. The entrance rules to become an *API* changed substantially in the early 1990s and in an effort to upgrade the standing of the profession the council has since decided that only solicitors, engineers or architects can now apply to take the entrance examination.

University courses in property tend to be specialized and attract those who already operate in the property market. For example, universities in Madrid and Barcelona offer postgraduate property courses in subjects such as property valuation.

13.2 BASES OF VALUATION

The main bases of valuation are market value, replacement/reinstatement cost and maximum legal value. Usually the *tasador* has to assess each of these values before selecting that to be reported to the client. Selection is not arbitrary as the reported value (*valor de tasación*) is clearly defined in the Decree on valuations of 30 November 1994. The definition of reported value (also called appraisal value) depends on the purpose of the valuation. For example, in mortgage valuations the decree advises that the reported value should be as follows:

1. for development or properties undergoing refurbishment, the gross replacement/reinstatement cost;
2. for properties tied to an economic exploitation, the lesser of market value and the net replacement/reinstatement cost;
3. in all other cases, including those development properties valued on the basis that they are completed, the lower of market value and the maximum legal value when applicable.

In addition, the decree specifies that, for reasons of prudence, *tasadores* must not value the overrented income when carrying out mortgage valuations.

13.2.1 Market value (MV)

This is described as 'the net amount which a seller could reasonably expect to receive for the sale of a property as at the date of valuation, assuming an adequate marketing period and assuming that there exists at least one potential purchaser who is correctly informed of the characteristics of the building and that both the purchaser and the seller act freely and without a specific interest in the transaction'.

Comparison of this definition with the '*Red Book*' (RICS, 1990) definition of open market value (OMV) highlights the following:

1. OMV is the 'best price' whereas MV is 'the net amount'. In addition, in the case of an overrented property, a chartered surveyor may value the overrented portion of the income whereas a *tasador* is not allowed to do so. For mortgage purposes the *tasador* is encouraged to give a 'prudent' price (or average price) rather than a 'best' price.
2. Under OMV the marketing period takes place before the valuation date, whereas under MV this is not specified.
3. Under OMV, the assumption is that values remain static between exchange and completion. In Spain it is unclear whether this is the case.

13.2.2 Replacement/reinstatement value

Gross replacement/reinstatement value is the sum of capital which is necessary to replace the building with a new one of the same characteristics as at the valuation date.

Net replacement/reinstatement value is the gross figure less the property's physical and functional depreciation at the valuation date.

13.2.3 Maximum legal value

This is the maximum legal selling price of a residential property under public legal protection as established in current legislation.

13.2.4 Reported value/appraisal value

This is one of the above values and is dependent upon the purpose of the valuation. The 1994 Decree on valuations gives a definition of the 'reported value' for each of the valuation purposes, for example, the 'reported' value for mortgage purposes is one of the three values described in section 13.2.

13.3 VALUATION GUIDELINES

There are two key guidelines: the Lease Law 29/1994 on commercial leases, the *Ley de Arrendamientos Urbanos* (LAU 29/1994 of 24 November) and the 1994 decree on valuations (Order of 30 November 1994) which deals with mortgage valuations, reserve assets of insurance companies and valuations of property funds. Both the law and the decree took effect on 1 January 1995 but the application of the guidelines on mortgage valuations was delayed until 1 April 1995.

13.3.1 Lease law 29/1944 (*Ley de Arrendamientos Urbanos*)

The 1994 Lease Law intends to remedy the distortions in the property market created by previous legislation dating from 1964 and 1985 (Keogh, 1994). Until this law the market had operated on three levels, namely leases signed before 1964 with open-ended contracts and frozen rents; those signed between 1964 and 1985 with open-ended leases and limited annual growth; and those signed after the 1985 Boyer Decree with lease lengths and rental levels agreed freely between the parties. As a result, the 1964 Lease Law fiercely protected the rights of the tenant whereas the 1985 Boyer Decree allowed total freedom in the negotiations for new leases which generally favoured the landlord. Such a legacy meant that there were severe divergences in rents paid. Leases based on the 1964 Lease Law gave the tenant automatic renewal and preferential rights to acquire the property. In addition rents were indexed and generally stayed well below their market level. The landlord was also responsible for most of the repairs. In investment terms, such a lease structure was very unattractive to landlords and encouraged owner-occupation and renting rather than leasing a property for investment purposes.

From 1985, as landlords and tenants were free to negotiate their own terms, landlords attempted to abolish the automatic right to renew whenever possible. The length of the lease was agreed by the parties and in many cases leases became shorter and rents started to reflect market levels more closely. At the same time, renting became less attractive to tenants. However, whereas the Boyer Decree brought Spanish leases in line with leases in other European countries, it did not apply to pre-1985 leases.

The 1994 Lease Law, which took effect on 1 January 1995, is an important turning point as new leases will, in time, abolish the previous lease structures. The new law essentially gives landlords the power to introduce rent reviews to open market value and terminate leases over a five to 20 year period. Since January 1995 phased rent increases will bring rents in line with open market levels, with phasing dependent upon the type and size of the tenant. For small shops, leases will expire in 20–25 years, with more generous provisions for family businesses. Leases on industrial properties will run for between 5 and 20 years with a rent review based on accumulated inflation after five and 10 years. Thus, in time, pre-1985 leases will become extinct and, as a direct consequence, the 1994 Lease Law should boost the letting market and investment market. Furthermore, it should boost liquidity, especially in the residential sector.

13.3.2 November 1994 Decree on valuations

This decree affects virtually all valuations carried out by the specialist valuation companies and the valuation departments within the lending institutions. It encourages the *tasadores* to follow the decree's guidelines on mortgage valuations, valuations for property funds and valuations of the reserve assets of insurance companies, even if the valuation is for a purpose other than that stated in the

1994 Decree. The *tasador* is obliged to clearly state whether the valuation follows the decree or not.

Property funds (a form of property unit trust) have recently been introduced in Spain. In January 1995 proposals were forwarded by four candidate funds, each of which was accepted, and formally launched in the same year. Property funds are governed by a number of rules among which the Decree of September 1993 is relevant to *tasadores*. The main rules are:

1. the valuation instruction must be for a minimum period of three years and a maximum period of nine years. In addition, the income derived from one instruction cannot exceed 15% of the total income of the valuation company;
2. the fund must be valued once a year by an independent valuation company registered with the Banco de España;
3. each property in the portfolio must be held for a minimum of four years;
4. a minimum of 70% of the fund's assets must be invested in property;
5. the fund should hold a minimum number of seven properties;
6. a single property cannot represent more than 20% of the value of the fund;
7. the fund is not allowed to market its properties but is allowed to refurbish them in order to attract tenants;
8. the fund can borrow up to 20% of its assets on the mortgage market.

Valuation of the asset reserves of insurance companies is required by the regulatory rules governing this business sector and approved by Royal Decree 1347/85 of 1 August (BOE 6/8/85) and the Royal Decree 1126/91 of 28 June (BOE 23/7/85). It is a requirement of insurance companies to seek valuations before insuring properties.

An additional aspect of the decree on insurance companies is the specification that revaluation should take place using the following schedule. Those properties which were valued between 1 January 1990 and 31 December 1991 should be revalued before the 31 December 1995; properties which were valued in 1988, 1989 and 1992 should be revalued before 31 December 1996, and those properties valued after 31 December 1992 should be revalued before 31 December 1997. In contrast, for the valuation of company accounts, litigation, mergers and acquisitions, sales/purchases and compulsory purchase there are no specific guidelines. In these cases valuers tend to refer to relevant norms affecting other types of valuations.

13.4 VALUATION METHODS

Normally a *tasador* will assess the reinstatement cost and the market value to arrive at the 'reported' value (*valor de tasación*). The choice of method depends on the guidance given in the decree on valuations.

13.4.1 Reinstatement cost method

Reinstatement cost is used to calculate the gross and net replacement costs of all property types. It applies to development properties whether at the project stage, in the course of construction or refurbishment, or properties which are completed or assumed to be complete. The gross replacement cost is the sum of the market price of the site and of the costs required to build a property with the same characteristics (capacity, use and quality) but with today's technology, materials and construction methods. The site value is calculated in accordance with Instruction III, Appendix 4 of the decree (most often its market value). The costs required to build include non-recoverable taxes, stamp duty, architect's and technician's fees, planning fees as well as administration costs of the developer and construction costs excluding non-structural erections which can easily be dismantled (in the case of older or historic buildings the valuer needs to assess the costs of the materials which lend the buildings their character). These costs are average costs and do not include the developer's target profit.

Net replacement cost, applicable only for completed properties, is the gross replacement cost less physical and functional depreciation. Physical depreciation is calculated in accordance with one of the following two methods. Linear amortization is the result of multiplying the replacement cost of the building (excluding the site value) by a coefficient, the latter having a value equal to the division of the age of the building by its life expectancy. The 1994 Decree on valuations states the life expectancies of various types of properties: 100 years for residential, 75 years for offices, 50 years for retail and 35 years for industrial and other properties having an economic usage (such as hotels). The second method involves the assessment of the costs to transform the property into a new one with similar characteristics. This approach can be used when linear amortization proves inadequate due to the age of the property or other reasons. Functional depreciation is calculated by deducting the costs which are necessary to adapt the property to its proposed use from the reinstatement cost excluding site value.

13.4.2 Comparative method

This method permits the determination of the market value of all types of property. Application of the comparative method involves the establishment of the qualities and characteristics of the subject property; analysis of comparable properties (real transactions or offers) on the basis of situation, use and type; qualification of the differences between the subject property and the comparable properties in reaching a conclusion on the adjusted rate (or yield) to apply to the property; and the application of the selected rate to the subject property calculating market value net of purchaser's costs.

The decree on valuations states that the comparative method requires evidence of at least three real transactions or, alternatively, evidence of six properties available on the open market. Furthermore, the valuer may not use evidence which is older than 12 months.

13.4.3 Capitalization method

There are a number of methods applicable to the valuation of income-producing property, with the decree on valuations offering guidelines for both let and unlet properties. Each of these, illustrating various stages of the valuation process, are considered below.

(a) Capitalization of expected rents, vacant properties

1. Assess future inflows until the end of the life of the building. In this respect the 1994 Decree on valuations stresses that future inflows must be prudently assessed. For instance, in the case of buildings where profits determine rental levels (e.g. hotels), the valuer will not assess what the maximum profits could be but rather what the average profits are likely to be. In the case of other buildings (offices and shops), the valuer needs to quantify the factors likely to impact on rental negotiations so as to assess the underlying rent.

2. Assess reversionary market value of the property at the end of its useful life. The market value of the property at the end of its useful life will be equal to the net reinstatement cost at the same point in time. This cost takes account of physical and functional depreciation. The site value will be based on its market value at the valuation date.

3. Select the rate of return as the safe rate plus a minimum of two additional basis points. For properties located in Spain, the safe rate will be the average rate on public borrowing with a two to six year redemption date. This is known as the *Rentabilidad de la Deuda Pública*. The average rate is that applicable over a time period varying between three and 12 months. The decree gives additional advice on how to select rates of return for properties located in other countries.

4. Calculate net present value (NPV). The 1994 Decree gives the detailed net present value formula (see below). The approach is, in effect, a short discounted cash flow. However, all inflows and outflows are discounted at a safe rate of interest which is not directly related to the property market. This reflects the fact that the property is not income producing, with the safe discount rate an expression of the uncertainty of future incomes.

The NPV is calculated according to the following mathematical formula:

$$\text{NPV} = \sum_{t=o}^{n} \frac{(\text{NI})_t}{(1+k)^t} + \frac{(\text{reversion value})^n}{(1+k)^t}$$

where NPV is the net present value, NI_t the periodic expected net income flow from rents (after landlord outgoings), k the discount rate (selected according to the advice in the decree) and n the number of periods to the end of the estimated holding period.

The tasador must justify and expound explicitly in the valuation report the hypothesis and calculation parameters used.

(b) Capitalization of net passing rent, for leased properties

The *tasador* must explain how the capitalization rate is chosen with reference to the state of the market, level of risk and characteristics of the property. However, the *tasador* is not totally free to assess the market capitalization rate as the decree specifies the minimum rates which can be applied. Again, this reflects the fact that the Spanish market value encourages 'prudence' and is not an assessment of the '*Red Book*'s' 'best price'. Minimum capitalization rates are updated annually by the Government in conjunction with the Banco de España and other organizations. For example, the following rates for property type and Minimum

capitalization rate were issued for the year 1995:

Residential: main residence	5%
Residential: second residence	9%
Offices	7%
Retail	8%
Industrial	9%
Parking	7%
Country properties	4%
Others	8%

These capitalization rates lead to a double discounting of second residences as these command lower rents and are capitalized at higher yields. The difference between the two levels of yield (5 and 9%) is large, a situation which is criticized by some *tasadores* as it does not always reflect the prevailing property market.

13.4.4 Residual method

The residual method is used to determine the market value of land with planning permission or of a property undergoing extensive refurbishment. The most commonly used approach is that of the dynamic residual method which can be considered in a series of stages as detailed below.

(a) Dynamic residual method.

1. Assess the best and most likely development potential. This can be based on the planning permission if it exists.
2. Assess construction dates, building time, marketing period.
3. Assess construction costs and other expenses such as marketing costs.
4. Assess value of the completed building. The starting point is the current market value assuming the building is completed. If the *tasador* estimates that the market is moving up the current market value can be increased by no more than the rate of inflation in the previous 12 months.
5. Assess cash flows during the construction period.
6. Assess capitalization rate: safe interest rate plus risk premium.
7. Calculate the market value of the property; the site value corresponds to the value of completed building less above costs.

The safe interest rate again corresponds to the average rate on public borrowing with a two to six year redemption. Regarding risk premium the 1994 Decree requires the following:

Residential: main residence	6%
Residential: second residence	10%
Offices	8%
Retail	10%
Industrial	12%
Parking	7%
Others	10%

However, the decree does not state whether these premiums should be updated annually. In all the stages within the residual method the *tasador* must justify and reason in an explicit manner the hypothesis and the calculation parameters used.

13.5 VALUATION PROCESS

The decree on valuations is undoubtedly raising standards. For instance, *tasadores* have to systematically inspect properties, check floor areas and justify their analyses of the property market, whereas previously these steps were not always taken. The valuation process detailed in this section emphasizes the key steps under the new decree.

13.5.1 Instructions

The various organizations involved in valuation work receive instructions orally or in writing, the latter being the more desirable situation. In the case of valuation companies, the majority of their clients are the lending institutions, in particular the mortgage sections of banks. However, following the 1994 Decree the work of *tasadores* extends to the newly-formed property investment funds. In addition, *tasadores* carry out valuations for insurance companies, property companies and individuals.

The principal clients of the estate agents (*APIs*) are purchasers/vendors of property. *APIs* are not allowed to carry out valuations in accordance with the 1994 Decree, unless they are also *tasadores*. As for chartered surveyors, their clients are predominately international companies and valuations are carried out on the basis of the RICS guidance notes. Chartered surveyors tend not to be *tasadores*, which places a limitation on the scope of their valuation work from Spanish clients.

13.5.2 Code of measuring practice

There is no code of measuring practice comparable to that of the RICS/ISVA, but definitions are stated in the Decree. There are three broad types of floor area: 'useful floor areas', 'built floor areas' and 'registral floor areas'. The 'useful floor areas' correspond, more or less, to net internal floor areas and includes the floor areas measured from the internal sides of walls, toilets and stairways, and half of the floor areas of external projections used for private purposes such as terraces and balconies. Exclusions are internal structural components, vertical structures,
horizontal conduits larger than 100 cm³ and floor areas having a height of less than 1.5 m.

The 'built floor areas' correspond, more or less, to the gross internal area. This is equal to the 'useful floor areas' defined above but without excluding internal structural components. It also includes external projections at 100% if for sole private use and at 50%, or other apportionment, if for common use.

The 'registral floor areas' are the areas stated in the property register. Such areas are usually assessed on one of the above bases. Floor areas stated in the property register take precedence over other floor areas unless they can be proved wrong.

13.6 PROPERTY ANALYSIS

This is comparable to the analysis which valuers carry out in the UK. The *tasador* inspects the property and assesses the site area, infrastructure, state of repair and general condition. In addition, the *tasador* analyses the lease details and the planning status of the property. Particular issues include: whether the lease is pre-1964, 1964–1985 or post-1985; the implications of the 1994 Lease Law on the lease contract (section 13.3.1); and passing rent, non-recoverable outgoings, and tenant and landlord covenants.

13.6.1 Planning analysis

The 1956 Planning Act, modified by the Acts of 1976 and 1992, forms the basis of the comprehensive town planning which operates in Spain (Riera and Keogh, 1995). Although a hierarchy of plans exists, paralleling in many respects the hierarchy of administrative structures at national, regional and local levels (Clifford Chance, 1995), it is only at the level of the municipality that comprehensive plan coverage exists. The general plan provides the core of the Spanish local planning system, it is a legally binding land-use plan formulated for the municipality or groups of municipalities (Riera and Keogh, 1995).

Plans are generally very detailed and if a planning application conforms to the plan the likelihood is that planning permission will be granted. Although the planning system is fairly rigid, developers may have recourse to special plans (*plan parcial* and *plan especial*) to amend existing plans. In addition, developers have some leeway where plans identify land available for development without stating what form the development should take. The valuer gathers information to assess the planning position of a property with reference to planning permission and neighbouring planning developments which may affect the property being valued. An acceptable planning application will be stamped *visado* (seen) by the relevant professional college and subsequently receive permission from the local authority. As planning permission must be initiated within six months, the valuer must carefully check the date of the planning permission before assuming that a valid permission exists.

13.7 MARKET ANALYSIS

Chartered surveying firms operating in Spain derive market knowledge from their own agency activities, which involves advising clients on lettings, sales, purchases, development and planning. From this knowledge the firms develop their own in-house property database which, supplemented by other data, provides valuers with very useful market information.

Valuation companies, through their clients the lending institutions, have a wealth of data on transactions which they utilize in their valuations. However, by law, these organizations cannot be involved in any agency or other fee income-producing activity. Thus, whilst holding an impressive database of property transactions they are removed from the mechanics and the knowledge of how deals are clinched.

Under the 1994 Decree on valuations the *tasador* must include evidence of three comparable transactions or, alternatively, evidence of six comparable properties on the open market. In addition, the evidence must relate to the previous 12 months and the *tasador* must identify the comparable properties in the valuation report and explain how they can be compared to the property being valued. As the decree only took effect in April 1995, for mortgage valuations, its impact is still not entirely clear. Smaller companies, in particular, find it difficult to comply as there is little exchange of market information amongst property professionals. At present, *tasadores* have to be inventive to obtain detailed comparable evidence and they generally enquire about the comparable properties on the market by pretending to be an interested party or by avoiding any searching questions from the owners/agents of comparable properties.

Analysis of lettings is based on pesetas per month per m². As there is no 'institutional' lease (full repairing and insuring lease), the landlord's and tenant's liabilities need to be carefully assessed. Deductions from the gross rent may include local taxes, insurance for the loss of rent, non-recoverable repairs and management. In the analysis of purchases and sales, it may also be necessary to deduct purchaser's costs. Transaction tax is at 6% and notary costs at *c.* 0.5%. In addition, there may be agency fees at *c.* 3% and often valuers give valuations which are exclusive of these costs.

A recent innovation, *Protips*, set-up in late 1994 by two chartered surveyors, is an on-line information system comparable to *Focus* in the UK. There is also a growing number of publications on the general state of the market. Indeed, chartered surveying practices operating in Spain issue market reports on a regular basis (Weatherall Green & Smith, 1995), as do the lending institutions and the valuation companies (Sociedad de Tasación SA, 1995). Furthermore, there is a wealth of general economic data from the daily press and regular publications from the banking sector. Trends, projections and historical data are clearly presented in the monthly publication *Boletín mensual del Banco de España.*

Example 13.1: Valuation example for mortgage purposes

Direct comparison approach
Assumptions:

Flat	Built area	100 m² (including terrace at 50%)		
Parking	Built area	30 m²		

State of repair: Good

		Flat	Parking
Valuation approach			
Prices from residential index:	Minimum	174 590	70 000
	Maximum	210 400	80 000

Comparable evidence
In accordance with the Royal Decree of 30 November 1994 there is a need to provide details of three transactions or six properties available on the open market in the previous 12 months.

Therefore, information is presented as shown in Table 13.1 in the valuation report of a valuation company.

Table 13.1 Comparable information as presented in a valuation report

Property	Source	Date	Floor areas	Price ptas/m²	Quality comparison
Flat comparables					
1. Calle A	Sale contract	11/94	95	190 526	Similar
2. Calle A	Verbal info.	11/94	122	174 590	Similar
3. Calle A	Offer	11/94	125	210 400	Similar
4. Calle A	Land registry	10/94	105	184 762	Similar
5. Calle A	Offers	10/94	110	180 000	Similar
6. Calle A	Sale contract	09/94	100	205 000	Similar
Parking comparables					
1. Calle A	Offer	11/94	30	76 667	Similar
2. Calle A	Offer	11/94	30	80 000	Similar
3. Calle A	Sale contract	10/94	30	70 000	Similar
4. Calle A	Land registry	10/94	30	70 000	Similar
5. Calle A	Offer	09/94	28	70 000	Similar
6. Calle A	Offer	09/94	30	71 429	Similar

Following the above presentation of data the *tasador* indicates that the analysis has considered comparable evidence in terms of location, floor area and obsolescence, and has also taken account of the dates of contracts or offers and can conclude that the value to be applied to the subject property is as follows:

Value of flat   190 009 ptas/m²
Value parking   72 786 ptas/m²

These assessed values, more or less, correspond to the average of the above comparables, though an element of subjectivity, or 'professional opinion', in adjusting the data is present. Indeed, there is criticism that it is far too precise to indicate a value to the nearest peseta per m².

Therefore the value of the subject property is

$$190\,009 \times 100 = 19\,000\,900 \text{ ptas}$$

+ 72 786 × 30	=	2 183 580 ptas
total	=	21 184 480 ptas
say	=	21 185 000 ptas

Net replacement cost approach

As most *tasadores* are architects they can draw upon their professional experience to assess construction costs. In the above example the information which would appear in a valuation report is as shown in Table 13.1. However, the 'reported value' selected is that obtained through the direct comparison approach and not the value calculated by the net replacement cost approach (Example 13.2). Therefore, the 'reported' value in this case is 21 185 000 ptas. It should be noted in the report that the valuation is only valid for six months from the valuation date.

Example 13.2: Valuation example of net replacement cost

	Flat	Parking
Price of land per m²	75 000	–
Construction cost	80 000	40 000
Additional costs	19 375	5 000
Depreciation	–9 937	–4 500
Net replacement cost	164 433 ptas/m² (built areas)	40 500 ptas/m² (built areas)

Capitalization method
Example 13.3: Valuation example for investment purposes

Example	office building
Floor area	2000 m²
Lease term	five years from 5/95
Rent	2000 ptas/m²/month = 48 million ptas/annum
Market rent	2500 ptas/m²/month = 60 million ptas/annum
Annual rent review	inflation index
Landlord's costs	10% of the rent stated in the contract
Capitalization	9% (discount rate), real discount rate after taking into account rental indexation
Residual value	70 years (for depreciation purposes)
Average occupation rate	100%
Average annual market growth rate	1% above inflation
Average contract term	five years (during stable periods)

It is assumed that the total annual rent is received in the middle of the year. Also, the purchaser's costs are not taken into account.

In arriving at the valuation, two periods are taken into account, namely up until lease termination and from this date until the end of the building's life cycle. In the first period the contractual rent is discounted and during the second period the existing market rental level is discounted at the beginning of each new lease contract.

First period: term

$$VA_1 = \sum_{i=0}^{4} \frac{48}{(1.09)^{(i+0.5)}}(1 - 0.10)$$

$$= 175.4 \text{ million ptas}$$

Second period: after term

$$VA_2 = \sum_{j=1}^{13} \left[\left(\frac{1.01}{1.09}\right)^5 \sum_{i=0}^{4} \frac{60}{(1.09)^{(i+0.5)}} \right](1 - 0.10)$$

$$= 469.3 \text{ million ptas}$$

Total capitalized value = 644.7 million ptas

(Source of valuations: Sociedad de Tasación SA)

13.8 CONCLUSION

The Royal Decree on valuations of November 1994, together with the Lease Law of November 1994, are changing the approach to valuation. Publication of valuation guidelines by the government has promoted the need for much greater professionalism. In this respect there has been a considerable improvement compared to previous practice as *tasadores* are required to explain more clearly how a value is arrived at. This has led to greater transparency as *tasadores* have to give details of comparative evidence. Also, valuation training is progressing as a result of these changes.

There is an important distinction in the nature of valuation work undertaken by *tasadores* and that done by chartered surveyors. The former are generally involved in mortgage valuations, particularly for residential purposes, the valuation of investment funds and the reserve assets of insurance companies, whereas the latter are predominately involved in valuation work for major clients on the basis of RICS guidance notes on valuations. The nature of valuation reports also differ with *tasadores* using reports which are highly standardized in comparison the valuation reports of chartered surveyors which are more detailed, particularly in relation to market information.

REFERENCES

Bardouil, S. (1995) Laying down the law. *Estates Europe*, **April 1995**, 10.

Clifford Chance (1995) *Investing in Commercial Property in Spain*.

Keogh, G. (1994) *The evolution of the Spanish property market post Boyer*. Paper presented at the Conference of the European Real Estate Society, Amsterdam 9–11 November, 1994.

Ministerio de Economia y Hacienda (1994) Royal Decree on valuations – Orden Ministerial de 30 Novembre de 1994.

RICS (1990) *Statements of Asset Valuation Practice and Guidance Notes* ('*Red Book*'), Royal Institution of Chartered Surveyors Books, London.

Riera, P. and Keogh, G. (1995) Barcelona, in *European Cities, Planning Systems and Property Markets* (eds J.N. Berry and W.S. McGreal), E & FN Spon, London, 219–43.

Sociedad de Tasación SA (1995) *Boletín anual del mercado inmobiliario*.

Weatherall Green & Smith (1995) *El mercado de oficinas*, quarterly publication.

Sweden 14

Stellan Lundström and
Erik Persson

In terms of population, Sweden is a relatively small country with slightly less than nine million inhabitants. The total property stock consists of three million tax-assessed units, of which 2.4 million are single-family units. The commercial property stock, including industrial buildings, comprises 170 000 tax-assessed units. In terms of area, this corresponds to 300 million m², with a market value of SEK1200 billion, distributed among multi-family dwellings, shops, offices and industrial property. The annual turnover in the commercial property market amounts to SEK50 billion. This takes the form of direct property purchases or the acquisition of shares in property companies. However, by the end of 1994, Swedish banks had taken over property valued at almost SEK100 billion in an effort to secure their claims following the property and financial crisis at the end of the 1980s. Currently the banks are in the process of gradually disposing of these property holdings.

The situation in the letting market for office and industrial property, which during the early 1990s was marked by high vacancy rates, weak absorption and more complex leases, has added new dimensions to property valuation. In this respect valuation has become more analytical in character. Currently (1995) Sweden is in a post-crisis reconstruction period, with the economy gradually improving. The inflation rate is low, 2–3%, and GDP is predicted to grow at *c*. 3% per annum for the next three years. However, unemployment and interest rates are still high and the Swedish budget deficit places constraints on the government's ability to act.

As recently as 1992 the Swedish property market was practically closed for foreign investors. However, it is now an open market and with the recovery in economy and membership of the EU there is a growing interest for Swedish property, especially from institutional investors.

14.1 THE MARKET FOR VALUATION SERVICES

Both the property market and the market for valuation services expanded during the 1980s, in particular the need for portfolio valuations in conjunction with cor-

European Valuation Practice. Edited by Alastair Adair, Mary Lou Downie, Stanley McGreal and Gerjan Vos. Published in 1996 by E & FN Spon, London. ISBN 0 419 20040 1

porate financial statements. This was reflected in the establishment of a number of new property companies. In addition, the practice of reporting estimated market values along with book values in the annual financial statements of property companies became more commonplace. This highly active market also led to an increase in the banking sector's needs for valuation data to assess credit-worthiness. As a consequence, the role of valuation has extended and has gradually become an autonomous profession in Sweden consisting mainly of independent valuers working in private consultancy companies. There is also a relatively large number of in-house valuers (*c.* 100) who are directly linked with banks, mortgage institutions, various state or municipal authorities. In total, the profession comprises *c.* 600 full-time valuers of which over half are involved in the valuation of single-family dwellings (*c.* 300–400) whereas *c.* 200 valuers are concerned with property in the commercial sector, namely offices, shops, industrial premises and multi-family dwellings. Part-time valuers dealing with both commercial and residential property are also active in the market, although it is more difficult to assess the exact number.

The valuation industry received a boost at the beginning of the 1980s when the Swedish property market began to attract the attention of institutional investors and, at the same time, several property companies gained a listing on the Stockholm Stock Exchange. Also, a number of new valuation firms were established, most of which have subsequently broadened their operations to include general consulting in real-estate economics. The largest companies in the market for valuation services are Catella AB, Ljungquist Fastighetsvärderingar AB, Forum Fastighets Ekonomi AB, Värderingshuset AB and Fastighetsekonomi.

As in many other European countries, Swedish valuers have been subjected to severe criticism arising from the property and banking crisis at the start of the 1990s. However, in spite of this, the profession has generally managed to maintain a rather favourable reputation due to the existence of a strong valuation organization and good academic training. Other professions, primarily accountants and business economists, have attempted to break into the valuation area but have achieved little success to date. Although the period 1990–1993 marked the deepest crisis in the Swedish property market since the 1930s, the market for services relating to real estate economics, of which valuation is an important component, remains buoyant. In particular, valuation in conjunction with the restructuring of property companies and banks, and the reorganization of the public sector's property holdings have been the main factors underlying the demand for valuation services.

The valuation of commercial property is now conducted primarily for the mortgage rating of property holdings taken over by banks, or for financial restructuring in connection with borrowing related to acquisitions. In addition, valuations are carried out in conjunction with annual financial statements, share valuation and stock exchange listings. Mandatory valuations of the entire Swedish property stock for assessment purposes are conducted regularly, with the resulting valuations used as the basis for various charges and taxes. In addition, valuations are carried out in connection with issues such as compulsory liquidation, expropriation and foreclosures.

The market for valuation services has changed gradually, with a greater use of general real estate economic analysis and consulting. Hence, traditional assessments of market value are increasingly supplemented by cash-flow, liquidity and risk analyses as well as by more sophisticated valuations of property portfolios. Buyers of consulting services increasingly require core data regarding the letting and property markets placing new demands on the competence of property valuers. Furthermore, property companies during the 1990s became driven by the need to maximize the net operating income of property. Together with the widening scope and consultancy role of valuers new requirements are placed on the level of expertise. Hence, the need for further education in real estate economics to supplement traditional knowledge of valuation.

The buyers of valuation services for commercial property consist primarily of property and building companies, institutional investors, banks, mortgage institutions and other financial players such as corporate finance companies, industrial companies and private property owners. A significant proportion of property valuations are also conducted on behalf of municipal property companies and other property owners in the public sector, due in part to the ongoing privatization and rationalization of operations within the public sector.

The price of a complete valuation of a conventional commercial building varies from SEK5000 to SEK50 000. The price is not fee based, as this would contravene current ethical rules. Most valuation companies apply a time-based or fixed price for their standard services, though for larger and more complex undertakings a price is agreed from case to case.

14.2 LEGISLATIVE OR REGULATORY RULES FOR VALUATION

Formal legal control exists only for public valuations, namely valuations for assessed value; valuations relating to various forms of compulsory liquidation; forced sales; and, to a certain extent, for the valuation of fixed assets in balance sheets and annual financial statements. Detailed regulations apply only for assessment purposes. In the other cases, only the principle regarding the applicable value category, its definition and, to a certain extent, recommendations regarding the appropriate valuation method to be used are governed by regulations.

For most commercial property valuation there is no regulatory context other than the fact that banks and institutions may have internal guidelines governing the valuation procedure for their in-house valuers. However, there are certain voluntary agreements regarding valuation procedure. The most important is the contract-based agreement between the Valuation Section of the Swedish Association of Real Estate Economics (SSF:V) and its members. In the membership contract for valuers authorized by the SFF there are mandatory rules governing how members are expected to behave and conduct their assignments as well as a Code of Conduct with ethical regulations.

It should be emphasized that the recommendations in both of these voluntary agreements are based on general principles. They are not designed to provide valuation guidelines in the same manner as those applying to assessment valuation. Nevertheless, the major valuation companies have developed schedules for more extensive reports. Similarly, most banks and credit institutions have developed frameworks and structures in an effort to gain a uniform standard for internal valuation reports.

14.3 CONTEXTUAL INFLUENCES

In Sweden there are three principal factors that have contributed to the development of valuation, namely the academic training of property valuers, the organization for valuers (the SFF) and the need for nationwide and periodically recurring assessment valuation. The tenure systems also have an influence on the valuation procedures.

14.3.1 Academic training of property valuers

Most valuers employed by the major valuation companies in Sweden have studied at the Department of Building and Real Estate Economics at the Royal Institute of Technology in Stockholm. The academic education is part of a 4.5 year academic programme, which is unique in Scandinavia. It has a curriculum structure similar to the program for British surveyors but the valuation content is strongly influenced by the development of real estate valuation in the USA. The course covers economics, real estate economics, finance, law, planning and building technology.

14.3.2 The Swedish Association of Real Estate Economics

The Swedish Association of Real Estate Economics (SFF) was established in 1964. According to its statutes, the association shall work to maintain a principled and professional body of valuers, satisfy the social need for quantitatively good valuation operations and work for the development of real estate valuation theory and methods. It shall contribute to the education of real estate valuers and supervise valuation activities and valuation techniques. Finally, the organization shall promote cooperation with national and international valuer organizations.

The Code of Conduct for valuers regulates professional practices and ethical rules. The regulations are similar to the corresponding rules established by TEGOVOFA while the ethical rules cover the broad area of professional conduct. More specifically, the latter covers professional competence requirements, the content of valuation reports, fees, relations with colleagues and the association, as well as publicity. The association also supports the publication of *Real Estate Terminology* (latest edition 1994) in which all relevant valuation techniques are defined and described, as well as including studies reflecting developments and practice in various areas of valuation. This publication can be regarded as the industry norm for Sweden.

14.3.3 Tax-assessment valuation

Since 1970, there has been a continual nationwide tax-assessment of property in Sweden based on general valuation theory and, in particular, the market value of property which is used as the basis for the payment of state property tax. Commercial premises are currently assessed every six years in conjunction with an extensive description and classification of each assessed property in terms of location, type of utilization, size, standard, age and lease situation. This procedure is extremely important for both the compilation and processing of market information.

14.3.4 Property tenure

The main form of land tenure in Sweden is freehold, though in the metropolitan areas in Stockholm and Gothenburg there is also a special form of leasehold, *tomträtt* (site-leasehold for land). *Tomträtt* can only be held for planned land owned by municipalities or state. In addition there are other different forms of subleases for buildings or land and, in particular, ordinary lettings for offices, retail and residential property. Apart from site-leasehold there are no assignation rights for subleases without permission from the property owner.

Typical lease conditions for commercial lettings are a three year leasing period followed by new negotiations, though the landlord and tenant can prolong the contract on unchanged terms. Annual adjustments of the rent take place according to the contract, with (normally) 75–100% indexation related to the consumer price index. The rent is in most cases a total rent which includes all operational costs (heating, electricity and taxes), repair and maintenance.

14.4 AUTHORIZATION OF VALUERS

In 1994 a decision was made regarding the authorization of valuers, including general valuers, authorized to value all types of property, valuers of single-family dwellings and valuers of agricultural property. Authorization is based on four requirements, namely academic education, practical professional experience, requirements regarding an up-to-date knowledge of the market through continual professional activities and independent status. To be approved as a general property valuer in the future, university training covering at least 3.5 years is required, of which 60 points must be within 'direct valuation related subjects'.

The task of a real estate valuer in creating an objective basis for decisions involving property is expressed in the rules governing authorized valuers. Special emphasis is laid on independence, of which there are three principal conditions. Firstly, an authorized valuer may not conduct valuation on behalf of internal customers. Consequently, valuers who work with banks, mortgage institutions, property companies, insurance companies or with public authorities, or in state or municipal employment, cannot gain authorization. Secondly, the valuer may not conduct assignments for the same customer to an extent that exceeds 50% of total workload during any one year. Thirdly, valuers may not engage in property agency activities.

In Sweden, the liability of valuers is only regulated by general legislation. The valuer is regarded as a professional expert and is assumed to have responsibility for information submitted. Prior to the introduction of authorization, the practice was that the valuer could only be held liable for direct errors regarding information relating to the valuation object. The cases tried so far are very few and have involved incorrect presentation of the layout of the property, its construction and so forth. Property valuers have not been held liable for damages resulting from a lack of market knowledge, though it is likely that greater demands will be imposed on authorized valuers in the future in this respect.

14.5 VALUATION CONCEPTS

The fundamental basis for all valuation is that the value of an asset originates from its potential future utility. This utility value can be transformed into a price through the market process which, in turn, allocates resources for optimum use within the prevailing political, social and economic framework.

14.5.1 Basis of valuation (value categories)

Three value concepts are currently used in Sweden: market value, income value (investment value) and depreciated replacement cost. Of these, market value is by far the most important concept and is in principle defined in accordance with TIAVCS' definition as: 'The likely price in the event of a sale of the property on the free and open market. The sale is assumed to have occurred at the date of valuation after the property has been offered for sale in the market in the customary manner' (based on translation of the Swedish definition). The market value concept is used in compensation legislation and for legislation governing property assessment. Moreover, as discussed, market value comprises an important complement to the book value in many corporate annual reports. Of course, no deduction is made for transaction costs in a given market value.

Despite extensive debate, the definition of market value has survived the banking and property crisis. As in other countries, there is a debate regarding mortgages and the need to calculate an estimated realization price or estimated future price. However, this has not gained widespread acceptance, though in various legal contexts there are references to the market value in present use and the market value in highest and best use, as a result of compensation regulations in planning and expropriation legislation. In conjunction with company valuation and valuation in insolvency situations, there is a need for a market value in the event of forced sale. The concept of a future market value has also been referred to in association with various development projects.

The income value is defined as the present value of the expected future return, however, this value concept has not been used extensively and, consequently, is of little importance. Nevertheless, there is a growing demand for individually adjusted income values, primarily from the financial sector, banks and so forth, and from companies who conduct active management of their property portfolios. By setting an income value in relation to market value, a basis is gained for decisions concerning the purchase and sale of property.

The calculation of production costs is used almost exclusively in valuations for insurance purposes and for cost calculations in construction. Apart from these, production cost estimates only appear in the valuation of specially designed industrial buildings such as those used in the chemical, forest-products and power-generation industries. In these contexts, the property valuer's knowledge of the market is incorporated as a depreciation factor.

14.6 VALUATION METHODS

In terms of method, and in accordance with international practice, there are three procedures for estimating the market value. Accordingly, value can be determined on the basis of comparative methods and the market analysis of prices in comparative sales; investment methods; and depreciated replacement cost methods. Land and buildings are very seldom valued separately (only for special leases of land and in some court cases) other than when depreciated replacement cost methods are applied.

14.6.1 Market value

(a) Comparative methods

In estimating the market value, direct comparative sales, i.e. an estimate of the market price on the basis of comparable objects, are given priority. This is done primarily by direct comparison. If there is a poor basis for this, the valuer's general knowledge of the market is utilized via various key figures, such as price per m^2 or the yield. The following characteristics are used for comparative purposes:

1. the lettable space;
2. assessment value of the property;
3. normalized net operating income;
4. estimated gross market rent.

There is generally satisfactory comparative material for residential and commercial properties. The observed prices can then be related to the lettable space in the form of kronor per m^2 or, if the valuer has a good market knowledge, through the utilization of a direct yield measure. This means that the observed prices for comparative properties are placed in relation to a normalized net operating income or to a market rent. For more common valuation objects, it is also possible to normalize prices at the determined assessed value.

Indeed, in the 1980s, valuers switched increasingly to yield methods and cash-flow based models with the former based in principle on the Gordon formula:

$$MV = f/(p - g)$$

where MV is the market value, f the net operating income, p the discount rate and g the growth in net operating income. The formula involves the perpetual capitalization of an assumed continual growth in net operating income, though in practice valuers frequently view the relationship as a simple one year measure.

Data for estimating the market value are available from public databases. However, for more unusual transactions and office premises, publicly available information may be insufficient. This is often due to the fact that the property sale is part of a larger business agreement in which the reported price reflects circumstances other than those relating to the property. In these circumstances the valuer's experience gains greater importance. A direct yield requirement comprises the most common method of transferring market knowledge to the individual object. The reported direct yield requirement is assumed to apply to a normalized net operating income. Adjustments are subsequently made for deviations in what is the actual outgoing rent, current vacancies and maintenance requirement.

(b) Market value based on cash flow

The market value of commercial property is based on the anticipated yield. Until the 1970s, the building residual and land residual methods were the most common forms of appraisal based on a perpetual capitalization using a life-cycle approach. However, with increasing inflation during the 1970s, the input parameters corresponded less and less with reality, as a result of which other procedures gained increased application.

Pure cash-flow analyses were developed in Sweden at the end of the 1970s. During the 1980s, such techniques gained more widespread acceptance for market value estimates, with cash-flow models applied primarily for result analyses. Arising from the influence of the financial sector, the property and financial crisis boosted the application of cash-flow analysis as a procedure to determine income value. In the steeply declining market of the early 1990s, analyses of leases and cash-flow have gained greater importance in connection with market-value estimates. Also, an illiquid property market with a substantial portion of forced sales has meant that there is greater focus on risk in the increasingly popular cash-flow analysis.

The typical cash-flow analysis shows the actual income stream and operational cost, repair, maintenance, taxes and capital costs for a five to 10 year period with a residual value at the end of the period. For market value purposes the capitalization rate is determined from market analyses.

The consideration of risk has not always been an obvious factor, especially when it involves valuations within insurance and property companies. The major valuation companies follow the spread in market yields through an analysis of reported prices. In cases in which the basic data does not provide a sufficient foundation for interpretation, the approach is to proceed from a model with a non-risk real rate of interest, supplemented by risk and depreciation increments. The objective is that the yield calculations should, as far as possible, be based on conditions in the property market.

(c) Market simulation

In cases in which the relevant market information is not available, market simulation is used. This procedure can essentially be described as a yield-based investment calculation in which the valuer attempts to simulate what a knowledgeable buyer would be expected to pay for the valued property. This process uses area and market letting information as well as data derived from cash-flow analysis.

In the absence of relevant market information the method has application, though there is a tendency for misuse due to simplification of the valuation process, facilitated by the increasing access to database computations. However, it should be pointed out that the method is risky since the valuer can construct a market value without any market evidence. The method imposes stringent demands on the valuer's expertise and integrity.

(d) Uncertainty

The valuation statement is usually concluded with an indication of the uncertainty intervals for the estimated market value. How such an interval is calculated varies largely from case to case, ranging from a simple percentage to more advanced statistical analysis or calculations based on probable variations in the input value parameters.

14.6.2 Income value

The income-value method is based on a calculation of present value. This is conducted in the same manner as a customary investment calculation. Calculations of individual income values is expected to increase in the future. Income value can be determined by using two basic procedures, either a standard investment calculation through the capitalization of a normalized income for the first year or alternatively through some form of cash-flow model.

An income value is calculated on the basis of the conditions provided by the customer. This means an individual adjustment of both the cash-flow forecast and the yield requirement. Calculation of the model requires basic data on incoming and outgoing payments, length of the calculation period, discount rate and a residual value.

14.6.3 Depreciated replacement cost model

As previously indicated, the determination of the production cost as the basis for an estimate of market value is used (apart from the insurance context) only for the valuation of specially designed industrial premises. In this context, knowledge of the property valuer is incorporated in the depreciation factor. Production costs are also applied in setting the assessed value for industrial buildings with no alternative uses.

14.6.4 Development trends

The decline in the letting and property markets in recent years has accelerated the development of new decision-making models. The rapid progress in information technology has played a major role in this development. Analysis primarily involves various types of market and feasibility studies incorporating macro-economic indicators relevant to households, business and industry.

14.7 MARKET INFORMATION

By international standards, access to property-related data is unusually good in Sweden. The principle of public access to information has been long established and the existence of a database-integrated information system that includes all property allows for a high degree of market transparency. The Swedish Land Data Bank System (LDB), which is an official register of real estate, contains information about the following:

1. title and deeds;
2. location of the property, address and coordinates of both the land and the building;
3. size;
4. owner's name and address;

5. layout information;
6. encumbrances, mortgages;
7. entitlements;
8. tax-assessment value.

The data in the property register relating to owner, mortgages, entitlements, plans and taxation values for any property are public documents in Sweden. Accordingly, this type of information can be fed into databases and serves as a source of information for market analysis and property valuation.

In addition, there is the Real Estate Tax Register which contains tax-assessment data with information in accordance with the LDB system, plus coded descriptions of owner category, location, number of buildings and the size of the building, age, standard and actual rent on the taxation date. This register is also databased and public.

Information from property assessment is also in the public domain and can be linked up with general physical and legal data as well as price observations from the property market. This provides a unique opportunity to create extensive and widely available price statistics as the basis for an estimate of market value. These types of statistics are at the disposal of all the major valuation companies.

The third register is the Land and Property Price Register. This contains information concerning all land transfers, including purchases and sales. The register contains information about forms of transfer, buyer and seller, acquisition date and purchase price. Again, the register is databased and public.

These data are published regularly. In addition, various companies can subscribe to computer files for their own data-processing and publications. Individual companies can either access the various databases via their own terminals or order individual files at a very low cost. A number of major valuation companies have developed their in-house systems based on official data. Indeed, it is possible to access information from public databases regarding layout, type of building and mortgages on the property. This type of area-based information can be combined with geographical information systems (GIS) to provide a basis for an increasingly popular service in the form of market analyses and general descriptions of the economic base in various areas. Thus, information can be processed in accordance with ready-made frameworks, however, it should be stressed that the utilization of GIS is as yet in an early stage and that there are no ready-made low-cost routines adapted for valuation purposes.

In addition, the largest valuation companies systematically compile market information on rents, yields and vacancies. There are also companies which provide information in the form of area-based key figures for rents, vacancies and yield requirements. This type of information is available for the 100 largest regions in Sweden and include an analysis of the major market transactions.

14.8 VALUATION REPORTS

In this section the content of a normal valuation report for commercial property is presented. It is important to note that for individual cases (and firms) there may be considerable variation from this compilation and emphasis can vary substantially among the various headings.

14.8.1 Contents in a normal valuation report for commercial property

1. **The assignment** Client, purpose of valuation, value category, date of value and special assumptions and/or limiting conditions.
2. **Sources of information and inspection** Official sources, maps, special information from the client. Observations from inspection.
3. **Property description** Owner, tenure, easements and other legal regulations, location, surroundings, planning, building descriptions (more detailed technical descriptions preferably in appendix), need of immediate repair, different kinds of lettable areas, vacancies, assessment. Evaluation of the location and the property.
4. **Property related economic data** Leasing contracts, actual rents, rent losses, operating expenses, taxes, assessed value, loans, interests. Estimated market rents for the subject property.
5. **Area and market descriptions and analyses** Population, industry, services and communications for the municipality and the district, market rents and market vacancies, property market situation, supply and demand. Evaluation of the area and the markets.
6. **Cash-flow analysis** (if applicable) To illustrate net operating income (NOI) before and after debt service over a calculation period and with assumptions concerning inflation, rent and cost development, vacancies, discount rate.
7. **Applied valuation procedure** A short description of applied valuation methods
8. **Estimation of market value** From:
   (a) analyses of direct comparable sales by using key data in different approaches namely net capitalization method (NOI/yield), area method (price per m²), gross multiplier, related to assessed value, other appropriate procedures depending on the situation;
   (b) using key data from general market experience;
   (c) market simulation by investment method from discounted cash-flow using market adjusted variables.
9. **Sensitivity analysis** To illustrate uncertainty and risk
10. **Final value estimate**
    (a) Summary with final value, uncertainty interval, key figures.
    (b) Limiting conditions if necessary.
    (c) Appendices.
    (d) Maps and photos, easement regulations, economic reports, comparable sales, etc.

14.9 CONCLUSION

The market for valuation services in Sweden has changed substantially following the crisis in the property market in the early part of the 1990s. This has, amongst other matters, resulted in new players with alternative ideas and preferences. Indeed, of particular importance is the increased influence of the financial sector. This development has broadened the concept of valuation with more emphasis on analyses and consultancy, the latter having implications for changes in the valuation profession. Similarly, a more internationalized market is another factor affecting the development of valuation practice and techniques. The recent authorization of valuers has highlighted quality and competence in the valuation process. Clearly, the Swedish professional body of valuers will need, in the future, to address, a more demanding market for its services but can look forward to facing greater challenges and more stimulating assignments.

FURTHER READING

Bejrum, H. and Lundström, S. (1986) *The Real Estate Economics of Rented Residential Property, Forecasts and Valuation*, Catella AB, Stockholm (Swedish).

Forsberg, M. and Karlsson, A. (1994) *Commercial property valuation – a comparative study between England and Sweden*. Diploma work, Department of Real Estate Economics, Royal Institute of Technology, Stockholm (English).

Hall, B. and Persson, E. (1994) *Authorization of Swedish Valuers*. The Swedish Association of Valuers (English).

Institutet för värdering av fastigheter (1994) *Terminology, Real Estate Economics and Property Right*, AB Svensk Byggtjänst, Stockholm (Swedish)

Lundström, S. (1994) *Theoretical and empirical problems in valuation of distressed real estate in Sweden*. Paper, Building and Real Estate Economics, The Royal Institute of Technology, Stockholm.

Persson, E. (1993) *Principles and Methods in Property Valuation*, Catella AB, Stockholm (Swedish)

Valuation Board (1993) *Valuation Guidelines*, Valuation Board, Stockholm (English).

Switzerland 15

Martin Hoesli,
André R. Bender and
Philippe Favarger

Switzerland is a small country with densely populated inhabitable regions. Its surface area is 41 000 km² and the population totals seven million inhabitants (of whom almost 20% are foreigners), giving a density of 169 inhabitants per km². For the year 1993, the national income is estimated to have been 310 billion Swiss francs, or approximately 44 000 francs per inhabitant. The primary sector occupies less than 6% of the working population and the tertiary sector, whose role is constantly increasing, occupies nearly 60% of the population. Switzerland has always dedicated a sizeable part of the gross national product to the gross domestic fixed capital formation: 26.7% on average between 1948 and 1991. In addition, investment in property and construction represents more than 60% of this value. The Swiss property construction market is therefore more important than the size of the country's population would suggest.

As a result of the small area of the Swiss territory, and the very marked political wish to maintain a strong agricultural sector (more than a quarter of the entire surface of the country), the availability of building land is limited. The change of zones for construction use is subject to stringent federal and local laws. Moreover, a federal law that was introduced in 1993 strictly limits the sale of agricultural land. Thus, one may say that there is, strictly speaking, no free market in agricultural land. Consequently the price of land actually available for construction is very high.

As for costs involved in building construction, Switzerland has a reputation for building on a long-term basis, and this holds good for all types of private and public construction work. When one takes into consideration the high level of salaries, one can see that the cost per m² or m³ for Swiss construction (roads, hospitals, factories, subsidized accommodation, free market accommodation, single-family houses, etc.) is among the highest in the world. This is possible owing to the high standard of living of the population and as a result of the low mortgage interest rates which remained below 4.5% between 1930 and 1968, and indeed below 4% in the years 1940 to 1964 (Figure 15.1).

European Valuation Practice. Edited by Alastair Adair, Mary Lou Downie, Stanley McGreal and Gerjan Vos. Published in 1996 by E & FN Spon, London. ISBN 0 419 20040 1

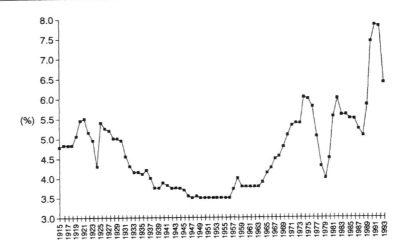

Figure 15.1 Interest rate for 'first-rank' mortgages, 1915–1993. *Source*: Swiss Statistical Yearbook and Swiss National Bank.

For a given building, it is possible to obtain up to three separate loans. The first one usually covers *c.* 60% of the value and has priority in case of default. In some cases, particularly during the late 1980s, the three loans could finance the total cost of the property. Obviously, the different ranking of the loans, and thus the different risk level, is associated with different levels of interest rates. As mortgage loans are high, the repayment period often extends over 50 years. In certain cantons the practice has even developed for 'first rank' mortgages actually being unrepayable. As a result the global mortgage debt in Switzerland is very high (nearly 500 billion francs, or 70 000 francs per capita).

In terms of stock, the value of existing real estate represented 870 billion Swiss francs in 1990 (Hoesli *et al.*, 1993), i.e. more than 50% of the national wealth. This figure is shared between 650 billion for the residential sector and 220 billion for the non-residential sector, and does not include public buildings (e.g. schools, hospitals, barracks) nor the real estate wealth owned by companies whose shares are quoted on the stock market. It is interesting to note that the share of real estate in the national wealth is very similar to that of other industrialized countries, as, for example, the USA.

15.1 INVESTMENT BY OWNERS AND TENANTS

One of the consequences of the high cost of accommodation is the relatively low proportion of residences occupied by their owners, probably the lowest in Europe. The rate stands at 31% nationally, but in the urban areas it is significantly lower (in the canton of Geneva, for example, it is only 11%). Currently several initiatives, both at cantonal as well as at federal level, are under way to expand owner-occupation. At the latter level it is important to mention that as of 1 January 1995, individuals can use part of the funds invested in their pension schemes to finance the purchase of their primary residence. The federal

Government set up many years ago a system which makes it possible to purchase a property with 10% of equity thanks to a partial guarantee – even some subsidies – by the State.

As far as cantonal initiatives are concerned, one should mention the desire very clearly expressed by one of the members of the State Council of the Republic and Canton of Geneva, in charge of housing affairs, to see the rate of owner-occupancy of properties rise within a reasonable time span from 11 to 20%. The success of these initiatives will, in the end, depend largely on what solutions can be found to reduce the cost of accommodation. For as long as the cost of accommodation remains more than five times higher than the family income before tax, it will remain difficult to encourage the acquisition of property without direct financial aid from the State. Moreover, the legal protection granted to tenants and the system of subsidies for rented accommodation aimed at the middle classes does nothing to engender in these people the necessary financial effort required of them to move towards the purchase of property.

The ownership of residential buildings is nevertheless to a large extent private: the State has, in the majority of cases, favoured private building at the expense of the construction of state-owned housing. There are, of course, exceptions, notably the city of Geneva, which is the largest property owner in the canton, holding approximately 5% of housing units in the city. The pension funds own a share of approximately 12% of residential wealth, which represents nearly 20% of their assets. Among the institutions owning property, it is worth mentioning the insurance companies and the mutual funds. According to various estimates, the share of real estate wealth owned by institutional investors and the State is around one-quarter.

Large companies usually own the buildings (commercial buildings and offices) in which they conduct their business. The remainder of commercial buildings and offices are owned by private investors who rent these buildings. Unfortunately, no statistics exist as to the relative share of each class of owner.

15.1.1 Characteristics of the Swiss property market

In general terms, the Swiss property market is relatively opaque and difficult to observe. It is in fact difficult, sometimes impossible, to obtain clear information concerning properties exchanged and above all concerning the price of transactions. Public information is essentially concerned with the location of lots exchanged, the date of transaction and the area covered by the actual building, but the price is only published in certain cantons. As a result, statistics concerning the property market are very fragmented. No national index exists, even for the price per m². The progressive computerization of the services provided by the authorities should permit, at least in those cantons where the transaction prices are quoted, the creation of property indexes of a more detailed nature.

The characteristics of the market have a clear effect on the methods of property valuation used in Switzerland. In fact, it is extremely difficult to relate these to market prices. Valuers tend rather to estimate the value of a property by applying the depreciated cost approach or by capitalizing the income from the property. As a result of the use of the former method, the recognized valuers are mainly architects. One should note that it is not necessary in Switzerland to follow any special training course, nor to pass any specific examination, before one may work as a property valuer and therefore this title is in no way protected by law.

15.2 LEGISLATIVE AND REGULATORY CONTEXT

15.2.1 Property valuation

Apart from fiscal legislation, there are no particular legal norms concerning property valuation. As far as fiscal matters are concerned, the norms of valuation are decreed at a cantonal and federal level. One could quote for example the Bernese norms on the 'Official Valuation of Buildings' (*Traité d'estimation*; *Schätzerlehrgang*, 1986), as this canton has recently gone ahead with a general revision of fiscal values. According to the Bernese law decree dating from 19 November 1986 concerning the general revision of official values of buildings and hydraulic forces, the official value of residential and commercial buildings should be established on the basis of revenue. In many other cantons, the fiscal value is found by making use of both the capitalization of income approach and the depreciated cost approach.

Different institutions and associations of valuers have decreed norms and directives related to the valuation of buildings.

1. The Union of cantonal valuers for the valuation of buildings, which is comprised of valuers working in Government agencies (*Union des experts cantonaux en matière d'évaluation des immeubles*) publishes a *Valuer's Manual*. The monetary value of the buildings as constructed should, in principle, be determined by applying the sales comparison approach. The heterogeneous nature of the buildings and the impenetrable nature of the market lead, however, to a combination of the income approach and the depreciated cost approach. If accounting data are available, it is the net income that should be capitalized. These valuers mostly conduct appraisals for taxation issues.

2. The central office for debenture bonds of the cantonal banks (*Centrale de lettres de gage des banques cantonales*) has adopted a new regulation since 1992. The regulation serves as a basis for the valuation of buildings subject to mortgages placed as security against loans from the central office. Residential buildings are to be valued on the basis of the income approach and the depreciated cost approach, with the greater weight being placed on the former method. To apply the income method, one should capitalize rents. For administrative and commercial buildings only the income approach is used.

3. The Swiss chamber of expert valuers (*Chambre suisse d'experts en estimations immobilières*) was created in 1986 following an initiative by the Swiss union of real estate valuers (*Union suisse des professionnels de l'immobilier*) and is comprised of independent valuers. This chamber has adopted the European professional code of ethics laid out by TEGOVOFA (The European Group Of Valuers Of Fixed Assets). It thus advocates evaluations that are very much market orientated and highly detailed. According to their tariff lists, the cost of an appraisal is made up of fees and costs (postage, visits, searches for documents, etc.). In the 1992 edition, the experts' fees were

around 175–225 Swiss francs for the expert and between 75 and 150 francs for secretarial services.

4. Other lenders in the real estate market, such as banks and insurance companies, often have internal directives. The value of the property is usually estimated on the basis of the depreciated cost approach and the income approach. The crisis of the 1990s has led numerous institutions to increasingly favour the income approach.

5. In company accounts, real estate assets are generally quickly amortized in order to create hidden reserves.

6. Court valuations are undertaken by independent valuers who can be members of the Swiss chamber of expert valuers.

15.2.2 Sale and purchase of buildings

The federal law on acquisitions of real estate in Switzerland by non-residents (*Lex Friedrich*) makes these purchases subject to an authorization. The authorization may be given if the building is used to house the purchaser's professional activity, under certain conditions if it is to be the secondary residence, or if it concerns social housing. The *Lex Friedrich* law is currently under revision. There are strong political pressures to abrogate this law but the outcome is uncertain, at least in the near future.

15.2.3 Protection of tenants

Tenants, especially tenants of residential units, are protected by law (*Code des obligations*). They may, in particular, demand the application of regulations that are relatively strict as far as rents are concerned.

The rents of commercial and administrative premises are often linked to the consumer price index if they are not related to turnover. For residential buildings, the indexation of rents [up to a maximum of 80% of the consumer price index (CPI)] is only authorized if the lease is signed for a minimum duration of five years, which is rather rare.

In residential units, the tenant may appeal against a rent increase. Such a rise may be justified legally by seeking to maintain the purchasing power of the capital that is exposed to risk (i.e. the equity). In any case, the rent increase cannot exceed 40% of the CPI. A rise in the operating costs and maintenance costs may also be passed on to the tenant. Lastly, the owners may demand an increased rent in the event of a rise in mortgage interest rates, and the tenant may demand a lowering of rent in the opposite case. Cantonal laws differ from one canton to another and some rents (e.g. those of subsidized housing) are more protected than others, which makes this field quite complex.

15.3 VALUATION TECHNIQUES

Generally speaking, the market value is estimated by computing a weighted average of the values obtained by using the depreciated cost approach and by capitalizing the rental income. For owner-occupied single-family houses and industrial real estate, most valuers generally rely exclusively on the depreciated cost approach.

15.3.1 The income approach to value

The income approach results from the application of financial theory according to which the value of an asset corresponds to the present value of the future stream of cash flows. To apply this method it is necessary to forecast future cash inflows and outflows. However, this method is seldom used in Switzerland, with the exception of some real estate mutual fund managers and real estate professionals.

From a theoretical point of view, the present value of a constant stream of cash flows until infinity is equal to the capitalization of the annual cash flow if interest rates are constant. In Switzerland this simplified formula is widely used. Most of the time valuers capitalize the gross rental income rather than the operating income (i.e. the income before interest and tax). The valuers justify the use of this approach by the wide variations in annual maintenance costs.

(a) Capitalization of the rental income

According to this approach, the value of a property is estimated as follows:

$$V = R/k$$

where V is the value of the building (*valeur de rendement, Ertragswert*), R the gross rental income (market rent rather than effective rent should be used; for residential real estate, the unit of comparison is the number of rooms, whereas for commercial and industrial real estate it is the number of m^2, i.e. the net surface area) and k the capitalization rate.

The capitalization of the rental income is based on the hypothesis that the operating and maintenance expenses are proportional to the value of the building. To account for these expenses, a premium is added to the required rate of return set by the investor. As a rule, heating charges are billed separately from the rent. In some cantons the caretaker's costs are also billed separately.

Valuers who have access to information on the sale of comparable properties (either because they also act as brokers or because they receive information from other brokers) use this market data to assess the rate of capitalization. When data are not available, a premium is usually added to a base rate. For a long time the mortgage interest rate has served as the base rate, but a growing number of experts suggest taking the yield rate of Government bonds as a base rate because of the growing effect of politics on mortgage interest rates. In addition, the recent wide variations in mortgage interest rates have led a growing number of experts to use average long-term rates and not the rate of the day.

There are a number of empirical rules to define the capitalization rate of which the best known are listed below.

1. Naegeli and Hungerbühler (1988) suggest adding between 1 and 5% to the 'first rank' mortgage interest rate, according to the type and age of the building. For buildings containing multiple apartments one adds 2–2.5% if they are less than 10 years old, and 2.5–3% if they are older than 10 years. For

commercial real estate and offices, additions of 2–3% and for industrial real estate 3–4% are made.

2. Haegi (1966) and Praplan (1978) utilize a premium of 1.5–3% above the average mortgage interest rate (first and second ranks). In this connection, Haegi quotes the former regulation for valuation used by the central office for debenture bonds of the cantonal banks. In the new regulation, reference is made to the 'current market rate': 'rates of around 0.5% to 2% higher than the average yield rates of the first rank mortgages are considered normal' (1993, Art. 13).

3. The official Bernese valuers (Association of Official Valuers for the Canton of Berne (1993, p. 61) suggest taking as base rate the average interest rate weighted between external funding and internal funds, and to add various premiums:
    (a) between 0.2 and 0.7% for the operating costs;
    (b) between 0.2 and 1.5% for maintenance costs;
    (c) between 0.1 and 0.5% for the rehabilitation provision;
    (d) between 0 and 0.3% for the vacancy risk;
    (e) between –0.3 and 0.3% for the various locational characteristics defined by Naegeli and Hungerbühler (1988).

4. The Union of Cantonal Valuers (1990) takes the base rate to be the average of the rates on borrowed funds and on internal funds, and they publish a range of premiums linked to the quality of construction and the building's age. For residential buildings:
    (a) between 0.7 and 2.7% for operating and maintenance costs;
    (b) between 0.5 and 0.9% for depreciation;
    (c) between 0% and 0.2% for vacancy risks;
    and for commercial buildings:
    (a) between 0.7 and 3% for operating and maintenance costs;
    (b) between 0.6 and 1% for depreciation;
    (c) between 0 and 0.4% for vacancy risks.

5. Haegi (1966) also outlines a rate of capitalization of between 5.5 and 7.5%. He quotes different sources, notably the directives of the cantonal banks, which propose ranges of rates or ranges of premiums linked to the mortgage interest rate according to the age and condition of the building. He does, however, draw attention to the fact that this kind of valuation is only approximate.

(b) The capitalization of the net operating income

This method is also based on the theory of a constant income over an infinite horizon. The net operating income is defined as the rental income minus the operating and maintenance expenses, which are supposed to be proportional to the rental income. In Switzerland this method is seldom used. Naegeli and Hungerbühler (1988) considers it inappropriate because the operating expenses are, in fact, very volatile over time, particularly the maintenance and rehabilitation costs.

To solve the problem of the volatility of costs, one has to estimate the expenses in the long term. Haegi (1966) draws from numerous examples a proportion of expenses (operating plus maintenance costs) totalling on average 35% of the rental income, with figures varying from 20% to 50%. Praplan (1979) quotes the practice of reserving between 25 and 45% of the rental income for expenses.

For the capitalization rate, the Union of Cantonal Valuers suggests the application of legal norms by assuming 60% of external funds (mortgage rate) and 40% of internal funds, without precisely indicating how to assess the rate of return required by the owner on the equity.

(c) Present value of future cash flows

Detailed forecasting of income and expenditure in the future is not widespread in Switzerland. The development of financial theory and computerization are however leading to a growing number of experts no longer accepting a simple capitalization of rental income.

Haegi (1966) outlines different methods originating in Germany, in particular the separation of the net operating income attributed to the land from that attributed to the building (a method recognized by American experts). The income attributed to the land is capitalized (constant to infinity), while the income from the building is forecast only for its foreseeable lifespan. This method has a limited use in Switzerland, notably because of the longevity of the buildings.

Fierz (1987) does not separate the income attributable to the land from the income attributable to the building, but suggests computing the present value of the income before deduction of projected maintenance and rehabilitation costs.

Some institutions, notably real estate mutual funds quoted on the stock exchange, compute the value of the buildings by calculating the present value of the future income stream. The net operating income is projected over a limited period of time (eight to 10 years) and the residual value at the end of the period is obtained by the standard capitalization procedure.

15.3.2 The depreciated cost approach

According to the depreciated cost approach, the value (*valeur intrinsèque*, *Realwert*) of a property is obtained by adding the net replacement cost of the building to the value of the land.

(a) The value of the building

The first course of action is to determine the gross replacement cost of the building, then to deduct a certain margin to allow for depreciation. The replacement value is generally estimated by multiplying the number of m³ as defined by the Swiss Society of Engineers and Architects (SIA: *Société suisse des Ingénieurs et Architectes*) by the appropriate price per m³. Two methods are usually employed to determine the degree of depreciation of a building.

The first consists in establishing a degree of depreciation (physical depreciation and functional obsolescence) in view of the life expectancy of the building or its composite parts (Peret *et al.*, 1987), which can then be applied to the replacement cost. There are many formulae to determine the nature of value over time, e.g. Naegeli and Hungerbühler (1988) or Praplan (1979) – Praplan also gives a range of life expectancy for each element of construction. On this subject, see also Association of the Official Valuers of the Canton of Berne (1993).

When the separation of the elements of the building is possible, one can apply a second method which consists of estimating the cost of restoring the building to its original state. This cost is then deducted from the replacement value. The MER (Merminod and Vicari, 1989) method, for example, permits a rapid valuation of the total costs required to restore the building to its original state on the basis of an appraisal of the various components of the building. A small adaptation of the MER method allows the valuer to obtain directly a rate of depreciation (Marco, 1993).

(b) The value of the land

Numerous valuers use data provided by the market which consists of estimating the value of the land in comparison with the sale of comparable lots. When such data are not available, experts can use the method developed by Naegeli and Hungerbühler (1988) which they call 'valuation according to the situational class' (*die Berechnung nach Lageklassen*, p. 43). This technique is, at first sight, quite astonishing, for it has no fundamental underlying theoretical basis. It is based on an empirical observation of a certain relationship between two pairs of elements:

1. the rental income and the value of the land (it should be noted that the relationship between the rental income and the value of the land also depends on the level of mortgage interest rates);
2. the value of the land and the total value of the property.

Naegeli thus defines eight classes of situation according to different criteria (general situation, accessibility, density of occupation, quality of the building, quality of location, quality of the environment). The part played by the value of the land in the overall value of a property is approximately 6% in class 1 and 50% in class 8. When the resulting gross yield (i.e. the ratio between the rental income and the total value) is 6.25%, then the ratio between the value of the land and the rental income is equal to the situational class number. This method of situational classification is also used in Germany. In Switzerland, it is practised by different cantonal administrations and also by a number of banks and insurance companies. It allows the calculation of the value of the land from a given value of the building.

Example 15.1

We consider a single-family house in the vicinity of Geneva. The following scores (on a scale from 1 to 8) can be given for the various criteria considered by Naegeli:

1. general situation   4
2. accessibility   2
3. density of occupation   4
4. quality of the building   3
5. quality of location   2
6. quality of the environment 4

The average score is: $(4 + 2 + 4 + 3 + 2 + 4)/6 = 3.2$. On this basis, Naegeli and Hungerbühler (1988) would conclude that the land:value ratio is 0.2, and the land:rent ratio 3.25.

15.3.3 Value proposed by the expert

It is generally considered in Switzerland that the market value (*valeur vénale*, *Verkehrswert*) of an income-producing property can reliably be estimated from a weighted average of the value obtained using the above two methods (depreciated cost approach and income approach). The unsolved problem is to choose the weights. The approach allows the appropriate value to be obtained only when the market elements are included, i.e. when using both methods separately. With the income approach, this means that the rental income and the capitalization rate depend on the state of the market at the time of the appraisal. When using the depreciated cost approach, the depreciation rate and the price of land selected by the valuer also depend on market conditions.

Naegeli and Hungerbühler (1988) propose a method which links the weighting coefficients to the difference (plus or minus) between the two value estimates (Table 15.1). This method is based on the assumption that the value resulting from the use of the income approach is more important than the one obtained with the depreciated cost approach. A building, never mind how beautiful, large or complex it may be, is worthless unless it is used and generates an income.

Table 15.1 Determination of the weights used to compute the property value (Naegeli and Hungerbühler, 1988)

Relative difference between the two value estimates (%)	Weighting coefficient of the income approach value (%)
0–9	50
10–19	67
20–29	75
30–39	80
40 or more	83

Example 15.2
The following data pertain to a single-family house (the appraisal is conducted as of the end of 1987):

Number of m³ as defined by the SIA	800 m³
Building cost per SIA m³	650 CHF
Depreciation rate	10%
Size of the lot	400 m²
Price per m² of lot	900 CHF
Other improvements	30 000 CHF
Various costs (as a percentage of total cost)	10%
Annual gross rental income	66 500 CHF

With the depreciated cost approach, the following value is estimated:

Reconstruction cost (800 m³ at 650 CHF)	520 000 CHF
– Depreciation (10% of 520 000 CHF)	52 000 CHF
+ Other improvements	30 000 CHF
+ Value of the land (400 m² at 900 CHF)	360 000 CHF
+ Various costs (10%)	85 800 CHF

| Value estimate with depreciated cost approach | 943 800 | CHF |

The income approach yields the following estimate of value:

Annual gross rental income	66 500	CHF
– Operating expenses (20% of rental income)	13 300	CHF
Annual net rental income	53 200	CHF
Capitalization rate	5.75%	
Value estimate with income approach	925 200	CHF

If the valuer estimates market value by computing an equally weighted average of the two approaches the following result is achieved:

Estimate of market value = (0.5 × 943 800) + (0.5 × 925 200) = 934 500 CHF

and the market value is estimated to be approximately 935 000 CHF.

15.3.4 Behaviour of various parties involved

As a general rule, the approach used to obtain an estimate of market value is that of the weighted average of the two methods discussed previously. Regarding the various parameters (coefficients of weighting, rate of depreciation of the buildings, capitalization of yield rate), each company or investor has their own particular method. According to estimates, 80% of the buildings owned by pension funds are valued at their purchase price (Böhm, 1992). Recently, this practice has been questioned and the idea of valuing the properties owned by pension funds at a value closer to market value has been developed, though most pension funds do not intend to sell their properties or even are restricted by law to do so.

The insurance companies regularly retain as a balance-sheet value the weighted average between the two values discussed above. Some annually calculate the value of their buildings based on the income approach.

Real estate mutual funds are required by law to determine the market value of their properties once a year. In order to do this, they strongly favour the income approach. As a general rule, their value estimates are rather conservative, which has led to complaints from some shareholders. A trial that was brought to the federal court has shown that for a particular mutual fund the appraised values were strikingly lower than the fair market value estimates. Some mutual funds compute the present value of the projected future cash flows of their properties, but the external valuers, who are mostly architects, favour the weighted approach as defined before. According to a number of valuers, the perspective of a mutual fund with regard to real estate valuation should be identical with that of a pension fund, since the long-term future income for both constitutes the main objective of the investment.

The banks carry out appraisals mainly in the context of mortgage loans; these appraisals are undertaken by both internal and external valuers. Again, the estimated value is a weighted average between the depreciated cost and income approaches. The weights are usually set at one-third to one-half for the depreciated cost approach and one-half to two-thirds for the income approach. It can be noted that banks increasingly use the income approach. The fiscal authorities carry out more or less regular appraisals for taxation purposes. Generally, the methods used are those described above, but across the 26 autonomous cantons there are almost as many methods as there are cantons.

15.4 INFORMATION SOURCES

15.4.1 Real estate market

No statistical information is obtained at a national level as far as real estate prices are concerned. Obviously, the census, which is conducted every 10 years, provides some interesting insights concerning the nature of residential real estate in Switzerland. The Federal Office of Statistics, mandated by the Federal Council to produce statistics on real estate transactions, published a general conceptual framework in 1994. It is hoped that in the near future reliable and useful data will be officially published.

Some cantons or towns publish data on real estate transactions, for example Basel, Genève, Zürich, Fribourg, Luzern and Ticino. The various statistics contain relatively good information concerning the volume of transactions, and types of sellers and purchasers. On the other hand, there is little information available about prices and, in particular, there are no data on yields. There is great reluctance to publish this kind of data and it is difficult to introduce change because of the power of the population expressed at elections.

15.4.2 Rents and vacancy rates

There are indications as to rents in the residential sector at the national level (Table 15.2 and Figure 15.2) and in certain cantons. Statistics on the level of rents for various submarkets (single-family homes, two-bedroom apartments, three-bedroom apartments, etc.) are taken from the federal census and complemented each year in certain cantons. At the national level, vacancy rates are unknown except for the year of the federal census and for residential buildings. In some cantons the statistics are collected annually. Vacancy rates are relatively low in Switzerland (close to 1% in the residential sector) although they have increased since 1990, particularly in the commercial real estate and office sectors. No official statistics are available regarding commercial rents and vacancy rates at the national level.

15.4.3 Construction prices

The level and progression over time of construction prices of residential properties are published in four cities: Zürich, Bern, Luzern and Genève. The Zürich figures for the price per m³ are given in Table 15.2 and Figure 15.2. The Zürich index is often used as a reference in Switzerland.

15.4.4 Interest rates

In its monthly bulletin the Swiss National Bank publishes the interest rates for mortgage loans and the yield rate on Confederation bonds (Table 15.2 and Figure 15.3 for the real rates).

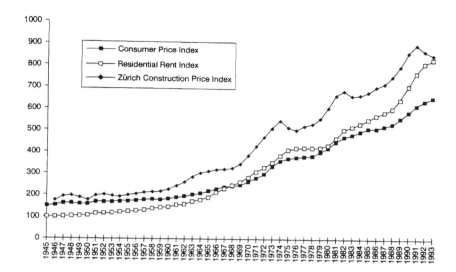

Figure 15.2 Price index, 1945–1993 (1993 = 100).

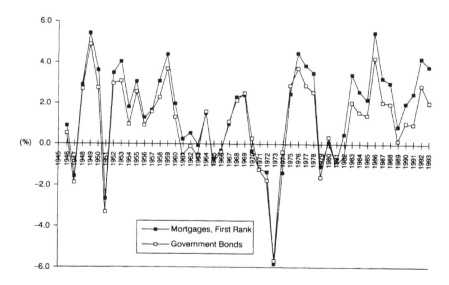

Figure 15.3 Real rates, 1946–1993.

Table 15.2 Statistical Information, 1946–1993

Year	Consumer Price Index December (8/1939 = 100)	Annual Inflation Rate (%)	Rent Index December (8/1939 = 100)	Construction Price Index Zürich (6/1939 = 100)	Mortgage first rank (%)	Government bonds (%)	Mortgage first rank (%)	Government bonds (%)
1945	151		102.0					
1946	155	2.6	102.0	176.6	3.6	3.2	0.9	0.5
1947	163	5.2	103.0	194.3	3.5	3.2	−1.6	−1.9
1948	164	0.6	105.0	197.2	3.5	3.3	2.9	2.7
1949	161	−1.8	107.0	189.4	3.5	3.0	5.4	4.9
1950	160.8	−0.1	108.8	179.4	3.5	2.6	3.6	2.8
1951	171	6.3	116.8	197.9	3.5	2.8	−2.7	−3.3
1952	171	0.0	118.7	204.3	3.5	3.0	3.5	3.0
1953	170.1	−0.5	120.8	197.9	3.5	2.6	4.0	3.1
1954	172.9	1.6	124.8	193.6	3.5	2.6	1.8	1.0
1955	173.6	0.4	127.8	201.1	3.5	3.0	3.1	2.6
1956	177.4	2.2	131.0	206.4	3.5	3.1	1.3	0.9
1957	181	2.0	134.1	212.9	3.7	3.6	1.7	1.6
1958	182.6	0.9	141.1	215.7	4.0	3.2	3.1	2.3
1959	181.5	−0.6	145.5	218.3	3.8	3.1	4.4	3.7
1960	184.7	1.8	148.8	227.0	3.8	3.1	2.0	1.3
1961	191.2	3.5	157.4	243.7	3.8	3.0	0.3	−0.5
1962	197.4	3.2	161.4	260.9	3.8	3.1	0.5	−0.1
1963	205	3.9	173.1	284.1	3.8	3.2	−0.1	−0.6
1964	209.8	2.3	179.3	302.1	3.9	4.0	1.5	1.6
1965	220.1	4.9	190.8	311.3	4.1	4.0	−0.7	−0.9
1966	230.2	4.6	213.5	318.6	4.3	4.2	−0.3	−0.4
1967	238.3	3.5	230.8	320.5	4.5	4.6	0.9	1.1
1968	243.5	2.2	246.3	324.2	4.6	4.4	2.3	2.2
1969	249.2	2.3	261.3	344.6	4.8	4.9	2.4	2.5
1970	262.7	5.4	281.3	384.2	5.1	5.7	−0.3	0.3
1971	280.1	6.6	307.9	427.3	5.3	5.3	−1.2	−1.2
1972	299.3	6.9	328.9	470.6	5.4	5.0	−1.4	−1.8
1973	335.0	11.9	351.4	512.8	5.4	5.6	−5.8	−5.7
1974	360.3	7.6	385.6	548.7	6.0	7.1	−1.4	−0.4
1975	372.7	3.4	413.0	517.0	6.0	6.4	2.5	2.9
1976	377.5	1.3	420.9	505.4	5.8	5.0	4.5	3.7
1977	381.8	1.1	422.1	524.3	5.1	4.1	3.9	2.9
1978	384.7	0.8	422.5	533.1	4.3	3.3	3.5	2.5
1979	404.5	5.1	424.2	560.6	4.0	3.5	−1.1	−1.6
1980	422.4	4.4	434.8	610.6	4.5	4.8	0.1	0.3
1981	450.2	6.6	467.7	667.9	5.6	5.6	−1.0	−1.0
1982	474.9	5.5	509.1	689.4	6.0	4.8	0.5	−0.6
1983	484.9	2.1	521.8	667.4	5.6	4.2	3.4	2.0
1984	499.2	2.9	536.1	670.2	5.6	4.6	2.6	1.6
1985	515.3	3.2	556.0	685.0	5.5	4.7	2.2	1.4
1986	515.3	0.0	575.3	708.4	5.5	4.2	5.5	4.2
1987	525.3	1.9	591.1	723.4	5.2	4.0	3.2	2.1
1988	535.7	2.0	607.9	756.7	5.1	4.0	3.0	2.0
1989	562.3	5.0	650.7	802.4	5.9	5.1	0.8	0.2
1990	592.3	5.3	712.8	866.5	7.4	6.4	2.0	1.0
1991	623.1	5.2	773.4	903.0	7.8	6.2	2.5	1.0
1992	644.5	3.4	818.1	874.2	7.8	6.4	4.2	2.9
1993	660.4	2.5	837.0	856.0	6.4	4.6	3.8	2.1

Average Annual Rates

1946–93	–	3.12	4.48	3.42	4.73	4.18	1.56	1.03
1964–93	–	3.98	5.39	3.74	5.41	4.88	1.37	0.87
1979–93	–	3.67	4.66	3.21	5.85	4.87	2.11	1.16

Sources: Swiss consumer price index: *Swiss Statistical Yearbook (SSY)* and *Monthly Bulletin Swiss National Bank (SNB)*; rent index: *SSY*; construction price index Zurich (up to 1960: August, 1961 onwards: october): *SSY*; mortgage rate first rank: 1946–86: *SSY*, five cantonal banks; 1987–93: *SNB*, New Mortgages, cantonal Banks; Government bonds (long term): 1946–52: *SSY (rendement moyen emprunts Confédération)*; 1953–82: *SSY, rendement moyen obligations Confédération, échéance, moyenne annuelle*; 1983–93: *SNB, rendement moyen obligations Confédération, moyenne annuelle.*

15.5 CONCLUSION

Due to the opacity and the small size of the real estate market, the comparison method is seldom used in Switzerland. Appraisers normally compute a weighted average of the cost approach and the income approach, with generally a higher weight based on the income approach. As regards the income approach, a capitalization of the income is undertaken. However, the discounted cash-flow method is beginning to be used by some valuers.

The Swiss real estate market is not very open to foreign investors as the purchase of property by investors not residing in Switzerland is subject to authorization by the appropriate state authority. Authorization is granted for commercial real estate used for professional activities, and for holiday homes. For income-producing properties the authorization can only be obtained for social housing.

REFERENCES

Association des estimateurs officiels du canton de Berne (1993) *AEC – Traité d'estimation: Directives pour l'estimation d'immeubles.*

Böhm, E. (1992) Wie Pensionskassen ihre Immobilien bewerten. *Schweizer Personalvorsorge*, **11/92**.

Centrale de lettres de gage des banques cantonales suisses (1993) Réglement d'estimation.

Fierz, K. (1987) *Wert und Zins bei Immobilien*, Schriftenreihe der Schweizerischen Treuhand- und Revisionskammer, Band 56, Zurich.

Haegi, A. (1966) *Die Bewertung von Liegenschaften*, Zurich, Polygraphischer Verlag.

Hoesli, M., Gacem, B. and Bender, A. (1993) Estimating the value of Swiss residential real estate. *Swiss Journal of Economics and Statistics*, **129**(4), 673–87.

Marco, D. (1993) *Valeur de substitution, vétusté, et valeur intrinsèque d'un bâtiment à l'aide de MER-OFL1*, Centre d'étude technique pour l'amélioration de l'habitat, Université de Genève.

Merminod, P. and Vicari J. (1989) *Manuel MER, Méthode d'évaluation rapide des coûts de remise en état de l'habitat*, Bulletin du logement no. 28, Berne, Office fédéral du logement.

Naegeli, W. and Hungerbühler, K. (1988) *Handbuch des Liegenschaftenschätzers*, 3rd edn, Schultess, Zurich.

Perret, F.L., Wieser Ph., Jaccard, P.A., Jahiel, H.B., Elci, M. *et al.* (1987) *Evaluation des biens immobiliers*, EPFL (Ecole polytechnique fédérale de Lausanne), Institut des transports et de planification, LEM (Logistique Economie Management) and ETHZ (Ecole polytechnique fédérale de Zurich) – Institut für Hochbautechnik – Abteilung für Architektur.

Praplan, R. (1979) *La vétusté*, Praplan, Genève.

Praplan, R. (1978) *Technique et pratique immobilières*, Praplan, Genève.

United Kingdom 16

Neil Crosby

Since the end of the Second World War there has been a fundamental change in the ownership and occupation of commercial and industrial property in the UK. The ownership of prime property was once in the hands of the large private estates, traditional institutions, such as the Church or the Oxbridge colleges, and small local property market investors or owner-occupiers.

The property companies dominated this change for the first 20 years following the war with the number of quoted companies rising from 35 in 1939 to 185 in 1964 (28 of these were involved in the residential market). Between 1964 and 1970, the number of companies declined on account of take-overs, amalgamations and liquidations, even though 10 new companies were formed. In 1992 the top 10 property companies had a market capitalization of £4222 million, in real terms this represents 117% of the 1964 value but only 33% of the 1970 value (Table 16.1).

Table 16.1 Publically quoted property companies (including residential)

Year	Number of companies	Market capitalization (£m) book values
1939	35	30
1958	111	
1962		800
1964	185	1296
1970	137	2764
	Market capitalization of top 10 companies	
1964		347
1970		1625
1992		4222

Sources: Fraser (1993); Guildstream (1973).

European Valuation Practice. Edited by Alastair Adair, Mary Lou Downie, Stanley McGreal and Gerjan Vos. Published in 1996 by E & FN Spon, London. ISBN 0 419 20040 1

The insurance companies and pension funds did not seriously enter the property market until the 1960s, in response to the decline in the attractiveness of bond investment as inflation was finally perceived to be endemic in the economy. This perception was not fully reflected in investment prices until the late 1960s. Figures 16.1 and 16.2 chart the progress of new money into property by the financial institutions in both nominal and real terms. They indicate a cooling of their interest in property during the 1980s.

The most recent development in the UK property investment market has been the involvement of overseas investors who, in 1987, contributed less than £300 million rising to nearly £2 billion in 1988. In 1989 and 1990 overseas investment ran at over £3 billion per annum but by 1992 it had fallen to around £1.3 billion, still substantially more than the pre-1988 levels (DTZ, 1993).

The emergence of property as an important home for the funds of the investing institutions caused a corresponding increase in interest in and analysis of the operation of property investment markets. There was virtually no research undertaken into these markets until the 1970s and property valuation techniques suffered the same neglect. However, during the 1980s, research into both markets and methods increased, especially as the initial surge of interest in property investment during the 1970s was tempered by less attractive returns during the early to mid-1980s relative to equities and bonds. The 1980s also saw a realization that the economic life of office and industrial property had reduced significantly and the expectation of refurbishment and redevelopment heightened the concern regarding property as an investment. Property investment performance in the 1960s and 1970s outpaced the alternatives but this has since reversed.

As with other investment assets, increasing concern often leads to a price re-rating, which in turn promotes a fall in total returns due to inclusion of price or value change as an element in the measurement of return. On an historical per-

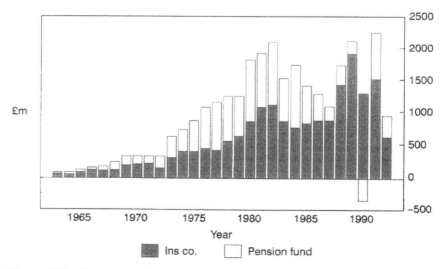

Figure 16.1 New money into property – insurance companies and pension funds 1963–1992. *Source:* CSO, DTZ Debenham Thorpe, IPD, Darlow (1983).

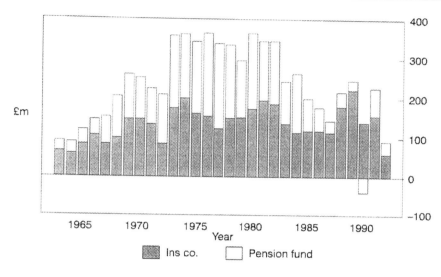

Figure 16.2 New money into property (1962) prices – insurance companies and pension funds 1963–1992. *Source:* CSO, DTZ Debenham Thorpe, IPD, Darlow (1983).

spective, investment yields of property generally fell during the 1970s but rose relative to other investments during the 1980s until the reverse yield gap between gilts and property, which had existed since 1960, was extinguished for a time in 1992 (Figure 16.3). These changes have contributed to the relative performance figures set out in Table 16.2.

Table 16.2 Comparative investment performance 1963–1992, total returns (% pa)

Years	Direct property	UK equities	UK gilts	Cash	Retail prices index
1963–1972	16.9	13.6	3.1	6.4	5.2
1973–1982	13.5	6.5	13.8	12.5	12.7
1983–1992	8.6	18.5	10.1	11.6	5.4

Source: Investment Property Forum (1994).

In 1990 the commercial and industrial property market went into recession and property capital values fell due to a combination of increasing yields and falling rents. The fall in capital values would have been worse than was actually recorded if lease lengths had been shorter and rent review provisions within leases not been upwards only. Overseas investors, particularly from Germany, also helped create some market activity. In the late autumn of 1993, the investment market began to recover with the financial institutions judging that the time was right to re-enter the property market; based upon an assumption that rental growth would appear in the future on the back of the recovery in the economy and a realization that the price of property was low in comparison with the other investment alternatives, especially since the UK's exit from the European Exchange Rate Mechanism.

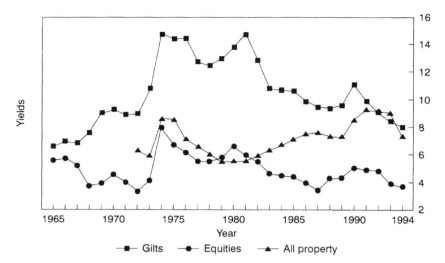

Figure 16.3 Investment yields – gilts, equities, property 1965–1994. *Source:* Hillier Parker Research (1993, 1994).

This recession has had implications for many aspects of the property market, not least valuation techniques. The falling market during 1990–1993 introduced the concepts of overrented properties (properties let on leases at rental levels which have since fallen but have no provision within the lease to reduce the rent to the prevailing market level) and lease inducements (the practice of offering incentives to tenants to take premises at rents that are thought to be higher than the prevailing real rental level). New valuation techniques were needed to deal with these phenomena.

The fall in property values also highlighted the issue of loan valuations. During the late 1980s, many banks lent significantly in the property investment and development market (see Figure 16.4). These loans were underpinned by market valuations of the property undertaken at or near the peak of the market. Many of these loans which were authorized by non-property experts relied heavily on the valuer's report. However, during the recession, the number of bankruptcies increased substantially (see Figure 16.5) leaving banks with properties which could only be sold at reduced prices.

The outcome of such volatile property market conditions over the recent past has been a reappraisal of both bases and methods of valuation. The largest institutional body representing valuers in the UK (The Royal Institution of Chartered Surveyors – RICS) responded by producing a working party report under the chairmanship of Michael Mallinson (RICS, 1994) which is likely to be the catalyst for some major changes in procedures and practices.

16.1 MARKET DATA

There is no freedom of information in the UK and, as a consequence, property market transactions data are not in the public domain. This creates difficulties in

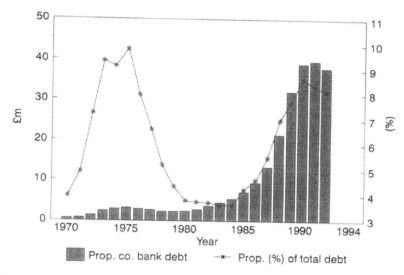

Figure 16.4 Bank loans to property companies outstanding debt 1970–1992. *Source:* CSO.

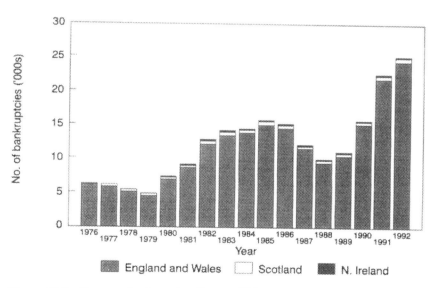

Figure 16.5 Company bankruptcies. *Source:* CSO.

researching commercial and industrial property markets and has resulted in some of the leading firms of property consultants collating information and publishing indices of property market value movements. As a result, there now exists a number of long-run property market indices with varying degrees of disaggregation. The largest of which, the Investment Property Databank (IPD), publishes a digest every year (IPD, 1994) and can be commissioned to produce data disaggregated down to a level of five properties, a limit which protects the confidentiality of the individual transactions. Morell (1991) identifies the make up of the different indices and the sources which include property consultants such as Hillier Parker, Jones Lang Wootton, Healey and Baker and Richard Ellis.

The published indices are related to a very specific part of the property market, namely investment property owned by many of the major institutions and property companies, and these cannot be described as whole property market indicators. Data on the latter is held at central government level by the Inland Revenue Valuation Office, who produce a market report but do not create indices.

Supply data is also restricted. The Central Statistical Office (CSO) used to produce commercial and industrial floorspace statistics but this series was suspended in 1986. Floorspace, occupancy and take up are surveyed for specific markets such as Central London offices and other major submarkets by individual firms of property agents and consultants, but the data is not coordinated and is incomplete.

The level of both property market and other economic data is also variable at a national, regional and local level. Local level statistics lack consistency and regional level data is less comprehensive than at the national level. A number of private organizations have taken advantage of this lack of consistency to collate and sell local market data, for example, *Focus*. This lack of comprehensive and freely available property market data hinders the valuation process by restricting the availability of transactions and creating obstacles to research.

16.2 THE LANDLORD AND TENANT RELATIONSHIP

A distinctive feature of the UK property market is the nature of the contract between landlord and tenant. The dominant tenure is the freehold interest which for all practical purposes is outright ownership of the property. The major restriction on development, including changing the use of property, relates to planning law. Freeholders can let the property to leaseholders (tenants) who have the right to occupy for the term of the lease, pass on the right to occupy subject to some restrictions in the lease (assignment) and sublet to other occupiers (subleaseholders), thereby becoming headleaseholders/landlords.

The increasing involvement of the institutions and property companies in the property market, allied to the long-term strength of the lettings market between 1960 and 1990, produced a situation where landlords could persuade tenants to enter into long-term contracts on terms which transferred many of the liabilities of property ownership to the tenants. Rents could be reviewed regularly to participate in market growth in nominal terms but rents could not be reduced in a downturn. Assignment of leases was possible but a contingent liability remained with the lessee if a subsequent tenant defaulted. This so-called institutional lease was normally for 25 years with upwards-only rent reviews every five years, on tenant full repairing and insuring terms with service charges to pass on any expenditure on common parts.

Some of the features of this lease have been challenged over the last few years by both tenants utilizing the oversupplied market and by government threatening to legislate on privity of contract (remove the contingent liability of previous tenants) and to outlaw upwards-only rent reviews. The latter threat caused some concern to the investing institutions and property companies as it attacked one of the sacred cows of the UK property investment market. Long leases with upwards-only rent reviews produce a long-term guarantee of income return with no risk of a fall except if the tenant defaults. The value of this guarantee has been fully appreciated in the current recession. However, tenant pressure has reduced the length of new leases (with some commentators suggesting that 15 years may become the new norm in the UK) forcing landlords to concede break clauses within these new leases. However, only a few landlords have given away upwards and downwards reviews (Investment Property Forum, 1993).

The rights of landlords and tenants on expiry of leases differ depending on which part of the UK the property is situated, for example, tenants in England and Wales are entitled to renew their leases on terms to be agreed (or decided in court if agreement cannot be reached) with landlords only able to regain possession on certain grounds (based on either tenants not undertaking their responsibilities under the lease or landlords needing the property for their own occupation or to undertake redevelopment). At rent review, a well-established procedure has evolved based upon arbitrators (valuers or occasionally lawyers), or expert valuers, determining rents if the landlord and tenant cannot agree. There is a plethora of case precedent in this area defining the meaning of various wordings within rent review clauses and determining the admissibility of evidence in rent review proceedings.

The various procedures and processes to be adopted for the different rent determinations on new lettings, lease renewals and rent reviews appear to have led to slightly different rental levels for the same property. The reliance on transactions leads some commentators and practitioners to believe that review rents lag the level of rents on new lettings. In a rising market they will be lower and in a falling market they may be higher (Crosby *et al.* 1993). Lease renewals are similar to a rent review in a rising market (a one-to-one negotiation with the spectre of a third-party determination) but take on more of the characteristics of a new letting in a falling market (where tenants can threaten to move to a plentiful supply of alternative premises if they do not obtain similar letting terms to new tenants).

16.3 VALUATION STANDARDS AND PROFESSIONAL LIABILITY

The way in which valuations are produced in the UK is regulated by means of both professional liability case law and guidance from the main professional organisations; the RICS, the Incorporated Society of Valuers and Auctioneers (ISVA) and the Institute of Revenues, Rating and Valuation (IRRV).

16.3.1 Valuation guidance notes

At present, the most influential guidance comes in the RICS 'Red Book' [the *Statements of Asset Valuation Practice and Guidance Notes* (RICS, 1990)]. The 'Red Book' is continually being updated and is mandatory on all members of the RICS, ISVA and IRRV carrying out valuations for the following purposes:

1. company accounts and financial statements subject to audit;
2. Stock Exchange prospectuses and circulars and for take-overs and mergers;
3. pension and superannuation funds, insurance companies, property unit trusts and unit linked property assets;
4. commercial property loans, debentures and mortgages, except those for the private purposes of lender or borrower.

The common feature with these valuations is that they are published and may be relied upon by parties other than those who commissioned the valuation. The 'Red Book' gives guidance on the appropriate basis of valuation, the reporting requirements and standards, and defines who can carry out the valuation. Although the 'Red Book' attempts to remove itself from a discussion of valuation methods, it does inevitably stray into advice on appropriate methodology from time to time. The basis of a valuation defines the target which the valuer seeks to achieve and, for certain purposes, the target needs to be very accurately identified to ensure that valuations for similar purposes are on a consistent basis. Methods of valuation represent the way in which the target is achieved and it is the responsibility of the valuer to choose the most appropriate method or methods to achieve the aim or target.

Although the majority of valuations do not come under the jurisdiction of the 'Red Book', many clients ask for some other valuations to be based upon it. Once a valuer has agreed to provide a 'Red Book' valuation, then departure from the principles enshrined in the book should only be with good reason. Although failure to undertake valuations under the conditions of the 'Red Book' would not necessarily be a prima facie case of negligence, evidence that the valuer chose to ignore the 'Red Book' without good reason would certainly not help the defence to a negligence claim.

The RICS is also developing a set of non-mandatory guidance notes for all valuations. This is the 'White Book' [the *Manual of Valuation Guidance Notes* (RICS, 1992)] and refers to the following:

1. valuations for buying and selling;
2. residential or commercial property loan valuations for the private use of the parties;
3. development appraisals;
4. fire insurance and related matters.

The 'White Book' restates the 'Red Book' bases of valuation but also goes further in developing practice papers giving guidance on how valuers should or could approach certain valuation problems. It also gives additional information on model conditions of engagement and 'White Book' guidance is set to evolve by the addition of similar practice papers looking at specific problems across the whole field of bases, methods and procedures related to property valuation.

However, at the time of writing, the RICS plans to merge the 'Red Book' and the 'White Book' to create a comprehensive (but continually evolving) guide to valuation practice. It is highly likely that the new 'Red Book' will give mandatory instructions on procedural matters and closely define the bases of valuation to be adopted for various valuation purposes. Guidance on valuation approach and method should not be made mandatory and left to the valuers' discretion.

There are a number of other statutory or regulatory standards which have to be observed. For example, valuations concerning mergers, take-overs or listings on the Stock Exchange have to comply with the Stock Exchange '*Yellow Book*' and '*Blue Book*' (Stock Exchange, 1993a, b) and the valuation of insurance company assets must take account of the Insurance Companies Acts. However, the RICS '*Red Book*' and '*White Book*', to a great extent, consolidate all of these requirements.

The '*Red Book*' and '*White Book*' therefore provide a comprehensive guide to the manner in which valuations are carried out in the UK. The two books provide, *inter alia*, information on model conditions of engagement, reporting and reviewing of valuations (including reporting of negative values) and bases of valuation as well as detailed guidance on the approach to valuing specialized items such as mineral bearing land, plant and machinery, goodwill and water rights. They also detail the differing statutory requirements of different owners where appropriate.

16.3.2 Professional liability

There have been a number of decisions in the courts concerning negligent valuations. In Singer and Friedlander Ltd v. John D. Wood and Co. (1977) (243 EG 212) the judge suggested that a valuation should fall within an acceptable bracket and further suggested 10% either side of the correct valuation would be permissible, extending this to 15% in exceptional cases. This case was decided on a valuation carried out in a period of boom prior to a fall in values. At the same time, the case of Corisand Investments v. Druce and Co. (1978) (248 EG 315, 407, 514) was heard and the judge decided that valuations had a speculative element in them and a valuer should be able to look ahead over the period of six to 12 months beyond the valuation date. The judge in this case also followed the permissible margin of error principle and suggested 15%.

In Mount Banking Corporation Ltd v. Brian Cooper and Co. (1992) (35 EG 123) the judge rightly questioned the validity of these previous two judgements. The right figure is not actually accessible and the correct test should be the exercising of proper skill and care. This case examined the methods adopted by the valuer and they were found to be competent. The legal position of valuers would now appear to be that the amount of the error is not the significant factor, but the basis, methods and procedures adopted by them will be scrutinized for professionalism and care.

However, given past experience, judges and other non-experts do sometimes appear to have difficulty with the concept that pricing valuations do not last for more than one instant in time. Valuers need to consider the additional information necessary to put the single valuation figure into context; perhaps by explaining the state of the market within which the valuation is undertaken.

16.4 BASES OF VALUATION

All the bases of valuation set out in the '*Red Book*' relate to the estimate of an exchange price at a single point in time. The bases allowed by the '*Red Book*' are:

1. open market value;
2. open market value for existing use;
3. open market value for alternative use;
4. depreciated replacement cost.

16.4.1 Open market value

Open market value is defined as the best price reasonably expected in a transaction completed on the valuation date assuming:

1. a willing seller (a hypothetical owner who is neither eager nor reluctant, i.e. not forced but not at a price which suits only him/her);
2. prior to the valuation, a reasonable period to market the property and complete all the necessary legal formalities was available;
3. during this period the state of the market was the same as at the date of valuation;
4. any bid from a special purchaser is excluded.

Open market value is used for investment properties, those held for future development and those declared surplus to a company's requirements, and it includes any existing alternative use (or 'hope value' for that use). It is a very well defined 'unrealizable' figure. Almost all property valuations to determine exchange price suffer from the problem that the valuation represents a single snapshot in time of an asset that cannot be sold in an instant. Formerly, the definition assumed that the marketing period took place from the valuation date into the future, also assuming no change in the state of the market during this period. The definition seeks to determine the sale price that would have been achievable if properties could be transacted in an instant thereby enabling the valuer to utilize up-to-date comparable transactions. Due to this seemingly irreconcilable problem, the British Bankers Association have recently persuaded the RICS to agree a '*White Book*' Valuation Guidance Note (VGN 12) which introduces a new valuation basis for commercial property loan valuations. The estimated realization price (ERP) is:

> The amount of cash consideration before deduction of costs of sale, and taking no account of any additional bid of a prospective purchaser with a special interest, which at the reporting date the Valuer considers could reasonably be expected to be obtained by a willing seller for the interest in the subject property on completion of an unconditional sale on a date assumed and stated by the Valuer, such date to be one following the period and method of marketing considered by the Valuer to be necessary to achieve that amount.

RICS, 1992, third amendments 1994

In addition to ERP, VGN 12 also introduces estimated restricted realization price (ERRP) which is exactly the same as ERP except the marketing period is restricted to one which is less than the valuer feels appropriate to the subject property.

ERP and ERRP are significantly different from open market value in one major respect. The marketing period is assumed to take place in the future and the market is not assumed to be static. The sale price will be affected by any changes in the market and the valuer must reflect them in the valuation. In effect, the valuer is being asked to forecast value change over the marketing period.

Whether this change in basis will give the bankers who forced it what they want is doubtful. All that has been achieved is to push the single snapshot in time to the end of the marketing period. The question now answered is, 'If a mortgage is granted today and foreclosed tomorrow, what price will be achieved?'. That will not save a bank which lends a high percentage of value at the top of the market from the consequences of a bankrupt owner or occupier in any subsequent recession.

VGN 12 also includes some guidance on additional information. It is suggested that the valuer includes advice on current and expected trends in the market for the type of property subject to the valuation and this is probably the key to sensible lending. If lenders had been informed in 1989 that the property market was very high relative to past trends they might not have been willing to lend so much; if they had taken no notice they would have shouldered much of the blame with valuers being less open to criticism.

16.4.2 Open market value for existing use

This basis is used for valuing non-specialized land and buildings which is owner-occupied for the purposes of the business which is operated out of the premises. It is also used for the valuation of non-specialized public sector property assets in continuing occupation. The accounting principle is the net current replacement cost of the asset by the business. The 'Red Book' definition is the same as open market value but with the additional assumption that the property will continue to be owner-occupied for the existing use. The property is assumed to be vacant. However, the falling property market of the early 1990s has introduced some difficulties of interpretation with this basis of valuation. The value of vacant properties has been particularly depressed due to difficulties of finding a tenant or an owner-occupier. Consequently, valuers have introduced a void period into their valuations (in some cases up to two or three years) before assuming occupation or income. However, while some valuers have assumed that owner-occupied properties are truly vacant (attracting a large deferment period and a significant write down of the value) others have assumed that the occupying company would immediately buy back the premises on the continuing occupation assumption (with the valuation excluding any period of vacancy). This issue has yet to be resolved by the Asset Valuation Standards Committee of the RICS who produce and amend the 'Red Book'.

The interpretation of the existing use provision is also difficult. The 'Red Book' implies that existing use does not mean the existing occupier or even the same business use. For example, it does not mean that a grocer's shop must be valued as a grocer's shop, any other shop use can be assumed. Existing use would appear, therefore, to mean existing planning use but the 'Red Book' states that this is also not true. The precise definition of existing use is not specified but it may mean the same planning use even if that particular use can be changed without permission.

16.4.3 Open market value for alternative use

The definition is the same as for open market value but assumes that the alternative use has been allowed. It is not appropriate for company or other accounts (basis on-going business) but it needs to be reported if materially different from open market value for existing use. If, for example, a company is taken over on the basis of a valuation to the existing use and subsequently the assets are sold off for a higher development value, the original shareholders have been misled as to the true value of the assets and the company. Conversely, the existing planning permission might be personal to the occupier and subject to a time limit, in that case the existing use value reported in the accounts might be significantly higher than the alternative use.

16.4.4 Depreciated replacement cost

There is some confusion within the UK valuation profession as to whether depreciated replacement cost (DRC) is a basis or a method of valuation. It is defined in the existing '*Red Book*' as a basis of valuation for properties which are not normally traded in the market. This is often the case for specialized properties in the private sector (for example, large industrial plants) and many properties in the public sector. The '*Red Book*' (which does not normally deal with methods of valuation) details the approach to this valuation, even though it calls it a basis of valuation rather than a method. The valuation is based upon a cost method; adding a site value to a cost of replacing the building, depreciated for age and obsolescence. In essence, the method suggests that the best way to assess how much the existing or similar occupier would pay for the land and buildings of a specialized asset is to assess the cost of buying the site for the existing use and building substitute premises, and then discounting for the fact that the new premises would provide better space. This seems to accord with open market value for existing use, therefore DRC is the best method for assessing open market value and should not be viewed as a basis of valuation. However, the '*Red Book*' affirms that DRC is a basis of valuation best suited to assessing the accounting concept of net current replacement cost.

For '*Red Book*' purposes, the valuation needs qualifying as 'subject to adequate potential profitability' of the business being operated from the premises.

16.5 APPLICATION OF METHODS OF VALUATION IN PRACTICE

The five basic methods used in the UK for assessing value are:

1. comparison of rents and capital values;
2. investment methods;
3. profits-based methods;
4. cost-based methods;
5. residual valuations for development.

16.5.1 Comparison

Reliance on comparables in assessing market value or price is well established in the UK. It has been confirmed by the courts and is largely unquestioned by the valuation practitioners. However, in both the recession of the early 1990s and a previous briefer, less severe downturn in the mid-1970s, transaction quantity fell and the valuation of assets by comparable techniques has been criticized.

Despite this, transaction evidence underpins almost all pricing valuation in the UK, including substantial inputs into all the other methods (especially the application of the investment method).

A good comparison is a recent transaction in the subject property or, alternatively, the same type of property which is similar in terms of location, physical characteristics and tenure. Due to the lack of freedom of information, valuers have to spend time collating and verifying information on transactions. During the recession in the property market, this process becomes more difficult due to the paucity of transactions, the use of confidentiality clauses where the parties to the transaction (usually the landlord in a rental negotiation) attempt to hide the precise details and the difficulty in interpreting the real level of value which is often disguised by a set of inducements to the tenant or the purchaser to keep the actual rent or price paid above the true market level. A hierarchy of evidence exists:

1. open market sales or lettings in the same property;
2. open market sales or lettings in a similar property;
3. agreed statutory prices (CPO) or lease renewals/rent reviews in the same or a similar property;
4. third-party determinations come last (and may not even be admissible in rental disputes).

In most cases the valuation is reduced to a unit of comparable information based on value per size unit. At present, practitioners still use imperial measurements but this is changing with planned metrication taking place during 1995/96. Detailed guidance is produced by the RICS and ISVA on measuring practice (RICS/ISVA, 1993) and, depending upon the type of property, the measurement of premises is to gross external area (GEA), gross internal area (GIA) or net internal area (NIA). Land is usually measured to site area (SA), defined as the total area of the site within the site boundaries measured on a horizontal plane. The normal units of value are price per m^2, yd^2, ft^2, ha or a. The following are an indication of the units for particular property types.

Property type	Unit of value
Offices	Price per ft^2 or m^2 NIA
Industrial and warehouses	Price per ft^2 or m^2 GIA or NIA
Business use	Price per ft^2 or m^2 NIA
Department or variety stores.	Price per ft^2 or m^2 GIA
Food superstores	Price per ft^2 or m^2 GIA
Retail warehouses	Price per ft^2 or m^2 GIA
High street shops.	Price per ft^2 or m^2 zone A NIA

Zoning of high street shop units is often carried out, especially in rent review and lease renewal negotiations. Zoning seeks to quantify the assumption that the floorspace at the front of the ground floor of a shop unit is more valuable than space at the rear of the shop, due to the power of the front area to attract shoppers into the unit and the reducing accessibility of the rear shop (see Figure 16.6). Zoning, where the second 20 ft (or thereabouts) of depth (zone B) is valued at a proportion (often one-half) of the first 20 ft (zone A) and the third 20 ft (zone C) is reduced by a further half, is not used for non-ground floors or away from the high street.

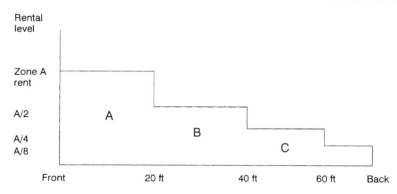

Figure 16.6 High street shop zoning.

Twenty foot zones are not standard across the whole of the UK with central London and Scotland (30 ft zones), and Northern Ireland (15 ft zone A and 25 ft zones for the remainder of the ground floor) being significant exceptions.

Metrication is causing some concern to shop valuers with 6 m or 6.1 m being the likely new zone depths adopted for most locations in the UK, with 9 m or 9.14 m for central London and Scotland.

Example 16.1: Valuation

Assuming the shop is 21 ft wide and 75 ft deep, and comparables show that the rental value is £100 per ft² zone A (based upon normal lettings on full repairing and insuring terms and five year rent reviews):

Zone A	21 ft × 20 ft = 420 ft² × £100	= £42 000
Zone B	21 ft × 20 ft = 420 ft² × £50	= £21 000
Zone C	21 ft × 20 ft = 420 ft² × £25	= £10 500
Remainder zone D	21 ft × 15 ft = 315 ft² × £12.50	= £3 938
Rental value of ground floor		= £77 438

Valuation, say £77 500 per annum.

16.5.2 Investment valuation

Of all the methods of valuation applied to property, the investment method has attracted most scrutiny and research in the UK. The name itself is a misnomer as the model applied to assess market value is a comparison technique, using yield as the unit of comparison. The basic model for a property let at its full rental value is simply rent divided by yield. This model, if converted to a discounted cash-flow (DCF) model, assumes the rental value remains static into infinity (perpetuity) and any prospect of refurbishment or redevelopment is also ignored in the cash flow. Not surprisingly, the yield is termed the all-risks yield (ARY), as all risks are implied within it and are not explicitly isolated. The mathematics are simply the summation of the present values of the constant income stream; the present value is £1 pa, which is called the years purchase in the UK. The yield is normally determined from comparisons of similar property transactions and not from first principles.

(a) Reversionary freehold interests

Conventional growth implicit market valuation approaches

On account of the nature of lease structures and rent review patterns in the UK, up to 1990 most investment properties would be let at rents which would be less than the current estimated rental value (ERV), sometimes termed the rack-rent. These properties are called reversionary and three adaptations of the basic rent/yield model have been in popular use to assess their market value; term and reversion, layer/hardcore and equivalent yield.

All three models are very similar variations on the same theme. Similarities include the fact that they all revert to the ERV only and rental values are not inflated above their current level. The only differences are that the term and reversion model splits the cash flow vertically while the layer/hardcore technique splits it horizontally (Figures 16.7 and 16.8). Both models apply different yields to the term and reversion or bottom slice and top slice based upon the perceived differences in the security of the income flow. The term is perceived to be more secure than the reversion and the bottom slice more secure than the top slice. These manipulations are thought by some practitioners and commentators to be irrational as, to be a true all-risks yield model, it is incorrect to isolate any particular risk when so many others are hidden in the yield. The equivalent yield model applies the same yield to both parts of the valuation (term and reversion or bottom slice and top slice) and it is therefore irrelevant whether vertical or horizontal slicing is adopted. It is the only defensible all risks yield approach.

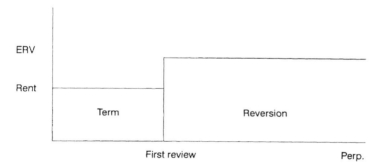

Figure 16.7 Income profile – reversionary freehold term and reversion.

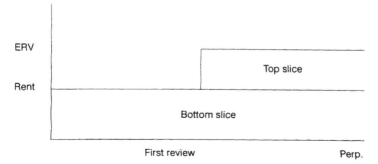

Figure 16.8 Income profile – reversionary freehold layer/hardcore.

However, it was not the most popular through the 1980s. A survey of 160 practitioners undertaken during 1988/89 (Table 16.2) identified that, although the majority of valuers used term and reversion, vertically-sliced approaches (53%), the valuers undertaking the major valuations of investments were predominantly using horizontally-sliced techniques (Crosby, 1991).

Table 16.3 Number of UK valuations by each method

	No. of respondents	No. of valuations
Term and reversion	95(53%)	8 840 (30%)
EY vertically sliced	21(12%)	2 850 (9%)
EY horizontally sliced	32(18%)	9 395 (32%)
Layer	30(17%)	8 595 (29%)
Total	178(100%)ª	29 680 (100%)

ªNote: This total of 178 includes a number of the 160 respondents who answered always or usually to more than one approach.

The analysis by number of valuers using each method indicates that over 50% of respondents used term and reversion while only 35% used horizontally-sliced approaches. By number of valuations this has changed to 30% for term and reversion, and to over 60% for horizontally-sliced approaches.

Given the nature of the valuers who use horizontally sliced approaches, if an analysis by capital value rather than by number of valuations had been carried out, it is assumed that the percentage of reversionary freehold interests valued by horizontally-sliced methods would have been much higher. By 1989, the majority of commercial and industrial property investments were valued by layer or equivalent yield horizontally-sliced valuation techniques.

The rationale for layer techniques
There is a practical argument for adopting the layer approach in a rising market. This is underpinned by the existence of upwards-only rent reviews within long leases. For example, if a high street shop or office block had been completed and let in 1988, it would probably have been on a 25 year full repairing and insuring lease with five year upwards-only reviews. By the end of 1992, 60% of the properties (by capital value) within the IPD were let on leases with over 15 years unexpired; a legacy of the property boom of the second half of the 1980s (Crosby et al., 1993).

An investor buying a reversionary freehold interest in 1988 would (on the back of significant rental growth in the previous years) be purchasing a relatively safe fixed-income stream for a few years up to the next review. On review there was perceived to be no chance of the rent falling below the current rent passing (upwards-only review) and little chance of it falling significantly below the estimated rental value. Given a long lease, this completely secure bottom slice, extending well into the future, could be perceived to be less risky than the reversionary increase to rental value. The top slice of the valuation suffers from risks in that the expected rental growth might not be realized and the estimate of current rental value might be incorrect. As it is a top slice income, any possible errors in these estimates will change its value out of all proportion to those errors; it is therefore a highly volatile cash flow. Within a conventional valuation, it is impossible to allocate rational yields to the top and bottom slices, hence the adoption of an arbitrary amount of 1 or 2% difference.

A typical reversionary freehold investment valuation using layer/hardcore, equivalent yield (horizontally sliced) and term and reversion approaches is set out in Example 16.2.

Example 16.2: A prime shop property let on a 25 year FRI lease in 1986 with upwards-only five year reviews at a rent of £100 000 pa. Value in 1988, when ERV estimated at £150 000 pa. Fully let ARY 5%.

Layer/hardcore

Bottom slice	£100 000		
YP perp. at 5%	20.0000		
		£2 000 000	
Top slice	£50 000		
YP perp. at 7%	14.2857		
PV 3 years at 7%	0.8163		
		£583 070	
Valuation before costs			£2 583 070
Less legal, valuation and stamp duty purchase costs of 2.75%			£69 133
Valuation after costs, say £2.5 million			

Equivalent yield horizontally sliced

Bottom slice	£100 000		
YP perp. at 5.5%	18.1818		
		£1 818 182	
Top slice	£50 000		
YP perp. at 5.5%	18.1818		
PV 3 years at 5.5%	0.8516		
		£774 194	
Valuation before costs			£2 592 376
Less costs at 2.75%			£69 382
Valuation after costs, say £2.5 million			

Traditionally applied term and reversion

Term rent	£100 000		
YP 3 years at 4%	2.7751		
		£277 509	
Reversion to current rental value	£150 000		
YP perp. at 5%	20.0000		
PV 3 years at 5%	0.8638		
		£2 591 123	
			£2 869 022
Less costs at 2.75%			£76 786
Valuation after costs, say £2.8 million			

The reason for the difference in the valuations is the choice of a very low yield on the term value in the last valuation. In the past, the added security of a lower contract rent was perceived to be an advantage in comparison with a tenant paying a full rent after the reversion. The major criticism of this is that the term has no growth potential and is therefore overvalued if a low growth implicit yield is chosen. However, this is a general criticism made of all of the traditional UK applications of investment valuation illustrated above and a number of growth explicit alternatives have been suggested.

Growth explicit market valuation models
These alternatives have not gained much support from practitioners until very recently. They have significant advantages over their conventional counterparts when valuing investment properties in a falling or fallen rental market (see section 16.5.2.b) but in a rising market these advantages are not so apparent. The most popular application is called short-cut DCF and a fuller discussion of the concepts underpinning alternative approaches is set out in Baum and Crosby (1995).

The short-cut DCF assesses the implied rental growth rate from the transaction price comparables after assuming the risk-adjusted target rate of return for the comparable property. This implied annual rental growth rate is then applied to the reversionary property's cash flow until the property is deemed to become rack-rented again (and so becomes identical to the comparable). The property is then notionally sold with the inflated rental value being capitalized at the all-risks yield. The approach is therefore still a comparable-based technique but it simplistically takes into account the prospective shape of the future cash flow and is still a pricing model rather than an analysis of price model. An illustration of the model applied to the previous example follows.

Implied growth rate formula

$$(1+g)^t = \frac{\text{YP perp. at } k - \text{YP } t \text{ years at } e}{\text{YP perp. at } k \times \text{PV } t \text{ years at } e}$$

where rental growth rate is $g\%$ pa, review pattern of comparable is t years, all-risks yield (ARY) of comparable is $k\%$ and equated yield, or target return, is $e\%$.

Assuming a target return of gilt or bond yields plus an additional risk margin, say 13% in 1988:

$$(1+g)^5 = \frac{20.00 - 3.5172}{16.67 \times 0.5428} = \frac{16.48}{10.86} = 1.518$$

$$g = 8.712\% \text{ pa}$$

Valuation

Term rent	£100 000	
YP 3 years at 13%	2.3612	
Value of term		£236 115
Reversion to ERV	£150 000	

Amount £1 3 years at		
8.712% $(1 + g)^3$	1.2848	
	£192 720	
YP in perp. at 5%	20.0000	
PV 3 years at 13%	0.6931	
Value of reversion		£2 671 292
Valuation		£2 907 407
Less costs at 2.75%		£79 954

Valuation after costs, say £2.83 million.

(b) Overrented freehold valuations

Since the beginning of 1990, the rental values of many properties (especially offices) have fallen. Due to the many long leases signed in the late 1980s with upwards-only rent reviews, the contract rents of these properties cannot fall. However, they are now so much above the true market rental level that even if rental values recover relatively quickly the contract rent will not be passed for a number of years. Heavily overrented properties let on long leases have become more like fixed-income bonds than growth investments, with the possibility of some reversionary value in the future. The strength of the tenant has become a paramount factor in valuation as the amount of rent payable over and above rental value is dependent upon the tenant not going bankrupt and handing back the lease.

The methods adopted to assess the market value of these overrented properties fall mainly into three camps.

1. The initial yield approach: this entails simply taking the passing rent and capitalizing into perpetuity at an initial yield, gained from comparables, gilt yields and the valuer's 'feel' for the market place.
2. Conventional reversionary valuation applications adapted for the different lease structures: the most popular (and most dangerous) by far is the reverse layer/hardcore method which is called the core and top slice approach.
3. Contemporary growth explicit market valuation models, such as short-cut DCF.

There has been a continuing debate regarding which techniques are more suited to the overrented problem (see, for example, Goodchild, 1992; Martin, 1991; Rich, 1992; Epstein, 1993; Crosby, 1992; Crosby and Goodchild, 1992). An illustration of all three methods is set in Example 16.3.

> Example 16.3: A central London office block let on lease with 17 years unexpired. The reviews are upwards-only every five years and the next one is in two years time. The current rent passing is £1 500 000 pa and the estimated current rental value is only £1 000 000 pa.
>
> There are a number of problems, the most basic being how the ERV is estimated in a market disguised by letting incentives. As no properties are let at their real rents, the next basic problem is the estimation of the all-risks yield. However, in applying the different methods, the ERV of £1 000 000 is the perceived real rental value and the all-risks yield of a

fully let property is estimated to be 6%. At the valuation date, the redemption yield on long-dated gilts is 7%.

Initial yield

Factors considered in determining the yield include the strength of the tenant and the unexpired term of the lease. If the tenant is very stable, there is no uncertainty in the rental level at each review because of the upwards-only rent review (uncertainty which exists when rental values are rising above passing rents) and the investment therefore has the characteristics of an illiquid bond. Assuming a small margin for this (gilts plus 0.5%), the valuation becomes:

Rent passing	£1 500 000	
YP perp. at 7.5%	13.3333	
Valuation		£20 000 000

Core and top slice

The core of the valuation is the current estimated rental value (ERV) which is expected to be maintained (by finding a new tenant), even if the tenant defaults due to the pressure of paying £500 000 pa over the real market value, with the assumption that the property could be relet at its current ERV. The ERV is capitalized at the all-risks (investment) yield on the assumption that it will grow in the future.

The top slice element is called the overage or froth. This is more risky than the core because it is totally dependent upon the tenant's ability to continue paying substantially over the real rental value. It is also a fixed amount with no growth potential, therefore it should be valued as if it was a terminable, risky, fixed income. The income flow is illustrated in Figure 16.9.

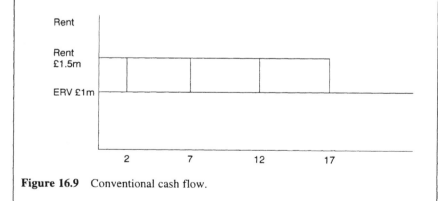

Figure 16.9 Conventional cash flow.

Assuming an equated yield (fixed-income property yield) of 10% (3% above gilts) and that the soundness of the tenant implies no substantial risk of default, the valuation becomes:

ERV	£1 000 000	
YP perp. at 6%	16.6667	
		£16 666 667
Overage	£500 000	
YP 17 years at 10%	8.0216	
		£4 010 777
Valuation before costs		£20 677 444
Less costs at 2.75%		£553 410

Valuation after costs, say £20.1 million; initial yield, 7.46%.

There are a number of flaws in this valuation. The most important is that the technique values some of the income flow twice. Figure 16.10 illustrates this, with the shaded part being the element which is double counted. The 6% ARY implies growth from the ERV and, while the rent passing is higher than the ERV, the growth at each rent review eats into the overage.

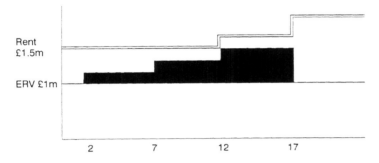

Figure 16.10 Double counting of income.

To amend the valuation, the valuer has to make assumptions regarding the growth in rental values from the existing ERV and when the overage is eliminated. These are precisely the assumptions behind the growth explicit alternative identified previously in this chapter.

Growth-explicit short-cut DCF
The cash-flow approach treats the term as a fixed-income cash flow and then reverts to a rack-rented property as soon as the ERV rises above the current rent passing (Figure 16.11).

The valuation requires an assessment of the rental growth rate implied by the all-risks yield. This in turn requires a target rate of return for a rack-rented property (based upon property risks above gilts). Assuming the equated yield of 10%, as in the core and top slice valuation, and the all risks yield of 6%, the implied rental growth rate can be calculated as follows.

Implied growth rate formula

$$(1+g)^t = \frac{\text{YP perp. at } k - \text{YP } t \text{ years at } e}{\text{YP perp. at } k \times \text{PV } t \text{ years at } e}$$

$$(1+g)^5 = \frac{16.67 - 3.790}{16.67 \times 0.620} = \frac{12.87}{10.34} = 1.244$$

$$g = 4.4668\% \text{ pa}$$

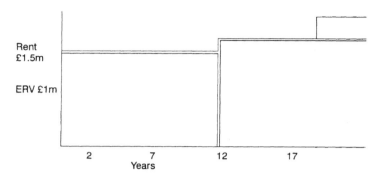

Figure 16.11   Growth-explicit short-cut DCF.

The growth rate can now be used to assess the date at which the ERV would overtake the rent passing of £1 500 000 if the implied growth rate was actually achieved.

£1 000 000 × (1.044668)² = £1 091 331
£1 000 000 × (1.044668)⁷ = £1 357 838
£1 000 000 × (1.044668)¹² = £1 689 429

This suggests that the first rent increase will take place at the review in year 12. The valuation is as follows:

Valuation

Term rent	£1 500 000	
YP 12 years at 10%	6.8137	
Value of term		£10 220 538
Reversion to ERV	£1 000 000	
Amount £1 12 years		
at 4.4668%	1.6894	
	£1 689 429	
YP in perp at 6%	16.6667	
PV 12 years at 10%	0.3186	
Value of reversion		£8 971 733
Valuation before costs		£19 192 271
Less costs at 2.75%		£527 787

Valuation, say £18.7 million, initial yield, 8.02%.

The above valuation identifies two parts, the term is a fixed-income bond investment with all the risk tied into tenant covenant. The reversion is tied to assessments of rental growth, which may be wrong, and the possibility that the property might be obsolete at the end of the lease, typical 'property' risks.

For this reason, the term yield can be varied within the valuation; reduced where there is a strong covenant (tenant), increased substantially where the tenant is suspect. If a very strong covenant is assumed in this case, using a yield of 8% on the term produces a higher valuation.

(c) Leasehold investment valuations

Due to the relatively small number of leasehold investment valuations in practice compared to the number of freeholds, leasehold valuation techniques are more of an issue to academics than practitioners. However, during the 1970s and 1980s, a number of investors made substantial returns from the UK property investment market by purchasing leasehold investment properties which they perceived to be significantly undervalued by pricing techniques.

Leasehold interests are periodic by nature with the termination of the interest governed by the expiry date of the lease from the freeholder. There must be at least two different leases to create a leasehold investment. The lessee holds the property from the freeholder via one lease and pays rent, and passes on the property to a sublessee by another lease and receives rent. The relationship between these two leases is fundamental to the value of the interest but conventional applications virtually ignore it. They determine the current difference between rent paid under the two or more leases and this income stream is capitalized until the end of the headlease. If the rents are less than full rental value, they are changed as in the freehold model, i.e. a reversion to full rental value but excluding any growth potential. Conventional applications of investment valuation methods are illustrated in Example 16.4. These conventional applications of investment valuation techniques to leaseholds are based upon the much criticized assumption that investors actually, or notionally, take out a sinking fund to replace the historic cost of the wasting asset at the end of the term. Interest on these funds has been assumed to accumulate at low rates of interest based upon the surety that the original purchase price must be recouped over the life of the investment.

Example 16.4: A leasehold shop property is held on a headlease with 12 years unexpired at a fixed rent of £10 000 pa with no further rent reviews. The property is sublet for the remainder of the headlessee's term at a rent of £30 000 pa with rent reviews in two and seven years time. The current rental value is estimated to be £35 000 pa. Fully let freehold shops sell for all risks yields of 6%.

There are three major variations of the conventional method; dual rate taxed, dual rate untaxed and single rate. They all adopt an all-risks yield based upon the freehold yield (due to the paucity of leasehold transaction evidence), increased for the extra risk of a leasehold. The shorter the unexpired term, the greater the perceived extra risk relative to the freehold. Assuming an adjustment by 2–8%, the valuations are as follows:

Single rate

Rent received	£30 000		
Less rent paid	£10 000		
Net income	£20 000		
YP 2 years at 8%	1.7833		
Term value		£35 666	
Reversion to ERV	£35 000		
Less rent paid	£10 000		
Profit rent	£25 000		
YP 10 years at 8%	6.7101		
PV 2 years at 8%	0.8573		
Reversion value		£143 814	
Valuation before costs			£179 480
Less costs at 2.75%			£4 936

Valuation after costs, say £175 000.

Dual rate untaxed

Rent received	£30 000		
Less rent paid	£10 000		
Net income	£20 000		
YP 2 years at 8 and 4%	1.7538		
Term value		£35 076	
Reversion to ERV	£35 000		
Less rent paid	£10 000		
Profit rent	£25 000		
YP 10 years at 8 and 4%	6.1240		
PV 2 years at 8%	0.8573		
Reversion value		£131 253	
Valuation before costs			£166 329
Less costs at 2.75%			£4 574

Valuation after costs, say £162 500.

Dual rate taxed

Rent received	£30 000		
Less rent paid	£10 000		
Net income	£20 000		
YP 2 years at 8 and 3% net taxed at 40%	1.1099		
Term value		£22 198	
Reversion to ERV	£35 000		
Less rent paid	£10 000		
Profit rent	£25 000		
YP 10 years at 8 and 3% taxed at 40%	4.4369		
PV 2 years at 8%	0.8573		
Reversion value		£95 094	
Valuation before costs			£117 292

Less costs at 2.75%	£3 226
Valuation after costs, say £115 000.	

The main reason why these valuations have come in for heavy criticism is that they were established prior to the 1960s when growth was not a significant factor in property investment. In the modern era, every single aspect of the valuation is suspect. The concept of a separate sinking fund is impractical and the inclusion of tax when the leasehold institutional market is dominated by tax exempt funds is irrational. If these were the only criticisms, the single rate approach would be acceptable. However, much more significant criticisms relate to the use of current profit rents and growth implicit all-risks yields. The combination of the leases can create a multitude of complex income growth structures which cannot be adequately hidden in the all-risks yield. The growth implication of a short-term all-risks yield is different to that from a perpetual all-risks yield and so it is virtually impossible to adapt and amend freehold yields for use in leaseholds (see Baum and Crosby, 1995).

The successful leasehold investors of the 1970s and 1980s used growth-explicit DCF approaches to determine the worth of leasehold investments and the short-cut DCF model approach for freeholds can be adapted for leaseholds, using implied growth rates from the freehold transaction evidence.

Contemporary growth explicit DCF market valuation

Assuming the freehold interest target rate of return is 10%, the implied rental growth rate formula can be applied to the freehold transaction evidence of 6% ARY.

Implied growth rate formula

$$(1+g)^t = \frac{\text{YP perp. at } k - \text{YP } t \text{ years at } e}{\text{YP perp. at } k \times \text{PV } t \text{ years at } e}$$

$$(1+g)^5 = \frac{16.67 - 3.790}{16.67 \times 0.620} = \frac{12.87}{10.34} = 1.244$$

$$g = 4.4668\% \text{ pa}$$

The second and most subjective stage of the appraisal is to adjust the target rate of return upwards for the extra risk of the leasehold investment. The cash flow is much more susceptible to variation on account of any errors in assessing growth (due to the top slice nature of the income) and much more of the cash flow is dependent upon getting growth relative to the freehold. If 15% is assumed, the present value of the prospective cash flow is as follows:

Years	Rent received	Growth at 4.467%	Inflated rent	Less rent paid	Net income	YP at 15%	PV at 15%	Present value
0–2	30 000	1.0000	30 000	10 000	20 000	1.6257	1.0000	32 514
3–7	35 000	1.0913	38 197	10 000	28 197	3.3522	0.7561	71 470
8–12	35 000	1.3578	47 524	10 000	37 524	3.3522	0.3759	47 288

| Valuation | £151 274 |
| Less costs @ 2.75% | £4 160 |

Valuation after costs, say £147 5000.

All the previous valuations are applications of investment valuation techniques to the question of price. They are primarily based on comparable transactions and the arguments for and against the different applications are based around which models make the best use of market evidence. They do not answer questions regarding the worth of properties, i.e. should a particular price be paid or how much should be paid for a property investment. The next section deals with the current state of appraisal for worth in the UK.

(d) Investment worth appraisals

Recommendation 25 of the Mallinson Report (RICS, 1994) suggested that the RICS should take the lead in codifying DCF techniques, developing new methodologies and information bases with the ultimate aim of reducing the valuer's dependence on the all-risks yield. There are no common standards regarding the use of DCF techniques although most major investors, property surveyors and consultants are now using growth-explicit DCF techniques to ascertain worth to set against price.

The approach to DCF by these investors and advisors is based upon a forecasting of cash flow over time in line with the models outlined in Chapter 3. Research during the 1980s and 1990s has focused on local property markets to enable appraisals of worth to be produced at the property-specific level. In the UK, a number of research consultancies have produced forecasts at the national, regional and local level for the different sectors of the commercial and industrial property market, furthermore, some institutions and firms have also developed their own models despite the data difficulties outlined in section 16.1.

There are two separate approaches to setting the target rate of return. Firstly, building up the return from an index-linked bond yield, adding for prospective inflation, obsolescence, real income growth or falls and risk. Secondly, basing the target rate on fixed income bond rates and adding for nominal rental growth rates and the other factors indicated for the first approach. Depreciation and obsolescence have been the subject of research by, among others, Baum (1992) and Salway (1986).

The information needs for an explicit DCF are a mixture of market and client-specific information. The former, which can be broken down into current and future data, should not be affected by the specific criteria of clients and is an attempt to quantify such factors as the current rent, rental value and lease structure, and the future rental value change, depreciation rates, redevelopment or refurbishment costs and exit yield forecast. Additional information on current and future costs (management, rent review, purchase and sale costs) is also incorporated. The client-based information includes factors such as holding period, loan facilities, taxation and target rate of return, many of which include grey areas (for example, holding period for an appraisal might be dominated by the current lease structure, the client might have specific redevelopment plans which do not match most profitable use or optimum time criteria, the client's costs may be different to the market standard, the exit yield is affected by the client's subjective view on holding period, etc.)

Due to the range of possible information that can be included in an explicit DCF, there is no accepted list of information or layout for this kind of valuation, with a number of organizations developing their own approaches. However, as the model is a genuine attempt to create a forecast of what will actually happen to the property over the life of the actual or prospective ownership, approximations are discouraged. For example, cash flows within implicit DCF market valuations continue to be assumed to be paid annually in arrears even though normal rent payment takes place quarterly in advance. As the all-risks yield is a comparison indicator, this continues to be tolerated in practice. In explicit DCF, cash flows are assessed quarterly in advance.

Example 16.5 illustrates a worth appraisal of an investment property, which requires the types of information as set out in Table 16.4.

Table 16.4 Typical information requirements for appraisals of worth

Type of information	Current information	Forecasts
Value	Estimated rental value Rents passing	Existing property rental value forecasts Location rental value forecasts Exit yield forecasts
Redevelopment	Costs of redevelopment	Inflation in building costs
Current lease	Number of tenants Lease expiry dates Rent review dates	Future voids
Holding costs	Management costs Review costs Purchase and sale costs	
Client-specific information	Discount rate Taxation Loan	

Example 16.5: A city centre office block was let eight years ago when first completed on a 25 year full repairing and insuring lease with five yearly upwards only rent reviews. The property is for sale at a price of £13 million and an appraisal of worth is required. The lease expires in 17 years time when a redevelopment is anticipated. Brand new buildings currently let for the equivalent of £1.25 million pa while the eight year old building is worth £1 million pa. Forecasts of rental growth are 6% pa for the location but a depreciating building is only expected to grow at 4% pa (in reality forecasts would need to be from year to year in the short term). Exit yields are estimated at 6% while building costs are forecast to grow by 5% pa.

Information
    Discount rate   10%
    Assumed growth rate (prime property in the location)   6%

Current rental value of a prime property in the location	£1 250 000 pa
Current rental value of the existing property	£1 000 000 pa
Rent review pattern	5 years
Purchase price	£13 000 000
Rent passing until next review	£750 000 pa
Unexpired term to next review	2 years
Unexpired term on lease	17 years
Depreciation: (a) Refurbishment/redevelopment period (holding period)	19 years
(b) Cost of rebuilding (% prime cap. value)	60%
ARY on sale of a prime building)	6%
Purchase costs (% of purchase price)	2.75%
Sale costs (% of sale price)	2%
Review costs (% of new rent)	5%
Management costs (% of income)	2.5%
Inflation in building costs	5%

Annual rental growth in existing property

Years	Growth	Vacancy levels
0–2	4% pa	0%
3–7	4% pa	0%
8–12	4% pa	0%
13–17	4% pa	0%
18–19		100% (redevelopment period)

Appraisal

Years	Gross income	Purchase, man. costs	Net income after voids	YP at 10%	Review costs	PV at 10%	Present value
0	–13 000 000	–357 500	–13 357 500				–13 357 500
0–2	750 000	–18 750	731 250	1.8427	0	1	1 347 486
3–7	1 081 600	–27 040	1 054 560	4.0249	–54 080	0.8264	3 463 146
8–12	1 315 932	–32 898	1 283 033	4.0249	–65 797	0.5132	2 616 219
13–17	1 601 032	–40 026	1 561 006	4.0249	–80 052	0.3186	1 976 411
						Present value	–3 954 238

Plus sale price after refurbishment/redevelopment:	Rental value in year 19	3 781 999
	YP perp at 6 %	16.66667
	PV at 10 %	0.163508
	Present value	10 306 452
	Net after costs	10 100 323
Less Refurbishment/ redevelopment costs:	Present cost	–12 500 000
	Inflated cost	–31 586 877
	PV at 10 %	0.163508
		–5 164 707
	Net present value	981 379

Given the assumptions regarding the future cash flow and a target rate of return which represents approximately 2% above the long-dated (over 15 year) bond redemption yield, the appraisal indicates that the price of the property is relatively cheap.

In the survey of valuation practice (section 16.5.2.a), only 30% of respondents indicated that they undertook DCF analysis to appraise price (Crosby, 1991). However, there was no indication whether this was a growth-explicit DCF (as above) or a growth-implicit cash-flow analysis. No detailed analysis of practice concerning explicit DCF appraisals has been undertaken in the UK but it would appear that DCF analysis is not widely used outside of the major property-owning institutions and companies, and the firms and consultancies advising those particular clients.

However, worth models should exert an increasing influence over the level of prices as the use increases. The logical extension of this view is that worth will one day equal price, however, this presupposes that pricing is dominated by logical rational investors all investing on similar subjective assumptions. This also suggests that short-term speculation on price changes does not exert any influence on price levels, something which does not appear to be excluded from other asset prices.

Risk adjustment to appraisal models has been covered earlier in this text and is not widely practised in the UK, other than the use of the risk adjusted discount rate as illustrated in Example 16.5.

16.5.3 Profits-based methods

There are a number of property types which have been specifically designed or adapted for a particular use and are transacted at prices which reflect the trading potential for that particular use. The 'Red Book' identifies these properties as hotels, public houses, cinemas, theatres, bingo clubs, gaming clubs, petrol-filling stations, licensed betting offices and specialized leisure and sporting facilities. The latter category includes properties such as theme parks, holiday complexes and leisure centres. Unless the property is let and held as an investment, or is surplus to the business requirements, the 'Red Book' basis of valuation is open market value for existing use. Where open market transactions of these types of properties exist, the preferred method of valuation is comparison but recent, similar comparables are often not available. These properties are usually valued on a profits method.

The profits method is based upon an estimate of the gross turnover of the business reduced or increased for potential changes by a different operator. This estimate is the product of the actual accounts and the valuer's expertise in assessing how efficiently the business is currently being run. The net profit of the business can then be assessed and then either capitalized directly using a multiplier which is purely comparative [termed the total earnings method by Colborne and Hall (1992)] or it can be split between a notional rental payment and profit for the running of the business. The rent can be capitalized as an investment and the profit can also be capitalized to value the goodwill attached to the property as distinct from the actual operator. This multiplier is also a purely comparative indicator. The valuation below illustrates both possibilities.

Example 16.6: A hotel has generated an average turnover of around £400 000 pa over the last three years with expenses of £300 000 pa. This does not include taxation, depreciation, owners' drawings, property loan servicing or rent (if appropriate).

Profits valuation

Gross turnover	£400 000	
Expenditure less rent	£300 000	
Adjusted net profit	£100 000	
Either: Rental value (40%)	£40 000	
YP perp. at 11%	9.0909	£363 600
Residual profit	£60 000	
Multiplier	3	£180 000
Valuation		£550 000
Or: Adjusted net profit	£100 000	
YP perp. at 18%	5.5	
Valuation		£550 000

A third method identified by Colborne and Hall (1992) is called the capitalized earnings method and it answers some of the criticisms of the other two approaches, which are based primarily on past turnover estimates and still require elements of comparison to determine the multipliers to apply to net profits. This method is based on a forward-looking cash flow over the next three or five years making explicit adjustments to the net profits for possible opportunities or threats to the particular business operated from the property. At the end of the period, the net profit is capitalized as in the total earnings method.

One of the major difficulties with the profits method is isolating personal goodwill from any value attached to the incoming purchaser being able to take over a business which is already running and can be compared with starting a new business from an empty property. This suggests differences between valuations where the property is owner-occupied and currently running as a business, a property let to a tenant and a vacant property. The investment value of a property let to a tenant would be as follows.

Investment valuation

Rent	£40 000
YP perp. at 11%	9.0909
Valuation	£365 000

The Mallinson Committee (RICS, 1994) expressed some concern at the inherent difficulties in applying profits methodology in practice, especially in the light of the Queens Moat case where a number of hotels were valued at widely differing figures in the early 1990s by two different firms of valuers. While accepting that the method was theoretically a more logical approach than some others, as it more closely followed the thought processes of buyers and sellers than, for example, comparison and implicit investment methods, Mallinson considered that the residual nature of the cash flows, coupled with the degree of subjective assessment of the likely effect of a different operator on the actual turnover and profitability, made an accurate estimate of exchange price more difficult. For these reasons, profits valuations are usually handled by valuers with a specialist knowledge of the particular business operated from the property.

16.5.4 Valuations based upon cost

Certain properties are infrequently, or never, traded in the market-place and are not occupied by a use which makes a profit (or the profit from the operation cannot be related solely to the occupation of the particular asset). In these circumstances, valuers revert to basing the value on the cost of providing the land and buildings. This approach is also the basis of insurance valuations which seek to identify replacement cost in the event of a fire.

The 'Red Book' has identified a particular cost-based approach to valuation as a specific basis of valuation called depreciated replacement cost (DRC). The 'Red Book' suggests that this basis is appropriate when the property is specialized and it is not practical to determine the open market value for the existing use. It also states that this basis represents the accounting concept of 'net current replacement cost'. The 'Red Book' identifies these properties as oil refineries and chemical works (where the buildings are no more than structures or cladding for specialized plant), power stations and docks (where the buildings and site engineering works are directly related to the business of the occupier and would have no value to anybody other than a company acquiring the undertaking) and properties located in particular geographical areas and of such construction, arrangement, size or specification that there would be no market for a sale to a single owner-occupier.

DRC is also the usual method of valuation for specialized public sector property assets such as some schools, libraries, sports and leisure centres, museums and galleries, cemeteries and crematoria, fire stations and public conveniences.

DRC requires estimates of land value in its existing use and the gross replacement cost of the buildings, before deductions for age, condition, obsolescence and other factors which would make the existing building less valuable than a new one.

Example 16.7: A 5000 m² specialist building occupying a town centre site which would take three years to construct.

DRC valuation

Land value in existing use		£375 000
Construction costs	£5 000 000	
Professional fees at 12%	£600 000	
Finance over construction period at 10% pa over three years (half costs), say	£925 000	
Replacement cost	£6 525 000	
Depreciation allowance	50%	
Depreciated replacement cost		£3 262 500
Valuation		£3 637 500

SAVP 3 of the '*Red Book*' provides detailed guidance on the approach to this type of valuation but Hicks (1993) and White (1994) highlight some of the problems faced by valuers following this guidance.

The land value should be assumed to have planning permission for the replacement of the existing buildings or a modern substitute. The determination of the land value needs to be based upon comparables but the reason for the valuation being undertaken by DRC is the lack of a market for the particular use. The '*Red Book*' suggests that this dilemma is solved by:

1. assuming a similar use to the actual use (for example, an oil refinery site can be assumed to be put to general industrial use); or
2. assuming a use which prevails in the vicinity of the property (for example, a museum surrounded by houses could be assumed to have a residential planning permission).

In assessing the cost of the buildings, the valuer should take account of the cost of a modern substitute to the existing building if this would cost less to provide the same floor area. As identified in Example 16.7, the cost of fees and finance should be allowed for in addition to the cost of construction. In accordance with the definition of open market value, the '*Red Book*' instructs the valuer to have regard to the cost of the building assuming the redevelopment period was commenced a few years ago and that the construction was finished in time for occupation by the valuation date. Both Hicks and White indicate that this produces a very different figure to that which would be produced if the construction was assumed to start at the valuation date. For example, they indicate that building costs have fallen by approximately 25% between 1990 and 1993 and interest rates have also fallen significantly. These assumptions applied to Example 16.7 would produce a valuation of approximately £3–3.1 million, a reduction of nearly 30%. In a market where building costs are rising, the opposite effect is apparent.

The '*Red Book*' suggests that obsolescence will normally be identified under three headings; economic (related to age and condition), functional (related to suitability for existing use) and environmental (related to a consideration of the use in comparison to the surrounding area and planning and environmental policies). The percentage reduction for depreciation caused by obsolescence can also be related to the remaining life span of the building compared to a new building or to the age of the existing building.

DRC valuations must be qualified. In the case of occupiers in the private sector, the valuer should qualify that the valuation is subject to the potential profitability of the business compared to the value of the total assets employed. The directors may feel that the balance sheet of the company cannot carry the property at the valuation and that some lower figure should be adopted. In the public sector, the qualification is subject to the prospect and viability of the continuance of the occupation and use.

16.5.5 Development valuation and appraisal

The appraisal of development sites in the UK is usually carried out using residual techniques, unless a supply of comparable sales is available. Given the individual nature of location and planning permission, directly comparable sites are often not available. The residual approach can vary from a simple assessment of site value based upon a deduction of development costs from the gross development value to a detailed assessment of the cash flow through a development situation. Although both variations are residual techniques in that the solution is a residue of income after expenditure, only the former is called the residual approach in the UK; the latter is called a discounted cash flow or a cash flow depending upon whether the cash flows are discounted to the beginning of the development period or accumulated to the end.

Example 16.8: A site with planning permission for offices is for sale. The permission is for a gross external area of 5000 m² which would generate 4000 m² of usable internal area. Development funding would be available at 10% pa and the block is expected to take two years to build, let and sell. Currently, offices of this type let at £200 per m² and sell for capitalization rates of 7%. The costs of construction are estimated to be £1000 per m².

Residual valuation

1. Gross development value (GDV)

Rental value of offices: 4000 m² × £200 =	£800 000
YP perp. at 7%	14.2857
	£11 428 571

2. Costs of development
(a) Site clearance and/or preparation	£ 50 000
(b) Costs of construction: 5000 m² × £1000 m²	£5 000 000
(c) Contingencies: 10% of (a) and (b)	£ 505 000
(d) Professional fees on construction at 12.5%	£ 694 375
(e) Finance charges: based upon half costs over construction period at 10%	£ 656 184
(f) Developer's profit at 15% GDV	£1 714 286
(g) Agent's and legal fees on sale at 2.75% of GDV	£ 314 286
Total development costs	£8 934 131

3. Residual for land purchase
	£2 494 441
Land acquisition fees at 4% of land price	£79 289
Interest on land and fees at 10% over two years	£432 919
Residual land value	£1 982 232
Land value, say £2 million.	

There is no set pattern to residual valuations as practised in the UK. Some valuers include a profit margin on holding the land over the development period, others do not take off a contingency sum for the risk that construction costs may be different to those estimated. Most valuers do not include any element of value change over the development period and some suggest that the GDV should be deferred two years as it will not be received until the end of the development period. This latter suggestion is incorrect as both GDV and development costs are deemed to be finally received and paid at the end of the development period (costs are rolled forward via the finance calculations which assume a crude draw down of finance throughout the development period). The interest on land is a form of deferment on both the development value and the costs.

The effect on the valuation of the risk that the costs and values may be different to those estimated is often tested by a sensitivity analysis. One of the major criticisms regarding the accuracy of the residual technique is that it is highly sensitive to changes in the construction costs or gross development value. For example, a 5% fall in the GDV would generate a fall in land value of nearly 20%.

Residual techniques are sometimes used to determine the anticipated profit when the land price is either known or estimated from direct comparable information. They are normally used in the initial stages of development when detailed costings have not been made. Although residual techniques do take into account the time span of development, they do this very crudely and, where detailed costings and timings are available, cash-flow techniques enable a more detailed and sophisticated view of the development to be taken.

Assume the site in Example 16.8 has been purchased for £2 million and costs and values are forecast to stay static over the development period of two years. The costs are expected to be drawn down from a loan facility at the end of each quarter. The actual construction costs including contingencies are expected to be incurred from the second quarter onwards, slowly at first with an increasing amount being spent in the middle of the development period before slowing down again towards the end of the two years. The preparatory costs will be in the first quarter.

(a) Cash-Flow Appraisal

The quarterly interest rate is:

$$(1.1)^{1/4} - 1 = 2.41136\%$$

End of quarter	0	1	2	3	4	5	6	7	8
Items £000s Land inclusive of acq. costs	2080								
Site prep.		50							
Consent costs incl. contin.			629	786	865	943	865	786	629
Fees	347								347
Sale price less fees									(11 114)
Outflow	2427	50	629	786	865	943	865	786	(10 137)
Previous balance	0.00	2427	2535	3225	4089	5052	6117	7129	8087
Int. at 2.4%	0.00	58	61	77	98	121	147	171	194
Balance	2427	2535	3225	4089	5052	6117	7129	8087	(1857)

Note: All calculations are taken to the nearest £ but only shown to the nearest £1000. Positive flows are shown in parentheses.

The cash-flow appraisal suggests that the profit at the end of the project will be £1.857 million, similar to the residual calculation which used a profit of £1.714 million to produce a land price of £1.98 million.

Cash flows can also be used to provide present values by discounting the quarterly inflows and outflows at the cost of borrowing. The present value of the profit is £1.537 million as illustrated below. Discounted cash flows are more likely to be used to determine land values at the beginning of the scheme than profits which are taken at the end.

Discounted cash flow (DCF)

End of quarter	0	1	2	3	4	5	6	7	8
Items £000s Land inclusive costs	2080								
Site prep.		50							
Consent costs incl. contin.			629	786	865	943	865	786	629
Fees	347								347
Sale price less fees									(11 114)
Outflow	2427	50	629	786	865	943	865	786	(10 138)
PV at 2.4%	1.000	0.9766	0.9537	0.9313	0.9095	0.8882	0.8674	0.8470	0.8272
PV outflow	2427	49	600	732	787	838	750	666	(8386)

The present value of the cash flow (profit) is £1.536 million. This could just as easily have been calculated by accumulating the cash flow to the end of the development (£1.857 million) and discounting this profit back to the beginning (£1.857 million × PV £1 eight quarters at 2.4%).

16.6 CONCLUSION

The valuation process in the UK is a long established one which has a strong institutional base within the RICS, ISVA and IRRV. Since the early 1970s it has been the subject of significant developments in procedural and methodology issues.

During the secondary banking collapse of the 1970s, it was realized that many property valuations were relied upon by the public in making many investment and other decisions and that the responsibilities of valuers to produce accurate and reliable valuations went beyond the duty of care to the immediate client. This resulted in the production of guidance notes which have become more and more detailed and precise as they evolved over the last 20 years. Despite this increasing institutional support for valuers, there have been many cases during the 1980s and into the 1990s of valuations which differed significantly from subsequent sale prices or from valuations of the same property by another valuer. Valuation inaccuracy in the present market does not often relate to valuers applying different bases of valuation to the same property, it is usually caused by different interpretation of the information. However, these bases are not always understood by clients and still cause confusion in a minority of valuers.

The recession of the early 1990s refocused attention on the issue of valuation bases and a substantial part of the Mallinson Report into commercial property valuations commented upon it. Preceding Mallinson, the problems with commercial loan valuations had already produced the new basis of estimated realization price (ERP) and Mallinson went further in advocating eight different bases of valuation depending on the role or property type to be appraised. Much of the debate which followed Mallinson revolved around those who feel that a minimum of different bases are needed to avoid confusion and those who believe that the basis of valuation should differ depending upon the purpose, despite the possibility of causing confusion among both providers and users of valuations.

The discussion on bases of valuation has obscured the very useful contribution the report made in a number of areas including the provision of additional information within valuation reports, the relationship between valuers and clients (including memorandum of instructions), the identification and disclosure of reasons why valuations may differ from sale prices or other valuations of the same property and the relationship between valuers and auditors of financial statements.

The emergence of more sophisticated owners and occupiers has precipitated the beginnings of a research culture into all aspects of property markets, including valuation methods. During the early 1970s there was some academic interest in the application of investment valuation techniques to an inflationary market and growth explicit alternatives to the conventional techniques were spawned. In 1976 the RICS commissioned a research project into valuation methods and it also concentrated on investment methods. Two reports followed edited by Trott (1980, 1986). During the 1980s more interest was shown in applying the alternative methodology in practice, with the concept of worth not necessarily equalling price gaining prominence. This has culminated in the 1990s with a much greater cross-fertilization of ideas between practitioners and academics.

There is no doubt that the recession of the early 1990s stimulated a healthy debate into all aspects of the valuation process. No method or basis has been immune to these investigations and other methods, besides investment, have now received attention, with the RICS sponsoring further research into cost- and profits-based methods and development valuations in addition to continuing work on investment valuation. During the recession the main research questions have related to valuation in thin markets, the valuation basis for loans, the valuation basis for accounts and the provision of information in valuation reports. However, the recession has highlighted the importance of the tenant and the contract under which they occupy. The UK has unique lease structures and this has created specialized valuation problems and a highly-developed legal framework. The value of substantial proportions of the UK property market is underpinned not by the usual property criteria of physical and locational characteristics, but by the term and provisions of the lease and the tenant's ability to honour them. This raises questions regarding the valuers' ability to interpret non-property information relating to tenants' covenant.

Valuation issues also figure prominently on the RICS's research agenda which includes topics such as valuation accuracy and the valuation of property assets where there are no transactions. In order to communicate the increasing volume of analytical material on property valuation, the number of academic and professional journals has expanded, ranging from the academically prestigious *Journal of Property Research* and *Journal of Property Valuation and Investment* to high circulation professional journals such as the *Estates Gazette* and the *Property Week*.

Many of the issues raised over the last 30 years have been addressed within Mallinson and the first draft of the combined '*Red Book*' and '*White Book*' circulated for consultation during 1995.

A number of other initiatives flowing from the Mallinson report, which paid particular attention to investment and profits-based valuation methods, are a committee to draft a paper on the formalization of a new basis of appraisal called worth (as distinct from price), suggesting a definition and some form of standard layout. This RICS subcommittee has parallels with developments in Australia and New Zealand, where attempts to codify DCF approaches are also underway.

Investigation of appraisal of worth combined with the discussions concerning commercial property loan valuations has raised the profile of the debate regarding forecasting of future property market movements within valuations and the valuer's ability to produce forecasts. Valuers in the UK have resisted any movement towards techniques which require forecasts on the grounds that they are not competent to determine future values. However, the availability of property market forecasts from various sources identified previously in this chapter has given the valuer the opportunity to develop the technical skills to incorporate increasingly sophisticated information bases into valuations and reports. In the wake of the recession, some clients are demanding more transparent valuations which include full information supporting the opinion of value.

However, perhaps the most significant development in UK valuation practice over the first half of the 1990s has been the increasing acceptance that conventional investment valuations applied to overrented properties do not provide credible solutions. Many leading practitioners in the UK have stopped using them for overrented valuations and this may precipitate a decline in their use for all situations in the future. This would signal a fundamental change in valuation methodology, the first for over 30 years.

POSTSCRIPT

In October 1995, the RICS in association with the Incorporated Society of Valuers and Auctioneers, and the Institute of Revenues Rating and Valuation, published a new '*Red Book*' entitled the *RICS Appraisal and Valuation Manual* (RICS, 1995). The new manual replaces the existing '*Red Book*' and '*White Book*' from 1 January 1996.

The new manual changes some elements of the material set out in this chapter, particularly within section 16.4 dealing with bases of valuation. The new manual details 10 different bases of valuation plus another four dealing with plant and machinery. For the first time in the UK, the international definition of market value is set out and interpreted. Open market value is redefined with 'best price reasonably expected' reduced to 'best price' and the addition of an assumption that the parties acted 'knowledgeably, prudently and without compulsion'. *Open market value with existing use* is renamed existing use value and follows the new definition of open market value with the additional assumptions of existing use for the foreseeable future and vacant possession. The definition of estimated realization price retains the assumption of a price 'reasonably' expected despite the test of reasonableness being excluded from the new open market value definition. The new manual requires that opinions of estimated realization price are to be reported alongside open market value. This will reinforce the opinion that estimated realization price, which will normally be higher than open market value when markets are rising and loans are being negotiated, does not provide lenders with the answer to the right question.

REFERENCES

Baum, A. (1992) *Property Investment Depreciation and Obsolescence*, Routledge, London.

Baum, A. and Crosby, N. (1995) *Property Investment Appraisal* 2nd edn, Routledge, London.

Colborne, A. and Hall, P. (1992) The profits method of valuation. *Journal of Property Valuation and Investment*, **11**, 43–9.

Crosby, N. (1991) The practice of property investment appraisal: reversionary freeholds in the UK. *Journal of Property Valuation and Investment*, **9**, 109–22.

Crosby, N. (1992) Over-rented freehold investment property valuations. *Journal of Property Valuation and Investment*, **10**, 517–24.

Crosby, N. and Goodchild, R. (1992) Reversionary freeholds: Problems with over-renting. *Journal of Property Valuation and Investment*, **11**, 67–81.

Crosby, N., Baum, A. and Murdoch, S. (1993) *Commercial Property Leases: A Critical Evaluation of the DOE Proposals*, Centre for European Property Research, University of Reading.

Darlow, C. (1983) (ed.) *Valuation and Investment Appraisal*, The Estates Gazette Ltd, London.

DTZ (1993) *Money Into Property*, DTZ Debenham Thorpe, London.

Epstein, D. (1993) Modern valuations. *Estates Gazette*, **9314**, 90–1; **9315**, 120–2; **9316**, 86–8; **9317**, 76–9.

Fraser, W. (1993) *Principles of Property Investment and Pricing*, 2nd edn, MacMillan, London.

Goodchild, R.N. (1992) Valuation issues for the 1990s. *Estates Gazette*, **Feb 29**, 85.

Guildstream (1973) *A Basic Review of the Sector and its Prospects*, Guildstream Research Services/Financial Times Business Enterprises Division, London.

Hicks, G. (1993) Overvaluation of specialist buildings. *Estates Gazette*, **9331**, 40–1.

Hillier Parker Research (1993) *Hillier Parker Rent Index Digest*, Hillier Parker Investment Research, London.

Hillier Parker Research (1994) *Average Yields*, Hillier Parker Investment Research, London.

Investment Property Forum (1993) *DOE consultation paper on commercial property leases: a response by the Investment Property Forum*, Investment Property Forum, London.

Investment Property Forum (1994) *Property Investment for UK Pension Funds*, Working Party Report. Investment Property Forum, London.

IPD (1994) *Property Investors Digest*, Investment Property Databank, London.

Martin, D. (1991) Valuation: Over-rented property. *Estates Gazette*, **Dec. 7**, 52.

Morell, G. (1991) Property performance analysis and performance indices: a review. *Journal of Property Research*, **8**, 29–57.

Rich, J. (1992) Valuation: Over-rented property. *Estates Gazette*, **9243**, 104–5.

RICS (1990) *Statements of Asset Valuation Practice and Guidance Notes* ('*Red Book*'), 3rd edn as amended, Royal Institution of Chartered Surveyors Books, London.

RICS (1992) *Manual of Valuation Guidance Notes* ('*White Book*'), 3rd edn as amended, Royal Institution of Chartered Surveyors Books, London.

RICS (1994) *The Mallinson Report: Commercial Property Valuations*, Royal Institution of Chartered Surveyors, London.

RICS/ISVA (1993) *Code of Measuring Practice*, 4th edn, Royal Institution of Chartered Surveyors Books, London.

RICS (1995) *RICS Appraisal and Valuation Manual* (new '*Red Book*'), Royal Institution of Chartered Surveyors Books, London.

Salway, F. (1986) *Depreciation of Commercial Property*, College of Estate Management, Reading.

Stock Exchange (1993a) *Admission of Securities to Listing* ('*Yellow Book*'), The International Stock Exchange, London.

Stock Exchange (1993b) *The City Code on Takeovers and Mergers* ('*Blue Book*'), 4th edn, The City Panel on Takeovers and Mergers, London.

Trott, A. (1980) *Property Valuation Methods: Interim Report*, Royal Institution of Chartered Surveyors/Polytechnic of the South Bank, London.

Trott, A. (1986) *Property Valuation Methods*, Royal Institution of Chartered Surveyors/Polytechnic of the South Bank, London.

White, P. (1994) Correcting for the overvaluation of specialist buildings. *Estates Gazette*, **9403**, 121–2.

CASE LAW

Corisand Investments v. Druce and Co. (1978) (248 EG 315, 407, 514).

Mount Banking Corporation Ltd v. Brian Cooper and Co. (1992) (35 EG 123).

Singer and Friedlander Ltd v. John D. Wood and Co. (1977) (243 EG 212).

European valuation perspective

PART
3

Conclusion and prospects 17

Mary Lou Downie and
Alastair Adair

17.1 INTRODUCTION

These accounts of national valuation processes, although they can convey little more than the tip of the valuation iceberg, clearly show that these geographically close countries, sharing a Western European cultural heritage, have developed valuation processes in response to common needs which, although similar in many ways, still display diversity in methods, definitions and sophistication. In many instances methods and ideas which appear to be common hide significant differences in interpretation and implementation. This chapter therefore attempts to highlight some common themes and to explore the differences which they mask. Most obvious among them are shared definitions of value and methods for arriving at them, particularly the strong underlying ideas of exchange price, comparative valuation methods and replacement cost. Many contributors dwell on the response of the profession to the recent market crisis and its desire for enhanced credibility. There are widespread moves towards codification of definitions, methods and best practice involving both professional organizations, educational provision and government regulation. These run parallel to increasing awareness of practices in other countries, through commercial networks and the influence of pan-European groups of valuers, such as TEGOVOFA and EUROVAL, as well as pressure from international clients. These themes are now considered in more detail.

17.2 THE CONCEPT OF EXCHANGE VALUE

The concept of exchange value or price underlies valuation in all the countries described. It is variously termed 'market value', 'open market value', 'actual market value' and other variations on the theme. These are all translations of indigenous terms, many of which are probably conditioned by the fact that all the authors speak English, at least as a second language and are likely therefore

European Valuation Practice. Edited by Alastair Adair, Mary Lou Downie, Stanley McGreal and Gerjan Vos. Published in 1996 by E & FN Spon, London. ISBN 0 419 20040 1

to have read valuation literature from the UK or USA in which the term 'open market value' is used. None the less, when the authors provide formal or informal definitions of the concept of value or even simply describe its interpretation informally it is plain that these countries all rely on the concept of exchange price as their main concept of value and that a good deal of effort has been invested by professionals, courts and legislators in search of a watertight definition of the concept. Some countries have achieved well-defined terminology enforced by strong professional bodies, such as the '*Red Book*' (RICS, 1990) in the UK, or by legislation, for instance, the *Wertermittlungsverordnung* (BGBL III, 1988) in Germany or the Decree of 1994 in Spain. Some countries have recently introduced definitions through their professional organizations, which have varying influence depending on the standing of the body concerned. In some countries, notably France, there are several versions of the definition, derived from common usage, legal judgements or from professional bodies. The value definitions promulgated by TIAVSC and TEGOVOFA are mentioned as influential in several countries, among them France, Portugal, Sweden and Switzerland. It is, however, not possible to assess fully from these accounts how quickly new definitions are assimilated within each country and whether they are implemented in all the submarkets there.

It is tempting to assume that valuers all over Europe have a clear 'exchange price' concept in common and that minor variations in the wording of definitions are incidental. In order to examine whether this is so it is worthwhile considering the ingredients of the definitions in question. They consist of the following distinct elements:

1. the property interest is offered for sale in the market;
2. there is a hypothetical willing seller under no compulsion to sell;
3. there is a hypothetical willing buyer under no compulsion to buy;
4. it sells at the best price which can be expected;
5. it sells at the average price which can be expected;
6. the price is paid in cash or a cash equivalent;
7. the transaction is conducted under normal business conditions;
8. the value relates to one specified date;
9. both buyer and seller are fully informed about the property's legal and physical characteristics;
10. the property is adequately marketed for an appropriate period;
11. the marketing period precedes the valuation date;
12. the marketing period follows the valuation date;
13. whether the marketing period precedes or follows the valuation date is unspecified;
14. the market is static during the marketing period;
15. the buyer has no special interest in the property.

Few of the definitions involve more than three or four items from this list but there are distinctions to be drawn between them, involving the contrast between (11) and (12) and (13) above, the particularly between (4) and (5). In fact, these issues were all raised recently in the Mallinson Report (RICS, 1994) and continue to be debated in connection with the redrafting of the '*Red Book*'. Mallinson revealed differences of opinion between UK valuers as to whether the open market value (OMV) definition requires an estimate of best price or of the average or repeatable price attainable in the market. Mallinson tested valuers' opinions by asking them to consider a range of likely bids for a property. The OMV definition clearly represents the top bid which could be 'reasonably expected', although not a maverick overbid nor an average bid from the middle of the expected range. The reason for preferring the highest bid as representative of exchange price is that such a bid will secure the purchase. The counter argument is that it may not be capable of being repeated and therefore is not representative of the price which could be achieved in the market. An alternative way of looking at the issue is to consider a set of sale prices of similar properties, excluding special purchaser transactions. If we consider that the various prices reflect the different views of value of subsets of willing buyers and sellers from the total set of those operating in the market-place, then OMV, by definition, is represented by the highest such price rather than the mean price. Although the discussion which followed the Mallinson Report has clarified this issue for the UK valuer, the opposite view is taken in some other countries. Germany epitomizes the contrast, where the *Verkehrswert* definition equally clearly involves seeking the average or repeatable bid as representative of exchange price. This in itself complicates the comparison of valuation and of values between countries, but the picture becomes confused as we look in more detail at practice elsewhere. In Belgium, although a best price definition is used, in practice average price is often reported, based on 'average' rather than market capitalization rates, in order to reduce tax liability. Reading the accounts of valuation methods and practices suggests that, in several cases, we cannot tell from definitions alone whether average or best price is in use but must look at implementation, i.e. at the methodology. In some cases, despite definitions specifying 'best price' or more likely not distinguishing between best and average price, it is in fact 'average price' that is used. This happens, as in Belgium, through adopting average capitalization rates, often derived by yield construction from money market rates or, as in Portugal and Germany, by taking the statistical mean of price data. The water is further muddied by adaptation of a definition to meet the varying needs of particular clients, as described in Spain where, if the valuation is for loan security, a more 'prudent' approach is taken.

The distinction between assuming that the marketing period runs before or after the valuation date is not made clear in most of the countries described. It is most important in countries with highly cyclical markets, where price rises are frequent and sizeable. This cyclical effect is likely to be most marked where there is an active speculative development industry, which has only been true of a limited number of submarkets throughout Europe until recent years. Most notable among these is the UK office market, particularly in the South East, and it is probably no accident that in the UK the exchange price definition specifically deals with the assumption. The difference between the two alternatives is seen as so significant here that the estimated realization price (ERP) definition has been suggested (RICS, 1994) to differentiate a subsequent marketing period from the OMV basis which assumes prior marketing.

Another topic of debate has been the assumption that there exist both a willing buyer and seller, a sensitive one in the illiquid, recessionary markets of the early 1990s when owners were unwillingly selling assets at depressed prices to alleviate their debt. Concern over this issue was fuelled by the introduction, by the EU, of a definition of market value for use in valuing insurance company assets (19/674/EEC), which is now embedded in national legislation throughout the member states. This definition requires the assumption of a willing buyer and seller, in contrast to the OMV definition (RICS, 1990) which assumes only a willing seller. Following clarification of the issue in the Consultation Draft '*Red Book*' (RICS, 1994a), this debate has lost its fire and the acceptance of the TIAVSC definition clarifies the issue.

The fact that these debates are now occupying so much time and effort within the relatively centralized valuation profession in the UK suggests that there is still a long way to go before valuers operating throughout Europe can come to a consensus on a definition of exchange value. In a tidy, unified Europe we might hope to move towards a single definition for all valuers to use and accepted by all clients. This would enhance cross-border communication in accounting, investment, performance measurement and lending, and thereby facilitate efficient resource allocation. However, strongly felt national identities and cultural differences between countries are likely to cast up obstacles to such an objective, as they have to so many other visions of European integration.

The contrast between German *Verkehrswert* and OMV as used in the UK provides an example of cultural differences impacting on this issue and illustrates why the professions in different countries may find difficulty in reconciling their value definitions and methods. The German inclination for systems which stabilize economic affairs and suppress inflationary trends is deeply seated, arising from the experience of hyper-inflation and associated social upheavals which troubled Germany earlier this century. This background makes good sense of the idea of the 'average value' or 'repeatable bid' version of the exchange price concept which is expressed in the application of the *Verkehrswert*. It leads the valuer away from the ever-rising overbid so characteristic of the inflationary UK property market of the 1970s and 1980s, and enshrined in its OMV tradition. In Germany, such a bid is not representative of *Verkehrswert* until it has become the norm. The valuation system should therefore tend to damp inflationary trends in property prices rather than exacerbate them, an effect entirely in accordance with German economic and social aspirations. In contrast, in the UK the public, media and many valuers still watch eagerly for signs of rising property prices as confirmation that the recession has ended and a prerequisite to the 'feel good factor', despite inflation having fallen to low single figures and having stayed there for four years. Inflating property prices are as much part of the UK aspiration as economic stability is part of the German. These expectations are reflected in the assessment of exchange price in each country.

Systems which require the property valuer to arrive at exchange price by reconciling depreciated replacement cost (DRC) with a market value derived from capitalizing investment income, for example, Germany, Sweden and Switzerland, could be interpreted as reinforcing this anti-inflationary effect, since the effect of a rising property cycle on the variables required for DRC is likely to lag its effect on those used in direct capital comparison or income capitalization.

Considering differences such as this between OMV and the *Verkehrswert* suggests that there may be opposition to adopting a common exchange value definition. German valuers are no more prepared to relinquish their belief in

Verkehrswert than UK valuers are to abandon OMV. Moreover, as we see in Belgium and elsewhere, even where definitions appear to be common, their implementation may differ. This has in fact been a problem in the UK, where much effort has been expended on tightening up definitions in order to achieve consistency of implementation.

The significance of disparities in exchange price definitions, and their implementation, lies in the uses to which the results are put. For example, the EU's first uniform market value definition (19/674/EEC) aims to introduce consistency in the accounts of insurance undertakings, thereby enhancing fair competition. The issue of uniformity in value definitions assumes more importance when the valuation will be relied on by third parties, other than the client or valuer, who are not party to the valuation brief and detailed report. This is recognized both in providing a value definition in the EC Directive and in the creation of the *'Red Book'* in the UK. The lack of consistency in application of definitions of value which are revealed here suggest that the objectives of the EU legislation may not be fulfilled simply by providing a common exchange price definition.

Performance measurement constitutes a use of valuations by a third party which not only depends for its usefulness on consistency in the basis of valuation but is of growing importance to the property investment industry. Comparison of the performance of property as an asset class between countries, regions and localities across Europe is increasingly used as the basis of investment portfolio decision-making, as described in Chapter 3. Systems of measurement have been set up in the UK and the Netherlands and also in France. Elsewhere, amenable sources of historic annual revaluation data are very hard to find. Initially the annual reports of the German open funds appear just such a useful time series of ready-assembled historic annual valuation data in the prime property market, being particularly attractive because of the lack of alternatives. However, their revaluations are constructed on the basis of the *Verkehrswert* using its 'average bid' basis, raising the question whether this will influence performance. It could be argued that rates of market movement, not the absolute level of capital value, are of most interest in making comparisons between performance in different locations. If 'average bid' levels of value move proportionately with the 'highest bid' levels on which performance may be based in, say, the UK or the Netherlands, then this difference in the valuation basis is irrelevant for this purpose. However, we do not know whether their movement is proportional and it is possible to hypothesize that, in a rising speculative market, 'highest bids' will accelerate ahead of 'average bid' levels, widening the gap between them and showing a higher growth rate, the effect being reversed in a falling market.

Theoretically, the use of the *Verkehrswert*, which includes the 'repeatable bid' idea, particularly if it operates together with a discretion to ignore reversionary increases in income, can have an interesting effect on the reporting of investment portfolio performance, smoothing out the peaks and troughs of the property cycle. It should give a less volatile picture of performance than using 'highest bid' values would do, fulfilling German economic aspirations by filtering out instability from the investment market-place. This effect could be applauded as beneficial compared to the volatility problems suffered in countries which use the 'highest bid' basis and follow every rise and fall of the property cycle, creating performance one year which is wiped out the next. Certainly, German investors find property attractive under German performance measurement techniques, as evidenced by the phenomenal inward cash flows of the open property investment funds in 1993 and 1994, despite falling rents in the Frankfurt office market.

Reading the accounts of valuation in each country suggests however that it may be impossible to differentiate between valuations carried out on the best price and average price bases. The lack of market data reported from many countries suggests that such subtle differences may be obscured in valuation tolerances, especially in recently inactive markets. As an example, the account of French practice suggests that both assumptions operate alongside one another, the resulting figures being indistinguishable. Indeed, in some countries, e.g. Switzerland, the market is so opaque that the principle of basing exchange price valuation on transaction data is routinely abandoned as hopeless and the valuer has no option but to fall back on a cost-based method or on yield construction. It is perhaps no accident that debate about the detail of value definitions has been loudest in the UK where the property market is often characterized as the most transparent in Europe and there is some hope of distinguishing the effects of different value definitions.

17.2.1 Cost-based valuation

There has been debate in the UK (RICS, 1994) whether depreciated replacement cost (DRC) is a basis of value or a method of valuation. There is little doubt from the accounts here that it is in widespread and frequent use in some of the countries documented. Whereas in Finland, France, Norway, Sweden and the UK, DRC is used only for specialist properties where there is no transaction evidence, in Germany, Switzerland, Spain and Portugal it is more widely used, usually in tandem with a comparative method such as income capitalization, the exchange value being a weighted average of the two outcomes. The weighting is dependent on the judgement of the valuer. The accounts from these countries suggest that this procedure is a legacy from property systems where transaction evidence was so scarce that, due either to low trading levels, secrecy or both, valuers had no alternative but to rely on the cost approach. As pointed out in Chapter 2, in property systems where owner-occupation predominates, and the planning system and land supply do not impose scarcity value, the method mirrors the reality of acquisition decisions where the choice is between the cost of building oneself a new property or buying a vacant older alternative.

The obvious professional to carry out this type of calculation was the architect or engineer, with first-hand experience of the costs and intricacies of building or adapting premises, and accordingly it was to these professionals that the task of valuation was entrusted. It is still this professional group which carries out valuations in the majority of European countries, so perpetuating the inclination towards a cost-based approach even after the advent of actively trading markets with improved levels of transactional evidence and investment activity. Germany, Portugal and Spain document clients' growing preference for comparative methods of arriving at exchange price, either by loading the weighting in favour of the capital comparison or income capitalization figure or by relinquishing DRC altogether where increased market activity allows. However, there is reluctance to abandon cost-based methods altogether and, as reported from Belgium, Germany, Norway, Portugal, Spain and Switzerland, even when the end result of a valuation is weighted almost entirely towards the outcome of a comparative method, the cost-based figure is retained as a 'check'.

This evolution towards comparative, transaction-based methods requires valuers to develop data collection systems and methods of analysis and to understand the functioning of the market-place. Just as architects and engineers became valuers because of their aptitude for cost-based methods, they may now feel uncomfortable with transaction-based ones. Some agency- or brokerage-orientated professionals argue that they are better qualified for the latter because of their intimate knowledge of the processes driving transactions. The clash between the two valuation traditions can be seen operating in Germany, where agency-based chartered surveyors of UK origin come into conflict with traditional German valuation methods implemented by professionals with an engineering or architectural training. This tension is beautifully illustrated in the account of the property boom in Portugal. This theme is returned to in section 17.8 below.

When DRC is used predominantly for valuing property in which there is no transactional market, any development is likely to be for owner-occupation and developers will not be involved as intermediaries between the user and the contractor. Then the basic equation will make no allowance for developer's profit:

$$DRC_1 = \text{land price} + \text{construction costs} - \text{depreciation}$$

However, when, it is used for valuing property in market-places where there is active trading and development activity, then the equation should be:

$$DRC_2 = \text{land price} + \text{construction cost} + \text{developer's profit} - \text{depreciation}$$

An allowance for developer's profit is expressly excluded from the calculation of DRC in Spain and the UK and is only expressly included in Portugal. It is not included in the calculation of *Sachwert* in Germany. Logically, there ought to be a discrepancy between the outcome of the comparative and DRC methods in markets which have speculative development activity but omit developer's profit from the DRC calculation. The latter would, prima facie, produce lower values than the former, as noted by Hoesli (1994). In practice, there is enormous difficulty in detecting responses in land price and development profit to short-term market movements, due to the time lag between user market activity and a development response, and the fact that so many variables are involved in the equation.

The DRC method does seem to give rise to rules of thumb. Two aspects of the method present themselves as prime candidates for the application of codified adjustments rather than adjustments based on market evidence or valuer's expertise. The first of these is the land value element of the calculation. Bearing in mind that DRC is most used for properties in which there is no active market, transactions in bare land with development potential are even less frequent, especially in urban areas, than are those in buildings, leaving the valuer with a thorny problem. Switzerland offers an extreme example of how a valuer might respond: by calculating the construction costs of a replacement building and assuming that the land value is a specified percentage of this figure, the percentage varying according to factors such as building type, location, etc., so arriving at the final valuation.

A second uncertainty is the deduction for depreciation. Again, various mathematical rules, usually linked to the building's age and the expected life of the building type, have been codified to assist valuers. To market-based valuers these percentage adjustments are anathema and render the outcome inferior to any transaction-based approach, however tenuous the transaction data on which it is based. Their obvious failure is in not accounting for economic obsolescence nor responding to the stage of the economic cycle which is an important influence on the quantitative effect of obsolescence (Salway, 1986). A valuer can make further adjustments to allow for these factors but it would appear that the very existence of codified rules for assessing depreciation are a temptation to valuers, particularly those with more tenuous links to the market-place, to investigate the appropriateness of the depreciation allowance or land value no further.

The outcome of these codified cost-based methods might be considered invalid as an estimate of exchange price. However, the uncertainty introduced by the lack of land value evidence is a natural outcome of the fact that DRC is most used for property types where there is no active market. This raises the question whether the concept of exchange price has any validity in a submarket where trading hardly occurs and could more logically be replaced by the concept of the property's worth. Returning to the debate which seeks to categorize DRC as a concept or definition of value, or a method of valuation, we might look to the descriptions of its use in each country for assistance. The fact that it is in widespread use in tandem with comparative methods for arriving at exchange price indicates that it is seen as a method of valuation rather than a value definition or concept. However, in some countries, such as Portugal and Spain, it is regarded as a concept of value distinct from exchange value and it could be argued that where the exchange value concept is unattainable due to the nature of the property, or lack of a trading market, then an alternative value concept, i.e. DRC, is the only viable approach to valuation. It could then be interpreted as a version of the concept of worth, as distinct from exchange price, as discussed in Chapter 2. It would therefore appear, from the collective evidence of the countries described here, that DRC is viewed both as a concept of value and as a method of valuation.

17.3 THE PROFITS METHOD OF VALUATION

The profits method of valuation is mentioned only by the authors from Finland, the Netherlands, Portugal and the UK for estimating the exchange price of specialized properties, the value of which depends on their trading potential. These are typically hotels, bars, cinemas and leisure facilities. It would appear that there is variation in the attention paid to income and outgoings, varying from detailed reference to the accounts in the UK to a simple multiplier of the gross takings in Portugal. It is interesting that the Portuguese chapter describes the method as the basis of transaction pricing during the period when property sales were so infrequent that comparative methods were not viable, mirroring the theoretical outline given in Chapter 2.

17.4 INCOME CAPITALIZATION

Although there appears to be common ground between countries regarding definitions of value and methods of valuation, significant differences can also be identified. Perhaps the most striking of these is the derivation of the capitalization rate or investment yield used in the income capitalization method, usually aimed at estimating exchange price.

17.4.1 Yield construction and yield analysis

In theory, the investment purchaser of a let building will pay a price such that their net rental income provides a return sufficient to compensate them for the opportunity cost of their money, allowing for the risk of the income stream compared to the risk of alternative investment media. By considering these factors, a valuer may be able to replicate the investor's judgements and so construct the appropriate investment yield. In practice, this process of yield construction is considered by many valuers to be too subjective to constitute a reliable means of finding exchange price. Valuers prefer the alternative, which is yield analysis. The relationship between the income and sale price is analysed to find the investment yield at which actual transactions were carried out. Several authors point out that, for this reason, the income capitalization method is a comparative method.

The choice between yield construction and yield analysis is seen as clear-cut by many valuers who consider that exchange price can only be arrived at by the latter approach and that in contrast yield construction, being subjective, gives rise to an estimate of investment worth. Yield analysis is considered to be essential to the assessment of exchange price of an investment property, being direct evidence of market behaviour and so providing it with validity. Although this view is likely to be strongly held by valuers in the UK and some other countries, a number of valuers in, for example, France, Italy, Norway, Portugal, Sweden and Switzerland, would be less positive. Accounts of yield construction come from Belgium, France, Italy, the Netherlands, Norway, Portugal, Spain, Sweden, Switzerland and the UK. In Belgium, France and the UK it is specified only for estimating investment worth or for valuing short-term fixed incomes. In Italy, Portugal, Sweden and Switzerland it is recommended as a second best, to fill the gap where no transaction evidence is available for yield analysis. In Spain it is required under the Decree of 1994 and here, as well as in Norway, Germany and Finland, minimum yields are specified by government, the central bank or professional organizations for loan security valuation and/or for acquisitions and portfolio revaluations by investment and insurance funds. The effect of this is to prevent values rising above a 'prudent' level during peaks in the investment market, so stabilizing the mortgage system and preventing funds from paying inflated prices for investments or showing temporarily inflated returns in their portfolios.

In Germany, the process of estimating the *Verkaufswert*, or long-term sustainable value, is well developed, as discussed in sections 8.13 and 4.3. This definition formalizes the estimation of a 'prudent' value, through the associated methodology of choosing a sustainable rental income, capitalized at a yield no lower than a floor specified by the lending institution and agreed with the Banking Supervisory Authority.

Yields are constructed on a variety of bases: the local or national government bond rate over different time horizons, the nominal interest rate adjusted for inflation, a weighted average of the interest rate on own and borrowed funds, or either of these rates individually. In all these cases a property-risk premium is added, varying according to the property type and even broken down into elements relating to the individual risks of the property. Some countries apply the yield to the income net of owner's expenses, others apply a yield to a gross rental income and make upwards adjustments to the yield to allow for various items of expenditure such as voids, operating costs, maintenance, refurbishment and so on. In addition, in countries such as France, where transfer costs are onerous, investment yields can be quoted gross or net of such costs, the difference being substantial. The overall effect of these variations in practice is that comparison of yields between countries is extremely complex and confusing, even before differences of tenure, income growth potential and security, national economic conditions and other variables are taken into account.

The various country chapters provide insufficient detail of yield construction methods, rent adjustment mechanisms and rental income growth patterns to assess the relationship between them. However, it would appear that many countries use, as a preference, growth implicit yields drawn from analysing the relationship between the initial rental income and the sale price. Chapter 11 describes the system of yield construction in Norway, where it is performed centrally by the Norwegian Surveyors Association. There the capitalization rate, I, is found by the equation:

$$I = d - g + r$$

where d is the nominal interest rate, g the rate of inflation and r a risk premium depending on the type of property. Since the pattern and rate of rental growth follows the movements of the consumer price index, this accords with the theoretical yield construction model outlined in Chapter 2. A similar approach is described for Sweden. Chapter 15 relates the use of mortgage rates or bond rates as the basis of yield construction in Switzerland, or a weighted average of the rate on borrowed and own money. It is unclear from the variety of methods described here how the resulting capitalization rate relates to the income growth pattern expected from the building.

There is an enormous variety in the tenure norms developed in these countries and in the factors which impact upon the extent and timing of rental growth, such as normal lease length, security of tenure, options to quit, rental adjustment mechanisms, the responsibility for outgoings and government intervention. It should be possible to make comparisons between the resulting income growth patterns and risks in each country and the appropriate allowance to be made in yield construction. This is, however, an enterprise which would require more detailed information than this book is able to cover. There is already some literature comparing lease structures in different countries (Lofstedt and Baum, 1993). The distinction between growth implicit and growth explicit yields does not arise in any chapter except the UK, despite the fact that in both the Netherlands and Sweden explicit discounted cash-flow projections are cited as methods for assessing exchange price. It would appear that this is a field requiring detailed research.

17.5 CALCULATION OF INVESTMENT WORTH

In practice, the choice between using yield analysis and yield construction appears to hinge largely on the availability of transactional data and is in all countries, except the UK, directed at estimating exchange value. There is, in fact, no evidence that the distinction between exchange value, based on yield analysis, and estimation of worth, based on yield construction, is in widespread use, although the accounts from Belgium, France, the Netherlands, Portugal, Sweden, Switzerland and the UK suggest that at least some valuers there concern themselves in estimating the likely selling price and the worth of investments to their client as an aid to decision-making. This distinction is dependent for its existence on a well-developed investment community which requires advice from valuers based on these ideas. This is not so in many of the markets in which valuers operate and is a relatively new phenomenon even in some major cities such as Madrid.

The UK has for some time enjoyed a relatively transparent market, a cohesive valuation profession and, in particular, a large and active investment market, driven by pension funds, insurance companies and public property investment companies. This scenario has facilitated the development of concepts of price and worth and definitions and methodologies for estimating them. The existence of a well-established academic community, supported by demand for higher education provision as the key to entering a distinct and regulated profession, has also been crucial.

In contrast to this situation, some countries do not have or are only now developing an institutional investment community for which publicly accountable valuations are important. In countries such as these, where operational property is largely owner-occupied, the evidence of investment-motivated transactions is scarce and often inaccessible due to confidentiality. Such conditions not only militate against the use of the income capitalization method but also tend to reduce the overall need for such valuations and for any distinction between price and worth.

UK valuers can also be grateful for the massive workload provided by the requirements of the accounting system and the large and active Stock Exchange. Revaluations for accounting purposes, frequent take-overs, mergers and launches of companies onto the Stock Exchange all provide not only opportunities for fee-earning valuation, but also an impetus for valuers to refine and develop their methods and definitions. In contrast to this, authors from several countries point out that companies there avoid revaluing their assets in order to avoid taxation. In Germany, take-over activity is rare due to the financial implications for the companies involved and widespread private ownership of industry reduces the need for public accountability and therefore for revaluations. It also provides a group of wealthy individuals with the resources to engage in investment activity which is hidden by the extremes of confidentiality.

It is for reasons such as these that levels of valuation activity differ between countries and accordingly the degree of development of the profession as well. Italy and Portugal have professions in the early stages of development, somewhat fragmented, without central coordination or regulation and only recently having a forum to promote debate and evolution of ideas and practice. The account of Portuguese valuation provides a short history of the development of the profession, from almost total absence of a market, where respected local individuals adjudicated over valuation issues, through to the conscious attempt of a young profession to develop its concepts, methods and practice in a market newly suffering the cyclical problems introduced by speculative investment and development.

17.6 PROPERTY MARKETS IN THE 1990S: THE CRISIS OF CONFIDENCE

One of the most notable themes running through the accounts of these countries is that of a valuation profession suffering a crisis of confidence and credibility, and under attack from other professionals who covet its workload and believe themselves better qualified to undertake it. One of the reasons for this is cited by some authors as the movement away from cost-based methods to market-based comparative methods. The latter involve knowledge of subjects which engineering and architectural education do not stress, such as the operation of the financial markets and economic analysis at the micro and macro levels. In addition, the international nature of some management consultancies and accounting firms ideally positions them to take on property consultancy, including valuation for international clients, whereas the descriptions here show many valuers deeply embedded in their home markets and specific local practices and processes.

17.6.1 The property market collapse and professional organization

A serious depression in commercial office values hit the prime markets of all the countries discussed during the early 1990s. This is largely in response to a phase of speculative overdevelopment in the late 1980s followed by economic recession: the classic market boom and bust. Several authors note this as the impetus for a reform of valuation practice in their countries. This is for many national professional organizations a necessity rather than a luxury, since the effect of the market collapse has been an increase in litigation against valuers, usually because of their valuation of property as security for a loan, followed by losses for the lender when the borrower defaulted and the property could only be sold at well below the valuation figure. The litigation has in some cases led to substantial damages being paid by the valuer, some of which, in the UK courts, are described in Chapter 16. The result is that professional indemnity insurance premiums, compulsory for valuers in the RICS and for many others, are rising to the extent that valuation becomes non-viable at the level of fees which clients are prepared to pay.

The response varies from one country to another, but falls largely into two main categories. The first of these is the consolidation of professional groups, which can be achieved by tightening the qualifications for membership or even seeking government regulation of the use of the title 'valuer'. In Spain the title *tasador* (or valuer) is now regulated by Decree, Finland is instigating a public register of authorized valuers with educational and experiential qualifications, and in Norway some sort of state licensing or certification system is proposed. The Finnish system will require three years experience and a relevant degree or no degree and 10 years experience. Valuers in France require no particular education but often have a degree from one of the Grandes Écoles and for IFEI membership need a university diploma or seven years experience. There are signs that the government there may legislate to regulate valuers and protect clients. NVM membership in the Netherlands now requires completion of a two year seminar course. Valuers in Norway have no educational requirements before entering the Norwegian Surveyors Association and for Portugal there is no professional organization to join. *Tasadors* in Spain require a five to six year university degree in architecture or engineering, followed by in-house practical training in valuation and must belong to a registered valuation company. However, this is required only to carry out mortgage valuations or portfolio valuations for investment or insurance companies, valuations for other purposes are unregulated. In the UK membership of the RICS requires a three or four year undergraduate degree or a one year postgraduate degree with a syllabus closely controlled by the institution, followed in both cases by two years supervised professional training and an assessment of professional competence. The ISVA has similar requirements. In many of these countries valuation is not confined to the members of the professional associations, although valuation for certain purposes, notably public investment companies and mortgages, often is. In Germany, the members of the valuation committees valuing the assets of the open property funds have to be approved by the Banking Supervisory Authority.

A second defensive response to the criticism of the profession which resulted from the market downturn is to codify practice and ethics by publishing authoritative manuals. The existence of manuals of valuation practice is mentioned in Finland dated 1991, France, the Netherlands, Norway dated 1993, Switzerland and the UK. These cover terminology, definitions and methods of valuation, reporting, etc. Some, for instance the '*Red Book*' and '*White Book*' produced in the UK, have avoided dictating methodology. In Finland and Sweden separate publications are mentioned dealing with terminology. It is noticeable that the necessity for these manuals is increasingly recognized, perhaps partly because valuers become aware of best practice and professional organization in other countries. Codes of practice are noted in Finland, France, the Netherlands, Norway, Sweden and the UK. These deal with the relationship between valuers, ethical behaviour, fees, etc. All these are aimed at raising the professional status of valuers and developing consistency of practice to reassure clients that high standards are being maintained.

Professional organizations vary in the sanctions they can exercise against members infringing their rules. In the UK expulsion from the RICS is a sanction against unethical behaviour which is exercised as necessary. Very little is said about the exercise of sanctions against members of other organizations, but there would appear to be a trend towards government regulation of valuation, for instance in France, Spain, Finland and Norway, which must be accompanied by some type of disciplinary action, as it is in Spain where the Banco de España can impose fines. The Banking Supervisory Authority in Germany can withdrawn approval either from individual members of an open fund valuation committee or from the valuation department of a mortgage bank which fails to adhere to the valuation guidelines agreed with the authority, although this is unheard of.

The international organizations of valuers, TEGOVOFA, TIAVSC and EUROVAL, appear to have been influential in disseminating discussion of value definitions and methods and codes of practice. The acceptance by the RICS of the TIAVSC definition of 'market value' for inclusion in the '*Red Book*' is an example. It is probably a happy coincidence that the discussion they started was timed to help with the reformulation of practice prompted by the property market crash in Europe. It would appear likely, from the accounts given here, that this discussion, having started, will not be capable of early resolution and that evolution in the regulation of valuers, refinement of manuals of practice and codes of conduct will continue.

As well as the influence of the international organizations of valuers, spurred on by the Single European market and the internationalization of investment activity, the force of the RICS cannot be ignored. This body initially operated within the UK and has now spread its influence to Ireland, Germany, France and the Netherlands, in all of which it has recognized higher education courses as a route to membership. This consciously evangelical policy, aimed at extending the institution's influence, follows the establishment by many of its members of offices, notably in France, Germany, Belgium and Spain. The first cohort of German postgraduates became fully fledged RICS Associate Members in summer 1995. It remains to be seen how the new membership of the Deutsche Verband Chartered Surveyors (DVCS) will develop their own national association and whether it will diverge from the parent body in the UK.

17.7 EDUCATION AND RESEARCH

The educational background of the valuation profession varies enormously throughout the countries described. The rising volume of high level valuation work available in new investment markets requires a corresponding extension of educational provision, which has been evident in the courses offered for RICS recognition in the Netherlands, Germany and France. However, there are sometimes obstacles to the provision of state funded courses to meet demand and it is significant that of these three, two are offered by private universities. In Germany, it is extremely difficult to establish new degree courses in state universities and it would therefore appear that the provision of opportunities will be limited.

However, the implications of the Single European Act mean that valuers face the prospect of greater commonality in professional qualification, education and training. This in itself does not provide a means of integrating valuers across Europe. Their training is currently diverse and it is difficult to select a model which has been successful in one country and adapt it to suit another (Jaffe, 1994). However, as professional bodies move to greater commonality in the education of valuers, so a standard European perspective will be fostered through the development of a common core syllabus. This could be adapted to the particular national and local circumstances and should be flexible enough to meet the traditions of real estate education in each country. Increasing provision of university courses aimed at the real estate profession is likely to have repercussions for research in real estate, as it has in the UK since university provision of RICS exempting degrees expanded in the 1970s, since it funds a growing body of academics engaged in researching the subject, including valuation practice and theory.

Kohnstamm (1995) argues that it is the task of academic researchers to create uniform valuation standards at national levels to accommodate cross-border investment advice. Indeed, educational links already exist between professional bodies and universities teaching real estate across Europe and, with the increase in research links between European academics from different countries, the exchange of ideas is accelerating.

17.8 CLIENT CHOICE AS AN INSTIGATOR OF REFORM AND CONVERGENCE IN PRACTICE

Instability in property markets in the 1990s has highlighted the inadequacies of valuation practice and initiated reviews of the profession in many national professional organizations: client dissatisfaction and potential loss of business to competitors has proved a compelling motivation to raise the level of technical excellence of valuations and their consistency within national borders. As investment increasingly operates across an international market-place, these effects are beginning to spill over into pressure for cross-border consistency as well. Dutch pension funds are active cross-border investors and have evolved expertise in their own and international valuation traditions. The creation of a detailed valuation brief, described by Hordijk (1994), applicable to property in any country, may be an indicator of future strong client-led evolution of the valuation process, especially in terms of the supporting data required in a valuation report. In 1994 approximately 20 leading Dutch institutional investors including ABP, Nationale Nederlande, PGGM and Rodamco, in cooperation with ROZ, the Dutch Real Estate Council, and Investment Property Databank, initiated a property performance index. It is underpinned by new valuation guidelines designed to produce consistent valuations, which may have far-reaching effects (Bardouil, 1995). The guidelines include a checklist for valuation content, procedures and methodology. Uncertainty over the veracity of values provided by valuers in other countries is a factor discouraging investors from diversifying their portfolios outside their home country and thereby limiting the risk and return management opportunities available to them. Client-led development of the valuation process could reduce this problem.

Other types of client, notably mortgage banks expanding their lending activity outside their home country, are also coming into contact with valuations carried out in the country of the property on which their money is secured. The German mortgage banks provide an example and their response is described in Chapter 4. Under the Mortgage Bank Law (BGBL 1 S 81) they are required to value the property to the definition of sustainable value or *Verkaufswert*. Although this is a definition of exchange price, it is fundamentally different from

OMV, as described in section 8.13. Recognizing the impracticality of communicating the idea of *Verkaufswert* to an RICS valuer in the UK, one solution is for the mortgage bank to commission a valuation to OMV with an extensive market report as backup and then recast the variables in-house to meet the definition required. The outcome of using this approach in several different countries will be that the valuers in German mortgage banks will have a good understanding of valuation practice in the countries in which they lend. Parallel practical education is likely to occur in various client bodies to the extent that, like the Dutch funds, they will be able to identify their valuation needs in terms of data, value concepts, definitions and methods. These can be based on their observations of best practice in a range of countries. Unless valuers respond to this type of client-led development of the valuation process they will lose the instructions of the larger and more internationally active clients. At present, valuers in the individual countries tend to continue using the traditional methods of valuation despite the identification of weaknesses in them (Baum and Crosby, 1995). Advances in methodology primarily depend on the initiatives of the professional bodies and academic researchers to promote change which will advance and strengthen practice (Kohnstamm, 1995).

As the larger international property consultants consolidate their position in mainland Europe they are likely to want to expand their activity beyond the core of agency and brokerage, particularly in view of the vulnerability of the income from such business in market recessions. Valuation work has the appeal of being less cyclical and is an obvious candidate for diversification of their services. For consultancies born in the UK of RICS parentage, as many are, the definitions of the '*Red Book*' and '*White Book*' and UK methodology will be used rather than local definitions and methodology. However, for local clients, familiar with local customs and perhaps bound to them by regulatory systems, it may not be attractive, or even possible, to use such valuations. It would not, for instance, be possible for a German mortgage bank to use an OMV produced by a chartered surveyor, yet an RICS member would be constrained by the '*Red Book*' to value to OMV or ERP rather than to the definition of *Verkaufswert*.

Nearly all discussions of improved processes of estimating price and worth nowadays refer to the issue of valuation fees and note that improved quality of service cannot be provided without a corresponding increase in fees from the low levels reached in the recent property recession, for instance Baum and MacGregor (1992). It may be that development in data collection and processing, which according to the accounts of these countries has a long way to go yet, can deliver significant improvement without a proportionate increase in fees. It is also possible that clients will be happy to pay higher fees for demonstrably more reliable and consistent valuations.

An issue raised in many of the descriptions of individual countries is that of valuer's independence from client pressure, whether in-house or external. Impartiality or independence from the client is mentioned as important to the credibility of valuations in Belgium, France, Germany, Norway, Spain, Sweden, Switzerland and the UK. This independence is often required only for certain types of valuation, for instance of the assets of investment funds, insurance companies and mortgage banks. In Sweden, Switzerland, Germany and Norway the valuer has the status of an independent expert or arbitrator and in several countries certain valuers are appointed by the courts to provide independent expert evidence when the need arises. This is described in Germany, Switzerland, France and Norway. In the UK the issue of independence has been under debate recently, as witnesses favourable to the party commissioning them have given conflicting evidence in court hearings considering valuation negligence. This has brought the expert witnesses into disrepute, with ensuing calls for the appointment of court-approved valuers unconnected to the parties in litigation. The question of independence has also surfaced in the context of conflict of interest where the agency interests of consultancies may conflict with their valuation and market research services. It is commonplace for UK consultancies to provide lucrative agency services in the same market-place where they carry out valuations for various purposes. There can be a conflict between the temptation to 'talk up' the market, to enhance agency income and to record the falls in exchange price of assets in the same market. The apparent solution is for valuation to be separated from agency/brokerage services, as it is in many European countries. However, it is this very separation which leads to difficulties in valuers acquiring not only transactional data as the basis for comparative valuations but also in understanding the forces driving price-making, which should be reflected in the valuation process. This conflict is observed by the author of the Portuguese chapter in section 12.5 and would appear to be an area which the profession needs to resolve. The creation of publicly available systems providing current detailed transaction evidence would reduce the pressure for agency and valuation services to be linked and increase the profession's ethical profile.

17.9 CONCLUSION

These accounts of the valuation process in 12 countries illustrate the potential for improvements in theory and practice in all of them. The dissemination of information about each other's different traditions is already underway and offers a rich field for practitioners and academics to research, debate and learn from. There are great difficulties inherent in communicating with valuers from other countries, not only the obvious problem of language, but difficulties in understanding each other's different traditions and the reasons for them. These include distinct economic and business cultures, the systems devised to implement their objectives, the differences of professional evolution and the client needs they serve. However, the pressure for valuers to expand their understanding is growing as clients discard the confines previously imposed on their businesses by national boundaries; if valuers do not also find ways of expanding their horizons they will lose fees to competitors who are willing to make the necessary effort and investment.

Agreement of value concepts, definitions and perhaps even methodology on an international basis appear to be a first step in the looked-for evolution of a consistent valuation process, aimed at maximizing the utility of valuations for clients and resulting in credibility for the profession. The establishment of communication between professional bodies is unlikely at present, since many of them see each other as competitors, and yet it is probably only by alliances between such groups that progress will be made. This may come about through the mediation of international groups such as TIAVSC. Communication between academic establishments is another possible source of convergence by means of the dissemination of theory and practice.

The obstacles to any standardization of the process of valuation across Europe are considerable. It is most likely that client pressure, perhaps exercised by defaulting to other sources of valuation advice, will be the main driving force behind unification of practice and consequent improvement in its quality. In the short term the greatest need is for an extension of research into different valuation processes, of which this book is hopefully just one of the first steps.

REFERENCES

Bardouil, S. (1995) *Dutch Property Index Prompts Valuation Overhaul*, Estates Europe, **3**(8), p. 1, Estates Gazette, London.

Baum, A.E. and MacGregor, B.D. (1992) The initial yield revealed: explicit valuations and the future of property investment. *Journal of Property Valuation and Investment*, **10**(4), 709–26.

Baum, A.E. and Crosby, N. (1995) *Property Investment Appraisal*, 2nd edn, Routledge, London.

Hoesli, M. (1994) Real estate as a hedge against inflation: learning from the Swiss case. *Journal of Property Valuation and Investment*, **4**(3), 51–62.

Hordijk, A. (1994) *Reducing the risk of property investment by a detailed valuation brief*. Paper delivered at the European Real Estate Society Conference, University of Amsterdam, November, 1994.

Jaffe, A.J. (1994) *Seven lessons about real estate education from the US experience*. Paper presented at the European Real Estate Society Conference, University of Amsterdam, November 1994.

Kohnstamm, P. (1995) Trends in European investment, performance and real estate education. *Journal of Property Valuation and Investment*, **5**(1), 51–8.

Lofstedt, C. and Baum, A.E. (1993) *A Comparative Study of Commercial Leasing Structures in Selected European Countries and the USA*. Working Papers in European Property, University of Reading.

RICS (1990) *Statements of Asset Valuation Practice and Guidance Notes ('Red Book')* as amended, Royal Institution of Chartered Surveyors, London.

RICS (1994) *The Mallinson Report: Commercial Property Valuations*, Royal Institution of Chartered Surveyors, London.

Salway, F. (1986) *Depreciation in Commercial Property*, College of Estate Management, Reading.

Index

Page numbers appearing in **bold** refer to figures and page numbers appearing in *italic* refer to tables. Where country names are included as subheadings they are listed after subject names, each section being in alphabetical order.

14199941R00200

Printed in Poland
by Amazon Fulfillment
Poland Sp. z o.o., Wrocław